PRACTICAL
AVIATION
LAW

PRACTICAL AVIATION LAW

J. SCOTT HAMILTON

FIFTH EDITION

Aviation Supplies & Academics, Inc.
Newcastle, Washington

J. Scott Hamilton is a member of the Embry-Riddle Aeronautical University faculty. He previously served as general counsel for the Civil Air Patrol, then as the national organization's chief operating officer. Prior to that, he served as senior assistant attorney general for the State of Wyoming. While practicing aviation law in Colorado, he also was a faculty member at the University of Denver College of Law, as well as Metropolitan State College of Denver. He is an experienced pilot and skydiver who served as a HALO instructor in the Green Berets. Hamilton is widely published on aviation law and has received many honors, including induction into the Colorado and Arkansas Aviation Hall of Fame.

Practical Aviation Law, Fifth Edition
J. Scott Hamilton

© 2011 Aviation Supplies & Academics, Inc.
All rights reserved.
Fifth Edition published 2011 by ASA.
Publication history: Fourth Edition originally published 2005 by Blackwell Publishing.
Other past editions—First, 1991; Second, 1996; Third, 2001.

Published 2011 by
Aviation Supplies & Academics, Inc.
7005 132nd Place SE
Newcastle, WA 98059
Email: asa@asa2fly.com
Website: www.asa2fly.com

Photo credits and acknowledgments. Unless otherwise stated, photographs used are © J. Scott Hamilton. Photos indicated throughout are courtesy of and copyright of the following organizations and are used with permission: p.19, NASA; p.20, (upper) Hyku Photo, (lower) © Eclipse Aerospace, Inc.; p.23, U.S. Customs and Border Protection; p.160, Library of Congress, G.G. Bain Collection; p.163, © Clay Observatory at Dexter and Southfield Schools, for Virgin Galactic; p.169, U.S. Navy; p.194, U.S. Army; p.279, provided by Denver International Airport; p.291, U.S. Air Force.

Cover: © rotofrank/iStockphoto

ASA-PRCT-AV-LAW5
ISBN 1-56027-763-7
    978-1-56027-763-7

Printed in the United States of America

2014   2013   2012   2011   9   8   7   6   5   4   3   2   1

Library of Congress Cataloging-in-Publication Data
Hamilton, J. Scott.
    Practical aviation law / J. Scott Hamilton.
       p. cm.
    Includes bibliographical references and index.
    1. Aeronautics-Law and legislation-United States. I. Title.

    KF2400.H36 2005
    343.7309'7-dc22
                        2004019630

CONTENTS

PREFACE

Practical Aviation Law is designed to be used in conjunction with the *Practical Aviation Law Workbook* as a university text for aviation law courses and, standing alone, as a reference guide for aviation business managers, pilots, mechanics, aircraft owners, and others involved in aviation by vocation or avocation.

Except for certain treaties having worldwide or at least multinational effect, the scope of the book is limited to the law of the United States and may have little relevance to the domestic laws of other nations. Neither does it attempt to explore the entire seamless web of the law— only those areas particularly applicable to aviation. I recommend that students considering a career in aviation business management also take courses in business law and aviation labor relations. While there is some overlap between those courses and aviation law, those give broader and deeper coverage of some of the legal concepts and principles studied here.

As the title suggests, this book takes a practical viewpoint. It aims to provide the reader with basic legal knowledge and perspectives along with an understanding of how the legal system works in relation to aviation activities. It aims to provide that in a form that can be applied to help you recognize and avoid common legal pitfalls, and to recognize when the moment has come to stop what you are doing and consult your lawyer. If this book had a subtitle, it would be *How to Avoid Aviation Lawyers and When to Call One.*

No book can hope to advise you what to do in every conceivable situation. In advising our clients, lawyers must take into consideration not only the law but also the facts and circumstances. In over thirty-five years of practicing law—in private practice, as government and later corporate counsel—I represented clients in well over three thousand aviation matters involving every subject in this book, and never saw two identical cases. While similar facts give rise to similar considerations, slight differences in the facts and circumstances often lead to major differences in the best approach to solving the problem. Examples in this book and its accompanying workbook are drawn largely from cases I encountered in my practice.

The law itself is also in a constant state of change. Even as I write, the Congress of the United States, fifty state legislatures, and a vast number of administrative agencies are daily making changes to statutes and regulations, while hundreds of federal and state courts are writing and publishing case decisions on the interpretation, application, and constitutionality of those laws and regulations, along with decisions that modify, clarify, or sometimes confuse the common law. Simultaneously, U.S. diplomats are negotiating with their foreign counterparts new or amended treaties to be ratified by their governments. Such changes as have occurred since the fourth edition of this book was published are the main reason for this expanded and updated fifth edition.

While this process of continual change keeps the lawyer's work from becoming routine to the point of boredom, it also means that what was good advice yesterday (or the day this book went to press) may no longer be good advice today. While the fundamental legal principles discussed in this book are less susceptible to sudden obsolescence than, say, a text on the Internal Revenue Code and IRS Regulations, *you are cautioned not to attempt to solve actual individual legal problems on the basis of information contained in this book.* Finding yourself faced with an actual legal problem, you should recognize that the time has come to consult your lawyer.

Acknowledgments

I would like to thank the following people for their encouragement, advice, and support, without which I would not have undertaken and persevered with the writing of this text and the related workbook and teacher's manual. These acknowledgments should not be construed to imply an endorsement of this teaching system by any of the persons or organizations mentioned.

Dr. Stacy Weislogel, chair, Department of Aviation, The Ohio State University, one of the first to urge me to write this book.

Professor Gary Kitely of Auburn University, who recently retired as executive director of the University Aviation Association, an organization that consistently provides a wonderful forum and source of information to those of us who teach aviation-related courses in colleges and universities. He was a source of encouragement not only in the drafting of the original manuscript for the first edition, but also in the continuously expanded international law coverage of each subsequent edition.

Dr. Rex A. Hammarback, director, University of North Dakota Aviation Foundation and formerly a professor in UND's renowned aviation program, who after I had explained my concept for the book said simply and directly: "If you write it, I'll use it."

Hon. John E. Faulk, NTSB administrative law judge (retired), a practicing attorney with the Trachtmann law firm in Melbourne, Florida, and an adjunct professor in the School of Aeronautics at the Florida Institute of Technology. Many of his recommendations based on his classroom experience using this teaching system have been incorporated as improvements to each successive edition.

Professor Terri Haynes, Chadron State College, Chadron, Nebraska. She deserves particular credit for strongly encouraging me to avoid "legalese" jargon wherever possible in favor of plain English to make the book as clear and understandable as possible to students and other readers having no previous training in the law.

Jonathan Stern, Esq., partner in the Washington, D.C. office of the world-renowned Schnader, Harrison, Segal & Lewis law firm and editor of the American Bar Association's *Aviation Litigation Quarterly*. Jon has been especially helpful in providing materials, insights, and updates on the continuing evolution of international law governing airline liability.

Bill Behan, president, AirSure, Ltd., Golden, Colorado. Bill continues to be a reliable source of information on developments in the ever-changing field of aviation insurance.

John and Kathleen Yodice, a father-and-daughter team in the Yodice & Associates law firm in Bethesda, Maryland, who do yeoman service for general aviation as legal counsel for the Aircraft Owners & Pilots Association and other clients and have proved themselves reliable sources of insights into recent developments in FAA enforcement, aviation medical, and airport and airspace access issues.

Professors Robert Kaps of Southern Illinois University (Carbondale) and Timm Bliss of Oklahoma State University, co-authors with me of the new *Labor Relations in Aviation and Aerospace* textbook and study guide with supplemental readings, published by Southern Illinois University Press, and Professor Jack Panosian of Embry-Riddle Aeronautical University's Prescott, AZ campus, who strongly encouraged that effort. All three of them also use this *Practical Aviation Law* text and motivated me to expand the coverage of Chapter 17 of this fifth edition to provide students a broader taste for that topic.

The Lawyer-Pilots Bar Association, Southern Methodist University's *Journal of Air Law and Commerce*, and the University of Denver's *Transportation Law Journal*, each of which consistently provides wonderful forums and opportunities for attorneys and others interested in aviation law to share knowledge and ideas in print and face-to-face in an atmosphere of professional collegiality. They continue to contribute greatly to the advancement of the legal profession and the quality of legal service to aviation clients.

Colleagues teaching aviation law courses at numerous colleges and universities who provide feedback and suggestions that contribute to the continuous improvement of each successive edition of this teaching system.

My students, past and present, who continue to relentlessly question, challenge, and demand clear explanations and sound reasoning, rightly refusing to settle for less.

Not unlike the airline industry, the publishing industry is in change as companies merge, are acquired, go out of business, or adjust their scope and market focus. Through all this change, successive editors at Iowa State University Press, Blackwell Publishing Professional, and now Aviation Supplies & Academics have recognized the need for this teaching system and its periodic updates, turning my vision into the solid reality you are now holding in your hand.

My family, who encouraged me in this project and more-or-less cheerfully tolerated the many hours I spent sequestered writing and updating this work (often after a full day of practicing aviation law or teaching), and especially my wife Charlotte, who did most of the typing of the original and subsequent manuscripts.

The credit is theirs; the errors are mine.

Notes on the Text

Unless otherwise noted, all opinions expressed herein are entirely my own and do not necessarily reflect the views of my employers, past or present.

All photos and illustrations are by the author, unless otherwise credited.

The use of proper language and phraseology is of crucial importance in the law. The primary use of *italics* in the text is to alert you to a word or phrase you need to understand to grasp the concepts under discussion, though italics are also occasionally used to give special emphasis to a point.

PART I

ADMINISTRATIVE LAW

1

Regulatory Agencies and International Organizations

If you are involved in aviation, you will deal with administrative agency regulations far more frequently than any other area of the law. Indeed, you will probably be confronted with making decisions based on the Federal Aviation Regulations (FARs) on a daily basis. Those regulations also establish standards of legal behavior by which a judge or jury may later decide whether you and your employer are legally liable for negligence in the event of an aircraft accident. Hardly any aspect of aviation today is unaffected by these regulations. That is why we begin with an examination of administrative law, with particular attention to the role of the Federal Aviation Administration (FAA) in administering the federal program of air safety regulation.

Since the 1920s, Congress has created a plethora of regulatory agencies to administer the many federal programs it has initiated. Indeed, federal agencies continue to grow and multiply, under Democratic and Republican administrations alike. We start here with an overview of the numerous administrative agencies most directly involved with some aspect of aviation, distinguishing them from each other according to the specific role played by each in regulating aviation.

The ease with which civil aircraft cross national borders, air transportation's key role in the global economy, and recent horrific effective use of civil airliners as weapons of terror have made the regulation and development of civil aviation a continuing subject of not only national but also international concern.

This chapter also introduces the International Civil Aviation Organization (ICAO) and the International Air Transport Association (IATA), organizations that, although not technically regulatory agencies, play an important role in harmonizing technical standards for civil aviation worldwide.

FEDERAL ADMINISTRATIVE AGENCIES

The terrorist attacks of September 11, 2001, shook the United States to the core. Few industries—indeed, few aspects of American life—were untouched, though some were more deeply affected than others. Civil aviation, having been so infamously and effectively abused in these attacks as a weapon of terror, has borne the brunt of these changes.

One of the results of the attacks was the most sweeping reorganization of the federal government in over a half-century.

Transportation Security Administration (TSA) (*www.tsa.gov*)

Barely two months after the attacks and for the express purpose of improving security in all modes of transportation, including civil aviation, Congress enacted the *Aviation and Transportation Security Act of 2001*, creating the Transportation Security Administration (TSA). The TSA was originally established as an operating agency of the Department of Transportation (DOT), but moved into the Department of Homeland Security (DHS) when that agency was created.

Previously, operators of airports served by commercial airlines had been responsible for airport security, relying primarily on contractors, with some FAA oversight. The new law brought the responsibility for day-to-day screening of airline passengers, baggage and cargo into the federal arena, under the TSA, which immediately set about hiring and training security personnel. Most of the new federal screeners were the same individuals previously employed by those contractors that had been performing the function prior to its federalization. With a change of uniform and some additional training, they returned to the same work.

The TSA also took over from the FAA the responsibility for inspecting and testing security measures at airports, with the added responsibility for the same at other transportation facilities, including foreign aircraft repair stations. Congress also empowered the TSA to receive, assess, and distribute intelligence information related to transportation security. The new agency was directed to develop plans, policies, and strategies for dealing with threats to transportation security and to coordinate countermeasures with other federal agencies. Congress also ordered that the federal Air Marshal program be beefed up and that steps be taken to increase the availability and use of explosive detection systems at air carrier airports.

Under the Secure Flight Program, the TSA is now responsible for maintaining the terrorist watch list and related No Fly and Selectee lists. The "watch list" of known and suspected terrorists is a uniform list used to identify persons who should be prevented from boarding (the No Fly List) or who should undergo additional security scrutiny (the Selectee List). The TSA began taking over the responsibility for the pre-boarding matching the names of airline passengers against these lists from the airlines in early 2009.

Transportation Security Oversight Board (TSOB)

Congress' initial investigation into the terrorist attacks revealed that various federal law enforcement agencies had clues that, if assembled together and investigated coherently, might have revealed the plot and enabled prevention, but that these agencies tended to hoard, rather than share, potentially crucial intelligence information. In an effort to address that shortcoming, the Aviation and Transportation Security Act also created the Transportation Security Oversight Board (TSOB), an extremely high-level panel composed of the Secretaries of Homeland Security, Transportation, Defense, and Treasury; the Attorney General, and the CIA Director (or designees of any of the foregoing), along with a Presidential appointee representing the National Security Council (NSC). The TSOB was made responsible for assuring the coordination and sharing of intelligence relating to threats against transportation.

Department of Homeland Security (DHS) (*www.dhs.gov*)

Next, Congress and President George W. Bush created the new Department of Homeland Security (DHS), now the largest federal department. Paralleling President Truman's epic 1947 merger of all branches of the U.S. armed forces into a new Department of Defense (DoD) to better coordinate the nation's defense against military threats, 24 federal agencies were brought under the new DHS to protect the nation against further terrorist attacks and respond to natural disasters. Agencies

---

brought into the DHS include the following (*italics* indicate the agency's former home in the federal bureaucracy):

Secret Service

Coast Guard (*Department of Transportation*)

U. S. Customs Service (*Department of the Treasury*)

Immigration and Naturalization Service (INS) (part, from *Department of Justice*)

Transportation Security Administration (TSA) (*Department of Transportation*)

Federal Protective Service (*General Services Administration*)

Federal Law Enforcement Training Center (*Department of the Treasury*)

Animal & Plant Health Inspection Service (part, from *Department of Agriculture*)

Office for Domestic Preparedness (*Department of Justice*)

Federal Emergency Management Agency (FEMA)

Strategic National Stockpile & Disaster Medical System (*Department of Health and Human Services*)

Nuclear Incident Response Team (*Department of Energy*)

Domestic Emergency Response Teams (*Department of Justice*)

National Domestic Preparedness Office (*FBI*)

CBN Countermeasures Program (*Department of Energy*)

Environmental Measures Laboratory (*Department of Energy*)

National Biological Warfare Defense Analysis Center (*Department of Defense*)

Plum Island Animal Disease Center (*Department of Agriculture*)

Critical Infrastructure Assurance Office (*Department of Commerce*)

Federal Computer Incident Response Center (*General Services Administration*)

National Communications System (*Department of Defense*)

National Infrastructure Protection Center (*FBI*)

Energy Security and Assurance Program (*Department of Energy*)

The Aviation and Transportation Security Act originally assigned the attorney general responsibility for screening all aliens applying for training at U.S. flight schools for security risks. Due to comparatively low fuel costs, prevalent VFR weather, and abundant suitable airspace, the U.S. (and particularly Florida and the desert southwest) was a popular destination for large numbers of foreigners wishing to learn to fly (and land). This new requirement hit U.S. flight schools—many of which were heavily reliant on foreign students—hard and hundreds closed their doors. This screening duty was later transferred to the new DHS and limited to students desiring to learn to fly aircraft with a maximum certificated gross takeoff weight of more than 12,500 pounds. As required by Congress, DHS now gives quick service to these prospective foreign students, acting on them within five days.

Aviation security law is discussed in much greater detail in Chapter 15.

Department of Transportation (DOT) (*www.dot.gov*)

The U.S. Department of Transportation houses a variety of federal agencies dealing with policy and regulation of various means of transportation of people and goods. DOT agencies having jurisdiction over various aspects of transportation include the Federal Aviation Administration (FAA), Federal Highway Administration (FHWA), Federal Motor Carrier Safety Administration (FMCSA), Federal Railroad Administration (FRA), Federal Transit Administration (FTA), Maritime Administration (MARAD), National Highway Traffic Safety Administration (NHTSA), Pipeline and Hazardous Materials Safety Administration (PHMSA), Research and Innovative Technology Administration (RITA), St. Lawrence Seaway Development Corporation (SLSDC), and Surface Transportation Board (STB). The head of the agency is the Secretary of Transportation.

The DOT issues foreign air carrier permits to foreign airlines designated by their nations to provide service to the United States pursuant to treaty. The DOT consults with the State Department in the approval process. Permit issuance requires presidential approval. The President may disapprove a specific foreign carrier only for foreign relations or national security reasons. Such permits have occasionally been denied or withdrawn in the application of U.S. foreign policy, as when Aeroflot's permit was suspended following the Soviet Union's invasion of Afghanistan.

Federal Aviation Administration (*www.faa.gov*)

In the Federal Aviation Act of 1958, Congress made the FAA primarily responsible for the safe and efficient use of the nation's airspace. The agency's influence on the entire aviation industry is pervasive.

The FAA Administrator is the head of the agency, and likely the single most influential person in U.S. civil aviation.

For many years, the FAA (and its predecessor, the Civil Aeronautics Authority or CAA) enjoyed independent agency status within the federal bureaucracy, an arrangement that afforded the administrator direct access to the president. But now that the FAA is but one of those many divisions of the DOT, the Secretary of Transportation is the sole voice for all of these subordinate agencies in the president's cabinet. Some aviation interests still feel that the development of sound aviation policy has suffered as a result of this organizational structure. A parade of proposals to liberate the FAA from the DOT has come before Congress, but none has passed and as the years go by, it appears even less likely that one will.

For several decades, the position of FAA Administrator was one of the plums of political patronage. The administrator served at the pleasure of the president, and turnover in the position was frequent, averaging about every two years—hardly sufficient time to accomplish anything in so ponderous a bureaucracy. Now, however, the individual appointed to the position is assured a 5-year term in office.

The FAA's activities cover a wide range, and include:

1. Regulation

The FAA regulates aviation safety, airspace use, and, to a certain extent, aircraft noise. The primary laws promulgated and enforced by the FAA are the Federal Aviation Regulations, found in Title 14 of the Code of Federal Regulations (14 CFR). This pervasive body of regulations addresses every conceivable aspect of aviation safety. Additionally, through those regulations prescribing airworthiness standards for the certification of new aircraft, the FAA has established aircraft noise limits. These regulations, developed in consultation with the Environmental Protection Agency (EPA), deserve credit as the primary incentive for development of the quieter high bypass ratio fanjet engines that came into use on the second generation of airline transport jets—the Boeing 747, Lockheed L-1011, and McDonnell Douglas DC-10. In comparison, the straight turbojet engines used on the first generation of jet transports, such as the Boeing 707, Douglas DC-8, and Convair 880, were positively thunderous. Indeed, as we'll see in Chapter 13, that first generation of airline jets (whose noise was not regulated by the FAA) appears largely responsible for creating the widespread enmity that persists today between airports and their noise-sensitive neighbors. Although these noisy "Stage 1" jets are now banned from flying in the U.S. unless retrofitted with quieter new technology engines of "hush kits," the legacy of public hostility toward airports engendered decades ago by their noise remains an effective obstacle to the development of new and the expansion of existing airports in this country.

The FAA also recently imposed noise limits on propeller-driven light and commuter aircraft receiving FAA type certification in 2006 and later, based on criteria developed by the International Civil Aviation Organization (ICAO, discussed later in this chapter).

Congress has also given the FAA sole regulatory authority over suborbital spacecraft, in the Commercial Space Launch Amendments Act of 2004, intended to encourage private enterprise investment and participation by avoiding overregulation of this developing area of commercial activity, recognizing that spaceflight is inherently more risky than flight in the atmosphere. That authority is now exercised by the FAA's Office of Commercial Space Transportation.

In addition to the FARs, the FAA from time to time issues other mandatory orders having the force and effect of law on the subject of aviation safety. The primary examples are Airworthiness Directives (ADs), which are FAA orders requiring some inspection or modification of previously certified aircraft. An AD is usually issued when operating and maintenance experience reveals the need to change some element of the design or fabrication of a particular type of aircraft or component to improve flight safety. The need for such an improvement may be revealed by an accident (or series of accidents), or by reports of difficulties experienced or observed by aircraft operators, inspectors, and mechanics in the field.

2. Certification

It is virtually impossible for a person or business to participate in any aspect of civil aviation in the United States without first obtaining one or more certificates from the FAA. The FAA certifies not only flight crew members—including pilots (student, sport, recreational, private, commercial, and airline transport), flight engineers, flight instructors, flight navigators, and ground instructors—but also airmen other than flight crew members, including air traffic control tower operators, aircraft dispatchers, mechanics, repairmen, and parachute riggers. The FAA also issues a great variety of ratings to accompany these certificates, as well as aviation medical certificates required of pilots and air traffic controllers (discussed in greater detail in Chapter 3).

The agency also certifies air carriers and commercial operators, including domestic, flag, and supplemental air carriers; foreign air carriers operating in the U.S., commuter and on-demand operators, rotorcraft external load operators, agricultural aircraft operators, and airports serving certificated air carriers; pilot schools and aviation training centers, aircraft and component repair stations, and aviation maintenance technician schools.

Additionally, each civil aircraft of U.S. manufacture is the product of three separate FAA inspection and certification processes. An aircraft manufacturer intending to introduce a new aircraft design into the marketplace must first produce prototype aircraft that are subjected to an intense program of both flight and static testing to prove the design's conformity to the certification standards contained in the FARs. Once this test program is completed to the satisfaction of the FAA, an FAA *Type Certificate* is issued, approving the design. Next, the manufacturer's production facilities and quality assurance program are submitted to FAA scrutiny. The agency must be convinced that the manufacturer's production and inspection methods are adequate to ensure that each aircraft produced will precisely replicate the design for which the type certificate was issued. Once this is accomplished, the FAA issues a *Production Type Certificate* and manufacturing can proceed. Next, each aircraft produced is inspected and tested for conformity with the original design and receives an FAA *Airworthiness Certificate* before being delivered to the customer. Subsequent modifications and improvements to the design require additional FAA certification, through amendments to the Type Certificate, by issuance of a *Supplemental Type Certificate*, or by a one-time field approval for modification of an individual aircraft under an FAA Form 337.

3. Registration

The FAA also operates a single centralized registry for all civil aircraft in the United States and for certain powerful aircraft engines and propellers. The FAA Aircraft Registry in the FAA Aeronautical Center in Oklahoma City maintains files on every aircraft that has ever been issued an "N-number" signifying U.S. registry (*see* Fig. 1.1). The files include the entire history of the sequence of owners of the aircraft and other legal interests in the aircraft, such as liens and encumbrances.

Fig. 1.1. If it has an "N-number," a title search through the FAA Aircraft Registry and the International Registry can reveal who owns it and who has recorded liens against it.

The utility and importance of this registry is explored in greater detail in Chapter 11.

4. Security

The Aviation and Transportation Security Act transferred the FAA's former air carrier security function to the TSA, but in that Act, Congress ordered the FAA to improve flight deck security by requiring airlines to strengthen flight deck doors and keep them locked except as necessary to permit authorized persons to enter or exit, and to develop guidance for training flight deck and cabin crews to deal with threats. Congress also ordered the FAA to explore the use of video monitors in the cabin, along with methods to prevent disabling of the aircraft's transponder in flight (as the 9/11 hijackers had done, to make tracking the aircraft more difficult) and improved methods for cabin crews to alert the flight deck of security breaches and other emergencies.

5. Cartography

Responsibility for the production of government aeronautical charts, once the domain of the Department of Commerce's National Ocean Service (NOS) has been transferred to the FAA. Along with that transfer of responsibility, over 300 NOS employees were transferred to the FAA's

National Aeronautical Charting Office (now called the Aeronautical Navigation Products Department or "AeroNav").

6. Education

The FAA educates members of the aviation community on new developments and matters pertaining to aviation safety through a system of publications, such as the Advisory Circulars (AC), and through safety seminars and recertification programs for flight instructors, pilot examiners, mechanics holding inspection authorization, and others. The FAA also trains its own employees at the FAA Academy in the Aeronautical Center in Oklahoma City and numerous programs at its various facilities.

7. Funding

Under the Airport Improvement Program (AIP), the FAA distributes federal matching funds for the construction of new airports, the improvement of existing airports, and related airport planning. These funds are appropriated by Congress from the Aviation Trust Fund comprising the proceeds of aviation fuel taxes paid by general aviation and passenger ticket taxes paid by persons traveling on U.S. commercial airlines. This funding program administers a trust fund currently valued at approximately $15 billion, generally expended at a rate of over $3 billion per year, and is discussed in greater detail in Chapter 13.

8. Investigation

The FAA investigates virtually all civil aircraft accidents in the United States, as well as some accidents outside the country involving U.S. built civil aircraft, in connection with the agency's air safety regulation and enforcement function. As more fully discussed in Chapter 10, the FAA also performs the on-site investigation of general aviation aircraft accidents under delegated authority on behalf of the National Transportation Safety Board (NTSB). The NTSB, however, has the exclusive authority to make the federal government's official finding of the *"probable cause"* of all civil aircraft accidents, regardless of whether the factual investigation was conducted by NTSB or FAA personnel.

The FAA also investigates incidents in which aviation safety may have been jeopardized but no accident occurred, as when two aircraft pass within such proximity as to create a collision hazard. The FAA also investigates all reports of violations of the Federal Aviation Regulations.

This process of investigation and enforcement in connection with alleged FAR violations is described in detail in Chapter 2.

9. Operations

The FAA operates a great variety of aviation facilities and equipment, including:

a. The Air Traffic Control (ATC) System

This system includes airport control towers, radar approach control (RAPCON or Approach) facilities, en route Air Route Traffic Control Centers (ARTCC or Center), the Air Traffic Control System Command Center (formerly known as Central Flow Control), and Flight Service Stations (FSS). There are some control towers operated by private enterprise and local governments at airports that do not meet activity-level criteria to qualify for a federal control tower, but most control towers and all RAPCONs and Centers are FAA operated. (Fig. 1.2) At this writing, Lockheed Martin is operating the FSS under contract to the FAA.

Fig. 1.2. Most ATC facilities, such as this control tower at the Cheyenne, Wyoming Regional Airport are operated by the FAA, although some towers at airports that are not busy enough to qualify for a federal tower are operated by private corporations under contract to local governments. More privatization of the ATC function is possible, as lawmakers search for ways to reduce federal spending.

b. Radio Aids to Navigation

The FAA also operates a vast network of ground-based radio aids to navigation ("navaids"), including radio beacons guiding aircraft over long distances (such as VORs and VORTACs), non-directional beacons (NDB) for imprecise navigation to some airports, and others that lead aircraft precisely to the runway in all weather, such as instrument landing systems (ILS), microwave landing systems (MLS), and the wide-area augmentation systems (WAAS) to improve the accuracy and reliability of satellite-based global positioning systems (GPS). Lockheed Martin operates the WAAS satellite for the FAA. Other radio aids to air navigation are operated by the Coast Guard (Loran C, although the U.S. has announced its intention to discontinue that service in favor of satellite-based navigation) and Department of Defense, which operates the constellation of GPS satellites. Local governments also operate some navaids, particularly NDBs, and private industry also owns and operates some approach aids, with several airlines having proprietary ILS or MLS equipment at remote airports they serve. With the increasing industry reliance on GPS navigation and impending implementation of the next generation air traffic control system (NextGen), it appears likely that a phase-out of many of these ground-based navaids may begin in this decade.

c. National Airports

For many years, the FAA was the operator of two of the major Washington, D.C. air carrier airports designated as the "National Airports" (Reagan—formerly known as Washington National—and Dulles). These airports are now operated by the Washington Metropolitan Airport Authority. (Fig. 1.3.)

d. Aeronautical Center

The FAA's Mike Monroney Aeronautical Center in Oklahoma City is a major record-keeping and training facility. There, you will find the Aircraft Registry (discussed more fully in Chapter 11), which maintains the records of ownership and other legal interests in every civil aircraft ever registered in the U.S. (*see also* Fig. 1.1 and accompanying text); the Airman Records Branch, which keeps a dossier on every person ever issued an FAA certificate; the FAA Academy, which trains air traffic controllers, air safety inspectors, and other FAA personnel; and the Civil Aviation Medical Institute (CAMI), which reviews and develops

Fig. 1.3. Ronald Reagan Washington National Airport with national capitol building visible in the background to left of tower. (Washington Metropolitan Airport Authority photo)

medical certification standards along with drug and alcohol testing policy for persons in the aviation industry.

e. Technical Center

The William J. Hughes Technical Center (formerly known as the National Aviation Facility Experimental Center or NAFEC), located near Atlantic City, NJ, is the site of the scientific test base for FAA research and development, test and evaluation activities relating to air traffic control, communication, navigation, airports, aviation security, and flight safety. The facility is deeply involved in shaping the Next-Gen air traffic system. The FAA does no basic research on aircraft and flight system technologies, these being within NASA's area of research responsibility. Where FAA and NASA research and development (R&D) responsibilities abut or overlap, the two agencies work together closely to coordinate their efforts without duplication, conflict, or waste. Throughout the federal government there is increased emphasis on interagency cooperation. Examples in aviation include Safer Skies, an FAA initiative that involved a wide range of government and industry organizations in an effort to improve the safety record of general and commercial aviation. The initiative is developing recommendations for changes in training, technology, and procedures with the goal of reducing general aviation accidents. The Safer Skies initiative also lead the FAA, NTSB, NASA, and a variety of industry associations to form the General Aviation Data Improvement Team (GADIT) to gather better data on general aviation accidents, especially those involving human factors. Another example is the Advanced General Aviation Transport Experiments (AGATE), a consortium of industry, higher education, and government entities (organized by NASA and including the FAA) focusing on developing technologies for general aviation. AGATE is intended to help revitalize the general aviation industry by advancing the use of new technologies in aircraft and developing new training methods for pilots. A related NASA program, the Small Aircraft Transportation System (SATS), is discussed later in this chapter in the section describing that agency.

National Transportation Safety Board (NTSB) (*www.ntsb.gov*)

The National Transportation Safety Board is an independent federal agency whose primary responsibility is to investigate transportation accidents, determine the "probable cause" of the accident, and recommend to the appropriate regulatory agencies (in the case of aviation, the FAA) measures that might prevent similar accidents in the future. Like the Department of Transportation, the NTSB's duties cover a broad range of civil transportation modes, including aviation, highway, marine, pipeline, and hazardous materials transportation accidents.

The NTSB is one of the smallest federal agencies, having only about 300 employees, only a fraction of whom are trained aircraft accident investigators. Therefore, the board must frequently delegate its on-site aircraft accident investigation duties to the better-staffed FAA. This is done particularly in non-fatal general aviation accidents, to allow the NTSB field investigators to concentrate on airline and other high-profile civil aviation accidents.

Regardless of which agency's employees conduct the on-site investigation, it is always the NTSB that must analyze the information and make the official finding of the probable cause of the accident. This process is discussed in greater detail in Chapter 10.

The NTSB also has the responsibility for coordinating and integrating the resources of the federal government and other organizations (such as the American Red Cross) to support the efforts of state and local governments and the airline to meet the needs of airline disaster victims and their families.

The NTSB also serves as the first level of appeal in cases where the FAA has taken enforcement action to suspend or revoke a certificate or, under certain circumstances, to impose a fine. This process is discussed in Chapter 2.

National Aeronautics and Space Administration (NASA) (*www.nasa.gov*)

Although NASA's name most commonly brings to mind the agency's space exploration activities, NASA continues to make important contributions in the areas of aerodynamics and aviation technology. In aerodynamics, NASA research & development led to the supercritical airfoil now in general use on high-performance aircraft (in both wing and propeller cross sections) and the "Whitcomb winglet" (Fig. 1.4), both of which increase aerodynamic efficiency and conserve aviation fuels. Much of the basic research that led to successive generations of increasingly quiet and fuel-efficient high bypass ratio fanjet engines was done at NASA.

Fig. 1.4. Many airliners are sprouting winglets such as these, originally developed by NASA, to improve fuel efficiency.

The agency is also conducting research into alternative aviation fuels, helicopter blades made of shape-changing materials to reduce noise and smooth out the ride, blended wing/fuselage technology to improve the efficiency and reduce the carbon emissions and noise footprint of subsonic jet transports (*see* Fig. 1.5), and the design and propulsion of a second-generation (the British Aerospace Concorde, now retired from service, being the first) supersonic or hypersonic transport. NASA research and development efforts in aviation have also led to advanced flight control and aircraft deicing systems, along with improvements in civil aircraft airworthiness. NASA is now providing research support in connection with development of the NextGen ATC system.

NASA's general aviation research activities focus on:

- Propulsion, noise and emissions improvements to reduce environmental impacts

Fig. 1.5. NASA is currently researching a blended wing body design for quieter and more efficient transport category jets. Here, a subscale X-48B is seen banking over desert scrub at Edwards Air Force Base. (NASA photo)

- New flight deck displays to improve safety
- Advanced metals and composites for general aviation applications
- Aerodynamic improvements to increase aircraft speed, capacity, and fuel efficiency

Recent interrelated general aviation programs supervised or participated in by NASA include the Highway in the Sky program, intended to ease pilot workload and simplify air navigation through more sophisticated electronic displays; the Advanced General Aviation Transport Experiments (AGATE), focused on developing technologies for general aviation; and the Small Aircraft Transportation System (SATS) program, building on the others to demonstrate the viability of

Fig. 1.6. The ergonomically designed high tech "glass cockpit" in this very light jet (VLJ) exemplifies the ease of operation goals of the AGATE and SATS programs.
(Hyku Photo)

Fig. 1.7. Very light jets, such as this Eclipse 500, may fulfill the vision of NASA's SATS program of doubling the number of U.S. communities receiving air transportation.
(Eclipse Aerospace, Inc. photo)

using increasingly-sophisticated light general aviation aircraft (Fig. 1.6), including very light jets (VLJs) (Fig. 1.7), to affordably reduce many of the expected problems in the nation's transportation system, such as increasing congestion on highways and at major airports served by the airlines, by providing point-to-point transportation between the thousands of existing public use airports not served by the airlines.

NASA also administers the confidential Aviation Safety Reporting Program (ASRP), designed to identify problems in the National Air Transportation System, especially those related to air traffic control. This program is described in greater detail in Chapter 2.

Civil Aeronautics Board (CAB)

Formerly the powerful and pervasive regulator of airline economics, including routes flown and routes served by U.S. airlines and foreign airlines serving the U.S., the CAB was gradually wound down as a result of Congress' passage of the Airline Deregulation Act of 1978. The CAB finally ceased to exist on January 1, 1985.

Before deregulation, the Public Utilities Commissions (PUCs) of most states also exercised tight regulatory control over the economic aspects of intrastate operations of air carriers, duplicating the CAB's controls over interstate and foreign transport for air carriers operating within the states. For example, in Colorado there is a niche market for air transportation between Denver and the state's ski resort areas. One airline focusing on serving this market was Rocky Mountain Airways (RMA), which operated only within Colorado. Before adding or deleting service between any two points within Colorado, RMA was required to obtain a certificate of public convenience and necessity from the state's PUC. Before setting or changing the fare to be charged on any of these routes, RMA was required to obtain PUC approval. This duplicative, expensive, and time and resource wasting state regulatory process was specifically preempted by the Deregulation Act, which prohibited all states except Alaska (which, due to its size, geography, and extremely limited highway system, is uniquely reliant on commercial air transportation) from regulating federally certificated airlines.

This federal preemption does not, however, extend into the areas of registration and taxation of aircraft, so that state aircraft registration requirements and state personal property or specific ownership taxes on aircraft are lawful and commonplace. Typical state aircraft registration and taxation programs are discussed in Chapter 11.

Air Transportation Stabilization Board (ATSB)

Only 11 days after the terrorist attacks of September 11, 2001, Congress passed the Air Transportation Safety and System Stabilization Act to compensate victims of the attacks for their losses and to aid the recovery of U.S. airlines from the financial consequences of the attacks. Victim compensation provisions of the Act are discussed in detail in Chapters 8 and 9.

The Act created the Air Transportation Stabilization Board, composed of the Secretary of Transportation, Chairman of the Board of Governors of the Federal Reserve System (designated as Chair of the ATSB), Secretary of the Treasury, and Comptroller General of the United States (as a nonvoting member), or their designees.

The ATSB was empowered to issue up to $10 billion in federal loan guarantees to the airlines and to compensate the airlines up to $5 billion for direct losses resulting from federal action grounding the airlines in the wake of the attacks.

National Mediation Board (NMB) (*www.nmb.gov*)

Unlike most other industries, labor-management relations in the airlines (and railroads) are governed not by the National Labor Relations Board (NLRB) under the National Labor Relations Act, but by the National Mediation Board under the Railway Labor Act of 1926, made applicable to common carriers by air in 1936. The NMB supervises union efforts to organize workers, elections, and conducts the compulsory mediation procedures the RLA requires as a mandatory step toward resolving major labor-management disputes within the airline industry. These procedures are discussed in detail in Chapter 17.

National Labor Relations Board (NLRB) (*www.nlrb.gov*)

The NLRB regulates labor-management relations in all U.S. industries except the airlines and railroads. Thus, the NLRB supervises union organizing efforts and elections, and rules on unfair labor practice claims in the aerospace manufacturing industry and general aviation (except general aviation operators conducting common carrier operations, such as on-demand charters and emergency medical air transportation). The NLRB's regulations and procedures are discussed in some detail in Chapter 16.

Federal Trade Commission (FTC) (*www.ftc.gov*) and Department of Justice (DOJ) (*www.usdoj.org*)

The Federal Trade Commission and Department of Justice police all industries for anticompetitive practices. In aviation, this mostly involves airline and aerospace manufacturer mergers and acquisitions and collusion among competitors in price-fixing.

The Department of Justice is also responsible for investigation and prosecution of federal crimes relating to aviation, such as aviation security and bogus parts cases. Crimes relating to aviation are discussed in Chapters 2 and 15.

In the Aviation and Transportation Security Act, Congress also directed the National Institute of Justice, the research and development branch of the Department of Justice, to assess potential use of nonlethal weapons by flight deck crewmembers to temporarily incapacitate intruders.

Customs and Border Protection (CBP) (*www.cbp.gov*)

The Aviation and Transportation Security Act required all airlines providing international air transportation to the United States to secure their computer reservation systems against unauthorized access and to electronically transmit passenger and crew manifests to U.S. Customs prior to departure. Under the Secure Flight Program, implementation of which began in early 2009, the TSA now screens the names on these lists against its "watch list" of known and suspected terrorists to identify persons who should be prevented from boarding (the No Fly List) or who should undergo additional security scrutiny (the Selectee List).

The CBP's Air and Marine division, formed in 2005 to consolidate several federal law enforcement aviation programs, is the world's largest civilian law enforcement air force, with over 700 pilots operating more than 272 aircraft of 22 different types (including unmanned aircraft systems). (Fig. 1.8.) The division's mission is to detect, interdict, and prevent acts of terrorism and the unlawful movement of people, illegal drugs and other contraband toward or across the borders of the United States, and to conduct air operations in support of other federal, state, and local needs, such as disaster relief.

Fig. 1.8. U.S. Customs and Border Protection Lockheed P-3 Orion on offshore patrol. (Customs and Border Protection photo)

The State Department (*www.state.gov*) and the President

The State Department negotiates treaties between the United States and other nations. Examples relating to aviation include treaties relating to air piracy and air transport agreements providing for reciprocal international air service. Once the State Department has negotiated a proposed treaty, it must be approved and executed by the President and ratified by the Senate.

Foreign air carriers designated by their country to provide service to the U.S. under an international air service agreement must receive a foreign air carrier permit before commencing operations to the U.S. The DOT issues these permits, after consultation with the State Department and subject to presidential approval under limitations described above in our discussion of the DOT.

STATE ADMINISTRATIVE AGENCIES

State governments are also free to regulate commerce, so long as state rules do not conflict with federal law or unduly burden interstate or foreign commerce. (See Chapter 13 for detailed discussion of the application of this concept to the regulation of airport operations and airspace use.)

In one example of permissible state regulation, Florida's Department of Environmental Protection (DEP) initiated enforcement action against Embry-Riddle Aeronautical University (ERAU) for the age-old and then industrywide practice of "sumping and dumping." It is a crucial step in the preflight inspection of any powered aircraft to drain small fuel samples from the aircraft's various fuel sumps to check for water, debris, and other possible contaminants, as well as to verify (by color and odor) that it is the correct type of fuel for that aircraft ("sumping"). For virtually the entire first century of powered flight, it was routine practice throughout at least the general aviation community to then discard each small collected sample by pouring it on the ground ("dumping"). The problem is that fuel is toxic, flammable, and corrosive, which qualifies it as *hazardous waste*. Although most of such a small sample of dumped avgas evaporates, some (including the tetraethyl lead additive) remains to run off into the soil and water, making the practice an unlawful disposal of hazardous waste, punishable by a fine of up to $50,000 per day under Florida law—enough to motivate anyone to make a focused effort to break an old bad habit. In consideration of ERAU partnering with DEP and the Aircraft Owners & Pilots Association (AOPA) to develop an educational campaign to persuade pilots to break this old bad habit, the state reduced the university's fine for the past illegal practice.

INTERNATIONAL REGULATION

International Civil Aviation Organization (ICAO) (*www.icao.org*)

Although not technically a regulatory agency, the International Civil Aviation Organization, an organ of the United Nations headquartered in Montreal, has had a profound worldwide effect on aviation standards.

ICAO was organized in late 1944 at the Chicago Conference. There (with World War II still raging in Europe and the Pacific), representatives of 52 allied and neutral nations gathered to chart global civil aviation's postwar course.

The two specific goals of the gathering were:

1. *Establishment of international technical standards* for airworthiness certification, flight crew certification, communications, and radio aids to navigation, and

2. *Establishment of principles and procedures for the economic regulation* of international civil aviation's routes, fares, frequency, and capacity.

The delegates' philosophy was clearly expressed in the preamble to the resulting treaty, the *Convention on International Civil Aviation* (also known as the *Chicago Convention*):

WHEREAS the development of international civil aviation can greatly help to create and preserve friendship and understanding among the nations and peoples of the world, yet its abuse can become a threat to the general security; and

WHEREAS it is desirable to avoid friction and to promote that cooperation between nations and peoples upon which the peace of the world depends;

THEREFORE, the undersigned governments having agreed on certain principles and arrangements in order that international civil aviation may be developed in a safe and orderly manner and that international air transport services may be established on the basis of equal opportunity and operated soundly and economically;

HAVE ACCORDINGLY concluded this Convention to that end.

Today, virtually all nations (at least 185) have signed the Convention on International Civil Aviation and ICAO has succeeded famously in achieving the first goal. ICAO-adopted technical standards, known as international Standards and Recommended Practices (SARPs), are published in a series of documents known as *Annexes* to the treaty. The smooth and efficient functioning of international civil aviation is largely attributable to ICAO's work. Wherever you fly on earth, you have ICAO to thank for communication and navigation systems that are compatible with the equipment in your aircraft and for the ability to communicate with air traffic controllers in the English language (an area ICAO has targeted for further improvement, because ATC English capabilities still vary widely across the globe). ICAO has also developed internationally accepted standards for the transport of hazardous materials by air and is actively pursuing agreement to achieve international harmonization of aircraft certification and operating rules as a goal to help reduce airlines' operating costs.

ICAO's Technical Cooperation Programme provides technical expertise, consultation, training, and airport and airway equipment to developing countries.

Concerns over global environmental deterioration have brought ICAO into the mix of organizations and businesses collaborating to minimize aviation's impact on the problem (quantified as about 2% of the emissions contributing to global warming).

Accomplishments in the area of the Chicago conferees' second goal were less sweeping, but significant. At that 1944 conference, The United States sought basically a free global market for the airlines, proposing that the nations of the world agree to recognize the Five Freedoms of the Air (*see* Fig. 1.9).

Although much of the world might jump at such a generous offer today, to gain greater access to comparatively lucrative U.S. markets, in late 1944 the United States was poised to dominate the international airline industry at war's end. At the beginning of World War II, there were only 365 transport aircraft in the U.S., but by war's end the U.S. had produced over 300,000 aircraft, of which over 11,000 were transports such as the C-47 (DC-3) and C-54 (DC-4), most of which would be taken out of service and disposed of as surplus shortly after the war's end. In the same time period, the U.S. had trained hundreds of thousands of aircrew members, including pilots, navigators, and loadmasters, along with mechanics, weather forecasters, dispatchers, and other essential support personnel. Many of these had operating experience on inter-

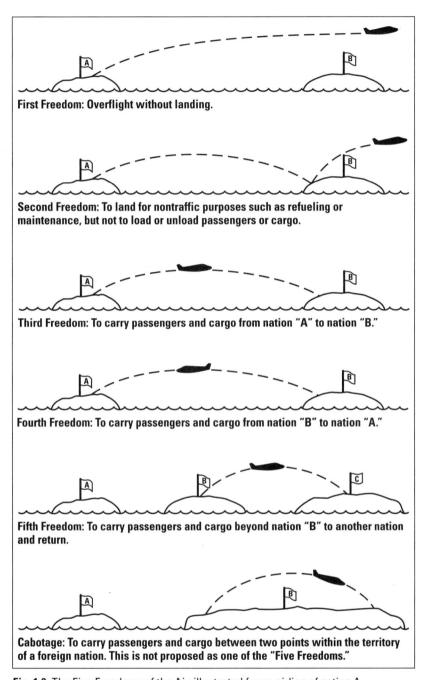

First Freedom: Overflight without landing.

Second Freedom: To land for nontraffic purposes such as refueling or maintenance, but not to load or unload passengers or cargo.

Third Freedom: To carry passengers and cargo from nation "A" to nation "B."

Fourth Freedom: To carry passengers and cargo from nation "B" to nation "A."

Fifth Freedom: To carry passengers and cargo beyond nation "B" to another nation and return.

Cabotage: To carry passengers and cargo between two points within the territory of a foreign nation. This is not proposed as one of the "Five Freedoms."

Fig. 1.9. The Five Freedoms of the Air, illustrated for an airline of nation A.

national routes and at foreign bases, and most would be mustered out of the armed forces and on the civilian job market shortly after the end of the war.

It would have required little more than a change of aircraft paint and crew uniforms to transform that military airlift fleet into civil airlines having a greater capacity than all of the other nations could hope to muster for many years. And unlike the other major powers on both sides of the war, America's aircraft manufacturing industry emerged intact, with plants undamaged, new designs in progress, and (with the abrupt cancellation of military orders) excess capacity to produce those new transports.

Thus it is not surprising that national protectionism prevailed over free market competition. The conferees agreed only on the principle of international sovereignty in airspace, providing that no scheduled international air service may be operated over or into a nation or its airspace without its permission.

A separate agreement known as the *Transit Agreement* was also signed at that time in Chicago by fewer than all of the conferees, agreeing to the first two Freedoms (overflights and nontraffic stops). Foremost among the nonsigners were the security-obsessed nations of the communist bloc. (Also understandable, considering the devastation they had received and were still receiving from Axis air power.) The other Freedoms were left to be negotiated between individual nations, although as part of the Chicago Conference, ICAO did develop a standard form of bilateral (between two nations) agreement for exchange of air routes. The form has been widely used since and is generally recognized as a significant contribution to the high degree of consistency in commercial international air service agreements for well over a half century. According to ICAO, over 3,500 bilateral air service agreements are in effect today.

Additional Freedoms discussed since the Chicago conference and included in some bilateral and multilateral (between more than two nations) air service agreements are:

- **Sixth Freedom:** The right to carry traffic from one nation through the homeland and on to a third nation.
- **Seventh Freedom:** The right to carry traffic between two foreign nations without going through the home country.
- **Eighth Freedom:** (Also called *cabotage*.) The right to carry traffic between two points in a foreign country, such as if a European

airline were permitted to operate commercial flights between New York and Los Angeles. If the origin and destination are located in geographically separated parts of that country, such as the route between Los Angeles and Anchorage, it is called *grand cabotage.*

In the United States, the President's National Commission to Ensure a Strong Competitive Airline Industry found that the prevailing bilateral agreement system was no longer conceptually sound or sufficiently growth-oriented in the global trade environment. The Commission recommended that U.S. negotiating efforts should focus on creating multilateral agreements.

Open Skies Agreements are the latest fashion in treaties for international air service. Unlike the bilateral agreements that were typical for many decades following the Chicago conference, open skies agreements (which may be either bilateral or multilateral) do not limit the service to be provided by airlines of signatory nations to specific city pairs (i.e., New York City–Paris), but give the airlines of both countries the right to operate between any point in one country and any point in another, as well as to and from third countries (*"beyond rights"*). Other features of open skies agreements designed to encourage competition include:

- **Free Market Competition:** No restrictions on number of airlines the signatory nations may designate to provide service under the treaty, or on capacity, frequency of service, or types of aircraft.
- **Pricing Determined by Market Forces:** A fare can be disallowed only if both governments concur—*"double disapproval pricing"*— only allowed for certain specified reasons intended to assure competition.
- **Fair and Equal Opportunity to Compete:** Carriers of all signatory nations may establish sales offices in all others, may convert earnings and remit them to the home country in hard currency and without restrictions, may provide their own ground handling services (*"self handling"*) or choose among competing providers, may arrange ground transport of air cargo, and are guaranteed access to customs services.
- **Cooperative Marketing Arrangements:** Designated airlines may enter into code-sharing or leasing arrangements with airlines of other signatory countries, with those of third countries, and even with surface transportation companies.
- **Liberal Charter Arrangements:** Airlines may choose to operate under the charter regulations of any signatory country.

- **"Seventh Freedom" Rights:** Some open skies agreements include authority for an airline of one signatory nation to operate *all-cargo* services between another signatory nation and a third country via flights not linked to the airline's homeland.
- **Safety and Security:** Each signatory government agrees to observe high standards of aviation safety and security, and to render assistance to the others in certain circumstances.
- **Dispute Settlement and Consultation:** The model text agreement (available on the State Department website, *www.state.gov*) includes procedures for settling differences that may arise under the agreement.

In 2007, the United States entered into an open skies agreement with the European Union. The agreement allows any airline of the E.U. and any airline of the U.S. to provide service between any point in the U.S. and any point in the E.U. The agreement favors U.S. carriers in that they are also allowed to fly between points in the E.U., while E.U. airlines are not permitted to provide service between points in the U.S. or own a controlling interest in a U.S. airline. The U.S. has concluded over 70 bilateral and multilateral open skies agreements to date.

First Freedom rights of overflight were granted by Russia beginning in 2001, allowing shorter and more efficient polar great circle commercial airline routes between North America and Asia, saving the airlines millions of dollars each year in fuel, staff costs, and landing fees at intermediate airports such as Anchorage.

Air piracy (hijacking and terrorism) has proved to be one of the most difficult and enduring problems facing ICAO. Such unlawful interference with civil aviation is hardly a recent phenomenon. The first reported episode occurred in 1784, when a young man forced his way into the basket of a Charliere (helium) balloon and demanded at swordpoint that he be carried aloft. ICAO statistics show that such incidents were extremely rare until 1968, when hijacking became a fad. Some 200 aircraft hijackings occurred worldwide from 1968 through 1970. The perpetrators were mostly criminals seeking to escape, mentally unstable persons, or political militants. A few acts of sabotage against airliners have simply been murders perpetrated in an attempt to collect on the life insurance of a targeted passenger. Politically-motivated terrorists have been responsible for the most recent hijackings and acts of sabotage against civil aviation, such as the blowing up of Pan Am flight 103 over Lockerbie, Scotland, and the hijacking of four U.S. airliners for use as weapons to perpetrate the most lethal terrorist attack in human history on the twin towers of the World Trade Center in New York City and the Pentagon in Washington, D.C. (The fourth aircraft crashed in rural Pennsylvania after the passengers, learning of the fate of the first three, attempted to regain control of the aircraft from the terrorists and prevented it from reaching its still-unknown intended target, no doubt saving others' lives in the process.)

The problem is one of global dimensions, which no single nation could effectively solve. Yet the frequent presence of a political motive for such acts has greatly complicated efforts to achieve global consensus on an appropriate approach to solutions. In such situations, although the nation whose airliner is attacked and others unsympathetic to the attackers' particular cause may view the attackers as terrorists or common criminals, others sympathetic to their cause may view them as heroic freedom fighters or even religious martyrs.

Given the level of factionalism and hatred in the world, it sometimes seems amazing that any agreements can be reached over such emotional and politically-charged issues, but under ICAO's leadership, about 100 nations have signed treaties agreeing to promptly return hijacked aircraft to their countries of origin, permit hijacked passengers to continue their journey as soon as possible, and hold suspected hijackers for investigation and either prosecute them under their own law or extradite them to the country whose aircraft was hijacked for prosecution under its law. While the threat has by no means been eliminated (because a significant number of nations have not signed the treaty and some continue to offer safe haven to hijackers and terrorists whose political agendas they support), significant progress has been made on the diplomatic front.

Meanwhile, as efforts continue to achieve world peace and improve international civil aviation safety and security, it appears certain that the role of ICAO will continue to increase in importance.

International Air Transport Association (IATA) (*www.iata.org*)

When the Chicago Conference failed to reach agreement on its second goal of regulating international civil aviation's routes, fares, frequency, and capacity, the international airlines formed their own trade association, the International Air Transport Association, to address these issues. IATA is also headquartered in Montreal. Initially operating primarily as a cartel to divide up markets and fix prices on international air routes,

IATA soon came into conflict with U.S. antitrust laws. As a result, the association discontinued that function.

Today, IATA's most important function is its clearinghouse in London, which rapidly settles accounts amounting to over $30 billion annually for interline transactions among member airlines and with their associated travel agents. (The Air Transport Association or ATA performs a similar clearinghouse function for U.S. airlines in domestic operations.) Without these clearinghouses, arranging travel requiring a change of airline would be an unbelievably complicated nightmare, particularly in the international arena where currency differences and fluctuating exchange rates add to the intricacy of the task.

IATA also works closely with ICAO on technical issues involving airline operations, safety, and security and has formed an alliance with the Flight Safety Foundation (FSF) to exchange information and promote the best airline safety practices.

IATA's *Aviation Training & Development Institute* offers a wide variety of courses in airline and airport management, aviation law, aviation security, airline safety, pilot selection, crew resource management, airport planning, and air navigation services. These courses are taught in 66 locations around the world, as well as by distance learning.

The association also publishes about 300 reference and training publications vital to the industry on topics such as safety, security, ground handling, transporting dangerous goods, and airport development.

2

FAA Enforcement

As we saw in the previous chapter, the Federal Aviation Regulations have always been the "law." The FAA employs thousands of aviation safety inspectors and hundreds of attorneys to enforce this body of law. Aviation professionals and general aviation operators are probably now more likely to encounter an FAA inspector than any other law enforcement officer.

The FAA issues certificates to a wide variety of specialized personnel (such as pilots, flight engineers and navigators, maintenance personnel, maintenance inspectors, air traffic controllers, aircraft dispatchers, ground and flight instructors, and parachute riggers); businesses (such as aircraft and component manufacturers, aircraft and component repair stations, commercial air carriers, air taxi and commercial charter operators, helicopter external load operators, and flight and aviation maintenance schools); operators of airports serving air carriers (most of which are regional or local governmental entities); and even products (such as individual aircraft, each of which receives an airworthiness certificate). The FAA also has the power to deny, suspend or revoke any and all of these certificates.

Because FAA actions to enforce the FARs are characterized as *administrative law* rather than *criminal law*, FAA inspectors are not required to advise suspects of their legal rights. In an effort to appear to be good cooperative citizens, aviators, maintenance personnel, aviation managers and others often make voluntary statements to FAA inspectors and air traffic controllers that are subsequently used by the agency to suspend or revoke their certificates or to punish them by imposing substantial fines.

The purpose of this chapter is to furnish a practical working knowledge of your legal rights in FAA investigation and enforcement situations. A separate course of study can and should be devoted to the organization and requirements of the FARs. Although the majority of the examples used in this chapter involve pilots, the same principles apply to actions against all individuals, businesses, and even public entities (such as airports serving air carriers) that may be charged with FAR violations.

A Range of Possible Consequences

When the FAA has reason to suspect that an individual or company has violated one or more of the Federal Aviation Regulations, the FAA can choose from a variety of penalties to punish the violator:

1. *Administrative Dispositions.*

When the FAA considers the violation to be minor, of little consequence but too serious to ignore altogether, it may dispose of the case administratively through the issuance of a warning notice or letter of correction.

   a. *Warning Notice.* Being issued a Warning Notice by the FAA is very much like receiving a warning from a police officer in a traffic case. The notice outlines the facts about the incident and indicates that it may have been a violation of the FARs but that the FAA has decided not to file formal charges.

   b. *Letter of Correction.* When a minor violation involves a condition that has since been corrected (for example, if the FAA inspector found an aircraft's ELT battery out-of-date and the owner immediately rectified the discrepancy), the FAA may issue a Letter of Correction outlining the facts of the incident or condition, stating that it may have been a violation of the FARs, but noting that in light of the corrective action taken, no enforcement action will be pursued.

The Letter of Correction is also used to provide for *remedial training* for some FAR violations, instead of punishment. This allows an individual suspected of a violation to submit to a course of remedial training (instead of having to face a certificate suspension or fine) if:

   a. The violation did not occur in connection with an operation for compensation or hire in air transportation, *and*

   b. The FAA is satisfied that you have a constructive attitude so that remedial training will probably lead you to a life of future FAR compliance, *and*

c. Your violation was not one that would indicate an underlying basic lack of qualification to hold your certificate, *and*

d. You don't already have a record of noncompliance with the FARs, *and*

e. Your violation was not deliberate, grossly negligent, or a criminal offense.

Unlike reexamination (discussed later in this chapter), remedial training does not include a testing component, so as long as you take the agreed training with an instructor of your choice during a time period that you and the FAA agree to, you will be off the hook with a Letter of Correction.

In my experience, most FAR violations are unintentional errors made by people who are really trying to comply with the regulations but make a human error. A little refresher training with an instructor never hurt anybody, and every client I have been able to help get into this program has come away feeling like a better pilot for the experience. And most importantly, remedial training doesn't result in an FAR violation going on your record. Presented with the option between remedial training and an enforcement action, I'd snap up the opportunity for remedial training every time.

If a Warning Notice or Letter of Correction is issued, this becomes a part of your airman record at the FAA Aeronautical Center in Oklahoma City. Warning Notices and Letters of Correction are automatically removed from your airman record two years after issuance. Meanwhile, this record is always consulted by FAA inspectors investigating alleged violations, and if it appears that the person or the company under investigation has a previous administrative disposition of record, a harsher penalty will be sought in the subsequent case, on the theory that "last time we were nice guys and gave him a break, and he obviously didn't learn his lesson from that, so this time we have to hit him harder to get his attention." Under current FAA policy, administrative dispositions are frequently used to provide remedial training to rusty individual certificate holders and under self-reporting programs for air carriers and manufacturers (discussed later in this chapter), but legal enforcement action in the nature of a certificate action or civil penalty is still taken quite frequently.

2. Certificate Action.

Where the violation is one of an operational nature (rather than, for example, a mere delinquency in record keeping), the FAA prefers to suspend or revoke the FAA certificate(s) held by the violator. The election between revocation or suspension—and, if suspension is elected, the duration of the suspension imposed—is determined by the FAA attorney handling the case, with the advice of the inspector who conducted the investigation and by reference to a table of sanction guidelines issued by the FAA's Washington, D.C., headquarters. Factors considered by the attorney in reaching this decision include:

a. *Precedent.* Penalties previously imposed by the FAA and upheld by the NTSB on appeal in similar cases serve as a guideline for future penalties.

b. *Current FAA Enforcement Priorities.* In the course of its safety-regulating duties, the FAA looks for patterns appearing in its investigations of accidents, incidents, and violations, and as a matter of policy focuses on certain types of misbehavior that may appear to be "getting out of hand" or causing particular concern. These receive increased emphasis in inspections and related enforcement actions. When an alleged violation falls within an area designated by FAA management for such special emphasis, penalties harsher than those previously applied for such a violation may be sought on the theory that precedent punishment has proven insufficient to deter such violations.

c. *Individual Considerations.* In selecting the sanction to impose on an individual violator, the FAA attorneys are also instructed to consider the following factors:

    i. The degree of hazard to the safety of other aircraft and persons or property in the aircraft or on the ground created by the alleged violation;

    ii. The nature of the violation (whether inadvertent or deliberate);

    iii. The violator's previous record (the FAA expects everyone to obey the law and have a violation-free record, so a previous violation is considered an aggravating circumstance that will lead to a harsher penalty in a later case, but a clean record is not considered a mitigating factor to reduce the penalty);

    iv. The alleged violator's level of experience (more-experienced pilots are expected to make fewer mistakes);

v. The attitude of the alleged violator (a positive attitude toward FAR compliance may soften the penalty, while a bad attitude may lead to harsher treatment);

vi. The nature of the activity involved (private, public, or commercial, the latter calling for a harsher penalty);

vii. Any ability of the alleged violator to absorb the sanction without any real impact (such as by taking an earned vacation during the period of suspension or an employer's offer to pay any fine imposed); and

viii. Whether the violation indicates an underlying lack of qualifications on the part of the violator to hold a certificate (either as the result of lack of skills or knowledge or an attitude of disrespect toward the FARs)

d. *The Horror Factor.* The FAA attorney's subjective "gut" feeling about the seriousness of the violation also plays a role in the selection of a penalty. Few FAA attorneys are pilots or have any other practical background in aviation, so this evaluation is often affected by views expressed by the investigating inspector and any sensational publicity that may have appeared in the news media.

3. Civil Penalties (fines).

The FAA attorney has the option of imposing a fine instead of taking certificate action in some cases. (Constitutional prohibitions against double jeopardy have generally been construed to allow the FAA to either impose a fine or to take certificate action, but not to do both for the same violation.) For operational violations, FAA enforcement policy generally encourages the use of certificate action against individuals and civil penalties against companies. However, if the FAA feels that the management of a certificate-holding company (such as an air carrier or repair station) is not making a serious effort to obey the FARs, it will not hesitate to suspend or revoke that company's operating certificate. A civil penalty may be the only punishment available against an FAR violator who is not required to hold an FAA certificate, such as the pilot of an ultralight vehicle or a skydiver.

If the FAA attorney elects to proceed with a civil penalty (fine), the agency may seek to collect a maximum of $1,000 per violation in most cases against individuals and some businesses, $10,000 per violation by air carriers and airport operators, or $250,000 for falsification of documents.

Most incidents give rise to more than one regulatory violation, if only because whenever an FAR is violated, the FAA almost always adds a residual charge of a violation of FAR 91.13 (careless or reckless operation) on the theory that it is careless or reckless to violate any FAR. For continuing operations, the FAA may count them on a per-flight or per-day basis. For example, if an airplane made a dozen flights after an AD was due but had not been performed, the operator could be fined $1,000 per flight for the overdue AD plus $1,000 per flight for a careless or reckless operation. In the alternative, if this situation was allowed to exist while the aircraft was operated over a period of thirty days, each day could count as a violation of each of these regulations. In either event the potential fine could quickly build to an astronomical number. If the violator is an air carrier or airport operator, multiply that result by ten.

4. Summary Seizure of Aircraft.

If the FAA charges you or your company with a violation and is concerned about your ability to pay such a fine, the agency also has the power to seize the aircraft involved and hold it until the fine is paid or bond is posted to cover the fine.

5. Reexamination.

If an accident, incident, or report of an FAR violation causes the FAA to be concerned about your competency, the FAA may require you to submit to reexamination in the area of concern. This may include a repetition of written, oral, flight, or other practical tests required for the certificate involved. The FAA must have some reasonable basis for requesting such reexamination, but if it does you have no right of appeal and *must* submit to reexamination, at your own expense.

If you do not submit to reexamination within a reasonable period of time, that in itself is an FAR violation for which the FAA may suspend or revoke your certificates. For example, if during IFR operations ATC observed you having some difficulty executing a published instrument approach procedure, wandering all over the sky, they might then require you to submit to another instrument flight test with concentration on instrument approach procedures as a condition of keeping your instrument rating. Before any reexamination, it is wise to spend some time with an instructor polishing your skills and updating your knowledge in the area in question.

Where an FAR violation caused the concern about your qualifications, the FAA can both require you to submit to reexamination and punish you for the violation by certificate action or fine. This is generally not considered to violate the constitutional prohibition against double jeopardy since the reexamination is not considered punishment.

INVESTIGATIONS

The FAA is required by Congress to investigate all reports of FAR violations, regardless of how far-fetched the initial report may sound. Most reports of FAR violations are investigated by FAA inspectors, usually those assigned to a Flight Standards District Office (FSDO).

The majority of FAR violations come to the attention of these FAA inspectors during the regular conduct of their duties, including aircraft accident investigations; routine checks (such as base inspections of aviation businesses); and airport surveillance (including ramp checks of aircraft operators and the hated "weekend duty" when the inspector on call for accident investigations may meanwhile roam around local general aviation airports, looking for problems like a cop on the beat).

The FAA's air traffic controllers are the second major source of reports of FAR violations. For example, if a flight operating under Instrument Flight Rules (IFR) deviates from an altitude assigned by the ATC, a report may be forwarded to the inspectors for investigation and prosecution as an FAR violation. In fact, the ATC computer program has a feature, officially named the Quality Assurance Program and generally called "the Snitch Patch," that *automatically* calls many deviations from clearances to the attention of FAA enforcement personnel.

ATC has caught and reported thousands of airspace violations since the terrorist attacks of 9/11/01 caused a dramatic increase in the designation (often on extremely short notice) of temporary flight restrictions (TFRs). Some of these errant pilots have been intercepted by fighters and escorted to a nearby airport (not usually the airport of intended landing), where they were met and interrogated by Secret Service agents eager to assure the pilot had no terrorist intent. FAA enforcement action has sometimes followed. (See Chapter 14 for more on airspace regulation.)

The third largest source of reports of FAR violations is the general public. Reports from the general public arise largely out of "buzz jobs," when a citizen is frightened or annoyed by low-flying aircraft, or low-flying aircraft spook livestock in a rural area. (Fig. 2.1.) Since the terrorist

Fig. 2.1. While the "buzz job" has a long history as the choice expression of exuberance by aviators, the public is no longer amazed or amused by such antics, more often responding with a flash of fear or anger instantly followed by the capturing of a picture or video clip on their cell phone or other photographic equipment, as seen here. The proliferation of small portable imaging devices in the hands of law enforcement officers and ordinary citizens has greatly increased the likelihood that low-flying aircraft and their pilots will be successfully prosecuted.

attacks of 2001, the general public has been particularly jumpy about low-flying aircraft, fearing that the pilot intends to crash into them or spray them with some lethal substance.

The FAA has a toll-free telephone number (800-255-1111) at its Washington, D.C., office for the Safety Hotline anyone can call to report FAR violations. The FAA promises to keep the caller's identity confidential if requested and begins a preliminary investigation of each report within one day. The FAA is also providing grant funding for a similar hotline operated by the National Air Transportation Association (NATA) for charter operators to report suspected illegal commercial operations in violation of FAR Part 135, a perpetual problem in the industry. The toll-free number for that hotline is 888-759-3581.

While the circumstances leading up to an FAA enforcement action are sometimes downright laughable, finding yourself the focus of one is anything but amusing. For example, a DC-3 freighter had just landed at a Florida airport and as the crew was taxiing to park, they noticed a group of young Civil Air Patrol (CAP) cadets drilling on the ramp to the immediate left of the aircraft's course. As the cadets paused to watch the proud classic airliner taxi grandly by, the captain said to the first officer: "Your aircraft." The first officer took the controls, responding: "I have the aircraft." The captain then opened the cockpit window, released his seat belt, rose, lowered his trousers and "mooned" the passing cadets, failing to first notice that the proud mother of one of the cadets was videotaping the drill and the taxiing DC-3. Mother was appalled. When she showed the videotape to the FAA, they were not amused, either, and issued an Emergency Order of Revocation of the pilot's airline transport pilot (ATP) certificate, alleging that he lacked the "good moral character" required to hold such a certificate, along with careless or reckless operation. At the hearing (more on this process momentarily) before a female NTSB Administrative Law Judge (ALJ), the videotape was shown several times, to the pilot's increasing embarrassment. By the conclusion of the hearing, the pilot's attorney was able to beat the moral character charge (the ALJ finding the "mooning" only a juvenile prank), but the judge found in favor of the FAA on the charge of careless operation (based largely on the first officer's testimony that he was laughing so hard he could barely steer the aircraft). She reduced the penalty accordingly to a 10-day suspension of the captain's ATP certificate, with credit for time served. The moral of the story, in this era of proliferation of personal digital and video cameras, and cell phones that can take and send digital photos and video clips, is that before doing something frisky with your flying machine, you should ask yourself: "How is this going to look to the FAA and the NTSB ALJ when (not if) they see it on video?"

The Crucial Moment (Ramp Checks, etc.)

Although you have the right to appeal the charges and have a hearing with your attorney present to represent you, as a practical matter the most crucial moment in the entire process is likely to be your first contact with an FAA representative. In my experience, people under investigation frequently make damaging admissions in early statements to the FAA, often not even realizing that they are under investigation for a suspected violation. Such admissions may later make it impossible for your attorney effectively to defend the formal charges brought against you.

Although on appeal the FAA will have the burden of proving its charges, your early admissions may be all that it takes. For example, in a violation alleged to have been committed by a general aviation aircraft operating noncommercially and under visual flight rules (VFR), the most difficult element for the FAA to prove on appeal may be the identity of the pilot-in-command of the aircraft at the time of the alleged violation (for example, in a simple low-flying case). If you have already admitted to the FAA that you were flying the airplane (although you may vigorously dispute charges that you were flying too low), that admission can be used against you on appeal. The testimony at hearing might go something like this:

FAA ATTORNEY: Inspector Stern, did you contact the Respondent, Mr. Badguy in the course of your investigation?

FAA INSPECTOR: Yes, Sir, I telephoned his home that same afternoon, and a person who identified himself as Mr. Badguy answered. I told him that we had received a complaint from a citizen that his plane was flying low over the town of Brooklawn earlier that day. He told me that he had been flying over Brooklawn about that time, but stated that he had been at least one thousand feet above ground level at all times.

Thus, the pilot provided the FAA the evidence needed to identify him as the pilot-in-command, an element that might have been impossible to prove without his admission.

Part of the problem here is the nature of the FAA inspector's job, which requires the kind professionalism of Dr. Jekyll when counseling individuals and companies involved in aviation to help us get the certificates we need and to stay out of trouble, then to transmogrify into the vicious Mr. Hyde and prosecute us to the fullest extent of the law when we are suspected of having violated an FAR. Another part of the problem is our attitude toward the FAA. From our earliest flight training, we are trained to think of the FAA as our friend. If we want to obtain a pilot certificate, add a rating to an existing certificate, or get authority to start an aviation business, we first go to see our friends at the FAA (the same inspectors who may later bring an enforcement case against us). If we find ourselves confused by an FAR and need guidance to interpret it, we consult our friendly FAA inspector. If we find ourselves in a dilemma in flight, perhaps in clouds with failing navigational equipment, we radio for help to our friends in FAA ATC. And each of these contacts is to be commended; for it is often only through such cooperation that we can live through many in-flight emergencies and remain in compliance with the regulations.

But many of the FARs are quite vague and subject to differing interpretations. Despite your best efforts to comply you may someday find, much to your chagrin, that an FAA inspector's interpretation differs from your own. As a result of this difference of opinion, you or your company may be temporarily or permanently deprived of the FAA certificates necessary to conduct your business (or at least prerequisite to your personal pleasure flying). For example, you may have undertaken a flight you believed proper under your authority as a commercial pilot only to find an FAA inspector later believes that you could not have legally performed the flight without also holding an air-taxi/commercial-operator certificate issued under FAR Part 135. Or, being human, you may simply make an inadvertent mistake that results in an FAR violation. In either event, the first contact you have with the FAA over this problem may be the most crucial moment in the entire experience. Yet unless you are in the habit of traveling around with your lawyer handcuffed to your wrist, which most of us are not, your first contact with the FAA—the most crucial moment in the entire case—will occur without your having the benefit of legal advice. In fact, it is very likely that you may not even realize until it's too late that your good old buddy from the FAA is talking to you this time in his Mr. Hyde enforcement role. If you committed some crime, such as holding up a convenience store, the first law enforcement officer to contact you during the course of the investigation would have to advise you of your legal rights before anything you said could be used against you in court. We've all seen those TV crime shows where the suspect is given the *Miranda warning* advising him of his rights. Most FAR violations, however, are not crimes and the courts have held that the FAA does not have to advise you of your legal rights before taking statements from you with the intent of using them against you to suspend or revoke your certificate. The courts consider such cases "merely administrative."

You have most of the same rights as a criminal suspect in that situation; it's just that the FAA doesn't have to advise you of those rights before interrogating you, so I will: *When questioned by the FAA, you have the right to remain silent. Anything you say can and will be used against you to suspend or revoke your certificate or fine you. You have the right to have your attorney present during any questioning.* (Unfortunately, you do not have the right to require the government to appoint an attorney to represent you if you can't afford one.)

While in a formal "ramp check" the inspector will usually identify himself as such, FAA inspectors are not required to identify themselves before striking up a conversation with you. Because of this, and because they are not required first to advise you of your rights, many people have given FAA inspectors enough information to hang them without even realizing that the person they were talking to was an FAA inspector. Indeed, in my experience, it is quite common for some FAA inspectors to try to trick people into confessing their participation in violations in order to perfect an otherwise difficult enforcement case. The seemingly friendly person who strikes up a conversation with you on the ramp some sunny weekend may well be an FAA inspector on airport surveillance duty hoping to get you to say something useable to prove an enforcement case against you. He doesn't have to identify himself unless you inquire whether he works for the FAA and request to see his FAA identification. After 9/11, in addition to their FAA ID, real FAA Inspectors now carry badges. They frequently begin an investigation by subterfuge since the law permits them to, and it's usually a lot easier than trying to get answers out of someone who knows what's going on, knows their rights, and has an attorney at hand.

My favorite example of this occurred in a small rural community. The town was having its annual July 4th celebration at a lakefront park, and a local skydiving club was invited to participate. Because the town might have been construed by the FAA as a "congested area" under the FARs, an airshow waiver was obtained from the FAA to permit the jump under certain conditions, notwithstanding the general FAR prohibition against parachuting over and into congested areas. A condition of that waiver was that the parachute jumpers must land in the lake. During his descent, one of the jumpers decided that he didn't really want to get his parachutes wet and have to go to the trouble of drying them out before repacking them. So he turned his parachute and steered to a landing in a cul-de-sac on a dirt road on the very fringe of town, where he landed safely without any perceptible danger to the three shanties in the neighborhood and their associated chicken coops. As he was gathering up his parachute, a beat-up old green pickup truck came bouncing down the road and pulled up beside him.

"Kind of missed your spot didn't you, sonny?" inquired the bib overall-clad driver.

"Nah, I just decided I didn't want to get my chutes wet," the jumper replied.

"Would you like a ride back over to where the other fellows landed?" offered the driver.

The jumper gladly accepted, and the friendly conversation continued during the ride, with the kindly old farmer asking things like: "What's your name? My, that's an unusual last name, how do you spell that?" and "Where do you work, George?"

As they were nearing the beach where the other jumpers had gathered, there was a lull in the conversation and the jumper took it to be his turn, asking: "What's your name?" followed by "Where do you work, Al?"

The answer to his final question was "I'm an FAA aviation safety inspector at the Denver Flight Standards District Office."

The truck stopped and the driver dropped the jumper off then went on to his office to file a violation that would prove unbeatable, given the jumper's admissions.

This example is only the most vivid and amusing of the great many I've seen in which people had no idea they were under investigation for an FAA violation until they had already made damaging admissions. I've seen other cases in which inspectors (without having first identified themselves) struck up conversations with people on airport ramps, in Fixed Base Operator (FBO) offices, or at social gatherings, or have telephoned and begun asking questions without revealing their purpose.

If, however, the person does claim to be an FAA representative, you should request to see his FAA ID and badge to verify the claim. Be sure to compare the face to the photo on the ID. In one case, FAA inspectors performing a base inspection on a major airline switched ID cards before going through the airline's security, and then hit the airline with a $20,000 fine for the security breach when they were allowed in. If the person claiming to be from the FAA can't produce an FAA ID and badge, or if the photo on the ID doesn't match the face of the person carrying it, call airport security or the police immediately.

Is there some way you can tell when your FAA inspector has made that switch from the kindly Dr. Jekyll who's your buddy to the vicious Mr. Hyde who is trying to take away your certificates? Is there some clue to alert you to the possibility that you are under investigation and your certificate may be in jeopardy? Yes, there is, and it is this: Someone from the FAA wants to talk to you about *history* (and by *history* I mean anything that has already occurred, whether years, months, minutes, or even seconds ago). Whenever an FAA representative wants to discuss history with you, an annunciator light should start flashing and bells ringing in your mind to alert you that you are probably now a suspect in an FAA enforcement case.

Now, of course, there is always the possibility that this particular FAA representative is writing the definitive history of aviation in the United States in her spare time and is only checking to be sure she has the facts straight for the chapter devoted to your role. But the probability of that is remote. The only other reason that someone from the FAA ever wants to discuss history is that they have been assigned the duty of building an enforcement case against you or the company you work for (or both).

One lawyer-pilot friend of mine, who had successfully defended numerous pilots to the embarrassment of her local FSDO, encountered an FAA inspector on the ramp as she was heading toward the FBO office at the conclusion of a flight. He wanted to ask her some questions. Recognizing a ramp check when she saw one and knowing that this individual was out to get her, she said she'd be glad to talk to him, but first she had to make a restroom stop (entirely plausible to any pilot). The inspector took a seat in the office outside the door when she entered the women's restroom, where she climbed out the window, got in her car and drove home. Whenever he finally realized he'd been tricked, he probably made a very nasty note in his file.

So there you are. The FAA inspector is in your face or on the telephone and wants to talk about history with you. The annunciator light is flashing and the bells are ringing in your mind, and you have that tightness in your throat that comes with recognition that the FAA is out to get you. Congratulations! At least you know what's going on, unlike many of the previous victims of FAA investigation and enforcement actions. But what are you going to do about it? Well, a good opener is always: "Why do you ask?" You may as well see if you can find out what this is all about, first, if you aren't already certain.

Then, you are on the horns of a dilemma. You know that you have the right to remain silent, that anything you say will almost certainly come back to haunt you by helping the FAA suspend or revoke your or the company's certificates (or both), and that you have the right to have your attorney present during any questioning. But your attorney isn't present, and the inspector wants to talk *now*. Additionally, you may suspect that if you exercise your rights and refuse to discuss the historical facts the inspector is looking for, she will make a little note in her file that "the suspect displayed a belligerent, uncooperative attitude," or something to that effect. You may fear that if the inspector decides you lack a constructive attitude, you may be denied the opportunity to participate in remedial training (instead of an enforcement action to suspend or revoke your certificates or fine you) and that you will be singled out for harsher treatment than normal. And that is exactly what may happen. You may have only two alternatives, both unpleasant (but not equally so): An angry inspector who may be unable to prove a case against you because you did not confess, or a happy inspector who can prove a case against you because you did confess. Pushed to that choice, I will go with the first choice every time.

Never discuss historical facts with the FAA without first consulting your attorney. You must be firm on that point. It is also, however, important to not appear disrespectful of the inspector, the FAA, or the FARs. It is definitely in your best interest to try to avoid the appearance of a bad attitude by maintaining a polite, soft-spoken presentation and professional demeanor toward the FAA inspector. You might try saying something like:

> "I really would like to talk to you about this, Inspector, but I think the professional thing for me to do in this situation is to consult my attorney first. May I have your business card, so that I can call you back after I consult with my attorney?"

Many FAA inspectors are not beneath persisting in trying to cajole you into telling them what they want to know in the face of your resistance, and they have been known to say things like:

> "Aw, shucks, I think you're blowing this way out of proportion. It's not that big a deal, and probably nothing will come of it. I've just had a file dumped in my lap, and I have to check it out. The sooner I get the answers to these questions so I can fill out this report, the sooner I can close the file."

So you relent and answer their questions. They write down the answers and close the file as promised. Then they put it in an envelope and send it to the FAA attorney who takes action to suspend or revoke your certificate. You appeal, and the FAA proves its case by using the answers you gave the FAA inspector. It happens every day. Don't be a chump. You must hold your ground and firmly but politely decline to discuss any historical facts with the FAA until you have consulted your attorney.

Another context in which that crucial moment of the first contact with an FAA representative may occur is by an invitation to telephone or visit the air traffic control tower or center. If you are personally invited (by the controller on the frequency or a line service person while you are securing the aircraft after a flight) to telephone or visit the ATC facility, that annunciator light should start flashing in your mind to alert you that you are probably suspected of an FAR violation. They aren't inviting you up there because they want to show off their new radar display to an appreciative taxpayer, and they don't want you to phone in so they can compliment you on the awesome skill you demonstrated in your crosswind landing. They want to talk to you because they think you have made a mistake.

Once again, you are on the horns of a dilemma. If you do telephone or visit the tower in response to their request, you may help them prove a case against you by identifying yourself as the pilot-in-command and by making other damaging admissions. If you don't, they may decide you lack a constructive attitude and attempt to come down harder on you.

My favorite example of the former occurred at Harlingen, Texas, then home of the Confederate Air Force (CAF), since renamed the Commemorative Air Force, a charitable organization that led the movement to restore and preserve American and foreign military aircraft of World War II vintage. A middle-aged commercial pilot flew his personal Piper Comanche on a personal pleasure trip to Harlingen for the CAF's big annual air show. He arrived VFR in VMC at dusk on the evening before the show. The flight was uneventful and there was no other traffic in the pattern when he arrived. He had not filed a flight plan, nor was one required. As he was tying down the Comanche on the line, a line service attendant from the flying service tapped him on the shoulder and said something like: "Pardon me, sir, but when you get done tying the aircraft down, they'd like you to pay them a visit in the tower." The pilot replied (probably with an audible gulp): "Tower? What tower?"

It seems that the pilot did not have the latest sectional aeronautical chart and thus did not realize that the airport had acquired an FAA control tower in the interim since the chart he was using had expired, so he had landed without establishing radio contact. Being an otherwise good and responsible citizen, however, he dutifully reported to the tower where he straightforwardly admitted his mistake, expressed sincerest apologies, and made it quite clear that he was mortified and had learned a valuable lesson. All in all, he found it a very frank and gratifying professional exchange with the controllers. He left believing that the problem was solved and that nothing would come of it. A few weeks later, the FAA instituted proceedings to suspend his commercial pilot's certificate for six months for the violation.

Then he contacted me for the first time. We appealed the case to the NTSB (more on how this process works later) and as the hearing was approaching, I was trying to figure out some way to defend this case and drawing a blank. After all, the guy had confessed, hadn't he?

Going over in my mind each element of the case the FAA would have to prove at hearing, I thought about how they would prove he was the pilot-in-command who had visited the tower and confessed. I expected that the FAA attorney would call as a witness one of the control tower operators who was present during this visit and would proceed to prove the identity of the pilot-in-command like this:

FAA ATTORNEY: Did you request that the pilot of the Comanche visit the control tower?

CONTROLLER: Yes, sir. I telephoned the flying service and asked them to send someone out and request that the pilot pay us a visit in the tower when he got done tying down his airplane.

FAA ATTORNEY: Did the pilot visit the control tower in response to your request?

CONTROLLER: Yes, sir, he did.

FAA ATTORNEY: And do you see that person present here in the courtroom, today?

CONTROLLER: Yes, sir, that's him in the green shirt, sitting over there next to Mr. Hamilton.

So I didn't bring my client to the hearing.

Sure enough, the control tower chief appeared as a witness and the questions and answers proceeded along the expected lines until the crucial question about recognition. Although my client was not present in the courtroom, the gallery was packed with a number of my students who had come to observe the proceedings. The tower chief paused, took his glasses out of his pocket and put them on, then studied each face carefully before he finally replied: "No, sir, I don't."

You could have heard a pin drop as the FAA attorney realized that he had walked into an ambush and was about to lose his case for inability to prove the identity of the pilot-in-command.

Then the darndest thing happened. The tower chief started rummaging around in his flight bag, pulling out unfiled approach-plate revisions, crackers, stale sandwiches, charts, tomorrow's fresh shirt—all the usual contents of the working aviator's flight bag. Suddenly realizing that everyone in the courtroom was staring at him as if he'd gone mad, he paused, turned to the judge and said: "But, Your Honor, while he was up there, he signed our guest book and I believe I have a copy of that with me." With some further rummaging in the bag, he found the copy of the relevant page from the "guest book," and the FAA introduced it as an exhibit. There, in the most legible handwriting you've ever seen, was my client's signature.

So we lost the case.

Current FAA enforcement policies require ATC personnel to report all observed FAR violations to the inspectors for investigation. Although once routine, controllers are no longer permitted to solve most problems by friendly chats with pilots.

If I get that invitation to visit the tower, I'll strongly *Roger* it and tie down the airplane, then if the situation permits, disappear as rapidly as possible, not waiting around to refuel or leave a trail of little exhibits-to-be like signed gas slips, car rental agreements, and so forth.

Another lawyer friend of mine who also does a lot of FAA enforcement defense work got a request to telephone the tower after landing at an unfamiliar airport. Trying to strike a careful balance between appearing to have a constructive attitude without giving the FAA ammunition to use against him in an enforcement case, he made the call. When the approach controller answered, he said: "Yes, Sir, and I'll need your name for our log." My friend laughed and replied: "I know why you need my name and I'm not going to give it to you, but if you think I did something wrong I'd sure like to know what it is so I won't do it again." The controller then explained the problem to him, he responded positively and appreciatively, and nothing further came of it. Once the airplane is at the chocks, you are no longer "air traffic" and thus no longer required to obey the orders of air traffic controllers (like to present yourself somewhere or call anyone on the telephone). You have a great deal to lose by showing up or calling and identifying yourself without first talking to your attorney. Don't fall for it!

Displaying Documents

Although you are not required to discuss anything with the FAA without having your attorney present, you are required by 14 CFR § 61.3(a) (1) and § 61.3(c) to have in your personal possession or readily available in the aircraft your pilot certificate, medical certificate, and government-issued photo ID whenever exercising the privileges of your certificate. You are required by 14 CFR § 61.51(i) to present your pilot certificate, medical certificate, government-issued photo ID and logbook to FAA or NTSB investigators or any federal, state, or local law enforcement officer for inspection upon reasonable request. Similar presentation-upon-request requirements apply to non-pilot holders of airman certificates, such as mechanics and repairmen (see, e.g.: 14 CFR §§ 65.89 and 65.105).

Unless you are a student pilot on a cross-country, however, you are not required to have your pilot logbook with you and it is probably best that you don't (even if you do, if you catch my drift). 14 CFR § 21.181(b) also requires that you make the aircraft's airworthiness certificate available for inspection by the FAA.

If you are operating under 14 CFR Part 91, these are the only documents you are required to present, and you are only required to *present* these documents for inspection, not to *surrender* them (unless the person making the request presents you with a written Emergency Order of Suspension or Revocation signed by an FAA attorney, described later). It is important that you exercise your rights here, as well. If the inspector starts to pocket or otherwise depart with your certificate and logbooks in her possession, you must insist upon their immediate return. Otherwise, you may later be held to have surrendered them voluntarily and given up all your rights to appeal any suspension or revocation of these certificates. Again, it may be necessary for you to firmly but politely insist upon preserving your rights in this regard. Present, but do not surrender, these documents. Present, but do not discuss anything about these documents without first consulting your attorney. If the FAA inspector ignores your protests and begins to depart the area with your certificates or logbooks anyway, scream bloody murder and get witnesses who can later testify that you did not voluntarily surrender these documents to the inspector. But do not under any circumstances lay a hand on the FAA inspector. You don't want to add a criminal charge of assaulting a federal officer, a felony under 18 U.S.C. 111, to your problems.

If you are operating under 14 CFR Parts 121 or 135, you will find that document production requirements are substantially greater than those described here.

Aircraft Inspection

During the course of ramp inspections, FAA inspectors routinely ask permission to board the aircraft. If you are operating under 14 CFR Part 135 or 121, the inspector must be granted immediate flight deck access upon request. 14 CFR Part 91 operators on the other hand are not required to grant FAA inspectors entry to the aircraft on oral request and should not grant such a request. Even if, as a gesture of kindness, you allow the inspector to board the aircraft to get in out of the rain, the inspector is not going to come aboard with blinders on. If anything appears amiss, the inspector's observations will be used against you later in an enforcement case. Even without your permission, inspectors may examine the aircraft's exterior without removing any inspection covers or opening cowlings or hatches. They can even press their noses against the Plexiglas and peek in from the outside. Just don't allow entry unless required.

It is not unusual for a difference of opinion to arise between the pilot and an FAA inspector over an issue of airworthiness during the course of a ramp check. The safest way to handle this is to call over a qualified mechanic to resolve the disagreement, if one is available. If not, you are on the spot: If you go ahead and fly, you may find yourself the guest of honor in an enforcement case for operating an unairworthy aircraft. But if you cancel your trip and later verify that your airworthiness assessment was correct, you will have suffered the inconvenience and consequences unnecessarily. If you feel confident that the aircraft is airworthy and that proceeding with your trip is worth the risk of an enforcement action, you can turn around and put the inspector on the spot. State that in your opinion, the aircraft is airworthy and you intend to fly it unless the inspector is so certain of her position that she is willing to issue a written Aircraft Condition Notice (FAA Form 8620-1). State that if she does, then you will defer to her judgment and not operate the aircraft until a qualified mechanic can inspect it.

The Letter of Investigation

Sometimes, you have no indication that the FAA is after you until you receive a letter from them in the mail. The *Letter of Investigation* (LOI) comes from an inspector at the Flight Standards District Office (FSDO) investigating a complaint or report of violation. The letter indicates that the FAA has received a report that you were involved in an incident in violation of the FARs. The letter will describe in short summary form what they believe you did, when and where they believe you did it, and will invite you to respond in writing within 10 days with your side of the story. Aviation lawyers call the LOI the "invitation to hang yourself," because a surprising percentage of recipients immediately sit down and (without the benefit of counsel) draft a complete narrative response and send it off to the FAA in the naive expectation that once the FAA sees their side of the story, the problem will go away. Fat chance! What almost always happens, instead, is that such writers give the FAA admissions against their own best interests that the FAA then uses to prove their enforcement case.

For example, the FAA LOI states that on May 31, 2009, the addressee was the pilot in command of Avitat Husky aircraft N2020BZ, and operated the aircraft over the Colorado River in the vicinity of Lake Havasu City, Arizona, at approximately 7:30 p.m. The letter goes on to state that the aircraft was observed flying at an altitude as low as 50 feet above swimmers and watercraft, contrary to Federal Aviation Regulations. The pilot's reply letter typically says something like: "When I flew my Husky over the river that evening, I never got below 500 feet AGL." Gotcha! The FAA may have had no proof of the identity of the pilot in command of the aircraft, so they sent an LOI to the owner hoping to draw him out. Sure enough, he fell for it and gave them a written confession that he was the pilot. That admission, of course, would constitute ample proof of the pilot's identity, sure to satisfy any ALJ.

Do not fall for the "invitation to hang yourself." Take it to your aviation lawyer immediately for advice. After considering your explanation of events, your lawyer may choose to craft a carefully worded admission-free response for your signature, respond on your behalf revealing that you are represented by counsel, or recommend no reply be sent.

When to Talk to the FAA

Talking to the FAA in *advance*, as when you don't understand an FAR and need an interpretation or other professional guidance to enable you to avoid committing a violation, is highly recommended.

And while you really are "air traffic" (while the aircraft is actually in operation and in communication with ATC) cooperate fully and be absolutely truthful in all communications. This advice applies even if you've made a mistake and fear that ATC has caught it. This is simply because any failure to be truthful could have far worse consequences than the suspension or revocation of your certificate.

Imagine that ATC has cleared you to climb and maintain Flight Level 380. Because of some distraction, you climb through your assigned altitude without leveling off, and ATC, noticing your mode-C encoder return, asks you to "say altitude." Realizing that you have made a mistake and that your certificate may be in jeopardy for violating an FAR by deviating from the clearance, you may feel a strong temptation to report level at 380 to avoid such troubles. The problem is that if you do that and succeed in conning the controller into believing that you really did not bust your altitude, the controller may not issue a deviating vector to the MD-11 that is coming at you head-on at Mach .85 plus your own airspeed at your real altitude. The consequences of that could make an enforcement case look like pretty light stuff. So I urge that as a practical matter you cooperate fully and report truthfully to ATC during all aircraft movements (from chock to chock you might say). But once the aircraft is stopped, they are on their own, and discussions of historical events should be deferred until you have first received the advice of your attorney.

You should also be careful to avoid getting into arguments with controllers on the frequency. Nothing is more certain to result in an enforcement case being filed against you than you jamming the frequency with some ranting filibuster over a difference of opinion with the controller. Carry out your responsibilities as pilot-in-command and do not accept clearances that would, in your professional judgment, endanger the safety of the flight. But save the debate until you're home safely back on the ground, you and the controller have both had time to cool off, and you've consulted your attorney. There is a better way to clear up past misunderstandings and prevent future conflicts with ATC. The radio frequency is not the appropriate forum for debate.

Additionally, it may benefit an air carrier or an aircraft and parts manufacturer to take the initiative to report violations to the FAA under certain circumstances. Under the Air Carrier Reporting and Correction Program, recently extended to cover manufacturers as well, the FAA will use a Letter of Correction instead of enforcement action if:

1. the carrier or manufacturer discovers that it has been operating in violation of the FARs in some respect,
2. the violations were not deliberate or intentional,
3. the violations do not indicate a basic underlying lack of qualification on the part of the company,
4. the company has already taken or agreed to take corrective action to prevent a recurrence of such violations, and
5. the company reports the violations to the FAA before the FAA learns about the violations from another source.

In such a case, it is to the company's distinct advantage to take the initiative to report its violations to the FAA before the FAA learns about them from another source, which is very likely. Competitors or disgruntled employees may tip off the FAA or the FAA may "hear it through the grapevine." The aviation community is close-knit, talkative, competitive, and keeps no secrets.

Even if the FAA does find out about the violation from another source before the company reports it, if the company takes immediate corrective action to prevent a recurrence of the violations, the agency will consider this action favorably to reduce any penalty to be imposed.

Immunity from Sanction: The NASA Report

If any occurrence during your operations results in an unsafe situation or causes you concern that the FAA or anyone else might think that you did something wrong (unless an accident or crime was involved), it is advisable to file an Aviation Safety Reporting Program (ASRP) report with NASA. There are three reasons to file this report: (1) You may make an important personal contribution to improving aviation safety; (2) you may receive immunity from sanction for an FAR violation; and (3) you have nothing to lose by filing the report.

The purpose of the NASA Aviation Safety Reporting Program is to identify problems in the National Air Transportation System to provide a sound basis for improving the system. The reporting form is free online at: *http://asrs.arc.nasa.gov*, at all FAA offices including Flight Service

(SPACE BELOW RESERVED FOR ASRS DATE/TIME STAMP)

IDENTIFICATION STRIP: Please fill in all blanks to ensure return of strip.
NO RECORD WILL BE KEPT OF YOUR IDENTITY. This section will be returned to you.

TELEPHONE NUMBERS where we may reach you for further
details of this occurrence:

HOME   Area _____ No. _____ - _____   Hours _____
WORK   Area _____ No. _____ - _____   Hours _____

NAME _____   TYPE OF EVENT/SITUATION _____
ADDRESS/PO BOX _____   _____
_____   DATE OF OCCURRENCE _____
CITY _____ STATE _____ ZIP _____ LOCAL TIME (24 hr. clock) _____

PLEASE FILL IN APPROPRIATE SPACES AND CHECK ALL ITEMS WHICH APPLY TO THIS EVENT OR SITUATION.

REPORTER	FLYING TIME	CERTIFICATES/RATINGS		ATC EXPERIENCE	
o Captain	total _____ hrs.	o student	o private	o FPL	o Developmental
o First Officer		o commercial	o ATP	radar _____ yrs.	
o pilot flying	last 90 days _____ hrs.	o instrument	o CFI	non-radar _____ yrs.	
o pilot not flying		o multiengine	o F/E	supervisory _____ yrs.	
o Other Crewmember	time in type _____ hrs.	o _____		military _____ yrs.	
o _____					

AIRSPACE		WEATHER		LIGHT/VISIBILITY		ATC/ADVISORY SERV.	
o Class A (PCA)	o Special Use Airspace	o VMC	o ice	o daylight	o night	o local	o center
o Class B (TCA)	o airway/route _____	o IMC	o snow	o dawn	o dusk	o ground	o FSS
o Class C (ARSA)	o unknown/other _____	o mixed	o turbulence	ceiling _____ feet		o apch	o UNICOM
o Class D (Control Zone/ATA)		o marginal	o tstorm	visibility _____ miles		o dep	o CTAF
o Class E (General Controlled)		o rain	o windshear			Name of ATC Facility:	
o Class G (Uncontrolled)		o fog	o _____	RVR _____ feet			

	AIRCRAFT 1		AIRCRAFT 2	
Type of Aircraft (Make/Model)	(Your Aircraft) _____	o EFIS o FMS/FMC	(Other Aircraft) _____	o EFIS o FMS/FMC
Operator	o air carrier o military o corporate o commuter o private o other _____		o air carrier o military o corporate o commuter o private o other _____	
Mission	o passenger o training o business o cargo o pleasure o unk/other _____		o passenger o training o business o cargo o pleasure o unk/other _____	
Flight plan	o VFR o SVFR o none o IFR o DVFR o unknown		o VFR o SVFR o none o IFR o DVFR o unknown	
Flight phases at time of occurrence	o taxi o cruise o landing o takeoff o descent o missed apch/GAR o climb o approach o other _____		o taxi o cruise o landing o takeoff o descent o missed apch/GAR o climb o approach o other _____	
Control status	o visual apch o on vector o on SID/STAR o controlled o none o unknown o no radio o radar advisories		o visual apch o on vector o on SID/STAR o controlled o none o unknown o no radio o radar advisories	

If more than two aircraft were involved, please describe the additional aircraft in the "Describe Event/Situation" section.

LOCATION	CONFLICTS			
Altitude _____ o MSL o AGL	Estimated miss distance in feet: horiz _____ vert _____			
Distance and radial from airport, NAVAID, or other fix _____	Was evasive action taken?		o Yes	o No
	Was TCAS a factor?	o TA	o RA	o No
Nearest City/State _____	Did GPWS activate?		o Yes	o No

NASA ARC 277B (January 1994)   **PILOT**   Page 1 of 2

Fig. 2.2. NASA Aviation Safety Report form.

Stations, or by writing to FAA Aeronautical Center, Distribution Section, AAC-45C, P.O. Box 25082, Oklahoma City, Oklahoma 73125.

A copy of the form is reproduced here (*see* Fig. 2.2), and NASA will accept a copy that you make out of this book. It is a good practice always to have at least one of these forms with you in your flight case. Electronic filing is also available at the website noted above.

The report is not only for use by pilots, but also air traffic controllers, maintenance personnel, and cabin crewmembers.

Filing a report may accomplish several things.

First, you *may make an important personal contribution to improving aviation safety.* Here's an example from a CFII client I represented: The day was marginal VMC with haze when the light twin was cleared for a practice ILS approach to runway 35R. The ATC clearance for the approach received from the airport control tower stated: "Piper 43 Tango is cleared for the practice ILS approach, runway 35 right; report power lines."

The pilot in the left seat was under the hood for the practice approach, while the instrument flight instructor in the right seat was keeping a careful lookout for other traffic. The instructor was being especially watchful this day because he was aware that in accordance with local noise-abatement procedures, departures were taking off toward them on the same runway (17L for these departures). The pilots had agreed that the flight instructor would handle the required call at the power lines since only he could see out the window and know when the aircraft arrived at this visual reference point about two miles from the runway threshold.

Meanwhile, however, things had gotten very busy at the airport and the air traffic controller was broadcasting nonstop instructions to a variety of aircraft in the area, with no breaks to permit reply. As the flight continued down the ILS past the power lines, the flight instructor was still awaiting an opportunity to broadcast his position report when through the haze he thought he saw something moving toward them on the runway. He ordered his student to execute an immediate missed-approach procedure (a climbing right turn on this particular approach) and the opposing traffic, a fast-moving Learjet, passed about fifty feet below and behind them, much too close for comfort. If the flight instructor had hesitated for another second before initiating a missed approach, a midair collision would almost certainly have resulted.

The flight instructor subsequently learned that this was not the first time something like this had happened at the airport. He immediately filed an Aviation Safety Report with NASA. As a result of his report, the standard clearance for practice ILS approaches to that runway when opposite-direction departures were in progress was changed to add the phrase "if unable, execute immediate missed approach." As a result of this change, the margin of safety was dramatically improved during these operations. That pilot's report may have saved others from having a midair collision there.

Second, you *may receive immunity from sanction for an FAR violation.* The FAA considers the filing of an Aviation Safety Report with NASA indicative of a constructive attitude that will make future violations less likely. Therefore, the FAA's policy, as set forth in FAA Advisory

Circular AC 00-46D, is that (with certain exceptions to be discussed momentarily) the FAA will not impose a fine or suspend or revoke a pilot's certificate for an FAR violation if such a report was timely filed. They may, however, issue an order to make your violation a part of your airman record. Such an order is appealable like any other if you believe you did not commit a violation.

In order to get the benefit of this possible immunity from sanction, you must mail or electronically submit the report within ten days after the incident. Upon receipt (whether by mail or electronically), NASA places its receipt stamp on the identification strip at the top of the form (*see* Fig. 2.2), snips off that strip, and mails it back to you as your receipt. Save this receipt, for it is now one of your most valuable possessions. If the incident results in the FAA taking enforcement action against you, brandishing this receipt is much like showing the cross to a vampire. It virtually stops them in their tracks (pretty strong magic).

Exceptions to this are that the violation must not have been deliberate (the Aviation Safety Report form is not a coupon good for one free buzz job) and must not have involved a crime or accident. Nor does it protect you where the incident indicates a lack of qualifications or competency, as discussed previously under the heading of "Reexamination."

Third, *you have nothing to lose by filing the report.* Except for reports involving aircraft accidents or crimes, NASA keeps these reports confidential and ensures the anonymity of the reporter and all other parties involved in a reported incident. With those exceptions, the FAA cannot find out about an incident from your filing of an Aviation Safety Report and the FAA is prohibited by 14 CFR §91.25 from using the report or any information derived from it for enforcement purposes.

The form itself is free and easy to fill out (I can tell you from my own extensive personal use of the form that it takes only a few minutes) and NASA even pays the postage. So it can't hurt and may help you to file an Aviation Safety Report whenever you encounter a condition or procedure you consider unsafe or you have the slightest clue that someone may suspect that you committed an FAR violation. When in doubt, fill it out! Don't wait to see whether the FAA is going to take action against you. It frequently takes longer than ten days for the FAA to let you know that they believe you have done something wrong. In fact, some inspectors seem to deliberately wait until after the tenth day following the incident before attempting to make the first contact with the violator, in hope that the violator will not feel motivated to file a timely Aviation Safety Report and will lose this chance for immunity.

If there was more than one FAA certificate holder involved in the incident, each should file a separate report. One report doesn't protect all who were involved, only the individual who filed it. The company operating the aircraft should also file a report since it can be charged with a violation as the aircraft's "operator," under the broad definition of "operate" in FAR 1.1.

FAA Aviation Safety Action Program (ASAP)

Another FAA program known as the Aviation Safety Action Program (ASAP), applicable to participating airlines holding 14 CFR Part 121 operating certificates and repair stations holding certificates issued under 14 CFR Part 145, also provides an opportunity for employees of those companies to avoid FAA prosecution for unintentional violations. The program, which is described in detail in FAA Advisory Circular AC 120-66B, is intended to increase the flow of safety information to both management and the FAA. It provides incentives to encourage employees of participating air carriers and repair stations to promptly disclose safety information that may include possible FAR violations without fear of punitive FAA sanctions or company disciplinary action. Participation in the program is voluntary. In order to participate, the airline or repair station and its labor unions (*see* Chapter 17) must enter into a Memorandum of Understanding (MOU) with the FAA. In order to seek immunity, the employee must report the event that may constitute an FAR violation to company management within 24 hours after the end of the duty day. Immunity from sanction under this program is neither absolute nor automatic. The circumstances of each case are reviewed by an Event Review Committee (ERC), typically composed of a management representative, a representative of the employee's union, and an FAA inspector from the Flight Standards District Office holding the company's certificate (Certificate Holding District Office, or CHDO). If the ERC determines that the event was inadvertent, did not involve an intentional disregard for safety, was not an intentional falsification (such as a record of repair to an aircraft), was not a crime, and did not involve substance abuse, the matter will be disposed of administratively, by a letter of correction or warning notice.

If the ERC does not reach unanimous agreement, the CHDO Inspector's opinion will determine whether the individual receives immunity from sanction.

The experience of companies and employee unions participating in the program has been somewhat mixed, and several airlines (including American, Delta, and Comair) dropped out of the program because employee unions complained that the process was abused by management, but the majority continue to participate.

Even if you are an employee of a participating company and choose to take advantage of this program, it is wise to also timely file a report with the NASA Aviation Safety Reporting Program described above.

Air Traffic Safety Action Program (ATSAP)

In 2007, the FAA and the National Air Traffic Controllers Association entered into a Memorandum of Understanding (MOU) to create a program for air traffic controllers similar to NASA's ASRP and the FAA/airlines ASAP programs. Known as the Air Traffic Safety Action Program (ATSAP), this program is designed to foster a voluntary, cooperative, non-punitive environment for the open reporting of safety-of-flight concerns by FAA air traffic personnel.

Reports must be submitted online at *http://atsapsafety.com* within 24 hours of the end of the employee's duty day. They are then routed through an Event Review Committee (ERC) process similar to that already in use in the ASAP program. If the Report is accepted, no disciplinary action can be taken, and the employee cannot be decertified, but the employee may be subject to an on-the-job safety check or additional skill enhancement training if recommended by the ERC.

Specifically excluded from immunity under the program are reports of events involving apparent noncompliance with applicable ATC directives that are not inadvertent, or that involve gross negligence, substance abuse, controlled substances, alcohol, intentional falsification, or criminal activity. Reports involving substance abuse, controlled substances, alcohol, intentional falsification, or criminal activity are referred to the appropriate FAA office or law enforcement agency.

Prosecution and Appeal

Under present FAA enforcement policies, violations by individuals not resolved administratively by remedial training, a letter of correction, or a warning notice almost always result in certificate action (suspension or revocation), while violations by companies that are not so egregious as to indicate that the company's management is not dedicated to FAR compliance more often lead to civil penalties (fines). We will now examine what happens once the case reaches the FAA's lawyers.

Certificate Actions

Notice of Proposed Certificate Action. If the FAA attorney decides that your violation calls for suspension or revocation of your certificate, you will receive a Notice of Proposed Certificate Action (NOPCA). This is a letter describing exactly what FARs you are believed to have violated and stating exactly what the FAA proposes to do about it (for example a 180-day suspension of your airline transport pilot certificate). You will be offered the choice to either:

1. Admit the charges and surrender your certificate,
2. Answer the charges in writing,
3. Request that the FAA go ahead and issue the proposed order to enable you to proceed with an appeal to the NTSB, or
4. Request the opportunity to be heard in an *informal conference* with the FAA attorney.

Informal Conference. This is a settlement conference. It's a chance to sit down with the FAA attorney and an inspector, let them get a feel for your attitudes and professionalism and be sure they understand what really happened and why you did what you did. If you select this option, you can and should speak freely because, with one exception, the FAA cannot use anything you say at the informal conference to prove its case against you if a settlement is not reached and you end up in a hearing before the NTSB on appeal. The only time any statement you make at the informal conference could come back to haunt you later would be if you tell a different story when you testify under oath at the NTSB hearing than you told the FAA in your informal conference. In that case, the FAA can use your prior inconsistent statement to impeach your credibility.

You should already have a lawyer by now, but if not, be sure to hire one to go with you to the informal conference. Remember: The FAA's lawyer is your adversary and cannot advise or help you. Your attorney will be able to obtain a copy of the FAA's evidence against you to review before the conference, so you'll know what you're up against. As a result of the informal conference, the FAA attorney may offer to reduce the period of suspension or to allow you to pay a fine instead of having your certificate suspended. Remedial training may still be an option. On rare occasions, where you can convincingly demonstrate at the informal conference that you did not commit the violation, the FAA attorney may agree to drop the case.

Order of Suspension or Revocation. If your attorney is unable to negotiate a settlement that you are willing to accept at the informal conference, the FAA attorney will soon issue an Order of Suspension or Revocation against your certificate. Unless the order is captioned as an *Emergency* Order of Suspension or Revocation (more about these later) it does not take effect immediately. You can defer the effective date of the order by filing an appeal with the NTSB within twenty days from the date the order was served on you. These orders are usually sent by certified mail to the address you have on file with the FAA at Oklahoma City and service is complete if anyone at that address signs for it. Your appeal must be filed within those twenty days; if it is, the effective date of the FAA's order will be postponed until your NTSB appeal is finally decided so long as your attorney carefully follows the board's Rules of Practice in Air Safety Proceedings. If you fail to file your appeal with the NTSB within twenty days after someone signed for the order at the last address you have on file with the FAA in Oklahoma City, the order becomes final and you can't appeal it. Therefore, it is very important that you make it a habit to comply with 14 CFR § 61.60, which requires you to give written notice of each change in your permanent address to the FAA Airman Certification Branch, Box 25082, Oklahoma City, Oklahoma 73125, or online via the FAA website. If you overlook that, the FAA sends you an order at the last address it has on file for you and whoever is living there now signs for it but doesn't get it to you within those twenty days, the order becomes final, and you lose your appeal rights. And don't think you can beat the system by not signing for certified mail from the FAA. If the order is returned to the FAA, they'll re-send it by regular mail to your address of record and the NTSB will hold that you were properly served.

Some young people attending college or working at jobs that require frequent moves continue to use their parents' or friends' addresses as their permanent mailing address with the FAA. This is fine, so long as you promptly receive mail sent there. But if you just let it pile up there and stop by and pick it up every few weeks or months, you may one day find that your certificate has been suspended or revoked and the deadline to appeal the order has passed.

NTSB Appeal. As soon as you receive the Order of Suspension or Revocation, take it to your lawyer to file the appeal with the NTSB. The FAA will file its order with the board as its Complaint, and your attorney will have to promptly file an Answer with the Board, stating which of the FAA's allegations you admit (if any) and which you deny. The board will assign your case to one of its administrative law judges (ALJs) to hold a hearing. There is one exception to this general right to appeal from an FAA suspension, revocation, or denial of a certificate: individuals who have been identified by the TSA as posing a security threat have no right to challenge the FAA's denial or revocation of their certificates through the NTSB appeal process.

Motion to Dismiss Stale Complaint. A statute of limitations is a specified time limit that begins to run from the date of the violation and beyond which no legal action can be taken based on the incident. There are no statutes of limitation applicable to FAA enforcement cases, only the NTSB's rather intricate *Stale Complaint Rule*, which provides, at 49 C.F.R. 821.33, that where the FAA's complaint (the order of suspension or revocation) is based on events alleged to have occurred more than 6 months prior to the agency's issuance of a Notice of Proposed Certificate Action, your attorney may file a *motion to dismiss stale complaint*. If the complaint does not present a legitimate issue as to your qualifications, the burden is on the FAA to satisfy the NTSB ALJ that there was good cause for its delay or that imposition of a sanction is warranted in the public interest, notwithstanding the delay. If the FAA fails to convince the ALJ of either of those, the judge may dismiss the FAA's complaint. Such a decision would then be appealable by the FAA to the full NTSB, through the process described later.

Discovery. Upon request from your attorney, the FAA will provide a list of witnesses and exhibits it intends to use at the hearing and copies of all previous statements it has received from those witnesses, along with copies of proposed exhibits, so that you will know what evidence you can expect to defend against at the hearing. You should expect to reciprocate and provide the same information regarding your intended defense.

Hearing. Eventually your case will be set for a trial-type hearing before an NTSB administrative law judge (ALJ) in a major city near you or near the place of the alleged violation (usually where the majority of the witnesses are located). All of these judges are lawyers and some of them are experienced pilots. They are based in Washington, D.C., Denver, Fort Worth, and Los Angeles, traveling over large territories called circuits hearing FAA enforcement and aviation medical appeals.

The hearing is show time, the *only* opportunity you (and the FAA) will ever get to prove your case. These are formal hearings, very much like civil trials. You are not entitled to a trial by jury in these cases. The NTSB administrative law judge alone will decide your fate. The FAA is required to put on its witnesses and exhibits first, having the burden to prove the violations charged. The FAA does not have to prove its case "*beyond a reasonable doubt*" as though it were a criminal case, only by a "*preponderance of the evidence*" (theoretically 50.1 percent) as in a civil trial.

Your attorney will have the opportunity to cross-examine the FAA's witnesses in an attempt to discredit their testimony. Once the FAA has presented evidence of each of its charges against you, the burden shifts to you to go forward with your defense, also through the sworn in-person testimony of witnesses and the presentation of exhibits. The FAA attorney has the right to cross-examine you and your witnesses to discredit your testimony.

In an extremely controversial development, the NTSB has taken the position that the board and its administrative law judges are bound by the FAA's own interpretation of the applicable FAR, even if that interpretation is announced for the first time during the course of the case under consideration. This is called "*due deference*." Aviation defense counsel are understandably outraged that the board would make a mockery of the most fundamental concepts of due process of law by taking the position that the law is whatever the FAA says it is, even if the agency never announced that interpretation before surprising someone by punishing them under it.

Once all testimony and exhibits have been presented, the judge will decide the case, usually giving you an oral decision then and there at the end of the hearing. The judge has several options. He may (1) find that the FAA has proved all of its charges and affirm the Order of Suspension or Revocation, (2) decide that the FAA has proved some but not all of its charges and reduce the term of suspension, (3) reduce a revocation to a suspension, (4) change the penalty from certificate action to a monetary fine, or (5) find that the FAA failed to prove its case and dismiss the Order of Suspension or Revocation. The ALJ cannot impose a harsher penalty than the FAA ordered. If either side is displeased with the judge's initial decision (sometimes both are), it may appeal that decision to the full board (the five political appointees in Washington, D.C.).

Appeal to Full NTSB. This is a paper appeal. Both sides must file written legal briefs with the board, arguing their positions and setting out their views of the governing law. As long as your appeal and brief are timely filed, your certificate remains in effect until the board decides the appeal. The only basic issues the full board will consider are: (1) Did the judge afford both sides a fair hearing? (2) Did the judge apply the correct law to the facts that were proved at trial?

Where witnesses at the hearing have testified to differing versions of events so that the judge had to decide which witness to believe, the board on its review will not reconsider that credibility choice. The board recognizes that the judge, who is able to look the witnesses in the eye and observe their gestures, mannerisms, and testimony, is in a better position to decide who to believe than the board, which has nothing more to go on than the written transcript of the testimony and the exhibits.

You will not get a hearing before the full board, nor is there any opportunity to present additional evidence not presented to the ALJ. The attorneys just mail legal briefs to Washington and eventually (at this writing about a year after the appeal to the full board was filed) the board's decision will arrive in the mail, unannounced. Either party may appeal the full board's decision to the U.S. Court of Appeals. (Note that you never get the opportunity for a trial to a court or a jury.)

Appeal to U.S. Court of Appeals. This is another paper appeal based largely upon written briefs filed by the attorneys for both sides, although the court of appeals will usually permit the lawyers to argue the case orally to the three-judge panel that will decide it. Again, there is no opportunity for either side to present evidence that was not considered by the administrative law judge.

This appeal does not automatically prevent the FAA's order from taking effect, but unless the NTSB found that you lacked the qualifications to hold the certificate, the board will grant your attorney's motion to stay the effectiveness of the order until the court of appeals decides the case. The court of appeals will eventually issue its decision by a written order. At this writing, most courts of appeals seem to be averaging about two years from appeal to decision. This decision is the end of the road for your appeal rights.

"**Taking It All the Way to the Supreme Court.**" Unlike lesser courts, the Supreme Court of the United States may pick and choose the cases it considers. The only way to get them to consider your case is through an arcane procedure known as a Petition for Writ of Certiorari (pronounced "sur-shur-err-eye"). This is really a paperback book your attorney must write and have printed to convince the Supreme Court that your case presents fascinating legal issues of nationwide import that cry out for the Court's attention. The Court typically receives between 7,000 and 8,000 such petitions each year, most from indigent and incarcerated prisoners who are relieved of the expense of a formal printing and may have nothing better to do with their time than sit in a prison's law library and generate petitions. In a typical year, the Supreme Court will choose to consider about seventy cases. Although it has been presented many opportunities to do so, the Supreme Court has never selected an FAA enforcement case for review. Face it: The odds are that the Supreme Court is not going to select your case, either.

Surrendering Your Certificate. If you don't appeal or you finally lose your appeal, you must physically surrender your certificate to the FAA for the suspension or revocation. It is not enough just to stop flying or exercising other privileges of your certificate. You will not begin to receive credit for the period of suspension until you have physically surrendered your certificate to the FAA. If you refuse to surrender your certificate at this point, the FAA will have the U.S. Attorney obtain an order from a U.S. District Judge for you to appear in court and explain why you have not surrendered your certificate. If you still refuse to surrender it, you may then be jailed for contempt of court until you do surrender your certificate.

Emergency Cases. If the FAA initially decides that permitting you to continue to operate during the appeal process would unreasonably endanger aviation safety, it can issue an Emergency Order of Suspension or Revocation. An emergency order is effective to suspend or revoke the certificate the moment it is delivered to the certificate holder. The certificate must be physically surrendered then and there, and continues to be invalid during the appeal process. Because this procedure effectively denies you the benefits of due process of law, the FAA typically uses emergency orders only in the most extreme cases of danger, as when an air carrier persists in operating unairworthy aircraft or an unqualified person continues to fly. For the same reason, the NTSB rules provide for extremely accelerated hearing and decision of these cases. In a nonemergency case, it typically takes about two years to go through the process of hearing and initial decision by the administrative law judge followed by briefing and a decision on appeal by the full board. In emergency cases, this entire process is required to be completed within sixty days. The recently enacted "Hoover Bill" (so-called because it resulted from an epic FAA abuse of its emergency authority in a case against legendary airshow performer Bob Hoover, which provoked a great uproar in the aviation community) was intended by Congress to provide some protection against FAA abuse of the emergency authority. Under this change in the law, a certificate holder who believes the use of the emergency authority is not justified has forty-eight hours from receipt of the emergency order to request the NTSB review the administrator's determination that an emergency exists. The board must decide that issue within five days. In the first 200 cases in which the FAA's use of the emergency authority was challenged, the NTSB converted only 3 into non-emergency cases, thus allowing the certificate holder to continue to exercise the privileges of the certificate pending the outcome of the appeal. This data has been interpreted by aviation defense attorneys as showing that the board continues to turn a blind eye to FAA abuse of the emergency power, while FAA attorneys cite it as proof that such abuse is extremely rare.

Getting Your Certificate Back

If your certificate is suspended, it will be automatically returned to you by mail at the end of the period of suspension. *Revocation* may sound as though your certificate is gone forever, but that is not necessarily so. If the revocation resulted from a drug-related conviction involving the use of an aircraft, revocation is permanent. The only and rarely used exception is if the FAA is convinced that allowing you to be recertified will facilitate law enforcement efforts (perhaps as an incentive to persuade you to testify against higher-ups in a smuggling operation or to enable you to work undercover as a government informant).

Revocation for an FAR violation not having a drug crime connection, however, means that (unless the FAA otherwise agrees) you will usually be prohibited from applying for recertification for one year. After that year, to regain certification you will have to take and pass each of the written, oral, and practical (flight or other) tests for each certificate revoked (but you still get credit for your previous flight time or other applicable experience).

However, if it was an airline transport (ATP) certificate that was revoked and if the basis for revocation was a falsification, recertification may be difficult. The FARs require that an ATP be of "good moral character." While probably no vaguer regulation was ever written, it is safe to say that the FAA usually views a person who previously obtained or attempted to obtain a certificate or rating under false pretenses as lacking in good moral character.

Civil Penalties (Fines)

As previously noted, the FAA may choose to punish FAR violations by fines rather than by suspension or revocation of certificates. Individuals may be fined up to $1,000 per violation, businesses and airport operators up to $10,000 per violation, and anyone (whether an individual or a business) up to $250,000 per violation for falsification of documents. Against individuals who do not qualify for an administrative disposition, the FAA prefers to use certificate actions for operational violations and will usually allow the violator to pay a fine instead only for isolated paperwork violations, such as failing to properly record a maintenance procedure actually performed. For violations committed by air carriers, air carrier airport operators, repair stations, and other aviation businesses who did not take advantage of self-reporting to obtain immunity, the FAA's policy generally prefers the use of fines. For example, in 2007 the FAA fined Southwest Airlines $10.2 million for operating 46 of its aircraft without having performed AD-mandated repetitive external and eddy-current inspections to detect fuselage fatigue cracking.

However, if the violator's actions appear indicative of a management disposition not to obey the law, the FAA will instead act to suspend or revoke the company or airport operator's certificate. Where the violator does not hold an FAA-issued certificate (such as a person flying or maintaining an aircraft without the requisite certificate, a parachute jumper or pilot of an ultralight vehicle, neither of whom is required to hold an FAA certificate), a fine is the only punishment the FAA can impose. (Fig. 2.3.)

Fig. 2.3. Because the FARs do not require a person to hold a pilot certificate to fly a single seat ultralight, this pilot may not, so the FAA's only recourse for a violation would be to impose a civil penalty (fine).

The procedure in these cases is labyrinthine and depends upon whether at the time of the violation you were acting in the capacity of an airman or aircraft mechanic and how much money the FAA is trying to collect.

In any civil penalty case, you will receive some sort of letter notifying you what the FAA believes you did, what FARs they believe you violated, the maximum amount of the fine allowed by law, and usually an offer to compromise the case for some specified lesser amount. Although in these cases, the FAA attorney is not required to offer you the opportunity for an informal conference, she will usually afford you such a conference if you request it. Just as in a certificate action case, the informal conference can be a good opportunity for you and your attorney to sit down with the FAA attorney and inspector and discuss the situation frankly but off the record in an effort to negotiate a settlement of the case.

If settlement efforts fail and the FAA is seeking to impose a fine of no more than $50,000, it will issue an Order Assessing Civil Penalty under FAR 13.16. If the violator was acting in the capacity of an airman or aircraft mechanic in commission of the violation, the appeal goes to the NTSB and follows the identical appeal procedure described earlier for certificate actions.

If, however, the FAA is seeking to impose a fine of more than $50,000, it must turn the case over to the U.S. Attorney's office with a request that they file a civil lawsuit to collect the proposed fine. These cases are filed in the U.S. District Court (the federal trial court) and are heard by a U.S. District Judge under the Federal Rules of Civil Procedure and Federal Rules of Evidence. The accused can even demand a jury trial. Again, appeal is to the U.S. Court of Appeals followed by a petition for certiorari to the Supreme Court of the United States, under the same procedures described earlier for certificate actions.

Falsification

It is both an FAR violation and a federal felony (major crime) to make a false statement on any federal form or in your pilot, aircraft, or propeller logbooks or other documents you maintain or present to the FAA to show FAR compliance, qualification for a certificate or rating, or to prove currency. If you succumb to the temptation to exaggerate your experience or qualifications in your logbook or on an application for a certificate or rating, or falsify aircraft maintenance records, crew duty time, or training records, that folly may bring your aviation career to an abrupt halt, and you may find yourself spending years in prison.

For the FAR violation, the FAA will revoke every certificate and rating you hold (whether the particular certificate or rating was obtained by fraud or not), usually by an emergency order taking effect immediately. For the federal felony the U.S. Attorney will file criminal charges against you, punishable by up to five years in a federal prison and/or a $250,000 fine. Nothing infuriates the government in general and FAA in particular more than being lied to. This is understandable because our aviation certification programs are in large measure an honor system, and the integrity of that system depends on each of us being absolutely truthful with the FAA. For that reason, the FAA and the Justice Department (of which the U.S. Attorney's office is a part) prosecute falsification cases with a special vengeance.

Other crimes involving aviation are discussed in Chapter 15.

CLEARING YOUR RECORD

Having an FAR violation on your record will put you at a competitive disadvantage for advancement in your aviation career. It may also increase the cost of your aircraft insurance, or even make you uninsurable.

Administrative dispositions, such as Warning Letters and Letters of Correction, are automatically deleted from your FAA airman record after two years.

Until recently, all other records and enforcement actions remained on your record forever. Now, under the FAA's expunction policy, cases closed with no enforcement action taken are cleared off your record within ninety days and enforcement actions resulting in suspension of your certificate are cleared off your record after five years. Only records of enforcement action resulting in revocation of your certificate stay on your record for the rest of your life.

Equal Access to Justice Act

If you prevail in an enforcement action brought against you and the FAA fails to convince the NTSB that the agency was substantially justified in bringing the charges, the Equal Access to Justice Act (EAJA) entitles you to recover your attorney fees and expenses from the government. The EAJA was intended to somewhat level the playing field between the awesome power of federal regulatory agencies and the individuals of modest means and small businesses they might otherwise oppress. To qualify, you must meet certain financial eligibility criteria set forth in the statute, and the statutory rate for reimbursable attorney fees is well below the current market rate for such professional representation. Nonetheless, it is both financially helpful and emotionally gratifying to receive such vindication after being victimized by agency heavy-handedness.

It should be apparent from this chapter that each of us involved in aviation, regardless of our role, has a strong personal incentive to understand, keep abreast of changes to, and meticulously comply with the FARs. This is both to prevent aircraft accidents (much more on this in Part II) and to avoid fines or a suspension or revocation of our valuable FAA-issued certificates. It should also be apparent that whenever your efforts to comply fall short of perfection, everyone involved should promptly file an Aviation Safety Report with NASA and consult an attorney knowledgeable in aviation law.

3

Aviation Medical Cases

You must hold a current FAA medical certificate in order to serve as a pilot or air traffic control tower operator (except that glider and balloon pilots may self certify that they have no known medical defects which would make them unable to pilot one of these aircraft, and a sport pilot candidate is not required to possess an FAA medical certificate, but may use a valid U.S. driver's license as proof of medical fitness. Any restriction on the driver's license becomes a medical restriction for exercising sport pilot privileges).

The FAA's scrutiny of applications for medical certification is heightening with increasing accumulation of medical and related data on citizens in computer data banks of various government agencies and increasing cross matching of this data between agencies. For example, in order to obtain an FAA medical certificate, you are now required to give the FAA written permission to access your driving record file in the National Driver Registry (NDR) database of traffic violations. This data is routinely cross-matched with information you provide on your application for an FAA medical certificate. Aviators who are unaware of this process and the potential consequences frequently succumb to the temptation to be less than candid on applications for medical certification, with immediate and catastrophic results to their aviation careers. Personal, financial, or employer imposed pressures may also lead a person who is not fully cognizant of the possible consequences to act as a pilot or required crewmember at a time when medically disqualified. The purpose of this chapter is to ensure that you have a practical working knowledge of how to analyze various aeromedical problems and dilemmas and arrive at the best solution or course of action.

I often see a classified ad listing an aircraft for sale that tells a tale of tragedy of Shakespearean depth encapsulated in the succinct phrase: *Must sell, lost medical.*

It's not often that I'm moved almost to tears by *Trade-A-Plane* but that one gets me every time. I always want to call them up and say, "Wait! Before you sell your aircraft, are you sure you've done everything possible to get your medical certificate back?" You see: you don't always have to take no for a final decision.

Sometimes the FAA can be persuaded to change its mind and reinstate your medical and in some circumstances the NTSB can order the FAA to issue or reinstate your medical certificate. We will now examine how the medical certification process and appeal procedure works. The procedure is very different from that of enforcement cases in important respects.

FAA HEALTH STANDARDS

Doctors and lawyers tend to communicate with our respective colleagues in our own professional languages, which are often largely unintelligible to outsiders. 14 CFR Part 67, which describes the medical standards and certification procedures for aviators, was written by doctors and lawyers in a not particularly readable mixture of the languages of both professions. To make sense of the specific FAA medical standards, it is helpful to bear in mind that each of these standards was designed to enable the FAA to answer the following basic questions about your health:

1. Can you see well enough to control the aircraft, see and avoid other aircraft, distinguish runways from taxiways at night, and recognize light gun signals in the event of radio failure?
2. Can you speak and hear well enough to effectively converse with other crewmembers on a noisy flight deck and with air traffic controllers?
3. Are you likely to suffer disorienting vertigo or loss of equilibrium in flight?
4. Are you likely to suffer a suddenly incapacitating medical event in flight?
5. Are you likely to operate an aircraft irresponsibly so as to endanger other people?

The specific medical standards in Part 67 are designed so that if you have any medical condition that would result in an unfavorable answer to any of these basic questions, you are not qualified for an FAA medical certificate. Therefore, your Aviation Medical Examiner (AME) should not issue you a medical certificate if you fail to pass the hearing and vision requirements of Part 67 or if you have a history or diagnosis of any of the following "specific disqualifying conditions":

1. Diabetes requiring insulin or other hypoglycemic medication for control. (If your diabetes can be controlled by careful attention to diet, you are not disqualified.)
2. Heart attack (myocardial infarction).
3. Angina pectoris (the crushing chest pain that is your clue that you are having a heart attack).
4. Other evidence of coronary artery disease (such as an irregular electrocardiogram (EKG).
5. Heart valve replacement.
6. Permanent cardiac pacemaker implantation.
7. Heart replacement (transplant).
8. A psychosis.
9. A personality disorder that has repeatedly manifested itself by overt acts.
10. A bipolar disorder (formerly known as manic depressive disorder).
11. Epilepsy.
12. A disturbance of consciousness without a satisfactory medical explanation of the cause.
13. A transient loss of control of nervous system function(s) without a satisfactory medical explanation of the cause (such as a so-called transient ischemic attack).
14. Substance dependence, abuse or misuse (including alcohol and a wide variety of drugs and controlled substances) within the previous 2 years.

Compare these "specific disqualifying conditions" to the previous basic questions the FAA is trying to answer about your health. The vision standards are designed to be sure that you can see well enough to control the aircraft, see and avoid other aircraft, distinguish runways from taxiways at night, and recognize light gun signals in the event of radio failure. Hearing and speech standards are to ensure you can communicate with other flight crewmembers on a noisy flight deck and with air traffic controllers.

Concern for risk of sudden and unpredictable in-flight incapacitation compels your AME to disqualify you if you have diabetes requiring insulin (putting you at risk of incapacitation by insulin shock), have suffered a heart attack or have coronary artery disease (which can lead to an incapacitating heart attack). The same concern requires your AME to disqualify you if are epileptic, or have experienced a loss of consciousness without a satisfactory medical explanation (so that your next seizure might happen while you're at the controls of an aircraft in flight).

Concern over potential irresponsible operation of aircraft endangering others disqualifies people having a psychosis or other psychiatric problems that have led to irrational behavior, as well as substance abusers.

A "history or diagnosis" of any one of the specific disqualifying conditions prevents your AME from issuing you an FAA medical certificate regardless of how good your health may otherwise appear during the examination.

There are also catchall subparagraphs that disqualify you for any other physical condition that in the opinion of the Federal Air Surgeon could make it unsafe for you to exercise airman certificate privileges or if you are taking any medication or undergoing any course of treatment that would adversely affect your performance.

Some examples of physical conditions the Federal Air Surgeon has found disqualifying under this "other physical condition" catchall, depending on severity and treatment, include arthritis, asthma, chronic lymphocytic leukemia, colitis, colon cancer, glaucoma and ocular hypertension, hepatitis C, hyperthyroidism, hypothyroidism, lymphoma and Hodgkin's disease, migraine syndrome, prostate cancer, sleep apnea and urolithiasis (kidney stones).

Examples of medications the Federal Air Surgeon presently considers disqualifying include seizure medications, as well as those medications such as Zyrtec that have label warnings of sedative effects.

Getting Certified When You Don't Meet the Standards

You may have a "history or diagnosis" of one of those specific disqualifying conditions or otherwise fail to meet Part 67 standards but now present no special risk. Perhaps you had a heart attack but then underwent heart surgery, quit smoking, went on a low cholesterol diet, and are following a good exercise regimen so that you are now no more likely to have another heart attack than anyone else of your age. Maybe you were able to beat an alcohol or drug habit. Maybe the history or diagnosis was erroneous (doctors are human and sometimes make mistakes too). Or perhaps the Federal Air Surgeon has disqualified you because in his opinion your condition, medication, or current course of treatment is incompatible with safe flying. Your treating physicians may strongly disagree with the Federal Air Surgeon's opinion. Shouldn't you be free to fly? Yes, and if you can convince the FAA that despite your medical history you are now fit to fly, you can.

Statement of Demonstrated Ability (SODA)

Pilots who have a static disability that is not expected to worsen may be certified through a process referred to as a Statement of Demonstrated Ability (SODA).

Let's start with the easiest ones: vision and hearing problems. If your vision doesn't meet FAA standards without eyeglasses or contact lenses but does with these lenses, all that may be required is for your AME to add this limitation to your medical certificate: *"Holder shall wear correcting lenses while exercising the privileges of his/her airman certificate."*

If you failed the color vision test, you may be able to get your medical certificate by arranging a test to determine whether you are able to distinguish between the red, green, and white of the control tower light gun that would give you directions in the event of a radio failure. If you can, you get your medical certificate even if your color vision isn't perfect. If your hearing is below standards but you can demonstrate that you can still hear and understand ATC instructions and flight deck conversation, you should be able to get your medical certificate, although it may have a limitation on it requiring you to use a noise canceling headset while flying.

If you have a below-the-knee amputation of a leg from an accident, but have a prosthetic limb which generally enables you to function normally, and your AME is of the opinion that this would present no problem with operating the aircraft's controls, she has authority to issue you a student pilot certificate with the limitation "For Student Pilot Purposes Only" to enable you to take a checkride with an FAA examiner. If you pass the checkride by demonstrating that you are in fact able to operate all of the aircraft's controls despite your disability, you will be issued a SODA.

Special Issuance

If your problem is a history or diagnosis of one of the specific disqualifying conditions listed above, but you can prove that in spite of that history you are unlikely to become suddenly incapacitated while flying (or to fly irresponsibly), you may obtain an FAA medical certificate by "special issuance." The burden will be on you and your doctors to convince the Federal Air Surgeon that you are now an acceptable risk to flight safety. If you succeed, the Federal Air Surgeon has the discretionary authority to issue you any class of medical certificate by special issuance, even though you don't meet the letter of the law.

The one exception to this is the diabetic who requires insulin injections to control the disease. Until recently, the FAA considered insulin-treated diabetes mellitus (ITDM) absolutely disqualifying for any class of medical certificate. No special issuance medical certificates of any class were granted to individuals with ITDM. In response to a petition from the American Diabetes Association, the FAA has now opened third-class aviation medical certification by special issuance to individuals with IDTM who haven't experienced any further complications, such as heart or kidney disease, neurological abnormalities, or vision problems. The conditions for special issuance to individuals with ITDM, which include stringent monitoring requirements, are available on the FAA's website. This change has opened up the joy and freedom of personal flying (under a student, recreational or private pilot certificate) to hundreds of such individuals, at this writing. Flight operations by these individuals are, however, limited to the United States, as ICAO has yet to adopt comparable rules. It continues to be the FAA's position that individuals with ITDM still pose too great a risk of sudden incapacitation to allow first or second-class medical certification as would allow them to carry passengers for hire.

Periodic renewal of medical certificates issued under this special issuance process, once as slow and cumbersome as getting the first special issuance, is now being expedited under the FAA's new "Quick-Cert" program. This program is part of the Federal Air Surgeon's goal to provide "same-day medical certification" to qualified applicants.

The safety record of pilots operating under specially issued medical certificates has proven every bit as good as that of the general pilot population over the years, so this enlightened and humane process of personalized evaluation is likely to remain a feature of aviation medical certification.

Reconsideration

Upon review of your application and completion of your examination, your AME has three alternative courses of action available: (1) if you appear qualified, issue the medical certificate; (2) if your qualifications are in question, defer the certification decision to FAA superiors, who review the question and decide whether to issue or deny your certificate; or (3) if you appear disqualified, deny your application.

If your AME defers issuance, the review process begins automatically without further action on your part, but if your AME denies you a medical certificate, you must request that he issue you a denial slip and forward your application to the FAA Aeromedical Certification Branch in Oklahoma City for reconsideration of the denial. If this step is not taken, you are considered to have withdrawn your application for a medical certificate.

If the Oklahoma City office also denies your application, it may be necessary for you to request further reconsideration by the Federal Air Surgeon in Washington, D.C., in order to preserve your appeal rights.

Suspension or Revocation

If while you hold a current medical certificate, the FAA learns that you are not medically qualified to hold that certificate, it may issue an order of suspension or revocation of your medical certificate. Such orders are usually issued on an emergency basis, since your qualifications are in question.

Appeal

If you receive a final denial of your application for a medical certificate from the FAA or the FAA issues an order of suspension or revocation of your existing medical certificate, you can appeal the decision to the NTSB. Your appeal will be heard by one of the board's administrative law judges, like the hearing you would receive on appeal of an enforcement case, as previously discussed in Chapter 2.

If the appeal is from an FAA order suspending or revoking your medical certificate, the FAA has the burden of proving by a preponderance of the evidence that you are not medically qualified. In the case of an FAA denial of your application for medical certificate, however, you have the burden of proving (again, by a preponderance of the evidence), through the sworn in-person testimony of qualified physicians supported by copies of your medical records, that you are qualified. In either case, if you convince the ALJ, the NTSB can order the FAA to issue you a medical certificate or set aside the FAA's order suspending or revoking your current medical certificate. From the ALJ, the route of appeal goes to the full board, court of appeals, and Supreme Court under the same procedures described for enforcement cases in Chapter 2.

Not all cases of denial, suspension, or revocation of a medical certificate are appropriate for appeal. If you have a history or diagnosis of one of the specific disqualifying conditions, and there is no real question that the history or diagnosis is accurate, appeal to the NTSB is futile. In that situation, the petition for special issuance is the only process by which you can have any hope of obtaining your medical certificate. If, however, the FAA position is based upon an erroneous or a subjective application of the catchall conditions, an appeal to the NTSB may succeed. If your physicians testify convincingly that your physical condition does not make you an especially risky pilot or that the medication or treatment you are taking is unlikely to interfere with your safe performance in flight, the NTSB may overrule the FAA.

Truth or Consequences

If you love flying, your periodic FAA medical exam is always a time for concern since you can't legally fly most powered aircraft as pilot-in-command without a medical certificate. So when you sit down in your AME's office to fill out the application form to obtain or renew your medical certificate, you may be tempted to omit some details of your medical history or otherwise fail to tell the whole truth on that form (Fig. 3.1).

While this temptation is understandable, it is a temptation you must resist. FAA medical certification is in large measure an honor system, the integrity of the entire process depending upon your truthfulness. If you succumb to temptation and obtain a medical certificate by false representations and are found out, the consequences will be horrendous.

As we saw in Chapter 2, it is both an FAR violation (14 CFR §61.59) and a federal felony (major crime) to make a false statement on any FAA form. For the FAR violation, the FAA will revoke not only your medical certificate but also all pilot and other FAA-issued certificates you hold, probably by an emergency order taking effect immediately. For the criminal violation, the U.S. Attorney will file charges against

Fig. 3.1. No one looks forward to taking an exam, and the periodic medical examination required to exercise the privileges of your pilot certificate is no exception. The temptation to cheat may always be present, but the potential consequences of giving false or incomplete information can be career ending.

you punishable by up to five years in a federal prison and/or a $250,000 fine. Nothing infuriates the FAA more than being lied to, and it and the Justice Department (of which the U.S. Attorney's office is a part) prosecute falsification cases with a special vengeance.

This extends not only to medical information called for on the application form but also to all questions on the form. For example, questions 18.v. and w. on the application form (*see* Fig. 3.2) ask whether you have a history of arrests and/or convictions of certain alcohol or drug related driving offenses or a history of other misdemeanor or felony convictions. The answers you give on this application will be automatically compared to information already entered in the National Driver Registry (NDR) database, which includes reports of traffic arrests and convictions from all fifty states. The National Crime Information Center (NCIC) computer database contains records of other arrests and convictions from all states as well as federal criminal arrests and convictions. If you have a record of an applicable traffic or other arrest or conviction but deny it on your application for an FAA medical certificate, these

Applicant Must Complete **ALL** 20 Items (Except For Shaded Areas)   **PLEASE PRINT**   Form Approved OMB NO. 2120-0034

Copy of FAA Form 8500-8
(Medical Certificate) or FAA
Form 8420-2 (Medical/Student
Pilot Certificate) Issued.

GG- 0000090

MEDICAL CERTIFICATE_____CLASS
AND STUDENT PILOT CERTIFICATE
This certifies that *(Full name and address)*:

| Date of Birth | Height | Weight | Hair | Eyes | Sex |

has met the medical standards prescribed in part 67, Federal Aviation Regulations, for this class of Medical Certificate.

Limitations

| Date of Examination | Examiner's Designation No. |

Examiner

Signature

Typed Name

AIRMAN'S SIGNATURE

VOID

1. Application For:
☐ Airman Medical Certificate   ☐ Airman Medical and Student Pilot Certificate

2. Class of Medical Certificate Applied For:
☐ 1st   ☐ 2nd   ☐ 3rd

3. Last Name   First Name   Middle Name

4. Social Security Number

5. Address   Telephone Number (   )

Number / Street

City   State / Country   Zip Code

6. Date of Birth   M M / D D / Y Y Y Y

Citizenship

7. Color of Hair   8. Color of Eyes   9. Sex

10. Type of Airman Certificate(s) You Hold:
☐ None   ☐ ATC Specialist   ☐ Flight Instructor   ☐ Recreational
☐ Airline Transport   ☐ Flight Engineer   ☐ Private   ☐ Other
☐ Commercial   ☐ Flight Navigator   ☐ Student

11. Occupation   12. Employer

13. Has Your FAA Airman Medical Certificate Ever Been Denied, Suspended, or Revoked?
☐ Yes   ☐ No   If yes, give date   M M / D D / Y Y Y Y

Total Pilot Time (Civilian Only)
14. To Date   15. Past 6 Months

16. Date of Last FAA Medical Application
M M / D D / Y Y Y Y   ☐ No Prior Application

17.a. Do You Currently Use Any Medication (Prescription or Nonprescription)?
☐ No   ☐ Yes (If yes, below list medication(s) used and check appropriate box).   Previously Reported Yes No

(If more space is required, see 17. a. on the instruction sheet.)

17.b. Do You Ever Use Near Vision Contact Lens(es) While Flying?   ☐ Yes   ☐ No

18. Medical History - HAVE YOU EVER IN YOUR LIFE BEEN DIAGNOSED WITH, HAD, OR DO YOU PRESENTLY HAVE ANY OF THE FOLLOWING? Answer "yes" or "no" for every condition listed below. In the EXPLANATIONS box below, you may note "PREVIOUSLY REPORTED, NO CHANGE" only if the explanation of the condition was reported on a previous application for an airman medical certificate and there has been no change in your condition. See Instructions Page

Yes	No	Condition	Yes	No	Condition	Yes	No	Condition	Yes	No	Condition
a.	☐	Frequent or severe headaches	g.	☐	Heart or vascular trouble	m.	☐	Mental disorders of any sort; depression, anxiety, etc.	r.	☐	Military medical discharge
b.	☐	Dizziness or fainting spell	h.	☐	High or low blood pressure	n.	☐	Substance dependence or failed a drug test ever; or substance abuse or use of illegal substance in the last 2 years.	s.	☐	Medical rejection by military service
c.	☐	Unconsciousness for any reason	i.	☐	Stomach, liver, or intestinal trouble	o.	☐	Alcohol dependence or abuse	t.	☐	Rejection for life or health insurance
d.	☐	Eye or vision trouble except glasses	j.	☐	Kidney stone or blood in urine	p.	☐	Suicide attempt	u.	☐	Admission to hospital
e.	☐	Hay fever or allergy	k.	☐	Diabetes	q.	☐	Motion sickness requiring medication	v.	☐	Other illness, disability, or surgery
f.	☐	Asthma or lung disease	l.	☐	Neurological disorders; epilepsy, seizures, stroke, paralysis, etc.				w.	☐	Medical disability benefits

Arrest, Conviction, and/or Administrative Action History --- See Instructions Page

Yes	No		Yes	No	
v. ☐ ☐		History of (1) any arrest(s) and/or conviction(s) involving driving while intoxicated by, while impaired by, or while under the influence of alcohol or a drug; or (2) history of any arrest(s), and/or conviction(s), and/or administrative action(s) involving an offense(s) which resulted in the denial, suspension, cancellation, or revocation of driving privileges or which resulted in attendance at an educational or a rehabilitation program.	w. ☐ ☐		History of nontraffic conviction(s) (misdemeanors or felonies).

Explanations: See Instructions Page

FOR FAA USE
Review Action Codes

19. Visits to Health Professional Within Last 3 Years.   ☐ Yes (Explain Below)   ☐ No   See Instructions Page

Date	Name, Address, and Type of Health Professional Consulted	Reason

— NOTICE —
Whoever in any matter within the jurisdiction of any department or agency of the United States knowingly and willingly falsifies, conceals or covers up by any trick, scheme, or device a material fact, or who makes any false, fictitious or fraudulent statements or representations, or entry, may be fined up to $250,000 or imprisoned not more than 5 years, or both. (18 U.S. Code Secs. 1001; 3571).

20. Applicant's National Driver Register and Certifying Declarations
I hereby authorize the National Driver Register (NDR), through a designated State Department of Motor Vehicles, to furnish to the FAA information pertaining to my driving record. This consent constitutes authorization for a single access to the information contained in the NDR to verify information provided in this application. Upon my request, the FAA shall make the information received from the NDR, if any, available for my review and written comment. Authority: 23 U.S Code 401, Note.

NOTE: ALL persons using this form must sign it. NDR consent, however, does not apply unless this form is used as an application for Medical Certificate or Medical Certificate and Student Pilot Certificate.

I hereby certify that all statements and answers provided by me on this application form are complete and true to the best of my knowledge, and I agree that they are to be considered part of the basis for issuance of any FAA certificate to me. I have also read and understand the Privacy Act statement that accompanies this form.

Signature of Applicant

Date   M M / D D / Y Y Y Y

FAA Form 8500-8 (9-06) Supersedes Previous Edition

NSN: 0052-00-670-6002

Fig. 3.2. FAA application for aviation medical certificate.

computers will compare notes and catch you and you will be prosecuted. You must answer all questions on the application form truthfully. These data-matching programs are credited with weeding out over 3,000 pilots with alcohol or drug problems.

In another example of agency cross-matching of computer records, in July of 2003 the U.S. Attorney's Office began Operation Safe Pilot, characterized as a "homeland security-type operation," that compared the FAA aviation medical applications of some 40,000 northern California pilots with the Social Security Administration (SSA) database of individuals receiving disability income payments. Where serious discrepancies appeared, such as pilots who had failed to report disqualifying conditions on their applications for airman medical certificates while drawing disability income payments from the SSA for such conditions as schizophrenia, bipolar disorders, and heart conditions, law enforcement action ensued. Following the review, the FAA immediately revoked the medical and pilot certificates of 14 pilots and 40 were prosecuted for federal crimes relating to their falsifications. This well-publicized result lead to congressional hearings, and the House Transportation and Infrastructure Committee urged the FAA to establish similar data-sharing programs with other federal agencies, within the bounds of the Privacy Act, to check for such false information.

Congress' concern was raised not only by the Operation Safe Pilot data-sharing experiment, but also by a near-simultaneous incident on the east coast where the lone professional pilot of an air taxi flight with four passengers aboard became incapacitated by a diabetic coma after takeoff from Martha's Vineyard en route to Hyannis, MA. Fortunately for all aboard, one of the passengers was a student pilot who succeeded in landing the aircraft (although gear up) at the Provincetown, MA, airport without injuries. Investigation of the incident revealed that the ATP-rated pilot had concealed his history of diabetes from the FAA for years. Not only did the FAA revoke his pilot and medical certificates on an emergency basis; he also entered a guilty plea to criminal felony falsification charges and was sentenced to 16 months in prison and 3 years probation.

Answering "yes" to any of the items on the application doesn't necessarily disqualify you from receiving a medical certificate. Those questions are on the form because the FAA is looking for clues that you may have one of the specific disqualifying conditions or another health condition that could make it unsafe for you to act as a pilot.

If you truthfully answer all questions on the application, depending on the severity of the reasons behind those "yes" answers, it may not even slow down the issuance of your medical certificate. But if you withhold the truth, the consequences can be horrendous, both legally to you and physically to you, your passengers, and other people and property below.

CHANGES IN YOUR HEALTH

What if your health changes for the worse while you hold an unexpired FAA medical certificate? Are you required to report the change to the FAA? Not until you next apply for a medical certificate and then only if one or more of the questions on the application form covers it. Are you required to stop flying? It depends. If what has happened to you since your medical was issued is one of the specific disqualifying conditions, a deterioration of your vision or hearing that puts you below FAA certification standards, or a condition, medication or course of treatment which unquestionably makes it unsafe for you to serve as a pilot, then 14 CFR §61.53 mandates that you refrain from exercising pilot privileges. You don't have to tell anybody, and you don't have to surrender your medical certificate, but you do have to stop acting as a pilot or other required flight crewmember (such as a flight engineer on some transport category aircraft). If you continue to exercise pilot privileges, you risk FAA enforcement action (that would almost certainly take the form of an emergency revocation of your pilot certificate) and your aviation insurance company would be in a position to deny coverage for any accident occurring during such operations (an exploration of aviation insurance is to come in Chapter 6).

If on the other hand the medical event does not fit within one of these categories, you have to use your own best judgment. If the medical problem is something that can lead to an unpredictable and suddenly incapacitating event in flight, you should stop flying. If your medical condition, medication or course of treatment may impair your judgment or ability to control the aircraft precisely, to see and avoid other aircraft, to understand and follow the instructions of air traffic controllers or otherwise perform competently as a pilot, you should stop flying. One of the responsibilities we have as members of the aviation community is to use good judgment and not fly when we don't feel up to it. Even if it may be technically legal, it just isn't prudent and as we will see in greater detail in Chapter 4, it may be negligence to do something that is not prudent.

If you are taking medication (whether by prescription or over-the-counter) ask yourself: "Can this drug affect my vision, alertness, judgment, or sense of balance?" If it's a prescription medicine, ask your doctor. If it's an over-the-counter medicine (such as a cold remedy), consult the label or package insert. The Physicians' Desk Reference (PDR), available

---

from most booksellers, is also a good reference to check. If the answer is yes, 14 CFR §91.17(a)(3) requires that you refrain from acting as a pilot or other required flight crewmember while you are taking the medication and until it is effectively out of your system. In order to predict when the medication will be effectively out of your system, the FAA and medical profession agree that the best rule of thumb is to wait twice the recommended dosage period after the last dose was taken. For example, if the instructions call for taking a dose every 4 hours, you could expect to be free of the medication's side effects 8 hours after taking the last dose. If the instructions call for a dosage range, such as every 4–6 hours, then you should use the longer period in making this computation and wait 2 x 6 = 12 hours. Then you are legal to resume flying unless the symptoms have returned. While you are reading the label or package insert watch for hidden alcohol, especially in cough syrups and liquid decongestants such as NyQuil™, which could also bring into play the 8-hour and other criteria of §91.17.

Do not fly if you have a cold or sinus infection. Changing atmospheric pressure encountered with climbing and descending can cause serious sinus and ear problems, including the risk of major permanent damage, and the pain caused by a sinus block may be so excruciating as to incapacitate you as a pilot. Use your best judgment, watching out for wishful thinking and rationalization, and don't fly if it wouldn't be wise.

Required Reports

You are not required to report a change in your health to the FAA before your next application for a medical certificate. You must, however, report any conviction for a drug or alcohol related traffic offense or the denial, cancellation, suspension, or revocation of your driver's license related to such an offense. Under 14 CFR §61.15(e), this report must be filed with the FAA Civil Aviation Security Division (AMC-700), P.O. Box 25810, Oklahoma City, OK 73125, within sixty days after the conviction or motor vehicle action. The interagency computer interface described earlier is keeping such a close watch in this area that the FAA sometimes issues an order of suspension or revocation for failure to make the report by the sixty-first or sixty-second day! The FAA and NTSB agree that you are required to make this report even if you aren't doing any flying, and even if you don't have a current medical certificate, for as long as you hold a pilot certificate. Don't forget!

Requests for Additional Medical Information

Whenever the FAA has some reasonable basis to suspect that you may not be qualified to hold a medical certificate, it can request that you furnish additional medical information or submit to further medical testing in the area in question. If you receive such a request, you are required to comply promptly and at your own expense. Failure to furnish the additional information requested is sound legal ground for the FAA to suspend or revoke your medical certificate under 14 CFR §67.31 until you provide the information.

Drug and Alcohol Testing

Mandatory drug and alcohol testing has become a routine requirement throughout the commercial aviation industry. The Supreme Court has found drug and alcohol testing (both in pre-hire screening and random sampling of employees) in transportation-related jobs to be constitutional.

Refusal to submit to a drug or alcohol test required by the DOT or FAA is grounds for suspension or revocation of your pilot certificate under 14 CFR §61.14(b) and §91.17(c).

Accident statistics show a significant correlation between alcohol and drug use and aircraft accidents, so the FAA has given very high priority to identifying pilots who abuse or are dependent upon alcohol or drugs and grounding them until they have recovered.

Get Help

The FAA's medical bureaucracy can be extremely frustrating to deal with, and it's easy to miss a crucial procedural step, or have your application get lost in the bureaucratic maze and seem to go around in circles for years awaiting a decision. An attorney who is knowledgeable in FAA medical certification procedures can be a tremendous help in evaluating your situation, choosing the best approach to the problem, and organizing and presenting the medical information to the FAA or NTSB in the most cogent and persuasive form.

Members of the Airline Pilots Association (ALPA), Aircraft Owners & Pilots Association (AOPA) and the Experimental Aircraft Association (EAA) can get help with medical certification problems through these organizations, as well. The "Members Only" sections of these organizations' websites are a good place to start.

To read more about FAA aviation medical certification standards and some valuable tips on how to stay in shape to pass your aviation medical exams, see Dr. Richard O. Reinhart's book, *FAA Medical Certification: Guidelines for Pilots (Third Ed.)*, published by the Iowa State University Press, now available in paperback.

PART II

AIRCRAFT ACCIDENTS

4

Basic Principles of Liability

The law is generally subdivided into categories of administrative, civil, and criminal law. In the preceding part, we examined the workings of administrative law, law made and enforced by administrative agencies in the aviation industry. We also touched on the criminal law implications of falsifying applications for FAA certificates and other records required by the federal government and for security violations. Criminal law aspects of aviation security, an area still undergoing change in the wake of the terrorist attacks of 9/11/01, will be further explored in greater detail in Chapter 15. For now, we will turn our attention to the civil law, which may be further subdivided into *tort* law and *contract* law. In this part on aircraft accidents, we will examine the workings of tort law and techniques available to reduce the risk of liability for the consequences of aircraft accidents. In the following part on aircraft transactions, we will examine contract law in the context of buying, selling, leasing, time-sharing, and managing aircraft.

This chapter introduces the basic principles of liability and procedures for civil litigation arising out of aircraft accidents, building the foundation for the other chapters of this part, which focus on risk management techniques useful to avoid such liability. The purpose of this chapter is to ensure that you have a working knowledge of the kinds of behavior you must refrain from to avoid such liability.

WHAT IS A TORT?

A *tort* is an act or omission that causes injury to another person by breach of a legal duty not arising out of a contract and subjects the actor to liability for damages in a civil lawsuit.

Whenever you read a headline like this one from a recent USA Today: *Jury awards $480 million to 3 hurt in plane crash*, you are almost certainly reading about a tort case. Chapters 5 through 10 will cover risk management techniques to reduce the impact of tort liability for aviation accidents, including selection of an appropriate form of organization for the aviation business, insurance, exculpatory contracts, and statutes and international agreements that limit the tort liability of airlines and governments. This chapter focuses on basic principles of tort liability.

Torts may be further subdivided into two kinds: *intentional torts* and *negligence.*

Intentional Torts

Intentional torts are all "acts" while negligence may consist of either an act or an omission. Some intentional torts are also crimes under federal, state, or local law, and may also be FAR violations. In such a case, the wrongdoer may be not only subject to a fine or imprisonment in a criminal action, but also ordered to pay compensation to the victim in a civil tort action, and fined or subjected to certificate suspension or revocation by the FAA or other federal and state regulatory agencies, all for the same misbehavior. The courts have generally held that this is not *double jeopardy*, which is prohibited by the Fifth Amendment to the Constitution of the United States, interpreting that provision only to prohibit the government from *criminally* penalizing a person twice for the same misdeed.

For example, state criminal charges including 110 counts of murder and 110 counts of manslaughter (one of each for each person killed in the crash) were filed against SabreTech, Inc., an airline maintenance contractor that shipped highly flammable oxygen canisters that were improperly packaged and not identified as hazardous material and caused an in-flight fire, and several of its employees in connection with the 1996 ValuJet DC-9 crash in the Florida Everglades, a crash that also gave rise to extensive civil litigation and FAA enforcement action. The state criminal action was ultimately settled for a $500,000 fine.

Meanwhile, a federal grand jury indictment charged SabreTech with several criminal violations of the Hazardous Materials Transportation Act in connection with the crash. In that case, the trial judge sentenced SabreTech to pay $2 million in criminal penalties and $9 million in restitution to victim's families (over and above the civil settlements already reached). This was the first time an aviation business was convicted of criminal charges arising out of a commercial jet airliner crash in the U.S., and some legal analysts suspect that the fine would have been much larger if the company had not already been in bankruptcy at the time. On appeal, the U.S. Court of Appeals overturned the $9 million portion of the sentence for restitution.

In the civil (tort) action, SabreTech and its insurers paid out some $262 million in settlements to the families of the victims.

In addition, the FAA initiated a $2.23 million civil penalty action against SabreTech for related FAR violations. The company settled that case by a compromise agreement to pay the FAA $1.75 million.

Now, let's look at some intentional torts that may arise in an aviation context, exposing a person and their employer to civil liability.

Battery

Battery is a harmful or offensive contact with another person with intent to cause the contact or apprehension of contact and without the consent of the other person (or where consent is obtained by fraud or duress). This could range from punching a person in the nose to uninvited sexually oriented contact.

Assault

An *assault* is simply an attempted battery that missed. If you tried to punch someone in the nose but he ducked and you missed, you have committed the intentional tort of assault.

Intentional Infliction of Mental Distress

The name of this intentional tort is an accurate description of what you are prohibited from doing. Here is an example: A flight instructor is aloft in a trainer with a student. The student pilot keeps repeating the same mistake. The flight instructor, in a fit of temper, reaches over and releases the student's seat belt while rolling the airplane into a very steep bank toward the student's side, grasps the handle of the cabin door beside the student, and threatens to expel the student. That is intentional infliction of mental distress.

False Imprisonment

Anyone can commit the intentional tort of false imprisonment; you don't have to be a law enforcement officer. *False imprisonment* consists of intentionally confining, restraining, or detaining another person against her will. This occurs most often in the aviation industry in the debt collection context when people or businesses resort to some use of force instead of litigation to collect a debt. Here's an example: An FBO's manager notices on the ramp an aircraft belonging to a person who owes the FBO some money. The manager sends a line service attendant out to block the aircraft's departure with a gas truck and bring the owner into the office. That's false imprisonment.

False Arrest

False arrest and false imprisonment sound so similar that fiendish professors are especially fond of asking you to distinguish between them on examinations. A *false arrest* is a false imprisonment carried out by a false or erroneous assertion of legal authority to detain the other person. An example of a false arrest would occur if the line service attendant in the previous example went out to restrain the debtor aircraft owner and found a very large, ill-tempered and imposing adversary. Deciding to outwit rather than attempt to overpower the owner, the quick thinking attendant approaches the owner from the rear, pokes a finger in his ribs and shouts: "Freeze! FBI! Lock your hands behind your head and come with me. Don't make any fast moves." This false assertion of legal authority ("FBI!") escalates this false imprisonment into a false arrest. The same might be true if you tried to make a "citizen's arrest" of someone you observed violating an FAR. The legal authority to perform a citizen's arrest is generally limited to felonies (major crimes like murder, robbery, or burglary) and does not extend to misdemeanors, violations of administrative regulations, or civil matters such as debt collection.

Trespass

Trespass is an intentional invasion of someone else's land. This intentional tort comes into play most frequently in aviation in the context of off-airport landings or landings on airports that are not open to the public, without prior permission of the owner.

Your intent can be determinative of whether you committed a trespass. If you are flying along and suddenly experience a catastrophic engine failure, pick the most suitable open area within gliding distance, and land there without permission, most courts would hold that you did not commit a trespass. That is because you did not intend to invade the landowner's property, but did so only in response to the emergency. At the other extreme, if you are out flying around and decide to land without prior permission in someone's field or on an airport not open to the public to practice your short or soft field landing technique or have a picnic, any court would agree that you were trespassing.

Something of a legal gray area exists in flight operations that are routinely expected to terminate in off airport landings, such as free flight in hot air balloons and cross-country glider flying. In the absence of a real and credible in-flight emergency, most courts would probably find these landings to constitute trespassing. Thus, in these operations, pilots and ground crews should take special care to obtain the landowner's permission before landing. (For example, by orally hailing the landowner from the low flying balloon or radioing the ground crew to go ahead to the farmhouse to request permission to land and before driving recovery vehicles into the landing area.) All possible care should be taken to avoid damaging standing crops and fences or frightening livestock in the landing and recovery efforts. A humble, respectful, and apologetic attitude, coupled with an immediate and sincere offer to pay for any damage caused by the landing and recovery crews, may appease the landowner and prevent a legal or physical confrontation.

Conversion

In legal language, this is not what a modifier does to your airplane to make it go faster. Think of conversion as being to someone else's personal property (such as their airplane) as trespass is to someone else's land. *Conversion* is defined as the act of assuming rights to personal property that are inconsistent with the rights of the owner or person entitled to possession (such as a lessee). As an example, if you somehow obtained a key and took someone's airplane joyriding without his permission, you would commit the intentional tort of conversion.

Conversion also sometimes occurs during improper debt collection methods. For example, an FBO manager spots an airplane belonging to a person who owes the FBO money on a competitor's ramp. The manager sends an employee down the line with a tug to pull the airplane back to the FBO's hangar and locks it up to hold it until the debt is paid. This may constitute a conversion. (Circumstances under which liens against aircraft for services, fuel, parts, etc., provided to the aircraft may be exceptions to the law of conversion are examined later in Chapter 11.)

An interesting feature of the law of conversion is that it gives the aircraft owner the option to sue for either: (1) money damages (for the consequences of being deprived of the use of the aircraft while it was in the converter's possession) or (2) a court order that the converter has bought the aircraft, compelling payment of its fair market value. (You took it; you bought it. Pay for it.)

The general theme you may have noticed running through these intentional torts is that the law encourages respect for the personal and property rights of others. The law frowns on resort to force or threat of force to resolve controversies instead of reason, persuasion, and (if all else fails) court procedures. When asked what he thought of Western civilization, Gandhi is reported to have replied: "I think it would be a good idea." The law of intentional torts is an effort in that direction, preferring the use of civilized means to dissolve disputes and seeking to avoid situations that may provoke violence.

Fraudulent Misrepresentation

Although found more frequently in contract litigation, a person or business can also sue for the intentional tort of fraudulent misrepresentation if deceived by a defendant who made a representation intended to deceive the plaintiff and with knowledge that the representation is false and damage results.

In the aviation context, this could apply if a mechanic, inspector, seller, or lessor knowingly misrepresented the airworthiness of an aircraft and a defect known to that mechanic, inspector, seller, or lessor caused an accident.

Negligence and Liability

Negligence is the most common form of tort involved in aircraft accident litigation. If there is a common theme running through all facets of American law—administrative, civil, and criminal—it is this: *You are responsible for the consequences of your actions.*

Negligence means failing to do an act that a reasonably careful person would do to protect others from harm or doing an act that a reasonably careful person would not do under the same or similar circumstances.

The four elements of a negligence case are:

1. a *duty* to be reasonably careful,
2. a *failure* to be reasonably careful,
3. which is the *proximate cause* of
4. *injury* to another person or her property.

If you are not reasonably careful and injure someone or damage his property, you will be found negligent and will have to pay the other person (or his survivors) for the damage you caused.

Let's examine each of these elements in greater detail in the context of aviation accidents.

Duty

Your duty to be reasonably careful to avoid harming others extends to anyone who might foreseeably be injured by your neglect. Whether you are a flight crewmember, an aircraft owner/operator, a manufacturer of aircraft or components, an airport owner/operator, an aircraft mechanic or inspector, an air traffic controller, or other person involved in aviation, you have a duty to be reasonably careful. That duty extends to everyone who could foreseeably suffer harm if you are not careful. This could include, for example, other flight crewmembers, passengers, people on the ground and their property, the owner of the aircraft, owners of any personal property carried aboard the aircraft, occupants of other nearby aircraft, and the owners of those aircraft and property carried aboard those aircraft.

Failure to Use Care

Who decides whether you were "reasonably careful" under the circumstances, and how? The jury or (if you do not request a jury) the trial judge decides whether you were reasonably careful. It is unlikely that either the judge or the jurors will have any aviation background. Instead, they will rely upon the testimony of aviation expert witnesses, the FARs, and other written guidance introduced as exhibits at trial.

If mandatory government standards such as an FAR or Airworthiness Directive (AD) state what you must do, then that is what is reasonable. Otherwise, the question the judge or jury must decide is what "a reasonably prudent person" in your position would have done under the circumstances.

Non-mandatory guidance such as the *Aeronautical Information Manual* (AIM) and Advisory Circulars (AC), along with the opinions of aviation expert witnesses who testify at trial are typically also considered by the jury.

Injury

Ordinarily, this must be real physical injury or property damage, not just frightening someone. If, however, you've inflicted mental distress which resulted in an emotional breakdown requiring hospitalization, that would be considered real physical injury.

Even if you were not reasonably careful, if your carelessness did not actually cause such harm to someone, you cannot be successfully sued for negligence. For example: you failed to perform an adequate pre-flight inspection, attempted to take off on almost empty fuel tanks, and fuel starvation caused the engine to quit on takeoff. But when it did, you were able to abort the takeoff without damaging the aircraft or harming its occupants or anyone else. In that situation, you could not successfully be sued for negligence since there was no injury. (But that will not stop the FAA from suspending or revoking your pilot certificate for careless operation under 14 CFR §91.13, inadequate pre-flight action under 14 CFR §91.103, or for your lack of the care, judgment, and responsibility required of the holder of a pilot certificate.)

Proximate Cause

Your neglect must have actually caused the injury, at least by setting in motion a sequence of events that would not otherwise have occurred. Indeed, most aviation accidents result not from a single mistake but from a series of errors that snowball and cause the accident. The legal concept of *proximate cause* is not the same thing as the NTSB's finding of *probable cause*. Nor will the NTSB's opinion of probable cause be admissible as evidence at trial. However, facts found by NTSB investigators during their investigation of the accident will be admissible at trial.

For example: A single engine general aviation aircraft flying from San Francisco to Denver reports an engine stoppage to ATC over the Colorado Rockies. The aircraft is substantially damaged attempting a forced landing, and its occupants are seriously injured. The NTSB is notified, and an investigator heads for the scene. Having first determined the time the aircraft took off from San Francisco and the time the engine stoppage was reported to ATC, and knowing the standard fuel capacity and burn rate for the type of aircraft involved, the investigator suspects fuel exhaustion. Arriving at the scene of the accident, the investigator sniffs around, but smells no avgas. He removes the overturned aircraft's fuel caps. No fuel runs out, nor can he find any trace of leaked fuel on the ground. Then, the investigator probes the fuel tanks with a dipstick, but still finds no fuel. A salvage crew dispatched by the owner's insurance company arrives on the scene to dismantle the aircraft and haul it out. The NTSB investigator watches as the aircraft's wings are disconnected from the fuselage and asks the salvage crew to stand each wing on end, root downward. No fuel runs out. Based upon these facts observed by the investigator, the NTSB later determines the probable cause of the accident to have been the pilot's inadequate pre-flight planning and failure to properly monitor his fuel supply, resulting in in-flight fuel exhaustion.

When the injured passengers sue the pilot for negligence, the NTSB investigator's testimony as to what he did and what he saw would be admitted into evidence. Then, instead of being able to use the NTSB's finding of probable cause as evidence, the plaintiffs would have to hire their own expert witness to analyze the facts found by the investigator and testify to an opinion of the proximate cause of the accident, based upon those facts. That opinion may, of course, well be the same one the NTSB expressed in its finding of probable cause.

There may be more than one proximate cause of an accident, and more than one person's negligence may be proximate causes of the accident. Consider this example: A student pilot is flying solo, shooting touch-and-go landings at a tower-controlled airport in a rented light trainer. The controller observes the student pilot turning onto a close in base leg that will bring the trainer into a position on final approach close behind a landing heavy jet. The controller, however, fails to instruct the student to extend downwind or to warn the student of the possibility of wake turbulence from the heavy jet. The student encounters the wake turbulence on short final, loses control of the airplane and crashes, destroying the rented trainer. Under these circumstances, a judge or jury might find that the student pilot, the student's instructor, and the air traffic controller each owed a duty to the aircraft owner not to allow the aircraft to encounter wake turbulence, to avoid risk of damage to the trainer. In this case, the judge or jury might find that the student pilot, the student's instructor, and the controller had each failed to exercise reasonable care to avoid this accident and that each of them proximately caused the accident: the student (by failing to recognize and avoid the potential wake turbulence encounter), the instructor (by failing to teach the student wake turbulence recognition and avoidance techniques), and the controller (by failing to warn and guide the student away from the observed danger).

Where multiple defendants are found negligent, some states allow judges and juries to apportion the percentage of negligence among them (as fractions of 100 percent) and to apportion the resulting damage accordingly. In these states, if the trainer that was destroyed was worth $150,000 and the judge or jury apportioned the negligence equally among the student, instructor, and ATC, then each would be liable to the aircraft owner for $50,000. Some states provide for *joint and several liability* in such cases, with no apportionment by the court. In these states, even if more than one defendant is found negligent, the victorious plaintiff can collect the entire judgment ($150,000 in this example) from any defendant found negligent. In these states, plaintiffs' attorneys often tend to follow the path of least resistance by enforcing their entire judgment against the defendant having the "deepest pockets" (the one most able to pay).

Negligent Entrustment

FBOs and other businesses and individuals who allow others to use their aircraft, whether through a commercial rental or simply allowing uncompensated use by a friend, face exposure to a subcategory of negligence known as *negligent entrustment*. Where the person allowed to take the aircraft has an accident causing injuries to others (or their property), and subsequent investigation reveals that the pilot was unqualified (as, for example, having an expired medical certificate or lacking the recent experience required for currency), some courts have found aircraft to be a *dangerous instrumentality* and FBOs have been held liable for the accident. Some courts are also expanding the scope of the law of *negligent entrustment* to apply to employers, such as air taxi operators, who negligently entrust their aircraft to unqualified employees.

Proof of Negligence

The procedure at trial is that the plaintiff (the person who claims to be injured) must first present evidence to prove each of the four elements of negligence to satisfy her *burden of proof.* Here, too, the proof must be by a *preponderance of the evidence* (51 percent), not *beyond a reasonable doubt.* There are, however, a few legal exceptions to this procedure that may lighten the plaintiff's burden of proof under some circumstances.

Negligence Per Se

Where the plaintiff can prove that the accident resulted from violation of an FAR that is intended to prevent such accidents, the FAR violation also constitutes civil negligence as a matter of law.

For example: 14 CFR §43.13(a) requires persons performing maintenance, alteration, or preventive maintenance on an aircraft, engine, propeller, or appliance to "use the methods, techniques, and practices prescribed in the current manufacturer's maintenance manual or Instructions for Continued Airworthiness prepared by its manufacturer, or other methods, techniques, and practices acceptable to the Administrator." Finding no such guidance on how to perform a particular task, a mechanic invents a solution, uses it to accomplish the fix without first obtaining FAA approval, and returns the aircraft to service. The repair fails, causing an accident. The FAA charges the mechanic with a violation of the quoted FAR.

If an FAA finding of the violation has already become final (either because the mechanic failed to appeal or defend an enforcement action, or because all appeals have been exhausted and the FAA's finding has been affirmed) that finding may be used in a subsequent civil trial to prove negligence. This is known as the doctrine of *res judicata* (the matter is decided). If not, the judge or jury may take the FAR into account and make a finding in the civil trial whether the regulation was violated. In either case, such a finding of negligence as a matter of law based upon an FAR violation is called *negligence per se* (negligence as such). Therefore, complying with the FARs and defending against charges of FAR violations takes on special importance in connection with related pending or potential civil litigation. Losing (or failing to defend) an FAA enforcement case arising out of an accident may also cause you to lose the civil suit!

Res Ipsa Loquitur

The legal doctrine of *res ipsa loquitur* (the facts speak for themselves) can be relied upon by a plaintiff to prove negligence, even if no one knows what really happened to the aircraft, if:

- the accident is not the sort of thing that normally occurs unless someone was negligent;
- the aircraft involved in the accident was within the exclusive control of the defendant (person or business being sued); and
- whatever happened, the accident was not caused by any fault of the plaintiff.

This doctrine effectively relieves the plaintiff of the burden of proving some specific act of carelessness proximately caused the accident. It has been used successfully by survivors of passengers where an airliner has crashed and the cause of the crash could not be determined, as when the aircraft was lost at sea.

Strict Liability for Defective Product

The seller of any product (including an aircraft or aircraft component) delivered in a defective condition unreasonably dangerous to the purchaser, an anticipated user, or other persons in the area of anticipated use is *strictly liable* for injuries to them resulting from the defect even if they were careful if:

- the seller is in the business of selling such a product; and
- the product is expected to be used without substantial change in the condition in which it is sold.

In such a case, negligence need not be proved and the seller is liable for resulting injury to users and others even if the seller exercised all possible care in the manufacture, inspection, and sale of the product and even if the seller had no contract with the injured person.

This strict liability applies to everyone in the stream of commerce from original component and airframe manufacturers through distributors and dealers, so long as the product left the hands of each in that dangerously defective condition.

It does not matter whether the defect is in the design or manufacture of the product, and may even apply where instructions for use of the product (such as the accompanying pilot's operating handbook or maintenance manual) prove inadequate.

And remember that in this context the term "product" includes not only the obvious, such as a compressor turbine, engine, rotor blade or aircraft, but also fuel and lubricants. Thus, businesses refining, transporting, and selling aviation fuels are exposed to strict liability for defects in the product.

This is *common law* (law made by judges deciding cases over the years, as distinguished from *constitutional law* made by citizens, *statutory law* made by legislatures, and *regulations* adopted by administrative agencies). The courts have always given high priority to protecting people's health and safety as a matter of public policy. In the area of product liability, the courts have reasoned that manufacturers of products and others in the stream of commerce (such as distributors and dealers) are in the best position to ensure that products delivered to customers are safe. The courts believe that the best way to motivate those businesses to exercise every possible effort to ensure safe products is to make them pay every time someone is injured by an unsafe product.

Note that this applies only to injuries and damage to persons and property, *other than the product itself,* caused by the defect. Damage to the product itself (such as a defective aircraft) is covered by warranty law, which we will discuss later in Chapter 11. Bear in mind also that strict liability for defective products applies only where the seller is in the business of selling such products and not to a private sale by an owner who is not in the business of selling aircraft. Even an airline that routinely sells many of its aircraft each year as it upgrades or "right-sizes" its fleet is not exposed to this strict liability if it sells a dangerously defective airplane, because the airline is in the business of carrying passengers and freight, not selling airplanes.

Strict Liability for Ultrahazardous Activities

The courts may also impose strict liability without regard for negligence where a nonparticipant is injured as a result of the defendant's conducting what the court considers to be an *ultrahazardous activity*. For example, if farm workers or nearby residents were poisoned by an aerial application of restricted-use pesticides, a court may deem that application to be an ultrahazardous activity and hold the aerial applicator strictly liable for the consequences, even if he had used reasonable care in the application.

Defenses

Once the plaintiff has carried the burden of proving negligence at trial, either by proof of the four basic elements or by proving negligence per se, *res ipsa loquitur*, or strict liability for a defective product or ultrahazardous activity, the burden then shifts to the defendant. To prevail, the defendant must then present evidence to rebut the plaintiff's proof and support any legal defenses asserted. Such defenses may include:

Sudden Emergency

Under the *sudden emergency doctrine*, the law recognizes that the stresses imposed by the sudden onset of an in-flight emergency situation may interfere with human decision-making. Imagine that you take off in a fully loaded multi-engine aircraft on a high density altitude day and an engine quits fifty feet over the lake at the end of the runway. Imagine, instead, that you have the luxury of a night to study the *Pilot's Operating Handbook* in the comfort of your library and draft an essay on emergency procedures in event of engine failure on takeoff. In which of these imaginary situations are you most likely to arrive at the right answer in time?

By applying the sudden emergency doctrine, the judge or jury weighing the reasonableness of your behavior may take into account the sudden emergency. Thus, an imperfect performance that might otherwise have been considered not reasonably careful could still be found not to constitute negligence in the face of a sudden emergency.

You do not, however, get the benefit of this reduced standard of care if your own prior negligence caused the emergency. For example: If the engine failure in our example resulted from fuel starvation caused by either your attempt to take off on almost empty fuel tanks following an inadequate pre-flight inspection, or your failure to select the proper fuel tank for takeoff because you did not follow the pre-takeoff checklist in the airplane flight manual, the sudden emergency doctrine would not relieve you of responsibility for the consequences of the resulting crash.

Assumption of Risk

The doctrine of *assumption of risk* may serve to relieve others of legal responsibility for harm befalling an injured person where it is proved that the injured person:

- knew and understood the scope, nature, and extent of the risk involved in the activity and
- voluntarily and freely chose to incur that risk.

Consider the following scenario: An aeronautical engineer who is a professional experimental test pilot and also holds an airline transport pilot certificate with flight instructor rating goes flying with a friend in the friend's aircraft, which is placarded against intentional spins. In the air, the engineer/pilot says, "I've heard that these babies really go flat in a spin and can't be recovered." The owner/friend replies, "Aw, that's an old wives' tale, and nothing could be further from the truth. It's very docile and easy to recover. Would you like me to show you?" The engineer/pilot enthusiastically replies, "I sure would!" The owner deliberately spins the aircraft and the spin goes flat. The owner is unable to affect a recovery and crashes, injuring the engineer/pilot. Under these facts, a judge or jury might find that, given his background, the engineer/pilot knew and understood the scope, nature, and extent of the risk involved and voluntarily and freely chose to incur that risk. The engineer/pilot having assumed the risk, his former friend (the owner of the aircraft) should not be held liable to pay for the engineer/pilot's injuries.

Contrast this scenario: The same owner has taken a friend with no aviation background flying in the same airplane. After takeoff, the passenger inquires about the placard: "What does this mean, 'intentional spins prohibited'?" The owner replies: "Oh, that's a bunch of FAA bull. This baby spins and recovers like a dream. Here, I'll show you." The owner deliberately spins the aircraft, the spin goes flat, the owner is unable to recover, the airplane crashes, and the passenger is injured. Under these facts, a judge or jury would almost certainly find that the injured passenger, having no aviation background or knowledge, was unlikely to have known or understood the scope, nature, and extent of the risk of spinning that airplane and did not voluntarily and freely choose to incur that risk. Thus, the doctrine of assumption of risk would not apply to relieve the owner of legal liability to pay for this passenger's injuries.

Plaintiff's Contributory and Comparative Negligence

If the plaintiff's negligence was also a proximate cause of the accident, this fact may reduce the extent of the defendant's liability or relieve the defendant of all liability. Most states have now adopted a *comparative negligence* approach. This allows the judge or jury to decide what percentage of the proximate cause of the accident was attributable to the defendant and what percentage resulted from the plaintiff's own (contributory) negligence, and then apportion liability for the plaintiff's injuries accordingly. A few states, however, still follow the harsh and old-fashioned *contributory negligence* approach, which holds that if the accident was even slightly the fault of the person injured, that person is not entitled to any compensation from anyone else, no matter how negligent that someone else may have been.

Among states having the more modern comparative negligence laws, two different general approaches to the apportionment of liability are found. In some states, the jury simply makes a finding of percentages and then apportions liability for the plaintiff's injuries accordingly. In states following this approach, the result is pretty simple. Say a jury in one of these states found that an accident was caused 60 percent by the defendant's carelessness and 40 percent by the plaintiff's own carelessness. If the jury further found that the plaintiff had suffered $1 million in injuries (medical expenses, lost income, etc.), then by applying the 60–40 split, the defendant would be liable to pay the plaintiff $600,000 and the plaintiff would have to bear the other $400,000 of loss. Other states draw a line, usually at 50 percent. In these states, if the jury finds the plaintiff's contributory negligence accounted for 50 percent or less of the cause, the apportionment process described above applies, but if the jury finds the plaintiff's contributory negligence to have been more than 50 percent of the cause, the defendant has no liability.

Under the humanitarian doctrine of *last clear chance*, a defendant cannot rely upon the plaintiff's contributory negligence to escape liability if the facts show that even though the plaintiff was negligent, the defendant had the last clear chance to extricate the plaintiff from a position of peril. This is another example of the courts striving to protect people's health and safety. Thus, if a pedestrian carelessly steps out in front of your car as you are approaching a green light, you must still step on your brakes and try to avoid running over the person. Likewise, an air traffic controller observing on radar an aircraft receiving ATC services descending below a minimum safe altitude in a mountainous area is encouraged to alert the flight crew of their error before an impact with the ground results.

Fig. 4.1. Manufacturers of aircraft designed to government specifications for military use, such as this C-17, may be shielded from suit by the government contractor defense.

Government Contractors

The *government contractor defense* shields manufacturers from liability for injuries and death to both military and civilian personnel caused by the manufacturer's products that are ordered by the government *for military use.* (Fig. 4.1) The defense protects the manufacturer only from design defects, and not manufacturing defects. Liability for design defects cannot be imposed upon a civilian manufacturer of military equipment if:

- the United States approved reasonably precise specifications;
- the equipment conformed to those specifications; and
- the manufacturer warned the United States about any dangers in the use of the equipment that were known to the supplier but not to the United States.

The defense continues to protect the manufacturer even after the equipment passes into civilian hands.

Statutes of Limitation

All states have statutes of limitation that impose time limits on how long a person has after an injury to file suit or be forever barred. These vary from state to state and according to the nature of the case.

Statutes of Repose

Statutes of repose impose time limits on how long after a product is manufactured the manufacturer may be held liable for injuries caused by defects in the product (whether in design or fabrication and whether brought under a strict liability or a negligence theory).

Under the provisions of the *General Aviation Revitalization Act (GARA)* passed by Congress in late 1994, there is now a federal 18-year statute of repose for FAA-certified general aviation aircraft having less than twenty seats (Fig. 4.2). This means that the original manufacturer cannot be held legally liable for injuries caused by one of these aircraft that is more than eighteen years old. GARA does not apply if the manufacturer deliberately concealed the defect, nor does it apply to claims by passengers receiving emergency medical transportation or persons on the ground who were injured by an aircraft accident. As new parts and equipment are added to the aircraft as replacements or upgrades, a new 18-year period begins to run *for that part or equipment, only.* Before GARA's enactment, about $40,000 of the cost of a new general aviation aircraft was attributable to the "tail" of potential liability for aircraft produced long ago. (In the U.S., today's fleet of single-engine aircraft

Fig 4.2. When one of these new general aviation aircraft is delivered to its first buyer, GARA's 18-year statute of repose begins to run. Manufacturers of parts and equipment added later in the aircraft's life are protected by GARA beginning 18 years after each such item is installed.

has an average life of 28 years, so GARA eliminated the manufacturer's exposure to liability for more than a third of the average life of one of these aircraft.) Before GARA, that cost made it so difficult for U.S. manufacturers to compete against their foreign competitors who had entered the U.S. market more recently that Cessna suspended production of its piston aircraft line until Congress enacted GARA.

According to the General Aviation Manufacturers Association (GAMA), the number of product liability lawsuits brought against general aviation aircraft and component manufacturers has decreased dramatically since the enactment of GARA. One major general aviation aircraft manufacturer told the General Accounting Office (GAO, the investigative arm of Congress) that the number of open lawsuits the company was defending fell from a high of around 900 in the early 1980s to a total of about 80 in early 2001. Meanwhile, general aviation manufacturing rebounded, with shipments of piston aircraft, for example, increasing nearly fourfold between 1994 and 2000.

Although GARA has accomplished its intended purpose of revitalizing the production of general aviation aircraft in the U.S., it has had unintended (though foreseen) adverse side effects on other segments of the general aviation industry. These will be discussed in Chapter 6, Aviation Insurance. GARA has not had any beneficial effect on the average price of new single-engine piston aircraft (the largest segment of the new fixed-wing aircraft market), which has continued to increase, even when the price is adjusted for inflation.

Some states also have statutes of repose that may apply to aircraft larger than those protected by GARA. The state of Indiana, for example, has a 7-year statute of repose on all products. An accident that occurred there provides a good example of the working of a statute of repose. A DC-3 was taking off from an Indiana airport on a skydiving flight when, just after liftoff and as the landing gear was retracting, an elevator control cable jumped off a pulley under the flight deck floor and jammed. The flight crew kept the aircraft's wings level, reduced power, and successfully bellied the airplane into a cornfield. Unfortunately, on impact one of the propellers separated from the engine, penetrated the aircraft's fuselage and injured one of the jumpers. The jumper's attorney then sued everyone in sight, including McDonnell Douglas (the Douglas Commercial Airplane Company had delivered the airplane to the U.S. Army Air Corps about forty years earlier, as a C-47). McDonnell

Douglas's attorneys moved for an order to dismiss the manufacturer as a defendant, based upon Indiana's statute of repose. The trial court agreed that the Indiana statute governed the case, and dismissed the claims against the manufacturer under the statute of repose because the product had been first sold more than seven years previously.

Exculpatory Contracts

In some comparatively rare circumstances, individuals and aviation businesses can protect themselves from potential liability for aviation accidents beforehand through contracts with voluntary participants. These contracts are discussed in Chapter 7.

International Law

International treaties govern the tort liability of airlines in international flight operations. These are covered in detail in Chapter 8, along with special legislation enacted to protect the airlines and others from litigation arising out of the terrorist attacks of 9/11/01.

Employers' Liability

An employer is said to be *vicariously liable* for torts committed by its employees within the scope of their employment. As an example: An airline flight crew descends below decision height (DH) on an ILS approach in bad weather without having the runway in sight. They allow the aircraft to descend into a stand of trees short of the runway, causing a crash. Because the crew's negligent approach was conducted *within the scope of their employment* by the airline, the airline is also liable for the consequences and must pay for the passenger injuries and deaths that result. The crewmembers also remain personally responsible for the results of their negligence, and they (or their estates if they are killed in the crash) can be sued along with their employer. Vicarious liability adds the employer as a responsible party but never relieves the individual employees of personal liability for their negligence.

If the employee is not doing the employer's work, but is "off on a frolic of his own," then the employer is not vicariously liable for the employee's negligence.

Damages and Attorney Fees

A defendant's potential liability in tort cases is generally limited to *compensatory damages*, the sum that will compensate the injured persons or their survivors for the consequences of the accident. This may include resulting medical expenses (both past and future), lost earnings, and pain and suffering. Reading a headline like *Jury Awards Smith $10 Million Verdict in Plane Crash*, many people reflexively equate Smith's victory to winning the lottery. Close examination of the facts, however, will usually show that Smith suffered horrible and lasting injuries that have left her confined to a wheelchair or bed, unable to earn a living or enjoy most of the activities she had before the accident. She is in constant pain and faced with incredible expenses for medical care, past and future. You can be pretty certain that if someone from the Eyewitless News Team were to shove a microphone into Smith's face and say, "Can you tell our viewers whether you would rather have this $10 million or be medically restored to the health you enjoyed before the crash?" Ms. Smith would much prefer to be her old self. But unfortunately the capability of the medical profession to restore broken bodies is still far short of omnipotence, so an award of money is the best a court can do to compensate the victim.

In fact, the judgment rarely accomplishes even that. The plaintiff's lawyer will usually have undertaken the case on the basis of a contingent fee, whereby the lawyer is paid only in the event of victory and then a percentage of the amount collected (typically in the range between 25% and 50%). This is not necessarily a bad thing, since these cases demand a tremendous amount of work and investment of expense by the plaintiff's lawyers and most injured people could not afford to hire attorneys to represent them in these cases if they had to pay the attorney's usual hourly rates. But the practice does result in plaintiffs actually receiving something less than full compensation for their injuries because of the so-called *American Rule*, which says that under most circumstances, win or lose, each party to a lawsuit is responsible to pay her own attorneys' fees. Personal injury litigation is not a get-rich-quick scheme. In most cases, the most the injured person can hope for is to receive compensation for her injuries, less her attorney's fee.

An exception (and it is a very rare exception) to this is in cases where the jury is allowed to award *exemplary or punitive damages*. In most states, juries are allowed to impose these damages over and above the compensatory damages only where the defendant's negligence was so extreme as to indicate a wanton and reckless disregard of the possible consequences of his actions. Thus they are called "exemplary" damages (to hold the wrongdoer up as an example to others that society will not tolerate that kind of behavior) or "punitive" damages (to punish the wrongdoer). Exemplary and punitive damages are the same thing; some states use one phrase and some use the other. In order to get an award of exemplary or punitive damages, the plaintiff's attorney must convince the jury that the wrongdoer just didn't give a damn whether anybody got hurt or killed. It isn't enough that the defendant was simply negligent.

For example: An airliner crashes due to a defect in its design. The manufacturer's business records reveal that it knew about the problem and the potential for catastrophe long before the accident, but rather than acting to correct the defect, the manufacturer chose to cover up the problem. A jury might well find that kind of behavior indicative of a wanton and reckless disregard for the possible consequences of its failure to remedy the problem, that the manufacturer just didn't care whether anyone got hurt or killed, and might award exemplary or punitive damages. It really takes something that outrages the jury to get punitive damages, and juries are surprisingly difficult to outrage.

Litigation Procedures

The first notice you get that you've been sued should come in the form of a *Summons and Complaint*, usually handed to you by a process server. When that is received, it is time to stop what you are doing and contact your lawyer immediately. Lawsuits are like ball games: If you don't show up on time to play, you lose by default. Your lawyer typically has only twenty days to file a well-considered *Answer* with the court. If you blow that deadline, the plaintiff may get a judgment against you by default, depriving you of your opportunity to defend yourself against the charges.

Discovery

Before trial, your lawyer will have the opportunity to find out what the other side's case is all about and they'll have the opportunity to learn about your defenses through *discovery*, including:

- written *interrogatories* (questions to be answered in writing),
- *depositions* (sworn testimony by prospective witnesses), and
- the examination of documents and other physical evidence (by a *motion to produce*).

Indeed, until discovery has been conducted, it is usually extremely difficult for your attorney to advise you realistically of the strengths and weaknesses of your and your opponent's positions and thus whether a settlement offer should be made (and if so, in what amount). Discovery can be very expensive and time consuming, but it is a crucial part of the litigation process.

Motions

If potentially fatal legal or factual weaknesses in either side's case appear at any stage, the attorneys may bring these to the court's attention by filing or stating a *motion*. Motions alert the court to an issue that may be properly resolved at that point, argue the moving party's view of the matter, and ask the court to rule on the issue. The opposing party has the opportunity to respond with counterarguments. Some motions, such as a *motion for summary judgment* or a *motion to dismiss* may dispose of the entire case.

Trial

Trial may be to the court (that is, a judge sitting without a jury) or to a jury (except in cases brought against the federal government, as we'll see later in Chapter 9). In cases tried to a jury, the jury listens to the evidence presented by both sides, and then the judge instructs the jury about the applicable law. The jury then retires to the sanctuary of the jury room to debate which witnesses they found most credible and which side's version of the facts most believable; decide which side proved its case by *a preponderance of the evidence*; relate the facts they believe true to the legal framework provided by the judge; and reach a decision on the outcome. If the jury's decision is not obviously legally flawed, the judge will then enter the jury's decision as the judgment of the court. Appeals may follow.

Alternative Dispute Resolution

Litigation is a very expensive and often-inefficient way to resolve disputes, so that many people and businesses are now turning to alternative methods of dispute resolution including *arbitration*, *mediation*, and hybrid approaches, with some success.

While such creative new approaches present attractive alternatives to the costs inherent in litigation, probably the most cost-effective approach is to prevent the accident through strict adherence to the FARs, rigorous training programs, meticulous inspection and maintenance, and habits of uncompromising care. Prudence pays. After all, if the accident doesn't happen, you don't get sued. Another beauty of accident prevention is that you don't need to hire a lawyer. You already know how to do it. In the next three chapters, we will examine other techniques you can use to control the risk of liability for aviation accidents. This field is generally referred to as *risk management*.

5

Organizing the Business to Limit Liability

In my observation, far more aviation businesses have failed as a result of poor business practices than from poor aviating. This chapter examines the selection of a form of business organization to protect owners from personal vicarious liability for torts committed by other employees of the business in the scope of their employment. It also examines attitudes, approaches, and practices that I have often seen bring aviation businesses to grief.

The purpose of this chapter is to provide you with an appreciation of the value of selecting and maintaining the appropriate form of business to protect the owners of the business from such liability and to provide you with a practical working knowledge of how to manage a business to avoid the most common and dangerous legal pitfalls.

FORMS OF BUSINESS

The form in which your aviation business is organized is one factor that can be used to control the potential consequences of legal risks inherent in doing business. The primary forms of business organization are:

- sole proprietorship,
- general partnership,
- limited partnership,
- limited liability company (LLC),
- limited liability partnership (LLP), and
- corporation.

While the form of your business cannot protect you personally from liability for your own negligence or intentional torts, it may protect you from vicarious personal liability for torts committed by employees of the business in the scope of their employment and from debts of the business.

In a *sole proprietorship*, the business is owned by a single individual who is personally responsible for debts of the business and (under the principle of vicarious liability discussed in the preceding chapter) for torts committed by employees of the business while acting within the scope of their employment. Thus, people who choose to do business as sole proprietors continually risk not only what they have invested in the business but all of their personal assets (including homes, airplanes, cars, and everything else they may own) in the event of an accident or difficulty in paying business debts. While the freedom to "be your own boss" afforded by the sole proprietorship is greater than that in any other form of business organization, it comes with a very high risk attached.

The same personal exposure to liability applies to each of the partners in a *general partnership*, and even *limited partnerships* are required to have at least one general partner whose personal assets are at risk for business liabilities (although the limited partners enjoy protection from personal liability similar to that afforded shareholders of a corporation).

Until recently, the *corporation* was the only form of business in which no owner (shareholder) of the business took on the added risk of vicarious personal liability for torts committed by employees of the business or debts of the business. In recent years, however, states have adopted laws permitting a business to be organized as a *limited liability company (LLC)* or *limited liability partnership (LLP)*, all of whose owners enjoy the same protection against personal liability as the shareholders of a corporation. (Although relatively new to the U.S., the LLC is hardly a bold experiment, having existed in Europe and South America since the 19th century.) Tax considerations of the particular enterprise drive the choice between a corporation, LLC, or LLP as the more appropriate form of business (a properly formed LLC or LLP can possess both the limited liability of a corporation and the pass-through tax treatment of a partnership). However, not even a corporation, LLC, or LLP will protect you from personal liability for the consequences of your own negligence.

Consider this scenario: One of your company's charter pilots is flying the president of your local bank, the most prosperous physician in the county, and a high-rolling investor to the Big City for a meeting. Severe icing is encountered on the approach and the pilot loses control of the aircraft, crashing into a schoolyard full of children playing at recess. There are no survivors aboard the aircraft and many of the children are killed or injured. Assume further that for some reason the accident is either not covered by your aircraft liability insurance policy (more on this in the next chapter) or that the losses are in excess of the amount covered by that policy. If the business is a sole proprietorship or a general partnership, the sole proprietor or general partners can be held personally liable for the pilot's negligence that caused the accident and could lose everything he/they have. If the business is a limited partnership, only the general partner risks being held vicariously liable for the pilot's negligence and losing everything, with the limited partners' maximum risk being that their investment (their share of the business) will become worthless. But if the business is a corporation, LLC, or LLP, its owners (the corporation's shareholders) have no exposure to personal vicarious liability for the pilot's negligence that caused the accident. The worst that can happen to them is that the accident will bankrupt the business so that their investment (stock) becomes worthless.

Obviously, the corporate form, LLC, and LLP afford the best protection against personal liability arising out of vicarious liability for torts committed by a business's employees and for debts of the business. While such protection is a very important consideration in choosing the form of your aviation business, it is by no means the only consideration. Other considerations that also bear upon selecting the appropriate form for your business include capitalization requirements and tax considerations.

Choosing the optimum form for your business before you begin operations is an important risk management step. You should consult both your accountant and your lawyer to help you reach an informed decision on the choice. The professions of law and accountancy are very similar to the practice of medicine in that prevention can be far more cost effective than subsequent attempts to cure a situation that has been allowed to get out of hand. The initial organization of your aviation business is a prudent occasion to invest in preventive lawyering and accountancy.

FORMING AND OPERATING A CORPORATION

If you choose to incorporate the business, inquire whether your lawyer would be willing to serve as the corporation's *agent for service of process*. If the corporation is sued, this is the person upon whom the process server must serve the Summons and Complaint, the first representative of the corporation to find out about the lawsuit. As mentioned in the previous chapter, your attorney may have only twenty days (and even less under some circumstances) to file an Answer or other pleading with the court. Having your attorney as the corporation's agent for service of process can eliminate the possibility of someone getting a default judgment against the corporation because the Summons and Complaint were not delivered to the corporation's attorney in time.

The *articles of incorporation* are to a corporation what a constitution is to a nation. They are the most basic document expressing what has been created. Although most states allow you to create a corporation by filling in a very simple form and paying a small filing fee, you will probably find that the cost of having your attorney draft original customized articles of incorporation is well worth the modest additional cost. When the state accepts your articles of incorporation and issues a *certificate of incorporation*, the legal equivalent of a birth in the family occurs. The law recognizes the corporation as a "person" having rights and an existence separate from and independent of its owners (unlike any other form of business organization). Sole proprietorships and partnerships are considered to be identical to their owners.

This birth alone, however, may not be sufficient to protect you from personal liability for the torts of the corporation's employees or for corporate debts. That is because of the *alter ego doctrine*. Under that doctrine if, notwithstanding the fact of incorporation, you continue to *operate* the business as though it were a sole proprietorship or partnership, a plaintiff's attorney may later be able to "pierce the corporate veil" to reach your personal assets to satisfy liabilities or debts of the business. The key to avoiding such a revolting turn of events is to take great pains to make it obvious to the public, including customers and suppliers of the business, that they are dealing with a corporation. (The same is true of an LLC or LLP.) This is done by carefully following the "duck rule."

It is said that if you come upon a creature in the wild and it looks like a duck, quacks like a duck, waddles like a duck, and leaves a slippery trail of spoor like that of duck, you may safely assume that the creature is a duck. This is the duck rule. To ensure that people know that they are dealing with a corporation, you must be sure that the business looks like a corporation, quacks like a corporation, waddles like a corporation, and leaves the trail of spoor left by a corporation.

No single factor discussed here automatically determines whether a plaintiff can pierce your corporate veil. The issue of whether the business was really being operated like a corporation rather than a sole proprietorship or partnership is a complex question of fact that the judge or jury will ultimately decide, based on many factors. But ignoring any of these factors increases the risk that a plaintiff's attorney will succeed in piercing the corporate veil to reach your personal assets.

Looking Like a Corporation

Here are some essentials of looking like a corporation.

Showing the Corporate Name

A corporation's "last name" must always be *Incorporated* (or the abbreviation *Inc.*), *Corporation* (or the abbreviation *Corp.*), or *Limited* (or the abbreviation *Ltd.*). The latter is not the same thing as an LLC or a limited partnership, but is one acceptable way of denominating a corporation. One of these becomes the legal last name of this new person, the corporation. You always use both your first name and your last name in business dealings. Corporations must do the same thing. Remember: You're trying to be sure that everyone you're doing business with knows he is dealing with a corporation. Every piece of paper that has the business's name on it must include that official last name because that puts the person on notice that he is dealing with a corporation. The same is true of signs around your facility, on the aircraft, and on other equipment. (Fig. 5.1.) Wherever the corporate name appears, the entire correct legal name should appear.

One single sign, website, or piece of paper not conforming to this rule can put your corporate protection in jeopardy. The plaintiff can present that piece of paper as an exhibit at trial and testify: "You can see from this that I had no reason to know that I was dealing with a corporation." This problem most often comes up when a business that began as a sole proprietorship or partnership later incorporates, simply adding Inc., Corp., or Ltd. to the previously used trade name. Frugal managers may decide to use up all the old stationery, invoices, checks, and other printed forms before having the corporate last name added at the next printing. Others have been known to deliberately omit the corporate last name for aesthetic reasons. Such an approach may defeat the liability limiting purpose of incorporating the business.

Fig. 5.1. Although the "Inc." on this FBO's sign looks like an afterthought, it should suffice to put the public on notice that they're dealing with a corporation.

Once the corporation is formed, every last blank piece of letterhead, form, check, and other office and shop supplies having the old name (which does not reflect the corporate status) should be shredded, then burned. If even one escapes, Murphy's Law ("if anything can go wrong, it will") dictates that you will see that piece of paper later, at trial, as Exhibit A in the plaintiff's attempt to pierce the corporate veil to reach your personal assets. And update the name on the corporate web site immediately.

Adequate Capitalization

There is no hard-and-fast rule on how much capitalization (money and assets) is required for a corporation. But the more you strive to keep it an empty shell having no assets exposed to potential claimants, the more likely it is that a judge or jury will pierce that corporate veil to reach your personal assets. Your attorney and accountant can help you decide what assets should be held in the corporation's name, given the nature and circumstances of your particular business.

Multiple Shareholders

While a single shareholder may legally own a corporation, this is another factor a judge or jury could consider as one brush stroke in the big picture of whether it was really being operated as a corporation. Having more than one shareholder makes the business look more like a real corporation to most people.

Quacking Like a Corporation

If your nickname is "Buzz" and you start your business as a sole proprietorship under the trade name Buzz's Flying Service, then later incorporate the business, you need to change your way of talking and writing to people. You must carefully avoid giving them the impression that they're really still doing business with good old Buzz and not with this new faceless corporate person, Buzz's Flying Service, Inc. For starters, make it an office policy that anyone who answers the telephone now answers it with "Buzz's Flying Service, *Inc.* How may we help you?"

In your business conversations and correspondence, you must change your old style, now taking care to avoid personalization. Back when the business was a sole proprietorship, it was OK to say things like "*My* company can install that new synthetic vision equipment in your plane" or "I can't imagine why you haven't received payment for that last parts invoice but *I'll* take care of that today." If the business is really organized as a partnership, then it's entirely appropriate for you to say things like "*My partner,* Ace, can do an annual inspection for you." But if the business is a corporation, this kind of talk can be the undoing of your protection because it doesn't sound to the listener as though she is dealing with a corporation but with only you individually or with your partner or partners.

Remember: A corporation is a separate legal entity, a "person" in the eyes of the law, and its customers and suppliers must be put on notice that it is the corporation, not an individual or group of partners, they are dealing with. Thus, it would be more appropriate to say, "Yes, *the corporation* can install that color radar set in your airplane" or "I'll check on why you haven't received payment for that last parts invoice and see if *the corporation* can send you a check for that today." The word *partner* must be banished from your language. You may say, "Our shop fore-man, Ace, can do an annual inspection for you." Even if you and Ace are each the holder of 50 percent of the shares of stock in the corporation, you are not "partners." It may be a hard habit to break, especially if you have grown up in the rural West where *partner* often serves as a generic term of friendship or esteem (as in "Howdy, partner") rather than an expression of a form of business relationship. But if you want to get the most liability protection out of your corporation, you'll eliminate that kind of language.

The Corporate Waddle and the Corporate Spoor

This is a matter of acting like a corporation and leaving a trail of paper-work that shows it. Although a corporation is a person in the eyes of the law, only human persons can do the corporation's work.

How to Sign for a Corporation

Although a corporation can legally enter into a contract, it takes a human person acting on behalf of the corporation to sign the contract and write the check. If you are that person, you want to be sure that it is apparent to the world that you are signing that contract or writing that check only on behalf of the corporation, as its agent and not personally. There is only one proper format in which to sign anything if you are signing it for the corporation and not individually. This signature block must include three elements: the corporation's full legal name, your signature, and your corporate title (*see* Fig. 5.2). If you omit the first or third of these elements, you risk personal liability. On corporate correspondence, if the letterhead shows the corporation's full legal name, that need not be repeated in the signature block.

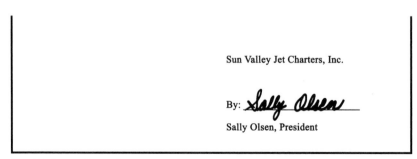

Fig. 5.2. Proper form of corporate signature.

Keeping Personal and Corporate Assets Separate

If you want the world to recognize the corporation as a separate person, then you must do so too. Don't put that person's money in your pocket. Care must be taken never to commingle personal and corporate funds or other assets, and corporate debts should never be paid directly from personal funds. Corporate debts should be paid only from corporate funds. If you pay them from your personal funds, that is not acting like a corporation but like a sole proprietorship. This is not to say that you can't find a way to get the money into the corporation to enable the corporation to pay its debts. The corporation can acquire funds in the following ways: (1) sale of shares of stock (capital investment), (2) income from operations, (3) debt (loans), and (4) sale or leasing out of assets.

For example, imagine that the corporation's hangar rent and payroll are coming due and the corporation is short of cash to make these payments (perhaps because especially horrible winter weather has severely cut back on income for the month's flight operation revenues). If you are a shareholder in the corporation and are in a financial position to help out, there are several ways you can do so without opening up the possibility of someone being able to pierce the corporate veil to reach your personal assets as a consequence. You could loan money to the corporation to cover its needs; you could buy some more stock in the corporation; or you could purchase assets from the corporation (and lease them back to the corporation if they are needed to continue operations).

Any of these transactions is proper since each respects the corporation as the separate legal person it is. Care must be taken, however, to document the transaction properly, leaving the all-important paper trail. If you choose to make a loan, then a *promissory note*, which includes a commercially reasonable rate of interest, should be filled out. If you choose to purchase corporate stock, the corporate minute book and stock certificate book should reflect that this transaction was handled in the manner prescribed in the corporation's articles of incorporation or bylaws. A properly signed and sealed *stock certificate* should be issued to you in exchange for the funds and the transaction recorded in the corporation's *stock certificate register*. If you purchase assets from the corporation, a *bill of sale* should be issued and the transaction reflected on the corporation's financial records. If you lease the purchased equipment back to the corporation, that should also be done by a written *lease*.

While all this is somewhat time consuming, it is the proper way of doing business and absolutely necessary to preserve the maximum personal protection from doing business in the corporate form. You can bet that if there's an accident that is not completely covered by the corporation's liability insurance, the plaintiff's attorney is going to examine your corporate books and records during the discovery process. He'll search in hope of being able to pierce the corporate veil to reach the personal assets of the owners (shareholders). If you have been careful to document each such transaction, that effort will be frustrated. Your corporate lawyer and accountant should be called upon to assure that these transactions are properly documented in the corporation's financial records, minute book, and stock certificate book.

Making and Documenting Corporate Decisions

Part of the process of acting like a corporation is making corporate decisions at the appropriate level and keeping the paper trail that proves that you have done so. Corporate decisions may be made at several levels: the shareholders, the board of directors, an executive committee of the board of directors, officers, or employees.

The powers, duties, responsibilities, and procedures for corporate decision making should be spelled out as clearly as possible in the articles of incorporation or bylaws. In normal corporate operations, the only decision the shareholders have the right to make is to elect a board of directors to govern the corporation. The board of directors elects officers. Typically, the board of directors makes decisions affecting corporate policy and major business decisions, while officers (such as a chief executive officer or CEO) execute that policy and make the day-to-day business decisions.

When in doubt whether a particular decision can be made by a corporate officer or should be referred to the board of directors, a good rule of thumb is to ask yourself: "Is this what the corporation is in business to do?" If the answer is "yes," then the officer can probably make the decision. If the answer is "no," then the matter should probably be taken up with the board of directors.

Take, for example, a full-service FBO. A customer wants to rent an airplane. If the corporation is in the business of renting airplanes, one would expect that the decision of whether to rent the individual an airplane could be made by an employee, following written corporate policy.

Suppose instead that the airport manager calls to inform the FBO that another enterprise on the airport is going out of business and the airport authority wants to know whether the FBO would like to take over and operate that facility under lease, in addition to or instead of the FBO's present facility. Although physical facilities are necessary to the corporation in operating its business, renting space from the airport authority is not what the corporation is in business to do. Moving or expanding is a big decision, a matter of policy. Therefore, this is a decision that is probably going to have to be made by the board of directors.

Whenever a meeting of the shareholders or the board of directors takes place, a written record (referred to as *minutes*) must be prepared. The minutes detail when and where the meeting occurred, who was present, and what was decided (it is generally not required to reflect everything that was discussed, only decisions that were reached). These minutes should be kept in the corporate minute book, the primary paper trail that serves as evidence that the corporation was operated as a corporation, with decisions being made in the proper manner at the proper level of authority. An empty or long-neglected corporate minute book turned up in the inquisitive process of discovery can be a powerful weapon to a plaintiff's attorney who is trying to pierce the corporate veil to reach your personal assets.

Duties to Employees

Regardless of the form of your business (whether a corporation, limited liability company, partnership, or sole proprietorship), the business has certain legal obligations toward each of its employees. These include a duty to provide *workers compensation insurance* and *unemployment compensation insurance, to pay agreed wages and withhold payroll taxes*, and to *provide a safe place to work*. Attempts by management to avoid carrying out these duties have brought many businesses to grief. Particularly in the small business just starting out, management may be reluctant to incur the expense and keep the records required to withhold payroll taxes and provide mandatory insurance. In such a situation, management may succumb to the temptation to call the people who work for the business *independent contractors* rather than employees, in an attempt to avoid the responsibility to provide the mandatory insurance and withhold payroll taxes. Such a decision may have catastrophic consequences.

Workers Compensation Insurance

In the popular mythology of American social welfare, state statutes compelling employers to provide workers compensation insurance coverage to compensate their employees for on-the-job injuries are celebrated as a great victory of the working class over exploitative employers. Actually, however, workers compensation insurance is far more advantageous to the employer than to the employee.

Because of the large number of businesses purchasing the insurance, it tends to be relatively inexpensive, although rates have risen substantially in the last few years, particularly since the terrorist attacks of 9/11/01 caused so many deaths of employees of businesses located in the World Trade Center.

The law of most states provides that if the business has covered its employees with workers compensation insurance, an employee who is injured on the job is prohibited from suing the employer for such injuries. If one of your mechanics or pilots backs into a spinning prop or is otherwise killed or injured on the job, you'll be instantly convinced of the value of workers compensation insurance in protecting the business from liability. This protection is well worth the expense and paperwork involved and in most states is mandatory for businesses having *any* employees.

Withholding Taxes

The Internal Revenue Service (IRS), like dynamite, is stronger than you are and has no friends. Revenue-collecting authorities have extraordinary powers not enjoyed by other administrative and law enforcement agencies. A friend of mine who practices tax law extensively sometimes makes the pseudo Freudian slip of referring to the IRS as the KGB. The analogy is entirely appropriate, given the extraordinary powers afforded revenue agents. For example, the IRS has the benefit of *hindsight review*. This means that even though a business considered certain workers independent contractors (and may even have obtained workers' signatures on contracts stating that they were independent contractors), the IRS may later decide that the person was really an employee for the purpose of the business's duties to withhold payroll taxes.

In making that determination, the IRS applies a *right to control and direct* test, examining a number of factors to determine whether a person is an independent contractor or must be considered an employee. Factors the IRS considers to favor a determination that a person is (or was) an employee (rather than an independent contractor) include if the person:

1. Is required to comply with company instructions about when, where, and how work is done;
2. Has been trained by the company;
3. Is integrated into the company's general business operations;
4. Must render services personally;
5. Uses assistance provided by the company;
6. Has a continuing relationship with the company;
7. Is required to work a set number of hours;
8. Must devote substantially full-time work to the company;
9. Works on the company's premises;
10. Must perform work in a preset sequence;
11. Must submit regular progress reports;
12. Is paid by the hour, week, or month;
13. Is reimbursed for all business and travel expenses;
14. Uses company tools and materials;
15. Has no significant investment in the facilities that are used;
16. Has no risk of loss;
17. Works for only one company;
18. Does not offer services to the public;
19. Can be discharged by the company; or
20. Can terminate the relationship (quit) without incurring liability.

Here is an all-too-frequent scenario: An FBO wishing to avoid the expense and paperwork inherent in insuring and withholding payroll taxes for its flight instructors elects to treat them as independent contractors. One day, IRS agents show up at the business and inquire into the whereabouts of one of these instructors, mentioning that the instructor didn't file federal income tax returns during the time he was instructing for the business. "Gee," the manager replies, "he left here a couple of years ago and I haven't seen him since, although I did hear a rumor that he was killed in the crash of a drug smuggling plane in Columbia, so you guys are probably out of luck." Undeterred, the agents explain that their investigation has further revealed that the business does not seem to have withheld payroll taxes for this individual or paid those taxes to the government, as required. "Oh, no, he wasn't an employee. He was just an independent contractor," the FBO manager explains. "We even require our flight instructors to sign a contract showing that. Here is a copy of the one he signed." Unfazed, the agents persist in their interrogation, gaining the manager's admissions that the flight instructor did give ground instruction in the FBO's classroom, had the use of a desk at the FBO, and used the FBO's FAA-approved syllabus to teach. The instruction was given in aircraft provided by the FBO, according to a schedule determined by the FBO's dispatcher. The instructor had to give the instruction himself; he couldn't send a buddy in to substitute for him if he had something else he'd rather be doing.

Applying 20/20 hindsight, the revenue agents may decide that under these facts the FBO had the "right to control and direct" this flight instructor's work. If so, the delinquent taxpayer was really an employee and the FBO, having failed to withhold and pay payroll taxes for this employee, must now pay those taxes to the IRS, with interest and penalties. If the business does not cooperate in promptly taking care of that obligation, IRS agents may freeze the business's bank accounts and seize its assets until the matter is resolved. It is not unusual in such a case for IRS agents in full SWAT team attire to show up at the business unannounced, armed with automatic weapons, to take over the property and lock up the hangars, offices, and aircraft.

And that's not all. If the business doesn't have the funds to pay this tax liability, the government can sell the business's assets to satisfy the debt. If the sale of assets still doesn't satisfy the entire tax liability, then if the business is a sole proprietorship or partnership, the proprietor or partners are personally liable for the balance due the IRS. If the business is a corporation, its directors can be held personally liable for unpaid tax liabilities of the corporation. The business and its owners (or in the case of a corporation, directors) can't even escape that tax liability by filing bankruptcy. Tax liabilities are, by statute, not dischargeable in bankruptcy.

It is therefore tremendously important for businesses (whatever their form) to resist the temptation to evade the duties owed to their employees and the government through the subterfuge of trying to call such workers independent contractors. This is not to say that a business can never have independent contractors. For example, if you take one of your business's airplanes to a paint shop to be painted, specifying the type of paint and design required and receiving a price quote for the job and an expected completion date, the paint shop would be a legitimate independent contractor. The work is being done at the independent contractor's facility, not your place of business, and the independent contractor is providing the paint, equipment, and labor. If the painter chooses to do the painting between midnight and 4:00 a.m., or to remove the paint by bead blasting instead of hand stripping, she may do so without consulting you. That is a legitimate independent contractor. If on the other hand you hire someone to paint the aircraft in your business's hangar, using your equipment, reporting for work at a specified time and working until an agreed quitting time, and doing the work under your supervision, that person is an employee. That cannot be changed even if you and she agree that she's an independent contractor and she signs a written agreement to that effect.

Lines of Defense in Risk Management

If you decide, with the advice of your lawyer and accountant, to form your business as a corporation, LLC, or LLP (to protect you from potential personal vicarious liability for torts committed by other workers), this should not constitute the entire risk management plan for the business. The problem of risk management is very similar to the problem of national security. France's experience with the Maginot Line showed that, to be effective, a defense must be in-depth and diversified. The same is true of business risk management strategies. While organizing the business as a corporation, LLC, or LLP is an important element in the risk management plan you develop for your business, it should not be the only one.

As we have already seen, your accident prevention program should be a primary facet of your risk management plan, since accidents prevented are lawsuits prevented. Liability insurance should also be a major element in your risk management strategy. (We will examine aviation liability insurance in the next chapter.) If you cannot purchase sufficient liability insurance coverage for a particular operation, exculpatory contracts (discussed in Chapter 7) may also enter into your risk management strategy.

6

Aviation Insurance

Adequate insurance must be a key feature of your risk management plan. To most of us, the language of insurance is a foreign language. Buying aviation insurance is like ordering in a French restaurant: If you can't read and speak the language, you can't be certain that you are ordering what you really want or that you've received what you ordered. Think of this chapter as a short but essential foreign language course.

The purpose of this chapter is to equip you with a working knowledge of aviation insurance sufficient to enable you to:

1. Determine the insurance needs of an aviation business or general aviation aircraft owner/operator and order the correct coverage.
2. Analyze the policy received to ensure that it actually includes all of the features which you ordered, adequately covers your needs, and contains no unanticipated pitfalls or other unpleasant surprises.
3. Recognize when changing circumstances make changes in insurance advisable.

INSURANCE FUNDAMENTALS

Let's first examine the cast of characters in the aviation insurance industry and see who plays what roles:

Sales

Aviation insurance is sold by agents, brokers, and directly by some insurance companies.

An insurance *agent* represents one or more insurance companies as a salesperson and is usually compensated on a commission basis by a percentage of premiums collected on policies sold. While also engaged in selling insurance, the *broker* differs from the agent in that the broker is not contractually bound to represent a specific insurance company but is free to represent you, the buyer, in shopping around to find the best available deal. The broker's compensation is also by commission. Some insurance companies, like Avemco, sell insurance directly to the customer over the telephone from national offices having toll-free numbers or online instead of through sales networks of agents or brokers.

Insuring and Underwriting the Risk

Insurance Companies

In general aviation, most policies are issued by a single insurance company. That company carries the entire risk (responsibility to pay for insured losses) under the policy.

Underwriters

Most airline insurance policies spread the risk over several insurance companies through the process of *underwriting*. This is generally done through a *clearinghouse* such as The Underwriters at Lloyds ("Lloyds of London") who, incidentally, wrote history's first aviation insurance policy. There, many insurance companies are represented. When a request is received to quote a rate to provide a particular insurance coverage for an airline, the clearinghouse affords the participating companies' representatives the opportunity to "subscribe" to cover a portion of the risk for a stated price. Once the various subscribed insurance companies' portions total 100 percent, the clearinghouse quotes the total price and, if the buyer accepts, issues the policy or a certificate of insurance.

Aviation Managers

Some insurance companies that write aviation insurance employ their own personnel to review applications received from prospective customers, decide whether the customer is an insurable risk, and determine an appropriate price for providing the requested coverage. Other insurance companies, however, contract that function to outside companies called aviation managers.

Claims

If you have an accident, you are required by the policy to immediately report it to your insurance company. The policy itself should state to whom the report is to be made. When in doubt, call the agent or broker who sold you the policy first. Claims on the policy will be investigated and settlement offers extended by an *insurance adjuster*. The adjuster represents the insurance company in determining whether the loss is covered by the policy and, if so, the monetary value of the damages and extent of the insurance company's obligation to pay.

Insurance Principles

There are two basic principles underlying all insurance: spreading the risk and minimizing the risk.

Spreading the Risk

There is an element of risk involved in all aviation operations. Aircraft accidents are statistically improbable events, but the financial consequences can be disastrous to an operator. Insurance serves to spread the risk of that unlikely but potentially catastrophic event over many similar operators, much as though all had contributed their premiums to a common contingency fund to cover such eventualities. By spreading the risk in this fashion, we enjoy a situation in which an adequately insured operator does not face the risk of financial ruin in the event of a single accident.

Underwriting accomplishes the same thing for the insurance companies, spreading the risk among the several insurance companies in the pool that underwrote the policy. It works. Even in the most disastrous aviation accident in history (the runway collision between two fully loaded airline 747s on a foggy day at the Tenerife Airport in the Canary Islands), not one of the insurance companies that had underwritten a portion of the insurance for the airlines involved suffered financial ruin. Neither did either of the airlines.

Insurance companies insuring airports, airlines, and other high dollar-value risks often reinsure a portion of their potential liability under the policy with another insurance company. *Reinsurance* may be done either on a pro-rata basis (with a result similar to the sharing of risks underwritten through a clearinghouse) or on an excess basis with the first insurance company required to pay, for example, all losses under a $20 million aircraft liability policy up to the first $10 million, with the reinsurer responsible to pay losses falling within the next $10 million of the coverage. Think of reinsurance as insurance for insurance companies.

Minimizing the Risk

Insurance companies have long recognized the value of accident prevention in avoiding claims against their policies. If the insurance company views the aircraft operator as "an accident looking for a place to happen," the operator may find it impossible to purchase insurance at any price. Among operators considered insurable risks, one factor used to compute the price (premium) of the coverage is the insurance company's best estimate of how likely this operator is to have an accident. Operators perceived as being the safest are able to purchase insurance less expensively than average operators, and below average operators may not be able to purchase insurance at any price. For business aircraft operators, implementation of a Safety Management System (SMS) can have an immediate favorable effect on their aircraft insurance rates.

Insurance companies ("*insurers*") expect the persons and businesses they insure ("*insureds*") to demonstrate an attitude of "*protecting the policy*," taking care to avoid accidents. If after issuing a policy the insurance company learns that the operator has reduced its pilot training program, is deferring maintenance, outsourcing maintenance to a substandard source, or otherwise reducing safety margins, the insurance company may become concerned that an accident is more likely than originally estimated. In that case, the company may cancel the insured's coverage, often on as little as ten days written notice (although if it does, the company must refund any unearned portion of the premium). If you ever have insurance canceled, you will find it much more difficult to buy insurance in the future. If one insurance company has decided you're a bad risk, others will be wary.

If you're going to be in the aviation business, then in addition to your accountant and lawyer, you need to develop a good working relationship with an insurance agent or broker who specializes in aviation insurance. Just as insurance is a foreign language to most of us, aviation insurance is a unique dialect within that language, not generally understood by people who don't live with it daily. An agent or broker who doesn't speak the dialect can get you in a lot of trouble, whereas one who does can keep you out of trouble. You'll still need to understand the rudiments of the language and the dialect yourself, so that you can communicate effectively with your broker or agent (or a direct writer) to order the insurance coverage you need and to confirm that you got what you ordered.

AVIATION INSURANCE COVERAGES

All prudent aircraft owners (whether in the aviation business, using aircraft in support of other business enterprises, or recreational flyers) should have *aircraft insurance*, including both *liability* and *hull* coverages. In addition to the workers compensation insurance and unemployment compensation insurance discussed in the last chapter, aviation businesses may also need *airport liability insurance*, including *premises liability* and *hangarkeeper's liability*, as well as *products liability*. *Prepaid legal services* or *loss of license insurance* may also be desirable to defend your personal pilot or mechanic certificate or protect your income during suspension or revocation. *Excess liability* coverage may also be prudent. We will now examine features of each of these types of insurance, with a particular focus on what you need to know in order to select and order appropriate coverages and ascertain that you have received what you ordered when the policy arrives.

Aircraft Insurance

A comprehensive aircraft insurance policy includes of two distinct types of coverage: *liability* and *hull*.

Liability Coverage

This covers your liability for injuries to others including passengers in the aircraft, persons and property on the ground, and other aircraft and their occupants. It generally does not cover flight crewmembers (who are expected to be covered by workers compensation insurance for professional pilots, and health and life insurance).

There are two types of *policy limits* that may be available in selecting the liability coverage in your aircraft insurance policy, *single limit* (also called "*smooth*") and *per person limits*. Under a $1 million single limit policy, the insurance will pay up to that limit for the total injuries of the total number of passengers and persons on the ground injured. Many general aviation policies have per person limits, such as a total limit of $1 million with a typical sublimit of $100,000 per person, per passenger, or per passenger seat. For the average 4–6 seat general aviation aircraft, such sublimit usually results in the $1 million total limit being mythical, beyond the reach of your injured passengers and persons on the ground. This is even truer when you consider that most general aviation trips are flown with less than all seats occupied. And it doesn't take much of an injury to eat up $100,000. For these reasons, most thoughtful people consider single limit liability coverage the more prudent buy.

Hull Coverage

This covers damage to or destruction of the insured aircraft resulting from an accident. It generally does not cover damage to the aircraft's engines in connection with an engine failure. However, if the engine failure leads to other damage to the aircraft, as in an ensuing off airport landing, that damage is not excluded merely by virtue of an engine failure having set the sequence of events in motion. Hull coverage may be purchased to cover:

- *all risks,*
- *all risks while not in flight,* or
- *all risks while not in motion.*

For helicopters (Fig. 6.1), coverage may be further broken down to include:

- *all risks while rotors are in motion* or
- *all risks while rotors are not in motion.*

Fig. 6.1. For helicopters, hull insurance may be purchased to cover all risks, all risks while rotors are in motion, or all risks while rotors are not in motion. As with fixed wing airplanes, only all risks coverage protects the owner/operator in any conceivable event that may damage an operable aircraft.

For operable aircraft intended to be operated, only *all risks* hull insurance will cover virtually anything that might happen to the aircraft. The lesser coverages, though a great deal less expensive, are suitable only for aircraft that are not operable and are not intended to be operated, such as aircraft undergoing long-term restoration, rebuilding, or modification that will preclude flight in the near future.

Valuation

The buyer of hull coverage may have a choice between methods of valuing the aircraft for purposes of determining the amount to be paid by the insurance company in the event of an accident resulting in a *total loss* of the aircraft. (An aircraft is considered a "total loss" when it is more economical for the insurance company to pay the entire value of the hull insurance and then sell the wreckage for salvage than to pay the cost to repair the aircraft. It is usually in the discretion of the insurance company to decide whether to treat a particular hull damage situation as a total loss or pay for repairs.) The most common valuation method is *stated value*. In a stated value policy, the insurance policy specifies the exact dollar amount the insurance company will pay to the aircraft owner in the event of a total loss. Rare (and possibly extinct) is the *current market value* policy. In contrast to stated value, a current market value policy permits the adjuster to take into account the current blue-book value of the aircraft at the time of the accident, along with factors peculiar to the aircraft (such as its general pre-accident condition, including paint, interior, engine times, and avionics installed or removed). The adjuster may rely on these factors to reduce the current market value below average blue-book values, lowering the settlement offer to the owner.

Given a choice, thoughtful aircraft owners prefer stated value hull coverage because it leaves no uncertainty as to how much the insurance company must pay in the event of an accident resulting in a total loss. Current market value policies have historically lead to controversy between the insurance company and the aircraft owner after a total loss, since the insurance adjuster's subjective assessment of the current market value of the aircraft immediately pre-accident may differ from that of the owner. This in turn frequently leads to a vexing, time-consuming, and expensive arbitration or litigation process (having an uncertain outcome) to resolve the controversy. The use of stated value hull insurance avoids this uncertainty and potential for controversy.

The value you choose to state for the hull insurance merits careful consideration, both beforehand and for as long as you own the aircraft. The insurance company will not allow you to overstate the value since that may motivate you to not protect the policy. On windy nights they would lie awake worrying that you might be out there helping your tie-down chains slip in order to turn a profit on the transaction. You should be careful not to understate the value, but state it at a figure that would purchase a comparable aircraft similarly equipped. Then reconsider whether that is still an adequate figure each year as you renew or replace your aircraft insurance. For many years now, the prices of used general aviation aircraft have been steadily climbing. This trend, along with improvements made to the aircraft in the interim (such as added or updated avionics equipment, an overhauled or remanufactured engine, or a new paint job and interior) may have substantially increased the value of the aircraft (and the cost to replace it with a comparable aircraft). The value stated in your hull coverage should be increased to reflect that increase in value.

If you have financed the purchase of the aircraft and not yet paid off the loan, the lender will insist you carry hull coverage. A savvy lender will also require that it be named as the *loss payee* (to whom the insurance company makes the check payable in the event of a hull damage claim). In the event of a total loss, upon receipt of the check, the lender will retain the balance owed on the loan and then pay any remainder to the aircraft owner. On receipt of payment for repairable damage, the lender simply pays the proceeds directly to the mechanic or repair station upon completion of the repairs. In either event, the lender's security (the aircraft or the insurance proceeds) is effectively in the lender's control, which makes it feel more secure (more to come on this point in Chapter 11 on buying and selling aircraft).

Regardless of the method of valuation employed in the hull coverage, once the owner accepts payment for a total loss under the hull coverage, the insurance company becomes the owner of the aircraft's remains ("*salvage*") if any.

Purpose of Use

Another fundamental choice you will have to make when ordering aircraft insurance coverage is your intended *purpose of use* of the aircraft (Fig. 6.2). In order of increasing premiums, typical purposes of use include:

Fig. 6.2. For some of the owners of these hot air balloons lifting off on an early morning launch, pleasure and business may be the appropriate aircraft insurance purpose of use; others may need limited commercial, commercial, or even special use coverage.

- *pleasure and business,*
- *industrial aid,*
- *limited commercial,*
- *commercial except instruction or rental,*
- *commercial,* and
- *special uses.*

The exact categories employed by your insurance company should appear in the policy itself, but the preceding are fairly typical industry-wide. Some insurance companies also rate *flying clubs* separately, at a rate somewhere between pleasure/business and limited commercial.

It is extremely important that you purchase coverage that will cover all purposes you may use the aircraft for, because if you have an accident during an operation conducted for a purpose other than one covered by the policy, it will not be insured. If after you have purchased your aircraft insurance there arises any change in the purposes for which the aircraft is to be used, this should alert you to reconsider whether the new purposes are covered by your existing insurance or you need to purchase additional coverage to encompass the change. Let's examine what specific types of operations are typically covered by the various purpose of use options.

Pleasure and Business

Sounds all encompassing, doesn't it? You'll either be using the aircraft to have fun or to make money, right? Well, it isn't as simple as it might look at first glance. Pleasure and business is generally defined to cover pleasure flying and personal flying incidental to or in direct connection with the insured's business, *excluding any operation for which a charge is made* (Fig. 6.3).

In other words, this does not cover any type of commercial operation. The "business" in "pleasure and business" is a situation in which you might be using an airplane much as you would a company car. Imagine, as an example, that your business is selling computer software and you have developed a software program for FBO management. Since all

Fig. 6.3. The "pleasure" in the pleasure and business purpose of use: the author's granddaughter enjoys a flight over the Rockies with grandpa in a Super Cub.

of your prospective customers (FBOs) are located on airports, you use an airplane to make your sales calls. But if you make a sale, you don't charge the customer for your flight. That's the only kind of business use this covers.

Industrial Aid

This coverage includes everything covered by pleasure and business as well as the transportation of your business's executives, employees, guests, and customers, again *excluding any operation for which a charge is made*. This is the appropriate coverage for most corporate aircraft, assuming that the aircraft is dedicated solely to corporate use and never rented or chartered to others.

The next two are really opposite sides of the same coin and easily confused.

Commercial Except Instruction or Rental

This covers all uses covered by pleasure and business plus industrial aid plus the transportation of passengers or cargo for hire, but *excludes commercial flight instruction or rental of the aircraft to other pilots*. If the business does only charters, cargo or mail hauling, and/or scheduled passenger carrying but never does commercial flight instruction and never rents its aircraft to others, this coverage is adequate (Fig. 6.4).

Fig. 6.4. This "freight dog" Grumman Goose amphibian is probably insured for commercial except instruction or rental purposes of use.

Limited Commercial

This is the flip side of the coin, the opposite of "commercial except instruction or rental." Limited commercial also includes all of the operations covered by pleasure and business plus industrial aid plus commercial flight instruction and aircraft rental to other pilots, but *excludes carrying passengers or cargo for hire*. If you're a freelance flight instructor working with your own or a customer's aircraft or an FBO not holding an 14 CFR Part 135 air carrier operating certificate, so that your aircraft are used only for commercial flight instruction and rental, this may be adequate coverage.

Commercial

Generally referred to as *full commercial*, this covers every kind of operation we have discussed: pleasure and business, industrial aid, carrying passengers and cargo for hire, commercial flight instruction, and rental to other pilots. This is the coverage needed by a full-service FBO, but even this may not cover some of the more risky operations considered *special uses*.

Special Uses

Flight operations that the insurance company believes involve a higher level of risk than those just described are rated as special uses and must pay a higher insurance premium. This might include agricultural aviation operations, operations requiring an FAR waiver, aerial firefighting, helicopter external load operations, helicopter flight training, banner and glider towing, fish spotting, power line or pipeline patrol, and emergency medical service helicopter operations (Fig. 6.5).

Pilot Qualifications

Another decision you will have to make when ordering the aircraft insurance (and should keep in mind for the future, to be sure that all flight operations continue to be covered by your aircraft insurance) is *pilot qualification requirements*, also referred to as an *open pilot warranty*.

Generally speaking, the premium you pay for your aircraft insurance policy varies inversely with the minimum qualifications of the pilots who will be permitted to operate the aircraft. The more qualified and experienced the pilots, the cheaper the coverage. For the same aircraft, a commercial instrument rated pilot with over one thousand flight hours,

Fig. 6.5. Emergency medical service helicopter operations frequently require landings in unprepared locations such as this dusty remote accident scene, often at night and in challenging weather. The higher level of risk these essential operations involve compels aviation insurance companies to rate them as a special use and charge a higher premium. (Less than a year before this photo was taken and less than a mile from this location, a similar EMS helicopter crashed when enveloped by blinding dust on a night landing at an accident scene.)

most of which were in the same make and model of the aircraft to be insured, would pay a much lower premium than a newly certified private pilot. If the aircraft has tail wheel landing gear, previous and recent tail wheel experience will be an especially important consideration.

Care must be taken to *never allow a pilot who does not meet the pilot qualification requirements of your insurance policy to operate the aircraft.* This has been known to trap not only private flyers who in gestures of generosity have allowed friends to fly their aircraft but commercial operators as well, not only exposing the aircraft owners to potential liability for negligent entrustment, as discussed in Chapter 4, but also jeopardizing the owners' aircraft insurance protection.

A typical scenario in which the commercial operator gets into trouble goes something like this: An air cargo business operating under FAR Part 135 has very strict qualifications for hiring pilots, and these are reflected in the company's aircraft insurance pilot requirements. These have helped the company obtain a relatively favorable price for this insurance. During the pre-Christmas rush, a major air express company calls seeking extra aircraft capacity. The big company offers a very attractive rate to the operator to help out, but the operator's present pilot compliment is already flying up to the limits of duty time permitted by the FARs. Rather than pass up what appears to be a golden opportunity, the operator temporarily hires additional pilots to handle this extra work and lowers its standards by hiring pilots who fall short of the pilot requirements of the insurance policy in order to meet this need. Operations flown by those pilots will be uninsured, and the insurer may cancel the policy out of concern over the insured's lowered standards.

This is not to suggest that the company should necessarily have passed up the opportunity. Only that whenever something changes in the way the company is doing business, management must consider whether the change will be covered by existing insurance or if expanded coverage must be purchased to encompass whatever is new. In this example, it might have been economical for the operator to pay an additional premium to lower the pilot qualification requirements of its aircraft insurance policy to take advantage of this business opportunity. Murphy's Law as applied to aviation insurance says that if you have an accident, it will happen (1) before your insurance policy becomes effective, (2) after it has expired, (3) within a policy exclusion, (4) during an operation for a purpose not covered by the policy, or (5) while the aircraft is under the command of an unqualified pilot.

Some pilots fall into lax habits of not logging all of their flight time (the FARs require only that you log flight time required to demonstrate currency). But as far as the insurance companies are concerned, if the time isn't in your logbook, you don't get credit for it for insurance purposes. So, if you got a price break on your insurance because you reported, for example, a thousand hours in type, but although you actually flew that time in type, you didn't log it all, you may actually be uninsured.

Endorsements and Exclusions

Insurance companies use *endorsements* to fine-tune the policy. Some of these are beneficial to the insured, while others may be detrimental. Some are ordered by the insured and require an additional premium, while others may be slipped in by the insurer and escape the notice of the insured until a claim is filed and the insurer uses the endorsement to deny coverage. Here are some examples:

Lienholder's Interest Endorsement

If you take out a loan to finance a portion of the purchase price of your aircraft, in order to protect its own interests the lender ("*lienholder*") will require that it be named the *loss payee* (to whom the insurance company will write the check in the event of a hull loss). The lender will also require you to purchase (at some additional premium) a *lienholder's interest endorsement* (also referred to as a *breach of warranty endorsement*) in favor of the lender and maintain that endorsement on the policy until the loan is fully repaid. This endorsement to the policy assures the lienholder that even if the circumstances of an accident are such that the insurance company would not have to pay the owner-operator, the insurance company will pay the lienholder the balance due on the loan. Thus, even if the aircraft is damaged while being flown by an unqualified pilot or otherwise outside the policy, the lender gets paid.

But there's a catch. Such endorsements usually provide that if the insurance company has to pay a lienholder under this endorsement for a total loss, the insurance company gets all of the lienholder's rights in return. Thus, if the lienholder is a bank that loaned you the money to finance a portion of the purchase price of the airplane, the insurer pays off the balance due to the bank. The insurance company then takes the bank's position on the promissory note you signed to borrow the money, and instructs you to continue to make those airplane payments (for your now destroyed aircraft), now to the insurance company rather than the bank. Operate outside the policy at your own risk: That is always a losing proposition.

Waiver of Subrogation Endorsement

Businesses that rent aircraft to others and wish to protect their customers from subrogation may do so by purchasing a *waiver of subrogation endorsement* to their aircraft insurance policy. Subrogation (the right of an insurance company that has paid a claim to sue anyone other than the insured who contributed to cause the accident) is discussed more fully later in this chapter.

War Risk Exclusion and Insurance

The typical *war risk exclusion clause* is Lloyd's form AVN 48B, captioned the "War, Hi-Jacking, and Other Perils Exclusion Clause." Although the exclusion has been included in most aircraft insurance policies since the reinsurers first required it in 1968, it has merited little concern on the part of domestic operators until recently. The new reality of terrorist activity within the United States using commandeered civil aircraft suddenly focused attention on the true breadth of this exclusion and brought home a realization of the exposure U.S. aircraft operators face for uninsured loss even in domestic operations.

This is a very broad exclusion, relieving the insurance company from responsibility to pay for losses resulting from a wide variety of mischief. Here's what it says:

This policy does not cover claims caused by:

War, invasion, acts of foreign enemies, hostilities (whether war be declared or not) civil war, rebellion, revolution, insurrection, martial law, military or usurped power or attempts at usurpation of power;

Any hostile detonation of any weapon of war employing atomic or nuclear fission and/or fusion or other like reaction or radioactive force or matter;

Strikes, riots, civil commotions or labor disturbances;

Any act of one or more persons, whether or not agents of a sovereign power, for political or terrorist purposes and whether the loss or damage resulting therefrom is accidental or intentional;

Any malicious act or act of sabotage;

Confiscation, nationalization, seizure, restraint, detention, appropriation, requisition for title or use by or under the authority of any Government, (whether civil, military or de facto) or by public authority;

Hi-jacking or any unlawful seizure or wrongful exercise of control of the aircraft or crew in flight (including any attempt at such seizure or control) made by any person or persons on board the aircraft acting without the consent of the Insured.

Furthermore, this policy does not cover claims arising whilst the aircraft is outside the control of the Insured by reason of any of the above perils.

The aircraft shall be deemed to have been restored to the control of the Insured on the safe return of the aircraft to the Insured at an airfield not excluded by the geographical limits of this policy, and entirely suitable for the operation of the aircraft (such safe return shall require that the aircraft be parked with engines shut down and under no duress).

If, as seems generally expected, acts of terrorism involving civil aircraft continue, then it is prudent for aircraft owners to consider the potential this exclusion creates for an uninsured loss of their aircraft. The solution is to add *war risk insurance* to the aircraft insurance policy (and even that does not cover the atomic or nuclear weapon scenario). In the past, most U.S. aircraft operators considered purchasing war risk insurance only when contemplating flight into areas of armed conflict in foreign countries, such as parts of South America, Africa and the Middle East, since standard aircraft insurance policies exclude losses resulting from acts of war or rebellion, or a variety of other hostile acts. Now, given the proven global reach of some terrorist organizations, it would be wise for aircraft operators to reconsider whether it would be prudent to add war risk insurance.

FAR Violation Exclusion Clause

Watch out for an *FAR violation exclusion clause*. This has become quite rare, but still turns up occasionally. This clause says that if the operation was in violation of an FAR, it is excluded from coverage by the insurance policy. The FARs are so sweeping in scope and in many instances so vaguely worded that it would be the very rare accident in which an industrious insurance adjuster could not find something about the operation arguably in violation of an FAR (if only 14 CFR §91.13, careless operation). You should consider an insurance company that includes such a clause in its policy suspect, since such companies tend to be the ones that resist paying claims. When you order the policy, be specific with your agent or broker that you will not accept a policy containing an FAR violation exclusion clause.

Ordering the Policy

When you order the policy, if you intend to operate the aircraft in the near future, you should assure that the agent or broker with whom you are dealing has the insurance company's *authority to bind coverage*. (Not all do.) If this is an agency or brokerage with whom the insurance company has had a good working relationship of some duration, the insurance company will show its trust and confidence by authorizing them to issue a *binder*, locking in the insurance coverage. Otherwise, the application and premium must be received and reviewed by the insurance company before coverage will take effect. See the opportunity for a Murphy's Law uninsured accident in the latter situation?

A checklist for use in ordering aircraft insurance appears in Figure 6.6. You should fill this out before you call your agent or broker or go online to shop, to be prepared to completely and accurately describe what it is you want to buy.

Reviewing the Policy

Once the policy arrives, you should make it a part of your discipline to immediately sit down under conditions that ensure you will not be distracted and read it. Read it carefully and thoroughly, using the same checklist you used to order it, double-checking to verify that you really got what you ordered. Although there is a refreshing trend toward "plain language" aircraft insurance policies, many are still written in convoluted insurance lawyer language difficult to decipher (and even what is "plain" to them may not be plain to you). You should, however, do your best to understand what the policy says. Make up a hypothetical accident. Go through the policy and figure out whether it will pay off for the accident and, if so, what will be covered and how much will be paid. Try several of these exercises until you feel comfortable that you understand how the policy works.

You may even find some surprises you can correct before Murphy's Law gets you. For example, my first airplane (a Cessna 175) was initially tied down outside on the ramp while I was wait-listed for hangar space to become available at our busy airport. One year, I changed insurance companies because my broker negotiated a better deal with a different company. He bound the coverage, and when the policy arrived I sat down that evening in my favorite easy chair and made myself read it. (Even though interpreting aviation insurance policies was part of what I did for a living, it was not a task I looked forward to, for duller prose was never written.) I was nearing the end of the policy when I turned to a page captioned *Hail Endorsement*. I had never seen one of these before, and my attention suddenly perked up. It seemed to say that if the aircraft was caught in a hailstorm but the damage did not affect airworthiness, the insurance would not have to pay more than 10 percent of the stated value of the hull for those damages. An airplane whose surfaces look like a golf ball may still be deemed airworthy, but its resale value will be drastically reduced. Murphy must have slept better than I did that night

AIRCRAFT INSURANCE CHECKLIST

General

    Purpose of use (check one)

        ____ Pleasure & business

        ____ Industrial Aid

        ____ Limited commercial

        ____ Commercial except instruction or rental

        ____ Commercial ("full commercial")

        ____ Special use (describe) _____

    Pilot qualifications

        Pilot certificate & ratings required: _____

        Minimum total flight hours or pilot in command (circle one)

        hours: _____

        Minimum time in make & model required: _____

        Other requirements (total tailwheel, turbine, etc.): _____

    Does broker have authority to bind coverage?

        ____ Yes

        ____ No

Liability Coverage

    Policy limits (complete all that apply)

        Single limit $_____

        Per passenger limit $_____

        Per occurrence limit $ _____

Hull coverage

    Risks covered (check one)

        ____ All risks

        ____ All risks not in flight

        ____ All risks not in motion

        ____ All risks, rotors in motion

        ____ All risks, rotors not in motion

    Method or valuation for total loss (check one)

        ____ Stated value: $ _____

        ____ Current market value ("blue book")

    Loss payee (check one)

        ____ Registered owner

        ____ Lienholder (name): _____

    Breach of warranty (lienholder's interest) endorsement required? (Check one)

        ____ Yes, in favor of (name of lienholder) _____

        ____ No

Exclusions

    FAR violation exclusion (check one)

        ____ No

        ____ Yes

War, Hi-jacking and other perils

        ____ No

        ____ Yes

        Other (describe): _____

War risk insurance desired?

        ____ Yes

        ____ No

Fig. 6.6. Aircraft insurance checklist.

because no hailstorm materialized before I could contact my aviation insurance broker first thing the next morning. I instructed him to contact the insurance company and either arrange to have the hail endorsement removed or cancel the policy and find insurance with another company not requiring such an endorsement, even if it cost more. He called me back shortly to advise me that the insurance company had agreed to delete the offensive endorsement from the policy and faxed me written confirmation the same day. I was very glad I had read the policy. Although the aircraft never did suffer hail damage, if I had overlooked that endorsement, it probably would have.

Keeping Your Coverage Current

Once you've ordered what you need and verified that you received what you ordered, don't just put the policy out of your mind. It's something you need to think about when things change. For example:

Airworthiness

If your aircraft ever requires a *special flight permit* (*"ferry permit"*) to be moved, think about your insurance coverage. Most aircraft insurance policies provide coverage only when the aircraft is being operated under a standard category airworthiness certificate. Therefore, operations under a special flight permit are not insured. You can probably purchase additional coverage for the ferry flight, but be certain that coverage has been bound before commencing operation under the permit.

Geographic Limits

If the aircraft is to be operated outside the contiguous (lower forty-eight) United States, check the geographical extent of your coverage as described in your aircraft insurance policy. Chances are you'll need to buy additional coverage to cover the proposed area of operation.

Warning of Policy Expiration

Another thing you should do to Murphy-proof yourself or your business is to maintain some kind of "tickler system" to alert you when your aircraft insurance policy is about to expire. Mark it on calendars; have it coincide with your annual inspection; do whatever works to be sure that you are reminded. We are accustomed to our insurance agents bombarding us with reminders in the mail and by telephone and e-mail when our insurance policies are expiring. After all, they do want to sell us another one and earn another commission. But they are not required by law to do that, and human beings (and our computers) sometimes make mistakes. If the policy expires without renewal, you know when the accident will happen.

Once you are comfortably satisfied that you have insurance that will adequately cover any conceivable situation, remain on guard to never let that fact enter into your safety decision making. Remember: The insurance company expects you to *protect the policy*. If they suspect that you are thinking along the lines of "So what if it doesn't make it; that's what we bought insurance for," your policy will be promptly canceled. Prevent accidents!

Airport Liability Insurance

If your business is located on an airport, you will also need *airport liability insurance*. This may include *premises liability* and *hangarkeeper's liability* coverages.

Premises Liability

This covers injury to nonemployees occurring at your place of business. For example: if your business is an aircraft repair station and a visiting customer slips on an oily spot in your hangar and falls, suffering injuries, this is the insurance that will pay for those injuries. Any business, no matter where it is located, should have premises liability coverage. It's just that if your business is on an airport, this coverage becomes a part of your airport liability policy.

Hangarkeeper's Liability

This insurance covers your liability for damage to other people's aircraft while they are in your care, custody, or control. This coverage pays off, for example, if a customer's airplane that is in your shop for work is damaged by an employee misjudging and backing another airplane into it with your tug, damaging one or both, or the hangar collapses under a heavy snow load, crushing the customers' airplanes inside. If you are inspecting or repairing others' aircraft and sometimes need to perform a maintenance flight check on those aircraft before approving them for return to service, *in-flight hangarkeeper's* covers any damage the customer's aircraft may suffer during such operations by your employees. You need hangarkeeper's insurance only if other people's airplanes are being stored or worked on in your facility. The hull insurance coverage of your aircraft insurance covers such potential damages to your own aircraft.

Product Liability

Although you'd normally think of this insurance in connection with manufacturers of aircraft and aircraft components, product liability coverage is also needed by all businesses that perform aircraft inspection, maintenance, or modification, or supply aircraft parts, fuel and lubricants. This insurance is needed to cover claims arising out of faulty workmanship, oversights in inspection, errors and defects in design or manufacture of goods sold, and faults in the quality, storage and delivery of fuels (including misfueling of piston-powered aircraft with jet fuel). For mechanics and repair stations, shops or modification centers, the coverage is sometimes referred to as *products and completed operations* coverage. To fully appreciate the importance of this insurance, take a moment to review the discussion of strict liability for suppliers of defective products in Chapter 4.

While the General Aviation Revitalization Act (GARA) discussed in Chapter 4 has succeeded in holding down the escalation in premiums for products liability insurance for manufacturers, the reverse has happened to servicing companies. Overhaul facilities and maintenance shops, and aircraft rental operations (none of which are protected by GARA) have been particularly hard hit. Attorneys representing plaintiffs in cases arising out of accidents involving older aircraft, precluded by GARA from suing the manufacturer, have turned for recompense to those who overhaul, maintain, and rent them to others. This has resulted in tripling and even quadrupling of premiums for these operators, a cost that has driven many small aviation businesses to close their doors (Fig. 6.7).

Aircraft Title Insurance

When purchasing an aircraft, it may be wise to purchase aircraft title insurance to protect against defects in the title that were not revealed by a title search of the records of the FAA Aircraft Registry and the International Registry. The title search process is discussed in greater detail in Chapter 11.

Fig. 6.7. General aviation aircraft maintenance shops have suffered from the effects of GARA, which has driven up their products liability insurance costs. Many smaller shops and shops with less than perfect loss histories have found it no longer economical to remain in business in the face of these increased costs.

Title insurance is most appropriate for corporate aircraft, as it is usually too expensive for transport category airliners and the cost is difficult to justify for light single engine piston-powered general aviation aircraft.

Prepaid Legal Services and Loss of License Insurance

Several aviation organizations, including the Air Line Pilots Association (ALPA) and Aircraft Owners and Pilots Association (AOPA), offer a *prepaid legal service program*, either as a benefit of membership or an additional optional service available to members for an additional fee. These plans will pay the cost of an attorney to defend you in the event the FAA acts to suspend or revoke your pilot or mechanic certificate. Some of these plans cover aviation-related consultation in other areas as well (such as an initial consultation in the event of an aircraft accident).

Loss of license insurance can provide you an income and the cost of learning another trade or profession in the event that the pilot, mechanic, or aviation medical or other certificate necessary to your current line of work is suspended or revoked.

Excess Liability Coverage

In each of the various liability coverages we have already discussed, your objective should be to purchase enough insurance to cover the worst-case scenario in your business. (For aircraft liability, an aircraft full of your wealthiest customers crashing into a convention center during a convention of millionaires; for hangarkeeper's liability, your hangar being full of the most expensive of your customers' aircraft when it burned down). You may find it impossible or prohibitively expensive to obtain that amount of coverage in these policies. If you find yourself in that situation, you should explore the cost and availability of an *excess liability* policy (also referred to as an *umbrella* policy).

This insurance becomes available to pay liability claims only after all other applicable policies (such as your aircraft liability insurance or hangarkeeper's liability insurance) have paid to their policy limits. For example, let's say you have $1 million of hangarkeeper's liability coverage. One of your employees fails to set the parking brake on the gas truck, which rolls into the hangar, collides with a customer's $20 million business jet and explodes. Your hangarkeeper's liability insurance company is responsible to pay for only the first million dollars of the loss. Unless you also have an excess liability policy in the additional amount of at least $19 million in this case, the remaining $19 million of the loss is uninsured, and your company is plainly vicariously liable to pay for these consequences of the employee's negligence.

CLAIMS

The real proof of your success in purchasing and maintaining the appropriate insurance comes when an accident occurs and you submit an insurance claim.

Duties

Every insurance contract places duties on both the insurance company and the insured.

As the insured, your duties to the insurance company include the duty to:

1. *pay premiums as they become due,*
2. be *truthful in all disclosures* made to the insurance company, and
3. *cooperate* with the insurance company during the investigation of a filed claim.

If the claim is covered by the policy, then the insurance company has the duty to *indemnify* the insured. This means the insurer must either:

1. defend the claim in court (if it believes that the plaintiff cannot prove you negligent or strictly liable) and
2. pay any resulting judgment up to the policy limit, or
3. settle the claim out of court for any amount up to the policy limit, *usually without the consent of the insured.*

Investigation and Determination of Coverage

An insurance adjuster will investigate the accident and carefully scrutinize the policy. This scrutiny will include (in the case of aircraft insurance) the insured purposes of use, pilot qualifications, endorsements, exclusions, and other conditions appearing in the policy, along with the facts and circumstances of the accident, to determine whether the claim is covered. If not, the insurance company has no obligation to defend or pay.

If you made false statements on the insurance application (such as failing to report a previous aircraft accident or exaggerating your pilot qualifications, however slightly) the insurance company may be legally able to avoid paying claims under the policy. The law in some states is that any false statement on an insurance application relieves the insurance company of the duty to pay for claims under the policy. In other states, the insurance company may escape liability only if there is some connection between the matter falsified and the cause of the accident. The only way to avoid such problems is to be extremely meticulous to tell the complete truth on insurance applications.

Subrogation

Most liability insurance policies provide that if the insurance company pays a claim under the policy, it has the right to pursue any claims the insured might have against someone else who caused or contributed to the cause of the accident. This right is called *subrogation*. In aviation, subrogation comes into play most frequently in the case of rented aircraft. Under ordinary negligence law, if a pilot operates a rented aircraft negligently, causing an accident that damages the aircraft, that pilot is liable to the owner for the cost of repair and lost rental income. If the owner's hull insurance pays the owner for the damage in that situation, that insurance company is said to be "subrogated to" the rights of the owner. The insurance company can sue that pilot for negligence (the policy may even permit the insurance company to bring that suit in the aircraft owner's name) to recover the money the insurance company paid the owner.

Businesses that rent airplanes to others and wish to protect their customers from subrogation may do so by purchasing a *waiver of subrogation endorsement* to their aircraft insurance policy. Another technique is to have the insurance company generically name renter pilots (who must also meet the pilot qualification requirements of the policy) as *additional insureds* on the policy. A few states require businesses renting aircraft to others to post conspicuous signs notifying renter pilots whether they are insured by or subject to subrogation under the business's aircraft insurance. Most states have no such requirement. If you are a renter pilot, you should personally examine the FBO or flying club's insurance policy to assure that you are personally protected from subrogation, either by being named as an additional insured on the policy or by a waiver of subrogation endorsement attached to the policy. If the business does not protect its rental customers in this fashion or if you rent from several different businesses, you would be wise to purchase *aviation nonownership liability insurance*. This insurance would pay or defend any such subrogation claim as well as claims made by passengers or persons on the ground suffering injuries or property damage if you have an accident while operating a rented aircraft.

Uninsured Risks

There are some aviation activities for which you cannot purchase liability insurance. At this writing liability insurance is not available for bodily injury to skydivers or hot air balloon bungee-jumping operations, at any price. In such a situation, the operator who chooses to engage in such operations without liability insurance may be able to obtain a measure of protection through exculpatory contracts, discussed in the following chapter.

It is also noteworthy that in some states, liability insurance companies are prohibited from paying punitive damages assessed against their insureds because that would interfere with the intended "punishment" effect of such damages actually being suffered by the insured. This is yet another compelling reason to always err on the side of caution in your training, inspection, maintenance and operating practices.

7

Exculpatory Contracts

Although exculpatory contracts are a rarely used risk management tool, inappropriate in most aviation operations, they can be extremely important for those that involve such a high level of risk as to be uninsurable. You should be aware of the availability of this risk management tool and know when its use is appropriate. The purposes of this chapter are: (1) to ensure that you recognize those unique circumstances where an exculpatory contract might be appropriate to limit potential liability and (2) to ensure that you appreciate the value of utilizing the services of legal counsel in a "preventive lawyering" role in drafting these and other legal documents.

An *exculpatory contract* is an agreement between the aircraft or airport operator and a participant in an aviation operation by which the participant agrees not to sue the operator of the aircraft or airport if the participant is killed or injured during the operation. These contracts can range in complexity from multi-page contracts typically signed today by sport skydivers (often after having viewed a video briefing by the skydiving center's lawyer on the serious legal import of the document) to the "fine print" on the back of a spectator's air show admission ticket.

Exculpatory contracts are among aviation's earliest risk management tools. In her book *Tailspins: A Story of Early Aviation Days*, Edith Dodd Culver describes her first flight in 1916 at one of Glenn Curtiss's flying schools near Newport News, Virginia (known as the Atlantic Coast Aeronautical Station), in a Curtiss flying boat (Fig. 7.1):

> "I must confess that I did feel some qualms when I was asked, before climbing into the flying boat, to sign my life away as it were—that is to sign a paper absolving the Atlantic Coast Aeronautical Station

Fig. 7.1. 1916 Curtiss flying boat on takeoff. (Courtesy Library of Congress, G.G. Bain Collection)

of any claim in case the flying boat crashed. But I learned that this was only routine practice for all passengers."

Today, an exculpatory contract is generally an appropriate risk management tool only where:

1. The operation is *not a common carrier* operation (such as carrying passengers for hire under the authority of an FAR Part 135 or 121 air carrier operating certificate);

2. The activity or relationship is *not* one in which the *law requires the operator to carry liability insurance* (the Federal Aviation Act of 1958 requires air carriers to maintain certain levels of liability insurance, and state laws require employers to provide workers compensation insurance for their employees); and

3. *Insurance*, although not required by law, is *not available* to the operator.

Exculpatory contracts are generally used in operations that are perceived by conservative insurance companies as being "out on the ragged edge," involving high risk or risks for which no actuarial statistics are available to the insurance company, constituting "unknown" risks. This has long included airlifting skydivers (Figures 7.2 and 7.3) or bungee jumpers, and motion picture "stunt" flying (as in one of the James Bond movies shot in the days before computer generated imagery, where a stunt pilot doubling for Agent 007 flies a tiny experimental BD-5J Microjet through a hangar while the hangar doors are closing, barely squeaking through at a 90-degree bank angle). Pilots of privately-owned former military aircraft ("warbirds," *see* Fig. 7.4) often require their passengers and customers to sign exculpatory contracts. Now, exculpatory contracts

Fig. 7.2. The author's daughter studies an exculpatory contract prior to making her first tandem skydive.

Fig. 7.3. She signed and found the thrill well worth the risk.

Fig. 7.4. Civilian operators of historic warbirds such as this WW II vintage Navy SNJ advanced trainer often take passengers for rides in connection with air shows and aviation gatherings. Requiring such passengers to first sign an exculpatory contract is commonplace.

may prove to be the primary tool to protect the burgeoning space tourism industry (Fig 7.5) from liability for passenger injuries.

If the potential income from an uninsurable operation is sufficient to entice you to engage in it without liability insurance, then you should consult your attorney to explore the possibility of protecting you from claims by other risk takers involved by having everyone sign exculpatory contracts beforehand. Such contracts, which serve to relieve the operator of legal responsibility for the consequences of her own or her employee's negligence, have been held void as a matter of public policy in the state of New York. In most other states the courts very closely scrutinize such contracts but enforce them if:

1. there is some *equality in bargaining power* between the parties, and
2. the subject matter is *not an essential of life* (such as food, medicine, medical care, shelter, public utilities, public transportation, or communications).

Some courts have upheld the fine print on the back of such things as admission tickets to races, air shows, and ski lifts as constituting valid exculpatory contracts, even where they have not been read or

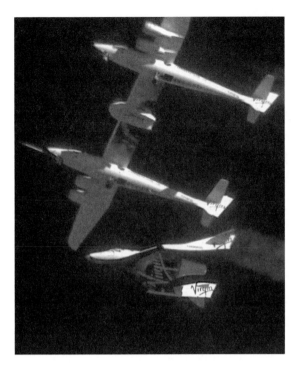

Fig. 7.5. If insurers shy away in the absence of a proven safety record, exculpatory contracts will also likely prove a useful risk management tool in the early years of commercial space transportation, such as the suborbital flights being offered by billionaire Richard Branson's Virgin Galactic whose spacecraft and mother ship are shown. (Photo by Clay Observatory at Dexter and Southfield Schools for Virgin Galactic)

signed by the purchaser. Much greater legal protection is afforded, however, by a full-size legible contract signed by the person giving up the right to sue. That contract should include a statement fitting into the doctrine of *assumption of risk*, previously discussed in Chapter 4, reciting that the person who is signing the agreement *knows and understands the scope, nature, and extent of the risk* involved in the operation (which may include personal injury or even death) and that the person *freely and voluntarily chooses to incur that risk* (for thrills or remuneration, as the case may be). The contract is even more compelling if it provides the person the choice between: (1) relieving the operator from legal and financial responsibility for accidents that may injure that person (including those resulting from the ordinary negligence of the operator and his employees and others whom the operator may wish to protect by the contract, such as an airport authority) or (2) paying the operator some additional price to be allowed to participate in the activity without waiving responsibility for negligence (but still assuming the risk).

The most effective format for this document requires the person giving up the right to sue to read it carefully and leave a trail of cross outs and initials throughout the document to indicate having read and understood the agreement and made conscious choices before reaching the signature line.

A word of caution: If the person signing the agreement is a minor, however, you get no protection since a minor can later legally disavow any contract he or she signed while a minor.

Each such contract should be handcrafted by your lawyer for your specific operation. This is another one of those preventive lawyering situations where it is very cost-effective to use your lawyer's skills and foresight to head off potential litigation. Frugal aviation business managers may be tempted to obtain copies of similar agreements relied upon by others who are or have been engaged in similar operations, then just change the name of the business or cut and paste favorite paragraphs from several such forms. This often results in documents that do not provide you the maximum available protection, at best, and may be the legal equivalent of what psychiatrists call "word salad" (nonsensical gibberish) affording no legal protection, at worst. Gathering other examples is fine, but then share them with your attorney for reference in drafting one for you; don't try to play lawyer yourself.

Some years ago, I drafted an exculpatory contract for a commercial skydiving operation in Colorado. The agreement was later upheld by the Colorado Supreme Court to bar a suit brought by a jumper injured during the company's air operations. Some of the rip-offs of that contract I've seen perpetuated by skydiving drop zone operators who obviously didn't have the assistance of legal counsel would be laughable if they were not so legally pathetic. That's a lot like doing your own surgery: If everything goes perfectly, you may save yourself some money. But the odds do not favor everything going perfectly, and you may create far more expensive problems than you started with. Of course this applies to all legal documents, not only exculpatory contracts.

Some states' courts hold that an exculpatory contract does not relieve an operator from liability for acts of gross negligence or willful or wanton misconduct. (Not all states recognize degrees of negligence, but this can be a problem in those that do.) For example: A Georgia company owned and operated several T-34 former military trainer aircraft it rented to customers interested in experiencing air combat maneuvering ("dogfighting"). With a company flight instructor on board, a pair of the aircraft would engage each other in simulated air combat. All customers were required to sign an exculpatory contract before the flight. On one such flight, one of the aircraft suffered a catastrophic structural failure of a wing spar, the instructor and passenger were unable to parachute to safety, and both were killed in the resulting crash. Litigation ensued, and the company asserted to exculpatory contract as a defense. There was evidence that the company had previously flown a sister ship to the accident aircraft from Georgia to Illinois with a suspected cracked wing spar and (conflicting) evidence that the spar on the accident aircraft was cracked. The court held that the case should go to trial and the jury should be allowed to decide whether this evidence showed that the company was grossly negligent or that its conduct was willful or wanton. If so, the exculpatory contract would not protect the company from liability, but if the jury found the company's negligence, if any, of the ordinary variety then the exculpatory contract would protect the company. Juries tend to be compassionate toward the injured and families of those who died, so if one of these cases reaches a jury it does not bode well for the defendant.

Bear in mind, too, that while some exculpatory contracts are better than others, the best exculpatory contract still does not provide you protection as good as adequate liability insurance. But if you are going to engage in operations that are uninsurable, the exculpatory contract is vastly superior to nothing and, coupled with organization of the enterprise as a corporation or LLC and a tight accident-prevention program, is an integral part of a risk-management plan having some depth and diversity.

It is also a good practice for an aviation business to have its legal counsel and insurance representative (broker or agent) review the company's risk-management program at least annually. The focus of this review is to ensure that your risk-management program still adequately takes into account any changes in the company's operations, along with recent developments in the law and in the insurance industry.

8

Airline Liability

While the general principles of liability and risk management previously studied apply to U.S. airlines in their legal relationship with domestic passengers, a higher duty of care (the *highest degree of care*) is imposed upon them in those operations. The legal relationship between airlines and international passengers (at least from the time the international passenger begins the process of boarding the aircraft until she has reached a safe place within the terminal at her destination) is governed by a different and unique body of law. This law includes a new international treaty known as the Montreal Convention that updates the old Warsaw Convention, which had already been modified by a contract known as the Montreal Agreement for flights touching the United States.

The purposes of this chapter are:

1. to acquaint you with the heightened legal responsibility of airlines and the use of airline tariffs as a risk management tool vis-à-vis domestic passengers, and
2. to enable you to recognize and avoid common mistakes that can deprive an airline of the protection afforded by international law, vis-à-vis international passengers.

The law that governs an airline's liability for injuries to passengers varies, depending upon whether the passenger is traveling on a purely domestic or an international (or partly international) ticket. In both cases, special legal obligations and protections apply to airline operations that do not apply to other flights.

AIRLINE LIABILITY TO DOMESTIC PASSENGERS

For the purposes of this discussion, we will define *domestic passenger* as an airline passenger whose ticket shows an origin and destination within the United States and whose *planned* routing does not include any stops outside the United States (Fig. 8.1).

When a domestic passenger is injured, the first question that must be addressed is whether the airline was acting as a *common carrier.* An operator is considered a common carrier if it represents to the public, either in writing (such as by advertising) or by its course of conduct, that it will (1) *carry for hire* (2) at a *uniform rate* available to (3) *all persons* applying (or cargo presented), as long as there remains unused capacity in the aircraft.

These characteristics distinguish common carrier operations from private or contract flying. A tariff in airline terminology encompasses the total agreement between the airline and the passenger or shipper, although the price (rate) is the predominant factor in most tariff discussions.

For the purposes of distinguishing between common carriage and contract carriage, a controlling question is often whether the price paid

Fig. 8.1. Any airline flight may include a mixture of domestic and international passengers and cargo. The airline's legal responsibility for passenger injury or cargo loss or damage can vary radically, depending on whether the passenger or cargo is deemed domestic or international.

for the trip is a standard price then in effect for the class of service on the flight or is a negotiated (haggled) price. If a passenger paid an airline's listed fare (for example: a $400 round-trip coach class from Los Angeles to New York), that looks like a common carrier transaction. Airline fare schedules have become profoundly complex computerized sliding scales designed to maximize revenue on each flight, up to the moment the aircraft door closes, and although no case law has yet appeared on the question, such programs would likely be found to satisfy the "uniform rate" test. (Less clear, and also unaddressed by the law, is the situation posed by purchasing tickets through such online intermediaries as Travelocity and Priceline whose advertising at least gives consumers the impression that the company is haggling with the airline on their behalf for the best price.) Contrast a member of a sports team traveling with the team that had negotiated a price to charter the aircraft to travel to a game. The latter appears more like contract carriage than common carriage. The reason this may be an important distinction is that under the common law, common carriers have been held to have the legal duty to exercise *the highest degree of care* to avoid injuring a passenger instead of the ordinary degree of care to be exercised by the hypothetical *reasonably prudent person* in our exploration of general principles of negligence in Chapter 4. Private and contract carriage is governed by that ordinary degree of care (Fig. 8.2). The highest degree of care standard applicable to common carriage is a tougher test. The courts have generally held that the highest degree of care standard requires that the airline and its

Fig. 8.2. Tulsa, Oklahoma-based Omni Air International operates only charter flights, such as this DC-10 disembarking Navy personnel returning from deployment. (U.S. Navy photo)

employees exercise *the greatest degree of human care and foresight possible* to ensure the passengers' safe conveyance.

Although this is a much tougher standard than ordinary care, it is not as tough as strict liability. The courts have shown a practical streak in applying the highest degree of care standard to particular situations, limiting it to a degree of care consistent with the practical operation and conduct of the airline's business. Thus, although a lawyer representing the family of a person killed in an accident resulting from structural failure of an airliner caused by an undetected flaw might argue that the highest degree of care standard required the airline to disassemble every aircraft and scientifically test every component of the aircraft between each flight, a court would recognize the impracticality of that. So the court would refuse to hold that the airline had breached its duty to exercise the highest degree of care by not implementing such a procedure.

At trial, the jury will listen to all of the (often conflicting) testimony of the witnesses (both eyewitnesses and expert witnesses) and will reach its own decision as to what really happened and why. Once all of the evidence (testimony, documents, and other physical exhibits) has been received, but before the jury withdraws to the secrecy of the jury room to deliberate, the judge will instruct them on the legal principles they must apply to the facts in order to reach a decision.

These *jury instructions* of the law can be crucial to the outcome. For example, the jury instruction given by the judge in a common carrier case is very different from that given in a contract carrier case. Consider the following scenario: Two jetliners take off from Dallas, Texas, bound for a college basketball tournament in Boise, Idaho. The first aircraft is an airliner operated by a commercial airline and the college basketball team and coaches are traveling on regular-fare tickets purchased for them by the college's alumni association. A few miles behind is an identical airplane owned and operated by a wealthy Texas oilman who is a dedicated alumnus of the school and great fan of its sports teams. The oilman has donated the use of his aircraft to transport his alma mater's basketball team and coaching team. The winds over the Rocky Mountains are westerly and in excess of thirty knots, with wind velocity increasing with altitude. As the two aircraft approach the Rockies, both flight crews observe lens-shaped clouds over the mountains. Both aircraft are experiencing a smooth ride and neither flight crew has illuminated the *fasten seat belts* sign. Suddenly, the first aircraft encounters severe clear air turbulence that throws unrestrained passengers about the interior of the aircraft, injuring some. A moment later, the same thing happens to the second aircraft.

Injured passengers on both aircraft subsequently sue the aircraft operators for negligence. In the separate trials of the two accidents, expert aviation meteorologists testify that these wind conditions would indicate the probability of development of a standing "mountain wave" along the eastern side of the Rockies. They would further testify that the fact that such a wave had already developed was confirmed by the crews' observation of altocumulus standing lenticular (ACSL) clouds. This mountain wave generated the severe clear air turbulence encountered by both aircraft. Pilot expert opinion testimony for opposing sides in both cases might then differ on whether a flight crew based in the Great Plains should have known how to recognize these indicia of mountain wave phenomenon, anticipated an encounter with clear air turbulence, and illuminated the *fasten seat belts* sign to preclude passenger injury.

In the case of the airline, the judge would instruct the jury that as a common carrier it had the duty to exercise the highest degree of human care and foresight consistent with the practical operation and conduct of its business to safeguard its passengers from injury. In that case, the jury would almost certainly find that included a duty to ensure that the flight crews were familiar with all meteorological phenomena they might encounter anywhere on the company's routes, and might well further find the airline negligent for not having done so with this particular crew.

In contrast, in the private carriage case of the second aircraft, a jury applying the lesser ordinary degree of care of a "reasonably prudent person" *might* find that reasonably prudent pilots based in the flatlands could be unaware of this mountain weather phenomenon without such ignorance constituting negligence. Admittedly, the latter case could go either way, but no one is ever certain what a jury is going to do in any particular case until it has done it. This example serves to illustrate the practical effect of whether the injured passenger was being transported by a common carrier or not.

This elevated standard of care does not apply to every conceivable situation in which a passenger might suffer injury as a result of airline negligence. Rather, the courts have generally limited application of this higher standard to the period between the times the passenger departs a safe place within the terminal to board the aircraft until she reaches a safe place within the terminal at the conclusion of the flight. Negligence of the airline and its employees could also conceivably cause injury to passengers at many locations within the passenger terminal, including the check-in area, concourses, boarding gates, and baggage claim area. The courts have generally held that the airline owes the passenger only reasonably prudent care within the terminal.

The defense of *assumption of risk* (*see* Chapter 4) is not available to airlines as a defense against suits brought by injured passengers (or survivors of passengers killed in an airline crash). This is because, recognizing the statistical evidence that commercial airline travel is the safest means of travel, the courts have held that the airline traveler cannot be considered to have chosen to incur some additional "known risk" by flying on an airline.

Air Carrier Risk-Management Tools in Domestic Operations

An airline can limit its liability for damage to or destruction of domestic passengers' baggage and shipped cargo, and may impose reasonable procedural prerequisites and timetables affecting litigation by passengers through its *tariffs*. Remember, the airline's tariffs (generally included in a *tariff book* that is available for review by passengers or shippers on request) contain all of the terms and conditions of the contract to transport the person or cargo, including (but by no means limited to) the price charged for the transportation. While, as we have seen, the law as a matter of public policy goes to great lengths to protect human health and safety, it is somewhat less stringent regarding personal property. There are two areas in which the airline can use tariff provisions as risk-management tools against domestic passengers: dollar limits on liability and privates statutes of limitation.

Limits on Liability

The airline may in its tariff set a dollar limit (typically on a per-bag or per-pound basis) on its liability for the loss or destruction of passenger baggage or shipped cargo. Because of the public policy that highly favors the protection of human health and safety, however, airlines are prohibited from placing dollar limits on the amount of their liability for passenger injury or death.

Private Statutes of Limitation

Laws that impose time limits on how long after an event a person may file a suit, or be forever barred from filing suit, are called *statutes of limitation*. Airlines are permitted to impose *private statutes of limitation* through tariffs. Most airline tariffs set deadlines for the passenger (or his survivors) or shipper having a claim against the airline (for either personal injury or loss or destruction of baggage or cargo) to notify the airline in writing of the claim and to file suit. The deadline for suit in the tariff may be less than that provided in the applicable public statutes of limitation. At least where the period contained in the private statute of limitations is not so short as to appear unreasonable, the courts enforce these tariff provisions and dismiss lawsuits that, although filed within public statutory periods, are filed after the deadline set forth in the tariff.

LIABILITY FOR INTERNATIONAL PASSENGERS

A passenger is considered an *international passenger* if that passenger's ticket shows either (1) an origin in one country and a destination in another country or (2) an origin and destination in one country but a planned intermediate stop in a different country.

Note again that it is generally the passenger's *planned* route as printed on the passenger's ticket that determines whether the passenger is a domestic or an international passenger. Thus, a passenger holding a ticket for a nonstop flight from San Diego to Anchorage is legally a domestic passenger. Overflight of a foreign country (Canada, in this case) en route between two points in the country of origin does not make the flight international, nor would an unscheduled stop in another country, such as an emergency landing. But a passenger on a flight from San Diego to Anchorage with a planned stop in Vancouver, British Columbia, Canada, would be an international passenger. A passenger ticketed from San Diego to Vancouver or from Vancouver to Anchorage would be an international passenger.

The Warsaw Convention—Laying an Enduring Foundation

The legal relationship between airlines and international passengers began with a landmark international treaty generally known as the *Warsaw Convention* and formally titled *The Convention for the Unification of Certain Rules Relating to International Transportation by Air*, a treaty now being rapidly updated worldwide by the new Montreal Convention discussed later in the chapter.

Application of the Warsaw Convention in recent decades often had bizarre, sometimes shocking, and often baffling consequences. Indeed, if any sense can be made of this treaty, it is only by putting it into historical context. The final version of the treaty was written and agreed to by the United States and many other nations in 1929. At that time, the international airline business was an infant industry. Visionaries saw that it held great promise to afford a better, safer, faster, and more comfortable way to travel, and thus to become a thriving industry if properly fostered and protected. But at that time, it was neither acceptably safe nor comfortable, nor were participant companies thriving.

The airline industry had experienced a fatality rate of forty-five passenger fatalities per 100 million passenger miles flown (compared to modern rates of consistently less than a minor fraction of one passenger fatality over the same distance). Perhaps the safest new transport on the line was the all-metal Ford Trimotor (Fig. 8.3), which is not remembered for the creature comforts its passengers enjoyed; the aircraft was incredibly noisy and neither adequately heated in winter nor cooled in

Fig. 8.3. When the Warsaw Convention was agreed to in 1929, this Ford Trimotor was the state-of-the-art airliner.

summer. It was also slower and had less range than most of today's light private aircraft.

But while the state of the art was then crude, it was also widely perceived as having great potential for improvement, a perception that has been borne out by history. In drafting this treaty, the various nations' representatives who participated in the process set for themselves the objectives of protecting and promoting the infant international airline industry. They agreed that this would best be accomplished by adopting an international treaty that would:

1. Protect international airlines from catastrophic loss in the event of a crash,
2. Promote airline safety,
3. Promote the availability of liability insurance to international airlines,
4. Provide uniformity of terms and conditions of transportation by air with those of other modes of transportation (ship, rail, bus, etc.), and
5. Provide a framework of internationally uniform law to govern international airline crashes.

A threshold problem faced by the delegates who drafted the treaty was that while all of these objectives were laudable, some of them tended to work against one another. For example, the same theory used to justify the imposition of strict liability against manufacturers of defective products (previously discussed in Chapter 4) would argue that safety is best promoted by making the airline strictly liable if a passenger is injured. But that approach would conflict with the objective of protecting international airlines from potentially catastrophic losses and promoting the availability of liability insurance. Thus, as in most legislation and treaties, compromises were reached between competing interests. In its final form, the treaty accomplished the following:

1. *A framework of internationally uniform law* was established. Treaty provisions standardized claims procedures in the event of international airline crashes. These procedures provide internationally uniform answers to these questions:
   a. In what nation's courts may a lawsuit arising out of the crash be brought? (*Jurisdiction*, in the international sense)
   b. What nation's law governs the crash? (*Choice of law*)
   c. When must the lawsuit be filed or forever barred? (*Statute of Limitation*)

The treaty provided that an international passenger can choose between four possible nations in which to bring a lawsuit for injury: (1) the nation of domicile of the airline, (2) the nation in which the airline has its principal place of business, (3) the nation in which the ticket was bought from the airline or from a travel agent, or (4) the nation that is the passenger's destination.

Except where specific provisions of the treaty apply, the forum court (the court of the nation where the case is being tried) applies its own choice-of-laws rules in deciding what law governs the litigation.

The treaty contains a globally applicable statute of limitations, providing that suit must be brought, if at all, within two years from the date of the conclusion of the passenger's trip, or its intended conclusion.

2. *Uniformity of terms and conditions* was achieved not only within the airline industry, but also among all transportation modes. Treaty provisions standardized the documents of transport (the passenger's ticket and, for cargo, the *air waybill*) in formats and contents similar to those already in widespread use for transportation by ship, truck and rail. This ensured that travel agents and shipping clerks accustomed to doing business with other transportation modes would quickly feel at home booking passage for customers or shipping goods on the airlines. (Neither the standardization of procedures nor the standardization of documents was particularly controversial. The rest of what the treaty did, however, was extremely controversial then, and that controversy did not abate during the seventy-five years between the treaty's ratification by the Congress of the United States and ratification of the new Montreal Convention to refine Warsaw.)

3. In an effort *to promote safety*, the treaty imposes *strict liability* on international airlines for *passenger injury or death* and substantially limits defenses that would otherwise be available to international airlines under the common law against claims for the loss or destruction of cargo.

4. Here is the most controversial provision of all: *To counterbalance strict liability and protect international airlines from catastrophic loss* in the event of a crash—and in connection with that, *to promote the availability of liability insurance to international airlines*—the treaty limited the dollar amount of the airline's liability for the injury or death of a passenger to the sum of $8,300 (U.S.) and (less controversially) $16.50 (U.S.) per kilogram for the loss or destruction of cargo.

The Association of Trial Lawyers of America (ATLA), an association of plaintiffs' attorneys, strongly opposed ratification of the treaty and continued relentlessly thereafter to lobby to persuade the U.S. government to withdraw from the treaty. ATLA's position was that even in 1929, this was a shockingly cheap price to pay for killing a U.S. citizen, and thus really operated to deny U.S. citizens who chose to travel internationally by air valuable legal rights.

After 1929, there were a number of other international conferences resulting in several treaties that changed some aspects of the Warsaw Convention between those nations, including from time to time raising the onerous limit of recovery for personal injury or death. But opposition in the United States, spearheaded by ATLA, long prevented the United States from signing any of these subsequent treaties. By 1965, that opposition had reached such proportions that the United States declared its intent to withdraw from the Warsaw Convention and to reconsider its prior grant of landing rights in the United States to the airlines of other nations unless those international airlines serving the United States would sign a contract with the U.S. government raising the limits of those airlines' liability for passenger injury or death.

The airlines met with representatives of the U.S. government on neutral territory in Montreal (home of ICAO) where they entered into the *Montreal Agreement*, a contract between the airlines and the U.S. government. The airlines agreed to increase the ceiling on their liability for injury or death of a passenger to $75,000 (U.S.) for those international flights "touching" the United States (originating in, terminating in, or having an agreed stopping place in the United States), regardless of the nationality of the passenger. International airlines wishing to subsequently enter the U.S. market were required to sign the Montreal Agreement as a condition precedent to such service.

Under the Warsaw Convention as modified by the Montreal Agreement, for international flights "touching" the United States, the airline was strictly liable for passenger injury or death, up to a maximum of $75,000 per passenger. Even that was not much money in the modern world.

Liability for International Cargo

The airline was also generally liable under the Warsaw Convention for the loss or destruction of air cargo to a maximum amount of $16.50

(U.S.) per kilogram. There were, however, five *defenses to cargo claims* that the airlines were permitted to use to defeat even that liability (the Montreal Agreement did not change any of the Warsaw provisions regarding cargo liability). These five defenses to international air cargo claims were:

1. The airline took *all possible measures* to prevent the cargo loss,
2. *Pilot or navigational error* caused the cargo damage,
3. The shipper's *contributory negligence* caused the damage to the cargo,
4. The loss, damage, or destruction of the cargo was caused by an *act of God, war, or state* or
5. The *nature of the goods* caused the damage.

Let's take a look at each of these defenses to international air cargo claims in some detail.

All Possible Measures

This defense might apply if, for example, the crash that destroyed the air cargo was caused by a terrorist bomb so sophisticated as to be undetectable by state-of-the-art baggage screening equipment properly employed by the airline.

Pilot or Navigational Error

This is bizarre. Remember: this is a *defense*. If the court found that pilot or navigational error caused the cargo damage, the airline didn't have to pay the shipper even $16.50 per kilogram! For example: An international airline flight was transporting a cargo of gold bars from a bank in the United States to a correspondent bank in Asia. The flight crew wandered off the published instrument approach to the destination airport and collided with a hill enveloped in clouds. A crowd of ordinary citizens reached the crash scene before the authorities, and by the time order was established, the cargo of gold was nowhere to be found. The cause of the accident having been pilot or navigational error, the airline had no liability to the shipper for the loss of this cargo. The only logical explanation for such a result is that pilots seeking airline employment in the late 1920s (when the treaty was drafted) tended to be men who had learned to fly in World War I and had maintained flight proficiency through barnstorming and other feats of aeronautical derring-do. Altogether, a rather wild-eyed bunch of desperados in the eyes of conservative Wall

Street investment banker types whose financial support was needed to promote the growth of the airline industry.

At least where only personal property (cargo) was involved, it appears that the drafters of the treaty intended to give an added measure of security or incentive to such investors. Knowing that the airline would not be held responsible for the consequences (at least to cargo) of whatever foolishness those daring young men in their silk scarves and flying leathers might commit with company "aeroplanes" might make the risk acceptable. (Remember: This defense applied only to cargo and had no bearing on the airlines' strict liability for passenger injury or death.)

Shipper's Contributory Negligence

This defense would apply if the shipper was shipping, for example, a rare and precious vase from China's ancient Ming Dynasty and merely shipped it in a crate without sufficient internal energy-absorbing materials to prevent breakage.

Act of God, War, or State

This defense would apply if the cause of the loss, damage, or destruction of the cargo were a major force of nature (or, *force majeure*). As examples: the aircraft was picked up from the ramp by a tornado, scattering the cargo to the winds, was shot down or blown up in the course of warfare, or was seized by government agents.

Nature of the Goods

This defense was most often applied in the case of shipments of perishable goods where the shipper did not take any special precautions to purchase refrigerated shipment and the goods spoiled in transit. The cargo simply spoiled because it was perishable; that was its nature.

Notice

The Warsaw Convention required the airline to deliver to the passenger a physical paper ticket (or to the shipper of air cargo, an air waybill) placing that customer on *notice* that the provisions of that treaty (as amended by the Montreal Agreement) applied to the flight. The airline was required to give this notice in a timely manner, allowing the customer the opportunity to take other measures to protect herself from loss (as by purchasing additional insurance). Attacking the inadequacy of the actual notice given to a passenger prior to a particular accident flight became a favorite technique used by plaintiffs' lawyers to attempt to break the meager limit of liability. A long line of cases developed interpreting the question of what constituted adequate notice under Warsaw in a great variety of factual scenarios.

Notice Must Be Readable

Under Warsaw, the notice was required to be printed in 10-point type on a good-quality paper with good-quality ink, using an excellent printing press. Smaller type, cheaper paper and ink, and inferior printing machinery would diminish the readability. If the warnings on the airline ticket (*see* Fig. 8.4) were not clearly readable without the use of a magnifying glass, courts could and often did hold that the airline failed to give the passenger adequate notice.

Delivery in a Timely and Proper Manner

Under Warsaw, for notice to be to be legally adequate, the ticket containing that readable notice was required to be delivered to passengers in a time and manner that permitted the passenger the opportunity to read and understand the warnings contained on the ticket and to take other measures to protect himself, as by purchasing insurance. In some cases, passengers received their tickets only at the last possible moment during the process of boarding, so that they had no opportunity to read the warnings on the ticket before the door closed and the aircraft was on its way. By then, there was no opportunity for the passenger, had he then read and understood the warnings contained in his ticket, to have purchased additional insurance to protect himself. In such a case, the courts held that the airline failed to give adequate notice.

Consequences of Inadequate Notice

If a court applying Warsaw found that the airline failed to give adequate notice to an international passenger who was subsequently injured or killed on the trip, the result could have serious financial repercussions for the airline and/or its insurers. In that situation, the airline was still strictly liable for the passenger's injury or death, but the airline was prohibited from availing itself of the dollar limitation on that liability it would otherwise have under the Warsaw Convention as modified by the Montreal Agreement.

If the court found that the airline failed to provide an international cargo shipper an air waybill adequately putting the shipper on notice,

ADVICE TO INTERNATIONAL PASSENGERS ON LIMITATION OF LIABILITY

Passengers on a journey involving an ultimate destination or a stop in a country other than the country of origin are advised that the provisions of a treaty known as the Warsaw Convention may be applicable to the entire journey, including any portion entirely within the country of origin or destination. For such passengers on a journey to, from, or with an agreed stopping place in the United States of America, the Convention and special contracts of carriage embodied in applicable tariffs provide that the liability of certain carriers, parties to such special contracts, for death of or personal injury to passengers is limited in most cases to proven damages not to exceed U.S. $75,000 per passenger, and that this liability up to such limit shall not depend on negligence on the part of the carrier. The limit of liability of U.S. $75,000 above is inclusive of legal fees and costs except that in case of a claim brought in a state where provision is made for separate award of legal fees and costs, the limit shall be the sum of U.S. $58,000 exclusive of legal fees and costs. For such passengers traveling by a carrier not a party to such special contracts or on a journey not to, from, or having an agreed stopping place in the United States of America, liability of the carrier for death or personal injury to passengers is limited in most cases to approximately U.S. $10,000 or U.S. $20,000.

The names of carriers, parties to such special contracts, are available at all ticket offices of such carriers and may be examined on request. Additional protection can usually be obtained by purchasing insurance from a private company. Such insurance is not affected by any limitation of the carrier's liability under the Warsaw Convention or such special contracts of carriage. For further information please consult your airline or insurance company representative.

NOTICE OF BAGGAGE LIABILITY LIMITATIONS

Liability for loss, delay, or damage to baggage is limited unless a higher value is declared in advance and additional charges are paid. For most international travel (including domestic portions of international journeys) the liability limit is approximately $9.07 per pound for checked baggage and $400 per passenger for unchecked baggage. For travel wholly between U.S. points federal rules require any limit on an airline's baggage liability to be at least $1250 per passenger. Excess valuation may be declared on certain types of articles. Some carriers assume no liability for fragile, valuable or perishable articles. Further information may be obtained from the carrier.

STAPLE
HERE

PRINTED IN U.S.A. BY RAND McNALLY   (3-85)   1290 ATB

REV 4-84

Fig. 8.4. Warsaw-compliant airline ticket notices and warnings.

1288 ATB (REV 4-25-89A)

NOTICE

If the passenger's journey involves an ultimate destination or stop in a country other than the country of departure the Warsaw Convention may be applicable and the Convention governs and in most cases limits the liability of carriers for death or personal injury and in respect of loss of or damage to baggage. See also notice headed "Advice to International Passengers on Limitation of Liability."

CONDITIONS OF CONTRACT

1. As used in this contract "ticket" means this passenger ticket and baggage check, of which these conditions and the notices form part, "carriage" is equivalent to "transportation", "carrier" means all air carriers that carry or undertake to carry the passenger or his baggage hereunder or perform any other service incidental to such air carriage, "WARSAW CONVENTION" means the Convention for the Unification of Certain Rules Relating to International Carriage by Air signed at Warsaw, 12th October 1929, or that Convention as amended at The Hague, 28th September 1955, whichever may be applicable.

2. Carriage hereunder is subject to the rules and limitations relating to liability established by the Warsaw Convention unless such carriage is not "international carriage" as defined by that Convention.

3. To the extent not in conflict with the foregoing carriage and other services performed by each carrier are subject to: (I) provisions contained in this ticket, (II) applicable tariffs, (III) carrier's conditions of carriage and related regulations which are made part hereof (and are available on application at the offices of carrier), except in transportation between a place in the United States or Canada and any place outside thereof to which tariffs in force in those countries apply.

4. Carrier's name may be abbreviated in the ticket, the full name and its abbreviation being set forth in carrier's tariffs, conditions of carriage, regulations or timetables; carrier's address shall be the airport of departure shown opposite the first abbreviation of carrier's name in the ticket; the agreed stopping places are those places set forth in this ticket or as shown in carrier's timetables as scheduled stopping places on the passenger's route; carriage to be performed hereunder by several successive carriers is regarded as a single operation.

5. An air carrier issuing a ticket for carriage over the lines of another air carrier does so only as its agent.

6. Any exclusion or limitation of liability of carrier shall apply to and be for the benefit of agents, servants and representatives of carrier and any person whose aircraft is used by carrier for carriage and its agents, servants and representatives.

7. Checked baggage will be delivered to bearer of the baggage check. In case of damage to baggage moving in international transportation complaint must be made in writing to carrier forthwith after discovery of damage and, at the latest, within 7 days from receipt; in case of delay, complaint must be made within 21 days from date the baggage was delivered. See tariffs or conditions of carriage regarding non-international transportation.

8. This ticket is good for carriage for one year from date of issue, except as otherwise provided in this ticket, in carrier's tariffs, conditions of carriage, or related regulations. The fare for carriage hereunder is subject to change prior to commencement of carriage. Carrier may refuse transportation if the applicable fare has not been paid.

9. Carrier undertakes to use its best efforts to carry the passenger and baggage with reasonable dispatch. Times shown in timetable or elsewhere are not guaranteed and form no part of this contract. Carrier may without notice substitute alternate carriers or aircraft, and may alter or omit stopping places shown on the ticket in case of necessity. Schedules are subject to change without notice. Carrier assumes no responsibility for making connections.

10. Passenger shall comply with Government travel requirements, present exit, entry and other required documents and arrive at airport by time fixed by carrier or, if no time is fixed, early enough to complete departure procedures.

11. No agent, servant or representative of carrier has authority to alter, modify or waive any provision of this contract.

CARRIER RESERVES THE RIGHT TO REFUSE CARRIAGE TO ANY PERSON WHO HAS ACQUIRED A TICKET IN VIOLATION OF APPLICABLE LAW OR CARRIER'S TARIFFS, RULES OR REGULATIONS

SUBJECT TO TARIFF REGULATIONS

Issued by the Carrier whose name is in the "Issued By" section on the face of the Passenger Ticket and Baggage Check.

Fig. 8.4. (Continued.)

the airline could not avail itself of either the dollar limit or any of the five defenses which would otherwise apply.

Interpreting the language of the Warsaw Convention, the courts held that once an airline "accepts" passengers by allowing them to board the aircraft, a later opportunity to read the ticket and buy insurance at an intermediate stop did not cure the lack of notice.

Remember: a person can be an international passenger if she buys a ticket for a flight between two cities in the same country but with a planned stop in another country, as in the earlier example of a flight from San Diego to Anchorage with a planned stop in Vancouver, British Columbia, Canada. What if the Canadian stop was inadvertently omitted from the passenger's ticket, even though the airline did plan for the flight to stop there? The courts held that since that omission deprived the passenger of notice that the flight was international in nature and that the limits of Warsaw applied, the passenger was an *international passenger without notice*. Therefore, if the passenger was injured or killed on the trip, the airline would be strictly liable for the accident, but with no artificial limit on the dollar amount of that liability!

Punitive Damages under the Warsaw Convention

There was a difference of opinion between U.S. courts on the question of whether international passengers are permitted to recover punitive or exemplary damages from the airline. There is a provision in the Warsaw Convention that followed the basic rationale used to allow the award of such damages in certain cases (see the earlier discussion of exemplary or punitive damages in Chapter 4). The Warsaw Convention provided that if the accident was caused by *willful misconduct* of the airline (or its employees acting within the scope of their employment), the airline remained strictly liable for the passenger's injury or death but without the artificial dollar limit). In the case of an air cargo claim, in a willful misconduct case the airline could not avail itself of the benefit of the $16.50/kg limit or any of the five defenses to cargo.

The standards for application of this willful misconduct exception closely followed the standards permitting an award of exemplary or punitive damages in domestic negligence cases. Generally, our courts allowed the willful misconduct exception to be applied where the airline or its employees committed an act or omission that they should have known would cause an accident or implied that they had a reckless disregard for whether the act or omission might cause an accident.

Consider the following scenario: An airline's flight crew experienced mechanical difficulty relating to the aircraft's airworthiness in a foreign country and called airline management to request authorization to have the repairs performed there before departure. Airline management denied permission and ordered the crew to proceed on schedule with the passengers aboard and with the aircraft in its present condition, so that the airline's employees can perform the necessary repairs at the company's maintenance facility in the United States. When the crew expressed reluctance to do so, management threatened them with firing on the spot unless they followed orders.

If the uncorrected defect caused an accident on the flight, resulting in passenger injuries, deaths and/or damage or destruction to air cargo, a jury might well have found that the airline's actions were so outrageous as to constitute willful misconduct. In that case, the artificial dollar limits on passenger injury and cargo damage would not apply, nor could the airline rely upon any of the five defenses to cargo. The result would be that the airline would be strictly liable for the actual dollar value of the losses suffered by the passengers and shippers.

One U.S. court of appeals held that the airline would still be liable for nothing more than that, since in its view international passengers may not recover punitive damages, but another held punitive damages available in that context. In such a situation, the U.S. Supreme Court is usually called upon to decide which interpretation is correct, but ratification of the new Montreal Convention, barring punitive damages, has made the issue moot for future accidents.

The courts further interpreted the Warsaw Convention, as amended by the Montreal Agreement, to include airline liability for passenger injuries and death resulting from hijackings and terrorist attacks.

Other Liabilities under the Warsaw Convention

By its terms, the Warsaw Convention applies only from the time the passenger begins "*the process of embarking*" until the passenger has completed "*the process of disembarking*." Judicial interpretations paralleled similar decisions on the question of when airlines are responsible to exercise the highest degree of care for domestic passengers. The courts determined that an international passenger has commenced the "process

Fig. 8.5. During the process of embarking or disembarking, treaties govern an airline's potential liability to international passengers while the airline owes the highest degree of care to domestic passengers.

of embarking" once that passenger has left *a safe place within the terminal* for the purpose of boarding the aircraft and has completed the "process of disembarking" upon reaching a safe place within the terminal on arrival (Fig. 8.5).

Bear in mind that the Warsaw Convention as modified by the Montreal Agreement (as well as the new Montreal Convention discussed in detail later in this chapter, and not to be confused with the Montreal *Agreement*) govern only the legal relationship between the airline and the international passenger or shipper of international air cargo. They have no bearing on the passenger's right to sue others who may have caused the accident, such as the manufacturer of a defective aircraft or the federal government for negligence of air traffic controllers.

Since the ticket the passenger is traveling under generally determines whether the passenger is a domestic or an international passenger, it is not unusual to have both domestic and international passengers aboard the same flight. For example, on a flight from Chicago to Mexico City with a planned stop in Dallas, leaving Chicago there might be some domestic passengers traveling on Chicago to Dallas tickets and some international passengers traveling on Chicago to Mexico City tickets. If an accident occurred on the Chicago to Dallas leg, the legal rights of the domestic passengers against the airline would vary radically from the rights of the international passengers. Imagine that the aircraft encountered an unforeseeable microburst moments after takeoff from Chicago and crashed, killing everyone on board.

Claims representatives for the airline's insurance company would almost immediately offer the heirs of each international passenger the full $75,000 limit of liability under the Warsaw Convention as amended by the Montreal Agreement. After all, there could be no doubt that the carrier was strictly liable for these international passengers' deaths, *regardless of the cause*, and the survivors of these passengers (assuming adequate notice and no provable willful misconduct on the part of the airline) had no incentive to file suit since $75,000 is the most they could recover under these circumstances. Such claims tended to be settled very quickly by full payment.

In contrast, although the heirs of the domestic passengers do not face any artificial dollar limits on the amount they can recover from the airline, they must first prove that the accident was caused by some negligence of the airline or its employees (under the highest degree of care standard). Unless they can prove that airline negligence caused the crash, they are entitled to receive nothing from the airline.

The Montreal Convention of 1999—Modernizing Warsaw

The Warsaw Convention accomplished its objectives (admittedly sometimes at considerable cost to injured international airline travelers or their survivors). Liability insurance is now readily available to international airlines, protecting them from catastrophic loss. Travel agents, shipping clerks, and customers now routinely and easily book air transportation for passengers and freight, more so now than for any other mode of transportation. A basic framework of internationally uniform law governing international airline passengers has avoided international legal chaos, and at least partly because of all of this, international airlines have made great progress in the over eighty years since the Warsaw Convention was agreed to. The international airline industry is no longer an infant.

In recognition of this accomplishment and today's realities, representatives of 118 nations and 11 international organizations gathered in Montreal in May of 1999 for the International Conference on Air Law on the Modernization of the "Warsaw System," hosted by ICAO. The delegates found it timely to reconsider whether all of the convention's provisions are still justifiable or if some had served their purpose and merited retirement. By the end of three weeks of discussion, debate, drafting and redrafting, a new treaty emerged. Formally titled *A Convention for the Unification of Certain Rules for International Carriage by Air*, it is generally referred to as the *Montreal Convention of 1999*.

By its provisions, the treaty would not take effect until 30 nations ratified it. This finally occurred in September of 2003, with the United States being the 30th ratifying nation. As in the past, many nations awaited ratification by the United States before making a ratification decision, since the U.S. refusal to agree to earlier efforts to amend Warsaw had rendered those international efforts largely wasted. Once the U.S. had ratified the treaty, ratifications flowed quickly from other nations, so that the Montreal Convention can now be considered universal.

Many writers credit initiatives by Japan's airlines, which in 1992 waived the protection of the Warsaw Convention's liability limits, for creating a climate for change that finally enabled this new treaty. In Japan's compensation culture, when a business causes harm to members of the public it is traditional for executives to promptly make public apologies and for the business to compensate the injured promptly and without resort to litigation. Yet levels of compensation received by Japanese airline accident victims are second only to the United States, and a close second at that.

The Montreal Convention of 1999 should be recognized as a tweaking, a fine-tuning of the Warsaw Convention, rather than a rejection and replacement of that system. The principle changes include:

1. For personal injury, Warsaw's strict liability approach survives, with changed limits. The airline is strictly liable for passenger bodily injury or death resulting from an accident occurring on board the aircraft or in the course of embarking or disembarking, for the *first 100,000 SDRs* (all monetary references are to Special Drawing Rights—SDRs—for ease of international currency conversion, with 100,000 SDR equaling $155,000 U.S., at this writing) of provable compensatory damages. This value is adjusted for inflation. SDRs are valued by the International Monetary Fund (IMF) by reference to the ever-changing values of a "basket" of the world's most stable currencies that presently

include the U.S. dollar, euro, British pound sterling and Japanese yen. The value of the SDR is posted daily on the IMF's website (*http://www.imf.org/external/data.htm*) and at *http://coinmill.com/ SDR_calculator.html#SDR17*. The currencies included in the "basket" are reviewed every five years to assure that it reflects the present relative importance of the various currencies in the world's trading and financial systems. SDRs are used as a point of common reference for valuation in many international treaties.

2. There is no artificial limit on the amount of recoverable compensatory damages *in excess of 100,000 SDRs* unless the airline proves itself free from any fault causing the accident. Warsaw's willful misconduct exception disappears.

3. Punitive damages are specifically precluded.

4. New documentation provisions allow the use of electronic ticketing and electronic air waybills. Warsaw's notice requirements disappear.

5. Cargo liability limitations are set at an *unbreakable* 17 SDRs per kg.

6. Warsaw's five defenses to cargo claims are replaced by these four. The airline is not liable if the destruction or loss of or damage to the cargo was caused by:

   a. Inherent defect, quality or vice of the cargo (similar to Warsaw's "nature of the goods" defense),

   b. Defective packing of the cargo performed by someone other than the carrier, its agents or servants (similar to the "shipper's contributory negligence" defense in Warsaw),

   c. Act of war or armed conflict (similar to the familiar "act of god, war or state" defense from Warsaw), and/or

   d. Act of public authority carried out in connection with entry, exit or transit of the cargo (seizure or damage by U.S. Customs in the course of inspection being an example).

7. Airlines are liable for delaying passengers and their baggage, to limits of 4,150 SDRs per passenger for passenger delay and 1,000 SDRs per passenger for baggage delay. These limits are breakable if the passenger proves the delay was the airline's fault.

8. For code-sharing flights, the passenger may recover from either the airline operating the flight or the airline whose code appears on the passenger ticket.

9. The passenger's principal and permanent nation of residence at the time of the accident is added to Warsaw's list as a fifth place

where suit may be brought (providing that the airline has a place of business there).

10. Where required by national law, the airline is obliged to make advance payments to meet the immediate economic needs of victims and their families (a routine practice in the industry today, even in the absence of any legal mandate).

11. Airlines are free to agree to higher limits or to waive the limits.

Attorneys practicing in this area of the law predicted that as more nations ratified the Montreal Convention, aviation litigation would diminish. Specifically, they forecasted that under Montreal, there would soon be:

1. No litigation over the loss, damage or destruction of cargo,

2. Little or no litigation by passengers and their families to recover full compensatory damages for injury or death,

3. Few, if any, attempts by airlines to avoid paying compensatory damages above 100,000 SDRs unless the airline clearly did not proximately cause the accident, and

4. An end to the (sometimes extreme) efforts by foreign passengers and their families to bring suit in the United States instead of their home countries.

These forecasts are proving accurate.

All treaties must be regarded as works in progress (though the progress on updating Warsaw seemed measurable in geologic time), and the Montreal Convention of 1999 is no exception. Like Warsaw, over the years Montreal is likely to become encrusted with judicial interpretations like the hull of a ship with barnacles. The trend of these decisions may reveal flaws in the treaty that will merit amendment, as may developments in the airline industry.

Most criticism to date has not been that the new treaty goes too far, but that it does not go far enough. Someday, no doubt, another will go farther, but will still fall short of perfection in the eyes of some critics, still be overtaken by events.

SEPTEMBER 11TH VICTIM COMPENSATION FUND OF 2001

Included in the Air Transportation Safety and System Stabilization Act of 2001, enacted by Congress shortly after the terrorist attacks, was a $10 billion fund for compensation of victims physically injured or killed as a result of the terrorist-related aircraft crashes and another $5 billion for compensation of air carriers for losses incurred as a result of the attacks. In order to receive compensation from the fund, victims (including families of those killed in the attacks) were required to waive their right to file or be a party to a civil lawsuit seeking damages for such injuries.

The fund was profoundly successful in preventing a litigation explosion from resulting from these horrific tragedies. Of the over 5,000 victims and their families, all but 95 elected to accept compensation from the fund in lieu of litigation. Those 95 sued, and all but 3 of those settled before trial.

9

Government Liability

There are many opportunities for employment by the federal government in aviation, both in the military and in the civil and career services. As in private industry, the most successful government employees will be those whose education and training have equipped them not only to avoid creating legal problems for their employer but also to assist coworkers in avoiding the kinds of mistakes that could bring adverse legal consequences upon the employer.

The purpose of this chapter is to provide you an understanding of the workings of the Federal Tort Claims Act in the aviation industry, to equip you to be a potentially valuable government employee, and to aid in your advancement to a civil service management or military leadership role within the federal government.

The common law, that body of law created by judges through hundreds of years of accumulated judicial pronouncements of what the law is, is a major source of the law in the United States and other *common law* countries. This is a part of our legal heritage from England, which spread its common law over much of the world through colonization. In much (perhaps most) of the world, however, the decisions of judges are not recognized as an original source of law. In these countries (*civil law* countries), only the law codified by the legislature or the executive branch is considered the law. Also, in civil-law countries, judges usually hear cases and find the facts without a jury. When the United States declared its independence from Britain in 1776, rather than risk the social and business chaos that might result from starting with a fresh slate, the new nation adopted the British common law of the time (with which it was comfortable and had no quarrel) as the common law of the United States.

This turned out to be a remarkably successful and practical approach to the problem, but with one peculiar twist: England was still a monarchy, so its common law included an artifact common to monarchies, the doctrine of *sovereign immunity*. This doctrine derived from less enlightened times when kings were considered appointed by deities. Deities, the line of reasoning went, were perfect. If a king did wrong, the appointing deity would be imperfect for having made the wrong appointment. Thus the king, having been appointed by a deity, could do no wrong. Since the king (sovereign) could do no wrong, he could not be sued by citizens claiming injury from an alleged intentional tort or negligence committed by the king (or by anyone in the government who was presumed to be doing the king's bidding). Under the doctrine of sovereign immunity, citizens could not sue their government.

THE FEDERAL TORT CLAIMS ACT

Remarkably, not only did the piece of legal baggage known as the doctrine of sovereign immunity slip into the common law of the United States through that early wholesale adoption, but with respect to the federal government it remained the law until after World War II when Congress passed the Federal Tort Claims Act (FTCA, pronounced "fitca") in 1946. Only 170 years after the Declaration of Independence, Americans were finally permitted to sue our federal government. FTCA allows suit "for injury or loss of property or personal injury or death caused by the negligence or wrongful act or omission of any employee of the government acting within the scope of his office or employment, under circumstances where the United States, if a private person, would be liable to the claimant in accordance with the law of the place where the act or omission occurred."

Liability, Generally

Under the FTCA, the federal government, like employers in the private sector, faces vicarious liability for the consequences of negligence committed by its employees acting within the scope of their employment. With a few exceptions to be discussed momentarily, the federal government is liable for the consequences of:

1. negligence (as previously analyzed in Chapter 4) of government employees who are

2. acting within the scope of their employment with the federal government
3. if a private employer would be liable for that employee's torts under the same circumstances.

Exceptions

There are several exceptions that distinguish the government's liability from that faced by employers in the private sector.

Geographic Limitation

The FTCA specifically excludes claims arising in a foreign country. This limitation has served to prevent the federal government from being sued, for example, for an accident that occurred at a U.S. Air Force base in Newfoundland that the United States operated under a long-term lease from Great Britain, since the lease did not transfer sovereignty over the area from Great Britain. Issues of liability for injuries arising out of U.S. military activities in the host nation are addressed on a nation-by-nation basis through separate *status of forces agreements (SOFA)* between the nations.

Combatant Activity

The FTCA does not apply to "any claim arising out of the combatant activities of the military or naval forces, or the Coast Guard, during time of war." Under this exception, a suit against the United States brought by the survivors of passengers and crew of an Iranian airliner shot down by a guided missile launched from a U.S. Navy cruiser which misidentified the plane as a threatening military aircraft during the 1988 "tanker war" in the Persian Gulf was dismissed by the court, which held that because of this exception such claims remain barred by the doctrine of sovereign immunity.

Activities Incident to Military Service

Congress also provided in the FTCA that the federal government is not liable for the negligent conduct of government employees if the person killed or injured was engaged in an *"activity incident to* [that person's] *military service."* This exception applies even during peacetime operations and has protected the federal government against suits in cases where, for

Fig. 9.1. Military personnel, such as this Army AH-64D Apache Longbow attack helicopter crew, are not allowed to sue the federal government for death or injury occurring while on duty. (U.S. Army photo)

example, a military air traffic controller negligently vectored a military aircraft into rising terrain at night, causing a fatal accident (Fig. 9.1).

Discretionary Function

Finally, Congress has specifically provided in the FTCA that the government would not be liable for the consequences of negligent or wrongful conduct by government employees performing a *discretionary function*. The courts have interpreted this proviso to draw a distinction between planning or policy-making activities of government employees and their operational decision-making. Planning and policy making do not subject the federal government to liability under the FTCA, even if the plan or policy subsequently causes an accident. Only operational decision making, if negligently done, may expose the federal government to liability for resulting harm.

With these exceptions, the federal government is vicariously liable like any other employer for consequences of the negligence of its employees occurring within the scope of employment. The act applies only to "employees of the government," which it defines to include "persons acting on behalf of a federal agency in an official capacity." FTCA liability does not extend to acts by independent contractors of the government. Although the cases are by no means unanimous, most courts have held that the federal government is not liable for the negligence of nonemployee designees who may be seen as doing the government's work. Thus, the government has usually not been held liable for the acts of Aviation Medical Examiners (AMEs), Designated Airworthiness Representatives (DARs), Designated Engineering Representatives (DERs), Designated Manufacturing Representatives (DMRs), or aircraft mechanics holding Inspection Authorization (IAs). As the FAA begins to certify individual U.S. civil aircraft and component manufacturers as Certified Design Organizations (CDOs), allowing them to type-certify new aircraft designs as airworthy in accordance with FAA standards but with minimal FAA oversight (similar to the type-certification process already in place in Europe that gives European manufacturers a competitive edge in the speed of certification and production of new designs), we can expect to eventually see litigation to test whether the federal government is liable under FTCA for any negligence of a CDO in the design and certification process.

Most FTCA aviation cases have arisen out of allegations of negligence by federal air traffic controllers.

Intentional Torts

The government is not liable under FTCA for intentional torts (*see* Chapter 4) committed by its employees, nor are those employees immunized by FTCA against personal liability for their intentional torts.

Punitive or Exemplary Damages

Under FTCA, the federal government (unlike a business in the private sector) is not exposed to the risk of punitive or exemplary damages.

Liability for Negligent Air Traffic Control

In early FTCA cases claiming ATC negligence, government attorneys argued that the government should not be liable because an air traffic controller's work is one continuous "discretionary function." The controller must continuously use judgment to issue heading vectors, altitudes, speed restrictions, and clearance limits to individual aircraft often having radically different performance capabilities, to avoid collisions and to make the entire mix of traffic being handled by that controller and receiving controllers downstream flow as smoothly as possible. The courts, however, rejected that argument, holding that what Congress intended by the discretionary function exception was to protect government and its *planners and policy makers* from being sued for the results of plans and policies that might later prove to have been unwise. The courts distinguished this from the admittedly high level of continuous judgment exercised by air traffic controllers, characterized by the courts as "mere operational details" not covered by the discretionary function exception. Thus, if the negligence of an air traffic controller employed by the federal government (there are some air traffic controllers at commercially operated air traffic control towers who are not federal employees) causes or contributes to an aircraft accident, the federal government may be held liable under the FTCA (Fig. 9.2).

Fig. 9.2. Most Federal Tort Claims Act cases involve claims of negligence on the part of air traffic controllers.

The "activities incident to military service" exception may also come into play in air traffic control cases if the person killed or injured was at the time engaged in an activity incident to military service. For example, imagine a military aircraft operating at night in clouds, receiving radar vectors from ATC. An ATC controller negligently vectors the aircraft into a mountain. The survivors of military personnel killed in the crash could not sue the federal government under the FTCA since they were aboard this flight incident to their military service. (They would not have been aboard the aircraft but for their military service.) If a similar accident occurred to a commercial airliner, passengers traveling under military orders would face the same bar. (But remember: This affects only the federal government's liability and has no bearing upon the liability of others whose negligence may have contributed to the crash such as the airline or aircraft manufacturer.)

In cases under the FTCA, government employees are held responsible to exercise the ordinary degree of care of the reasonably prudent person. In many ATC cases, the question of whether the controller carried out her duty may be resolved by reference to the *Air Traffic Controller's Handbook*, an FAA publication often referred to as the "controller's bible." The handbook instructs controllers how to handle most air traffic situations, even prescribing the exact phraseology to be used in most circumstances. For example, where a controller concluded a takeoff clearance with the phrase "watch the propwash," instead of giving the wake turbulence advisory specified in the handbook, and the departing aircraft encountered wake turbulence, lost control and crashed, the federal government was held liable for negligence under FTCA.

For situations not specifically addressed by the *Handbook*, the controller's actions would be subject to the ordinary negligence test: What would a reasonably prudent air traffic controller have done under the same circumstances? In that situation, the plaintiff's and the government's attorneys would offer the testimony of expert witnesses.

As in other negligence cases, the controller's negligence must have been a proximate cause of the accident for the government to be held liable. It is not enough that the crash occurred while the aircraft was under some measure of ATC control or even that a controller's performance was imperfect. Some negligence of controllers must have caused or contributed to cause the crash.

Liability for Weather-Related Accidents

At air traffic control facilities, federal employees monitor the weather, advise pilots and dispatchers of current and forecast weather, and often suggest alternate routing around severe weather. Where the government has undertaken to provide such services, its employees must do so in a reasonably careful manner. FAA Flight Service Stations (FSS) are now staffed by private sector employees of contractor Lockheed Martin, not covered by the FTCA.

Where federal employees significantly understated weather along a pilot's route, the federal government has been held liable. Examples include failing to report forecast icing conditions or understating their severity, reporting an incorrect altimeter setting, failing to report deteriorating runway visibility or braking action, or understating the severity of storms, as by reporting a known squall line as a "line of cells."

The FARs establish minimum visibility requirements for takeoff in commercial operations. No such takeoff minima are prescribed, however, for aircraft operating noncommercially under the general operating and flight rules of 14 CFR Part 91.

Although it is legal for controllers to issue clearances and for pilots of aircraft operating noncommercially to attempt to take off when visibility is below commercial minima, a takeoff attempt may still be imprudent. Despite the pervasiveness of the FARs, flying still requires pilots continuously to exercise their own judgment. Not every inadvisable action is specifically prohibited by an FAR (though in hindsight an act not specifically prohibited by an FAR may be deemed to have constituted careless or even reckless operation in violation of 14 CFR § 91.13).

Pilots should always bear in mind that just because a certain action is not specifically prohibited by the FARs, that does not necessarily mean that it's a good idea or would not be considered careless or reckless by the FAA or negligent by a jury. Crew fatigue, rusty instrument skills, questionable reliability of navigational avionics, or other variables may render imprudent an operation that would otherwise be considered routine. The pilot-in-command, bearing the ultimate responsibility for safety of the flight, constantly exercises judgment in the face of changing conditions. While the crew may never choose to ignore an FAR without fear of consequences both to their certificates and being found to be negligent per se, the fact that no FAR was violated is not proof that the crew was not negligent.

To the extent possible, the flight crew is responsible to consider not only the weather conditions reported to them but also their own observations. If the thunderstorm ahead is clearly visible to the crew by looking out the window or at the aircraft's on-board radar, Nexrad display, or lightning detector, the crew is obviously not justified in relying upon anyone else's assurance that the path ahead is clear. In such a situation, if the crew chooses to continue on that heading with catastrophic results, it is unlikely that the federal government's erroneous reporting of weather conditions ahead will be found a proximate cause of the accident since the true conditions were known to the crew. This is sometimes referred to as a *superseding* or *supervening cause.*

Comparative negligence concepts may also be applied in FTCA claims. For example: a Florida general aviation pilot operating his personal airplane on an IFR flight in IMC missed approaches at his primary and alternate airports, then crashed in a wooded area short of the runway at a third airport (Jacksonville International) on his third approach to that airport in heavy fog and was killed in the crash, along with his three passengers. When their families brought suit against the United States under the FTCA, the trial judge (plaintiffs are not entitled to a jury trial in FTCA cases) found that air traffic controllers were negligent in failing to provide the pilot weather information, but the pilot was also negligent in foregoing the options to retreat to an area where the weather was better, rather than persisting in repetitive approaches to airports in the same general area. Applying comparative negligence law, the court apportioned the liability, finding the negligence of the federal government 65% responsible for causing the accident and the pilot 35% responsible.

Liability for Negligent Airworthiness Certification

Each civil aircraft manufactured in the United States is the product of three separate FAA inspection and certification processes. First, the design must be proved to conform to aircraft certification standards contained in the FAR. At that point, the FAA will issue a Type Certificate approving the design. Second, the manufacturer must satisfy the FAA that its production and inspection methodology assures precise replication of the design for which the Type Certificate was issued, with each aircraft manufactured to acceptable standards of quality. The FAA issues the manufacturer a Production Type Certificate for the design once it is satisfied with the manufacturer's production facilities and quality assurance program, and manufacture can proceed. As each individual airplane is completed, it is inspected and tested for conformity with the approved type design and issued its own FAA Airworthiness Certificate before being delivered to the customer. Subsequent modifications and improvements to the design each require additional FAA certification, usually under a Supplemental Type Certificate or FAA Form 337 field approval. Negligence in any of these phases of certification may lead to liability of the federal government.

The FAA is shifting some of its present workload in this process to the manufacturers as they become certified as CDOs. It remains to be seen whether that shift will also relieve the federal government of FTCA liability for negligence by those CDOs in that process.

Where FAA written standards (such as those included in the FARs and internal agency orders and handbooks) exist, the courts have held that FAA employees engaged in the certification process are not performing a "discretionary function," because they do not have discretion to deviate from these written standards. Therefore, the federal government can be sued for negligence in certification of the aircraft under the FTCA. If, however, the government employee assured exact compliance with those written standards, it is unlikely that the government would be found negligent in certification of the aircraft because the rulemaking process by which those standards were developed would be considered a discretionary function.

In aircraft design and manufacture, much as in flight operations, FAA regulatory standards provide minima. On one hand, it is clearly both an FAR violation and negligence per se to certify as airworthy an aircraft that does not meet the FAA's standards. On the other hand, the fact that an aircraft design and a particular aircraft meet these published FAA technical standards does not bar a finding of negligence in design or manufacture or a finding that the aircraft was delivered in a dangerously defective condition. The manufacturer may still be found negligent or strictly liable for the consequences of an accident resulting from a design or manufacturing defect even if FAR standards were met.

Administrative Claim Prerequisite to Suit

Anyone seeking judicial relief for a wrong is required to first exhaust any administrative remedies the law provides. Under FTCA, a person is required to file an administrative claim for compensation with the federal government and await a decision on that claim before filing suit. If suit is filed before the claim is decided, the court will dismiss it.

9/11 Claims

The Victims Compensation Fund discussed in Chapters 1 and 8 has served to protect the United States from almost all litigation by victims of the terrorist attacks of September 11, 2001.

Personal Liability of Federal Employees

Unlike employees of private enterprise, individual federal employees enjoy protection from personal liability for the consequences of their on-the-job negligence. Federal law now provides that whenever a federal employee is sued personally for negligence in the performance of a federal job, the U.S. Attorney (the federal government's trial lawyer) will substitute the United States for the named employee as defendant, and defend the case in its own name. Any settlement or judgment will be paid by the federal government, not by the individual employee who may have been negligent. In private industry, both the employer and the employee can be held liable for the consequences of the employee's on-the-job negligence.

Federal employees enjoy a rare situation in American law in which a person does not face the risk of personal liability for his own negligence. This is a truly unique benefit of federal employment. That is not to say, however, that the agency cannot take administrative disciplinary action against the employee, including termination of employment.

State and Local Government Liability

State governments also enjoy the protection of the doctrine of sovereign immunity, though most if not all have adopted state legislation similar to FTCA, waiving that protection under certain circumstances. These state laws are not uniform, and vary widely.

10

Accident Notification, Reporting and Investigation

Every operator of business or commercial aircraft should have an accident response plan in place for guidance in the event of an aircraft accident. While using your best accident prevention efforts to avoid an accident, it would be imprudent to operate on the belief that your operation will never experience one.

The time immediately following an accident is one of the most stressful and chaotic periods the flight crew, maintenance personnel, and company management will ever experience. Yet statements made and actions taken in the minutes, hours, and days following the accident by all of those involved will have far-reaching consequences in many areas. These may include FAA enforcement actions against the operator, pilots, and mechanics involved; civil litigation and related questions of insurance coverage; and even criminal charges, as well as damage to the reputations of the company and individuals involved.

This time of stress, grief, and chaos immediately following an aircraft accident is the worst of all possible times to have to first address the question "What do we do now?"

This chapter lays out factors that should be considered in preparing that portion of your accident response plan that addresses what to do after the initial focus on rescue of survivors. The purpose of this chapter is to help you develop that portion of your accident response plan now, before the accident happens.

CONTROLLING THE RELEASE OF INFORMATION

After everything has been done to rescue survivors, focus should shift to securing and preserving the accident scene and wreckage and notifying those who must be notified in a timely manner, while assuring that any facts released are accurate. This damage containment effort is a necessary part of your overall risk-management plan.

Aircraft accidents excite people. Everyone wants to know what happened (especially news media determined to get "the scoop" first) and it may seem that everyone is asking at the same time. Everyone involved in the accident—and especially those most intimately involved, surviving flight crew—will be in some degree of shock, may feel overwhelming guilt and/or sadness, may have personal injuries, and will have the highest blood adrenaline level they've ever experienced. One effect of all this is a highly garrulous ("motor mouth") condition. It is in the nature of our training and personalities as pilots that whenever something goes wrong, we immediately start analyzing what went wrong and how we could have prevented it, and this process is certainly speeded up by the accident-induced adrenaline rush. The flight crew may have already arrived at one or more theories by the time they first encounter another person after the aircraft comes to a halt. Their theories are also more likely to be wrong, since speed generally decreases the accuracy of analysis (especially in a highly complex technical context such as an aircraft accident).

But the law bestows a special aura of truthfulness on *excited utterances* made by persons involved in the accident immediately after the accident. Anything you say at this point may be used later by the FAA, a plaintiff, or prosecuting attorney with devastating effect as an *admission against your interest* (and your employer's) in an FAA enforcement action, civil litigation, and even criminal prosecutions which may arise out of the accident. (In cases where criminal activity is suspected, the FBI may participate in the NTSB investigation and even, as in the 9/11 attacks, assume control of the investigation, with the NTSB providing requested technical support.)

Although it is rare in the United States, state or local prosecuting attorneys may even bring criminal charges (such as *murder* or *manslaughter*) against individual crewmembers or others whose conduct is believed to have led to the accident, seeking imprisonment. This happens more frequently in civil law countries, which tend to treat virtually all misbehavior as criminal and which usually do not have a system of negligence law intended to compensate victims. One recent example was Brazil's criminal prosecution of the American flight crew of a business jet that collided in flight with a commercial airliner (the business jet landed safely with damage while the airliner crashed with no survivors). Such prosecutorial behavior is, however, not unheard of in the United States, especially if the accident attracts a lot of public attention and the prosecutor is seeking reelection or higher office and believes the attendant publicity may help his prospects.

When improperly labeled oxygen generators shipped as air cargo started an in-flight fire that cost the lives of all passengers and crew aboard a ValuJet DC-9 in the Florida Everglades, criminal charges were filed against the shipper and several of its employees. (This accident and the outcomes of the numerous cases—administrative, civil and criminal—it generated is discussed in greater detail in Chapter 4.) For more on crimes relating to aviation, see also Chapter 15.

The media may be on the scene early and will diligently apply themselves to obtain every possible statement from crewmembers, other survivors, rescue personnel, and other witnesses. That is their job. Unfortunately, the popular press is notorious for failing to understand or accurately report the facts in aviation accidents, for lack of the most rudimentary technical knowledge. For example, if the pilot is heard to say: "the airplane stalled," this will most assuredly be erroneously translated by the media into a report that "the airplane's engine stalled."

Thus, your accident response plan should initially focus on precluding people under your influence or control, such as employees, from making any initial statements about what happened, then assuring that only verified facts, *not speculation*, are released.

As a lawyer who has had on more than one occasion to focus on controlling damages to aircraft operator clients resulting from an accident, I prefer that clients not *unnecessarily* notify or give statements to anyone and that required notices and reports be given no sooner and in no greater detail than required. But as an observant person, I must also acknowledge that appearing to "stonewall" the news media by refusing to discuss the matter ("no comment")—or even worse, disseminating information that later proves false—may have a devastating effect on public confidence in the aircraft operator or manufacturer. Hopefully, your company will have the assistance of individuals trained and skilled in public relations to assist in the development of that portion of your accident response plan addressing who is to respond to the news media, when and how, and to manage that response when the time comes.

One appropriate way to handle the inevitable barrage of news media inquiries without unduly offending the media is to patiently respond to each inquiry with a simple statement such as: "the accident is being investigated by the National Transportation Safety Board, who are the federal government's experts in aircraft accident investigation and who will determine the probable cause." Refer all inquiries to the NTSB. Do not allow persistent reporters to draw you into speculating on what happened.

NOTIFICATIONS AND REPORTS REQUIRED

In the event of an accident, do not file an Aviation Safety Report with NASA. As we saw in Chapter 2, NASA report immunity benefits do not apply if an aircraft accident was involved. If NASA receives a report of an aircraft accident, the report is not held in confidentiality but immediately forwarded to the NTSB, where it becomes a matter of public record that can then be used against you in FAA enforcement and civil litigation.

Your accident response plan should designate a specific person or office in the company to be notified first in the event of an accident and a person to whom all inquiries about that accident are to be directed. This enables the company to put its accident response plan into effect immediately.

You are not required to report accidents or incidents to the FAA, nor are you required to notify the NTSB of *every* mishap involving an aircraft. Because a report may trigger FAA enforcement action (FAA and NTSB personnel do talk to each other) and may provide evidence that can be used against you in related FAA enforcement cases and in civil litigation, the NTSB should be notified and written reports filed *only* when required by law.

The operator of a *civil aircraft* (including a *public aircraft*, operated by a federal or state agency) is required by law to *notify* the nearest NTSB field office *immediately and by the most expeditious means available* (usually the telephone) when there is an aircraft accident or certain other types of incidents. The operator is required to file a *written report* with the NTSB on a form provided by the board within ten days after an *accident*, but only if requested by the board for one of the *incidents* for which notice is required.

Crewmembers are required to attach a statement setting forth the facts, conditions, and circumstances of the accident or incident at the same time if they are physically able. Crewmembers who are incapacitated at that time are required to submit such a statement as soon as they are able.

The reference determining whether an aircraft mishap requires immediate notification and reporting is NTSB Part 830, Notification and Reporting of Aircraft Accidents or Incidents and Overdue Aircraft, and Preservation of Aircraft Wreckage, Mail, Cargo and Records (found in Title 49 of the Code of Federal Regulations). Under those regulations, the aircraft operator is required to give the NTSB immediate notice of an aircraft accident or certain specific incidents.

Accidents

To determine whether notice is required, the operator, in consultation with her attorney, must first determine whether the mishap is an *aircraft accident* within NTSB definitions:

> *Aircraft accident* means an occurrence associated with the operation of an aircraft which takes place between the time any person boards the aircraft with the intention of flight and all such persons have disembarked, and in which any person suffers death or serious injury, or in which the aircraft receives substantial damage.

Thus, if an aircraft undergoing inspection slipped off a jack and killed or injured a mechanic working under it, NTSB notification would not be required. Neither would notification be required if an unoccupied aircraft was blown over in a windstorm or damaged by a service vehicle. Nor is notification required if the aircraft was in operation (or at least passengers or crew were aboard intending to fly) but no one was killed or seriously injured and the aircraft did not receive substantial damage. The latter situation, however, requires that we consult more NTSB definitions. What is *serious injury*? What is *substantial damage*?

> *Serious injury* means any injury which: (1) Requires hospitalization for more than 48 hours commencing within 7 days from the date the injury was received; (2) results in a fracture of any bone (except simple fractures of fingers, toes, or nose); (3) causes severe hemor-

rhages, nerve, muscle, or tendon damage; (4) involves any internal organ; or (5) involves second- or third-degree burns, or any burns affecting more than 5 percent of the body surface.

Thus, simple cuts and bruises, broken noses, fingers, and toes not requiring hospitalization for more than forty-eight hours are not serious injuries.

Substantial damage means damage or failure which adversely affects the structural strength, performance, or flight characteristics of the aircraft, and which would normally require major repair or replacement of the affected component. Engine failure or damage limited to an engine if only one engine fails or is damaged, bent fairings or cowling, dented skin, small punctured holes in the skin or fabric, ground damage, damage to rotor or propeller blades, and damage to landing gear, wheels, tires, flaps, engine accessories, brakes or wingtips are *not* (emphasis supplied) considered "substantial damage" for the purpose of this part.

The second sentence of this definition serves to exclude many gear-up and other landing mishaps that have not caused serious injury.

Incidents

If the mishap was not an *accident* under the above definitions, you must next determine whether it is one of the specific *incidents* that require immediate notice to the NTSB. By NTSB definition:

Incident means an occurrence other than an accident, associated with the operation of an aircraft, which affects or could affect the safety of operations.

You are not, however, required to notify the NTSB of all incidents. You are required to notify the NTSB *only* if:

An aircraft accident or any of the following serious incidents occur—
1. Flight control system malfunction or failure;
2. Inability of any required flight crew member to perform normal flight duties as a result of injury or illness;
3. Failure of any internal turbine engine component that results in the escape of debris other then out the exhaust path;
4. In-flight fire;
5. Aircraft collision in flight.

6. Damage to property, other than the aircraft, estimated to exceed $25,000 to repair (including materials and labor) or fair market value in the event of a total loss, whichever is less.

7. For large multiengine aircraft (more than 12,500 pounds maximum certificated takeoff weight):

    i. In-flight failure of electrical systems which requires the sustained use of an emergency bus powered by a back-up source such as a battery, auxiliary power unit, or air-driven generator to retain flight control or essential instrument.

    ii. In-flight failure of hydraulic systems that results in sustained reliance on the sole remaining hydraulic or mechanical system for movement of flight control surfaces;

    iii. Sustained loss of the power or thrust produced by two or more engines; and

    iv. An evacuation of an aircraft in which an emergency egress system is utilized.

8. Release of all or a portion of a propeller blade from an aircraft, excluding release caused solely by ground contact.

9. A complete loss of information, excluding flickering, from more than 50 percent of an aircraft's cockpit displays known as:

    i. Electronic Flight Instrument System (EFIS) displays;

    ii. Engine Indication and Crew Alerting System (EICAS) displays;

    iii. Electronic Centralized Aircraft Monitor (ECAM) displays; or

    iv. Other displays of this type, which generally include a primary flight display (PFD), primary navigation display (PND), and other integrated displays.

10. Airborne Collision and Avoidance System (ACAS) resolution advisories issued either:

    i. When an aircraft is being operated on an instrument flight rules flight plan and compliance with the advisory is necessary to avert a substantial risk of collision between two or more aircraft; or

    ii. To an aircraft operating in Class A airspace.

11. Damage to helicopter tail or main rotor blades, including ground damage, that requires major repair or replacement of the blade(s).

12. Any event in which an aircraft operated by an air carrier:

    i. Lands or departs on a taxiway, incorrect runway, or other area not designated as a runway; or

ii. Experiences a runway incursion that requires the operator or the crew of another aircraft or vehicle to take immediate corrective action to avoid a collision.

13. An aircraft is overdue and believed to have been involved in an accident.

The initial notification *to* the NTSB should contain no more information than is required. The only information that is required to be given, if available, in the initial notification is:

a. Type, nationality, and registration marks of the aircraft;
b. Name of owner, and operator of the aircraft;
c. Name of the pilot-in-command;
d. Date and time of the accident;
e. Last point of departure and point of intended landing of the aircraft;
f. Position of the aircraft with reference to some easily defined geographical point;
g. Number of persons aboard, number killed, and number seriously injured;
h. Nature of the accident, the weather, and the extent of damage to the aircraft, so far as is known; and
i. A description of any explosives, radioactive materials, or other dangerous articles carried.

If the aircraft accident or incident is one requiring immediate notice to the NTSB, shortly after you give the required notice you will receive from the board the forms for submitting any required written reports. The aircraft operator is required to file the written report within ten days after an *accident*, but is only required to file a written report for an *incident* if the incident is one of those listed above and then only if requested by the board. Both the initial notification and the subsequent written notice should be directed to the nearest NTSB field office. NTSB field offices are listed under U.S. Government in the telephone directories in the following cities: Anchorage, Alaska; Atlanta, Georgia; West Chicago, Illinois; Denver, Colorado; Arlington, Texas; Gardena (Los Angeles), California; Miami, Florida; Parsippany, NJ (metropolitan New York, New York); Seattle, Washington; and Washington, D.C.

If the accident occurs outside the United States, notification and reporting requirements and definitions of accidents and incidents may be different. Notification of NTSB-equivalent officials of the country in which the accident or incident occurred is required under international agreements as well as local law. Operating company and crew are bound to abide by the laws of the country in which they are operating. Failure to comply with foreign local law can antagonize foreign governments, aircraft accident investigators, and law enforcement officers, having an adverse effect not only on the accident investigation, but also on the legal consequences to the operator and crew and the operator's welcome to continue operating in that nation. ICAO Annex 13, International Standards and Recommended Practices of Aircraft Accident Investigation, provides the general framework for aircraft accident investigations worldwide. Some nations take exception to some particular provisions, but Annex 13 is a good frame of reference for what to expect in the conduct of aircraft accident investigations globally.

Regardless of the location of the accident, flight crew who are members of a union should immediately notify their union of the accident. Union personnel can be of tremendous assistance in diplomatically protecting crewmembers from the press and preventing uncontrolled release of rumors, speculation, potentially damaging admissions, and inaccurate statements of fact. The Air Line Pilots Association (ALPA) wallet card of immediate post-accident advice is reproduced here as Figure 10.1 (*see* next page).

The operator's aircraft insurance policy must be consulted to determine the required time and procedure for reporting the accident to the insurer.

Some Techniques That Work

If a crewmember requires hospitalization, she will probably be on some form of pain medication, which may cloud her thought processes. Upon request, most hospitals will insure that the press and FAA and NTSB investigators are denied access to a crewmember while she is in the hospital.

Even though crewmembers may not appear to have suffered physical injuries that require hospitalization, they are certain to be in some degree of shock that may mask symptoms. Checking them into the hospital with instructions to hospital staff to restrict access can be helpful both to ensure their health and to protect them from interrogators. While the crewmembers are obligated to cooperate in the NTSB investigation, they should not be required to do so until it has been determined that they are

**WORLD-WIDE
ALPA HOT LINE**

USA (202) **797-4180**

CALL THIS NUMBER IMMEDIATELY
IF YOU ARE INVOLVED IN AN
ACCIDENT/SERIOUS INCIDENT
AT ANYPLACE OR ANYTIME
(COLLECT CALLS ACCEPTED)

*For any other safety related problem, call the
ALPA Engineering and Air Safety Department
TOLL FREE at 800-424-2470.*

ALPA PILOTS' SAFETY GUIDE

In the U.S. there is no legal compulsion for a pilot to give a
statement to the FAA or the NTSB or any other public authority concerning an incident or accident unless he is served
with a subpoena. Therefore, it is recommended that you
make no statements and accomplish the following, if possible:

1. Keep the crew together.
2. Obtain rest facilities *for ALL* crewmembers away from the
airport.
3. MAKE NO STATEMENTS ABOUT THE NATURE OF THE
DIFFICULTY.
4. Refer to the back of the ALPA membership card for your
rights of representation.

Outside the U.S. accident investigation procedures vary
greatly. In the event of an accident in a foreign country, you
are urged to call the Hot Line Number immediately and to
follow the above steps to the extent possible.

Fig. 10.1. ALPA
wallet card.

physically and mentally competent to answer questions in an intelligent
manner. Crewmembers should not be questioned if under the influence
of medication or the predictable wave of shock and guilt that inevitably
washes over them immediately following the accident. Crewmembers
should also refrain from making statements to medical personnel about
the cause or details of the accident, as these may be recorded in medical records and later afforded the special aura of truthfulness of excited
utterances, even if they're wrong.

Crewmembers should also be reminded, as discussed in Chapter 2
on FAA enforcement, that although they are required to show their
certificates to FAA inspectors or other law enforcement personnel on
request, they must be on their guard never to relinquish their certificates. Crewmembers should be cautioned to refrain from making any
statements to the FAA.

Once crewmembers are released from the hospital, if circumstances
require that they remain in the area, it may be prudent to check them
into a local hotel or motel as unobtrusively as possible under assumed

names. If they are allowed to return home, it may be worthwhile to arrange for the telephone company to provide crewmembers with a temporary unlisted number.

If the NTSB conducts an informal inquiry during the on-site phase of the accident investigation, the crewmembers should insist that the FAA representatives agree in writing that nothing the pilots say during the inquiry will be used against them in an enforcement action. If the FAA refuses to agree, the crewmembers may request that the FAA representatives be excluded from the informal inquiry.

Most airlines paint their logo on the vertical tail of every aircraft and their name along the top of the fuselage. In the most disastrous aircraft accidents, the tail is often the only identifiable portion of the aircraft remaining. To minimize the adverse psychological effect of airline travelers seeing the company's logo thus displayed in the inevitable long-running news coverage of the accident, some airlines have been known to paint over the name and logo as soon as the NTSB investigator in charge will permit.

Accident Response Plans

Aircraft accidents always expose the companies and individuals involved to the possibility of FAA enforcement actions, civil litigation, damaged reputations, and even criminal charges. Preparation and dissemination of an accident response plan and following that plan carefully can help control these adverse consequences. Excellent examples include the *Corporate Aircraft Accident Response Plan* published by the United States Aircraft Insurance Group (USAIG), available at: *http://www.usau. com/usau.nsf/doc/CorporateAccidentResponsePlan.pdf* and the *Emergency Response Manual* published by the Air Charter Safety Foundation (ACSF) (*http://www.acsf.aero*).

NTSB Family Support Services

The NTSB has received additional tasking from Congress to serve as the coordinator to integrate the resources of the federal government and other organizations (such as the American Red Cross) to support the efforts of state and local governments and the airlines to meet the needs of airline disaster victims and their families. Family counseling, victim identification and forensic services, communicating with foreign governments, and translation services are among the federal services the

NTSB can make available to help local authorities and airlines deal with a major airline disaster. In these disasters, a Joint Family Support Operations Center (JFSOC) is now routinely established under the NTSB's Federal Family Assistance Plan for Aviation Disasters to coordinate support to affected families.

PART III
AIRCRAFT TRANSACTIONS

11

Buying and Selling Aircraft

In my experience, most litigation over aircraft purchases arises because (1) the buyer and seller did not come to a clear agreement on all aspects of the transaction and failed to properly document the deal, particularly the aircraft's condition, (2) the buyer failed to commission an adequate prepurchase inspection and title search before buying the aircraft, and/or (3) the transaction was not properly documented and recorded with the FAA Aircraft Registry and the new International Registry.

State law largely governs the buying and selling of aircraft, with federal law only peripherally involved. Generally speaking, all sales and financing of products, including aircraft and aircraft components, are governed by state law. Fortunately, the law of all fifty states is now virtually identical in this area since all have adopted the Uniform Commercial Code (UCC) with few or no modifications. The UCC provides, however, that where a federal statute provides a system for recording documents of ownership and security interests in a specific class of products, federal law prevails. This is the case with aircraft under the Federal Aviation Act of 1958, as amended. As we saw in Chapter 1, the FAA Aircraft Registry in Oklahoma City maintains records showing the entire history of ownership and other legal interests in all aircraft of U.S. registry (that is, all aircraft having an N-number).

The UCC regulates business almost as pervasively as the FARs regulate aviation safety. The UCC is usually intensely studied in college-level business law courses. Because of the pervasive effect of the UCC on all business transactions, including aviation (and because in my observation more aviation businesses fail as a result of poor business practices than from poor aviating), I recommend that all students supplement this aviation law course with a business law course.

The sale of an aircraft raises legal considerations not only for the buyer and seller but also for any lender who may be financing the purchase for the buyer and any person or business that may already hold a security interest in the aircraft.

If you are the buyer, you want to know:

1. What am I really buying?
2. What are my legal rights if the aircraft turns out to be a lemon?
3. Am I getting clear title to the aircraft? (Fig. 11.1.)

State law governs the first two questions, as the law of *warranty* is covered by the UCC. The third question, governed by the law of *security interests*, is answered partly by reference to state law under the UCC and partly by federal law under the Federal Aviation Act.

From the seller's point of view, there are also warranty law considerations in selling an aircraft. Sellers want to know the nature and extent of their legal liability if the buyer later becomes unhappy with the airplane and suffers a condition lawyers refer to as "buyer's remorse."

Fig. 11.1. If you buy it, will you get clear title?

A lending institution (bank or finance company) financing a portion of the purchase price for the buyer will be concerned with these basic questions:

1. How can we assure that we will get paid, no matter what may happen to the aircraft in the future?
2. Will we have any exposure to being held liable if the aircraft is involved in an accident?

In this chapter, we will examine state, federal, and international law relating to these basic concerns of people in businesses buying, selling, and financing aircraft.

SECURITY INTERESTS

A *security interest* is a legal interest in an item of personal property that secures the payment of a debt. A person or business may acquire a security interest in an aircraft by loaning money to the purchaser and obtaining a written *security agreement* (Fig. 11.2) signed by the purchaser, by performing work or furnishing goods or services to the aircraft (*mechanics' and materialmen's liens or artisans' liens*), or by providing storage for the aircraft (*warehousemen's liens*).

If the aircraft owner does not pay the debt when due, the holder of a security interest has the right to take possession of the aircraft (or to retain possession, as in the case of a repair station that has completed an inspection, repair, servicing or modification of the aircraft but not yet received payment), even without resorting to judicial process, so long as this can be done without provoking a breach of the peace.

Thus, a security interest can be considered an exception to the tort law of conversion (discussed in Chapter 4). Indeed, the aviation industry has "repo men" who earn their livelihood by traveling around the country repossessing aircraft for unpaid holders of security interests (also referred to as *lienholders*). Like their counterparts in the automotive world, these people rely on stealth and speed to take the aircraft and spirit it away, often in the middle of the night, sometimes using bolt cutters to free locked tie-down chains or to gain entry to hangars. As long as the repossessor can get the airplane without a fistfight or shoot-out, the taking is legal in most states. It is obviously of great interest to buyers and lenders to ensure that the aircraft being purchased is not already subject to some unsatisfied security interest that might lead to the unhappy surprise of its being taken in a midnight repossession.

DEPARTMENT OF TRANSPORTATION
FEDERAL AVIATION ADMINISTRATION
CIVIL AVIATION REGISTRY
AIRCRAFT REGISTRATION BRANCH
P. O. Box 25504
Oklahoma City, Oklahoma 73125
AIRCRAFT SECURITY AGREEMENT

OMB Control No.2120-0042
08/31/2008

NAME & ADDRESS OF DEBTOR

NAME & ADDRESS OF SECURED PARTY/ASSIGNOR

ASSIGNED/NAME & ADDRESS OF ASSIGNEE

ABOVE SPACE
FOR FAA USE ONLY

Date: _____

A security interest is hereby granted to the secured party on the following described collateral:
AIRCRAFT (FAA registration number, manufacturer, model, and serial number):

NOTICE: ENGINES LESS THAN 750 HORSEPOWER AND PROPELLERS NOT CAPABLE OF ABSORBING 750 OR MORE RATED SHAFT HORSEPOWER ARE NOT ELIGIBLE FOR RECORDING.
ENGINES (manufacturer, model, and serial number):

PROPELLERS (manufacturer, model, and serial number):

SPARE PARTS LOCATIONS (air carrier's name, city, and state):

together with all equipment and accessories attached thereto or used in connection therewith, including engines of _____ horsepower, or the equivalent, and propellers capable of absorbing _____ rated takeoff shaft horsepower, described above, all of which are included in the term aircraft as used herein.
The above described aircraft is hereby mortgaged to the secured party for the purpose of securing in the order named:
FIRST: The payment of all indebtedness evidenced by and according to the terms of that certain promissory note, herein below described, and all renewals and extensions thereof.

Note bearing date of _____ executed by the debtor and payable to the order of _____ in the aggregate

sum of $ _____ with interest thereon at the rate of _____ per centum per annum, from date, payable in installments as follows:

The principal and interest of said note is payable in _____ installments of $_____ each on the _____ day of each successive month

beginning with the _____ day of _____ . The last payment of $_____ is due on the _____ day of _____ .

SECOND: The prompt and faithful discharge and performance of each agreement of the debtor herein contained made with or for the benefit of the secured party in connection with the indebtedness to secure which this instrument is executed, and the repayment of any sums expended or advanced by the secured party for the maintenance or preservation of the property mortgaged hereby or in enforcing their rights hereunder. Said debtor hereby declares and hereby warrants to the said secured party that they are the absolute owner of the legal and beneficial title to the said aircraft and in possession thereof, and that the same is free and clear of all liens, encumbrances, and adverse claims whatsoever, except as follows: (If no liens other than this mortgage, indicate "none".)

AC Form 8050-98(7/00)

Fig. 11.2. FAA aircraft security agreement form.

Perfection and Priority

Except for aircraft and engines covered by the Cape Town Treaty discussed below, filing the security agreement with the FAA Aircraft Registry perfects a nonpossessory security interest in an aircraft. If a lienholder who is not in possession of the aircraft fails to record a security

It is the intention of the parties to deliver this instrument in the state of _____.

Provided, however, that if the debtor, their heirs, administrators, successors, or assignees shall pay said note and the interest thereon in accordance with the terms thereof and shall keep and perform all and singular the terms, covenants, and agreements in this security agreement, then this security agreement shall be null and void.

Time is of the essence of this security agreement. It is hereby agreed that, if default be made in the payment of any part of the principal or interest of the promissory note secured hereby at the time and in the manner therein specified, or if any breach be made of any obligation or promise of the debtor herein contained or secured hereby, or if any or all of the property covered hereby be hereafter sold, leased, transferred, mortgaged, or otherwise encumbered without the written consent of the secured party may deem himself insecure, then the whole principal sum unpaid upon said promissory note, with the interest accrued thereon, or advanced under the terms of this security agreement, or secured thereby, and the interest thereon shall immediately become due and payable at the option of the secured party.

Upon default, secured party may at once proceed to foreclose this mortgage in any manner provided by law, or the secured party may at its option, and they are hereby empowered so to do, with or without foreclosure action, enter upon the premises where the said aircraft may be and take possession thereof; and remove and sell and dispose of the same at public or private sale, and from the proceeds of such sale retain all costs and charges incurred by secured party in the taking or sale of said aircraft, including any reasonable attorney's fees incurred; also all sums due him on said promissory note, under any provisions thereof, or advanced under the terms of this security, and interest thereon, or due or owing to the said secured party, under any provisions of this security agreement, or secured hereby, with the interest thereon, and any surplus of such proceeds remaining shall be paid to the debtor, or whoever may be lawfully entitled to receive the same. If a deficiency occurs, the debtor agrees to pay such deficiency forthwith.

Said secured party or his agent may bid and purchase at any sale made under this mortgage or herein authorized, or at any sale made upon foreclosure of this security agreement.

In witness whereof, the debtor has hereunto set _____ hand and seal on the day and year first above written.

ACKNOWLEDGMENT: NAME OF DEBTOR _____
(If required by applicable local law)

                                  SIGNATURE(S) (IN INK) _____
                                                   (If executed for co-ownership, all must sign)

                                  TITLE _____
                                                (If signed for a corporation, partnership, owner, or agent)

ASSIGNMENT BY SECURED PARTY

For value received, the undersigned secured party does hereby sell, assign, and transfer all right, title, and interest in and to the foregoing note and security agreement and the aircraft covered thereby, unto the assignee named on the face of this instrument at the address given, and hereby authorizes the said assignee to do every act and thing necessary to collect and discharge the same. The undersigned secured party warrants and agrees to defend the title of said aircraft hereby conveyed against all lawful claims and demands except the rights of the maker. The undersigned secured party warrants that the secured party is the owner of a valid security interest in the said aircraft. (A Guaranty Clause or any other provisions which the parties are desirous of making a part of this assignment should be included in the following space.)

Dated this _____ day of _____.

ACKNOWLEDGMENT: NAME OF SECURED PARTY (ASSIGNOR) _____
(If required by applicable local law)

                                    SIGNATURE(S) (IN INK) _____
                                                   (If executed for co-ownership, all must sign)

                                  TITLE _____
                                                (If signed for a corporation, partnership, owner, or agent)

THIS FORM IS ONLY INTENDED TO BE A SUGGESTED FORM OF SECURITY AGREEMENT WHICH MEETS THE RECORDING REQUIREMENTS OF TITLE 49, UNITED STATES CODE, AND THE REGULATIONS ISSUED THEREUNDER. IN ADDITION TO THESE REQUIREMENTS, THE FORM OF SECURITY AGREEMENT SHOULD BE DRAFTED IN ACCORDANCE WITH THE PERTINENT PROVISIONS OF LOCAL STATUTES AND OTHER APPLICABLE FEDERAL STATUTES. THIS FORM MAY BE REPRODUCED.

SEND, WITH APPROPRIATE FEE, TO: AIRCRAFT REGISTRATION BRANCH
                                           P.O. BOX 25504
                                         OKLAHOMA CITY, OKLAHOMA 73125-0504

AC Form 8050-98(7/00)

Fig. 11.2. (Continued.)

agreement with the FAA Aircraft Registry, a buyer who is not otherwise aware of that security interest (a *good faith purchaser without notice*) takes clear title, and the lienholder's security interest is unenforceable.

Sometimes there may be several security interests in an aircraft, having a total value that may even exceed the value of the aircraft. In such a case, if the aircraft owner is unable or unwilling to pay these debts, the question of *priority* among the holders of these security interests becomes important. Any unpaid lienholder may repossess the aircraft and dispose of it in accordance with general procedures set forth in the UCC.

The Code permits the sale of the aircraft in virtually any commercially reasonable manner, with notice of the sale to the aircraft's registered owner required before the sale can take place. If the proceeds of that sale are greater than the total of all possessory and recorded security interests, all lienholders receive the entire amounts they are still owed, and the surplus is then paid to the aircraft's pre-repossession owner. But if the proceeds of the sale are insufficient to satisfy all debts owed to lienholders, the following *order of priority* applies:

1. The person having *possession* of the aircraft under a possessory lien for parts, labor, materials, or services has first priority and is entitled to be paid in full from the proceeds of the sale before any other lienholder. This is an example of the old adage "possession is nine-tenths of the law."

2. As between the holders of *recorded* security interests (those who have filed documents with the FAA Aircraft Registry reflecting their security interests in the aircraft) priority runs from the date and time of *filing*, the rule being "first in time, first in right." Thus, after any possessory lienholder is paid in full, the earliest lienholder of record is entitled to be paid in full before the next, and so on down the line until the proceeds of the sale are exhausted.

Release of Liens

The prudent FBO, mechanic, or repair station will not release an aircraft after it has been worked on, stored, or fueled unless first paid by credit card, cash, or certified funds (a certified or cashier's check). However, if for some reason the business wishes (as to accommodate a long-time good customer claiming a temporary cash shortage), it may have the aircraft owner sign a promissory note for the amount due, secured by a security agreement, giving the creditor a security interest in the aircraft. Those documents should then be immediately filed with the FAA Aircraft Registry. If the aircraft is released without these, the lien is extinguished, but by following this procedure, the lien is preserved (although at a lower priority, behind other previously recorded security interests).

If the existence of an unsatisfied security interest (either recorded or possessory) is revealed by the title search or inquiry at the FBO, that does not necessarily mean that the purchaser should abandon plans to purchase the aircraft. The purchaser need only ensure that such lienholders are paid out of the proceeds of the sale and provide the buyer a *lien release*, which can then be filed with the FAA Aircraft Registry to clear that security interest off the aircraft's records.

CAPE TOWN TREATY—ADDITIONAL FILING REQUIREMENTS

Effective March 1, 2006, the Cape Town Treaty, formally titled *The Cape Town Convention on International Interests in Mobile Equipment* and its related *Protocol on Matters Specific to Aircraft Equipment* created the International Registry of Mobile Assets ("International Registry") and added additional filing requirements for security interests and leases in certain aircraft and components. The International Registry, although physically located in Dublin, Ireland, operates entirely via secured transactions online, existing for all practical purposes only in cyberspace and operating 24 hours a day, 7 days a week, and 365 days a year. Intended to facilitate financing and reduce financing costs for international aircraft transactions, the treaty creates an international legal process for repossession that enables a secured lender, following a default, to deregister the aircraft and obtain its export from a country that has ratified the treaty; to take possession or control of the aircraft or sell or grant a lease of the aircraft; and to collect and receive income or profits from the management or use of the aircraft.

Applicability

The treaty applies to interests in certain airframes, aircraft engines, and helicopters as well as railway rolling stock and space assets. *"Aircraft Objects"* covered by treaty requirements include only:

1. Airframes that are certified to carry at least eight persons (including crew) or over 2,750 kg (6,063 lbs) of cargo,
2. Helicopters that are certified to carry at least 5 persons (including crew) or over 450 kg (992 lbs) of cargo, and
3. Jet engines having at least 1,750 lbs of thrust and turbine or piston engines having at least 550 rated shaft horsepower.

For such aircraft and engines, the treaty's filing and registration requirements are not limited to international transactions, but apply to domestic transactions within the U.S., as well, where they augment FAA Aircraft Registry registration and filing requirements as an add-on. These requirements are not retroactive, applying only to transactions occurring on or after the treaty's effective date. There is no need to register transactions that occurred before that date with the International Registry and in fact the registry precludes that possibility.

Interests that can be registered under the treaty include security agreements, conditional sales contracts, a lessor's interest under a lease, assignments, bills of sale, subordination agreements, and subrogation agreements, along with amendments, discharges (terminations and releases), and extensions of any of these. Curiously, the treaty also allows registration of *prospective interests*, such as a transaction to accomplish any such listed interest that has not yet closed.

Perfection

Interests in aircraft and engines covered by the treaty are perfected by filing, but it is a two-step process requiring filing the documentation first with the FAA Aircraft Registry, and then with the International Registry. The International Registry will not accept documents not first filed with the FAA.

Priority

For aircraft and engines covered by the treaty, whoever registers their interest with the International Registry first has priority over all other interests. Thus, for example, a lender that files its security agreement with the FAA but fails to also register it with the International Registry risks losing its priority to a subsequent creditor that registered its interest with the International Registry, even if the subsequent creditor was aware of the prior lien. A prospective interest filed with the International Registry is effective from the date of filing, so long as the transaction is later completed.

Searching the International Registry

Purchasers of aircraft and engines covered by the treaty should search both the FAA Aircraft Registry and the International Registry to determine existing ownership and other legal interests, if any, in the property. In order to perform a search of the International Registry, a person must first obtain a *priority search certificate* from the registry for the particular aircraft or engine that is the subject of the inquiry. Title search companies routinely perform searches of both registries for their clients.

Release of Liens from the International Registry

As with perfection, the filing of releases is a two-step process, requiring filing with both the FAA and international registries.

WARRANTIES

A *warranty* is a statement or representation made by the seller regarding year of manufacture, make and model, equipment, condition, and title. State law under the UCC governs warranties. The UCC provides for two categories of warranties: *express warranties* and *implied warranties.*

Express Warranties

Express warranties are not required to be expressed in writing but may be created by oral representations made by the seller to the buyer during the course of negotiating the sale and need not be in any particular form. The UCC has the following to say about how an express warranty is created:

1. Express warranties by the seller are created as follows:
   a. Any *affirmation of fact or promise* made by the seller to the buyer *which relates to the goods and becomes a part of the basis of the bargain* creates an express warranty that the goods shall conform to the assignation or promise.
   b. Any *description of the goods* which is *made part of the basis of the bargain* creates an express warranty that the goods shall conform to the description.
   c. Any *example or model* which is *made part of the basis of the bargain* creates an express warranty that the whole of the goods shall conform to the sample or model.
2. It is not necessary to the creation of an express warranty that the seller use formal words such as "warrant" or "guarantee" or that he have a specific intention to make a warranty, but an affirmation merely of the value of the goods or a statement purporting to be merely the seller's opinion or commendation of the goods does not create a warranty.

Let's consider some examples of the creation of express warranties. In negotiating the sale of a used general aviation light twin-engine aircraft, the seller shows the prospective buyer the engine logbooks, which indicate that both engines have received major overhauls only 70 hours previously. This can be seen as both an *affirmation of fact* and a *description of the goods* that creates an express warranty that the engines have so recently benefited from such an overhaul. If the buyer inquires about the oil consumption of these engines and the seller states that he just returned from a long cross-country trip in the airplane and it did not burn any oil, this may also constitute an affirmation of fact creating an express warranty as to the low oil consumption. If the seller agrees to deliver the aircraft with a currently effective FAA Airworthiness Certificate, this can be seen as a promise or description of the goods expressly warranting that all FAR-mandated inspections are current and all ADs have been complied with.

If the aircraft is purchased based upon examination of a manufacturer or dealer's demonstrator model, the seller expressly warrants that the aircraft delivered will be identical to that demonstrator model, except as otherwise agreed between the buyer and seller.

Not everything the seller says about the airplane creates an express warranty. Some laudatory hyperbole is considered by the law *"mere commercial puffery"* that does not create a warranty. Examples would be statements like: "It's a great little airplane; you won't find a better one anywhere" or "It was owned by a little old lady who only flew it to church on Sundays" or "It's a fantastic bargain that won't be here long at this price; another guy just left to meet with his banker and if he gets back first with the money, it's his."

Although the UCC does not require that the seller's statements be put in writing to create express warranties, this is another one of those situations where it is prudent to call upon your lawyer to put the purchase contract, clearly expressing the warranties, in writing. Then if a dispute should later arise, the document is clear proof of what was agreed. Otherwise, you should not be surprised if the seller's recollection of the discussions differs from your own, and it may require the expense, exasperation, and unpredictability of a trial where a jury decides which of you is telling the truth to resolve the controversy. Have *your* lawyer draft the agreement; don't succumb to the temptation to save a little money by using a standard form offered by the other party to the transaction or one drafted by their lawyer. There is no such thing as a generic "fair" or "standard" aircraft purchase contract, and the contract I drafted when representing a seller was typically very different from the one I drafted when representing the buyer. If both sides use attorneys, then an agreement acceptable to both sides will surely be achieved (if it cannot, you may be better off not going through with the deal). Whether the other side uses their lawyer or not, you should always use yours.

Implied Warranties

The UCC also provides for implied warranties in certain circumstances. The two kinds of implied warranties under the UCC are an implied warranty of *merchantability* and an implied warranty of *fitness for a particular purpose.*

Implied Warranty of Merchantability

The UCC provides that unless specifically excluded (more on this shortly), the law implies a warranty that a product is "merchantable" *if the seller is a merchant with respect to goods of that kind* (that is, if the seller is in the business of selling aircraft, whether full-time or part-time). The law does not imply a warranty of merchantability if the sale is between private parties not in the business of selling aircraft. To be *merchantable,* the product must be, in the language of the UCC, "*fit for the ordinary purposes for which such goods are used.*" In other words, an aircraft must be fit for flight; it must be airworthy.

While the FARs do not define "airworthy," the NTSB and the courts have held this word to mean a great deal more than simply that the aircraft is capable of flight. To be airworthy, an aircraft must be in its original or properly altered (in accordance with the FARs) condition, as verified by the logbooks (Fig. 11.3).

Fig. 11.3. The fact that it will fly is not proof that an aircraft is airworthy. To be deemed legally airworthy, an aircraft must be in its original or properly altered condition, as verified by its logbooks and maintenance records.

Implied Warranty of Fitness for a Particular Purpose

The UCC implies a warranty of *fitness for a particular purpose*

> [w]here the seller at the time of contracting has reason to know any particular purpose for which the goods are selected and that the buyer is relying on the seller's skill or judgment to select or furnish suitable goods.

For example: A prospective buyer approaches someone offering a helicopter for sale (not necessarily a merchant) saying: "I don't know much about helicopters, but I own a construction company, and we need one for a major project. It must be capable of lifting a 10,000-pound 150-foot-tall steel power-line tower, then climbing up to 14,000 feet MSL and hovering there out of ground effect to place it at temperatures up to 90-degrees Fahrenheit." If the seller represents to the buyer that a particular helicopter will do that job and the buyer relies on the seller's representation, the seller has impliedly warranted the helicopter's capability to perform that function under those conditions, creating an implied warranty of fitness for this particular purpose. If it turns out that the helicopter won't do that job, the seller has breached the warranty and the buyer can return it for a full refund.

Disclaimer of Warranties

The UCC does, however, permit sellers to *disclaim* some warranties. Written express warranties cannot be disclaimed, but oral express warranties and implied warranties may. Such disclaimers are required to be in writing and conspicuous. All implied warranties can be disclaimed by the use of such approved expressions as "there are no warranties which extend beyond the description of the aircraft on the face of this agreement, including, but not limited to, any implied warranty of merchantability" or "the aircraft is delivered and accepted as is, with all faults," or other language that in common understanding calls the buyer's attention to the exclusion of warranties and makes it plain that there is no implied warranty.

When the buyer before purchasing the aircraft has examined it thoroughly (or has had the opportunity to examine it but refused to), there is no implied warranty covering defects that such an examination ought to have revealed. This should not deter you from commissioning the prepurchase inspection we're about to discuss because it's better to find out the true condition of the aircraft before buying it than to have to resort to warranty litigation when you discover a defect after you've bought it.

Breach of Warranty Claims

If a warranty is breached, the buyer must notify the seller and give him an opportunity to correct (*"cure"*) the problem. If the seller fails or refuses to fix the problem, the buyer may sue for breach of warranty. The suit may seek *specific performance* (a court order for the seller to correct the deficiency, at its expense), *damages* (judgment ordering the seller to reimburse the buyer the cost of repairs), or *rescission* (judgment ordering the seller to refund the purchase price and take back the aircraft). Such litigation can be expensive (perhaps prohibitively so for a relatively inexpensive aircraft), and its outcome is always something less than certain. If you have financed the purchase of the aircraft, you will have to continue to make your loan payments while the litigation is in progress.

HOW TO AVOID LITIGATION

As mentioned at the beginning of this chapter, most litigation over aircraft purchases gone sour can be attributed to these factors: (1) the buyer and seller did not come to a clear agreement on all aspects of the transaction and failed to properly document the deal, particularly the aircraft's condition, (2) the buyer failed to commission an adequate prepurchase inspection and title search before buying the aircraft, or (3) the transaction was not properly documented and recorded with the FAA Aircraft Registry. Let's look more closely at these.

Contract of Sale

To prevent the necessity for litigation over what warranties were or were not made or breached in the sale, it is in the interest of both buyer and seller to have a written purchase contract clearly expressing the warranties agreed to or excluded from the deal, written by your lawyer or negotiated between parties both represented by lawyers. Unless buying an aircraft known not to be airworthy for purposes of completion or rebuilding, buyers should not agree to contracts containing warranty disclaimers like "as is, with all faults."

If the seller is carrying the financing for the sale, it may offer the buyer a *conditional sale contract*. A conditional sale contract is a unique form of secured transaction typically providing that title to the aircraft does not pass to the buyer until the debt is paid in full. If the buyer misses a payment or is late in submitting a payment, the seller (still holding title) can legally repossess the aircraft and the buyer gets nothing back. While the secured lender in an ordinary financing transaction will usually work with a debtor facing financial difficulty, the seller under a conditional sale contract may look forward to the buyer's technical default to enable it to take back the asset. If the borrower in an ordinary secured financing transaction defaults and the lender goes through the repossession and sale process, any excess over the amount remaining due on the loan is refunded to the borrower. Not so under a conditional sale contract. Thus, buyers should be highly wary of entering into conditional sale contracts.

Prepurchase Inspection

It is much less expensive for a prospective buyer to learn all that can be learned about the condition of an aircraft before purchasing it than to pursue litigation claiming a breach of warranty later. Therefore, if you are considering purchasing an aircraft, you should hire an aircraft mechanic to perform a prepurchase inspection. The ideal person for the job would be someone you know and trust or who enjoys an excellent reputation (and has no relationship with the seller that might color his judgment). An airframe and powerplant (A&P) mechanic holding Inspection Authorization (IA) and having special experience and familiarity with the particular make and model of aircraft would be most desirable. This person should have access to the list of all airworthiness directives (ADs) and manufacturers' Service Bulletins (SBs) on the aircraft and its engines. There is no such thing as a "standard" prepurchase inspection. But if you really want to know what condition the airplane is in before you buy it, nothing less than an *annual inspection* ("*C check*" for turbine-powered aircraft) will provide you that level of detail. It is worth the cost, and you may be able to persuade the seller to split that cost with you (Fig. 11.4).

Reliance on a recent annual inspection signed off by an IA unknown to you or having a cozy relationship with the seller is unwise, as there are unfortunately some unscrupulous individuals in the industry who will sign off anything for a price.

Fig. 11.4. A shine is a good sign, but outward appearances can be deceiving. Only a thorough prepurchase inspection to annual inspection standards by an independent IA familiar with the make and model can give you a complete and reliable understanding of the aircraft's true condition.

Title Search

Because aircraft can so quickly travel from state to state and because Congress saw the need to enable buyers and lending institutions quickly and simply to determine who has what legal rights in an aircraft, the FAA Aircraft Registry was established at the FAA Aeronautical Center in Oklahoma City, Oklahoma. The Federal Aviation Act, which created the Aircraft Registry, requires that all documents reflecting ownership and security interests in civil aircraft be filed there.

Performing title searches at both the FAA Aircraft Registry and the International Registry should reveal not only who owns an aircraft but also all *recorded* security interests outstanding against the aircraft. You can access at least that portion of the Aircraft Registry that reflects current registered ownership through the FAA website. Several private companies in Oklahoma City, including an office of the Aircraft Owners and Pilots Association (AOPA), will perform a title search for you for a modest fee and quickly provide you a written report on the aircraft's ownership and outstanding recorded security interests. They typically back up their report with title insurance, protecting you against any error in their report (a benefit not available if you choose the online do-it-yourself approach). If you are borrowing to purchase the aircraft, the lender will require that you purchase a title search as a precondition of making the loan. But even if you are in the enviable position of being able to pay cash, it is still prudent first to purchase a title search to assure yourself that the seller is really the owner and that there are no lienholders who have not been paid and who may send the midnight repossessors to take the aircraft after you've paid for it.

For aircraft covered by the Cape Town Treaty, the title search should also include a search of the International Registry. Unlike the FAA registry, which is open to all to search without charge, the International Registry requires that the party performing the search first register (a process that may take several days) and pay a fee for access. Title search companies have already gone to the expense of registering with the International Registry and are positioned to search that registry for you more expeditiously.

One type of security interest that a title search may not reveal is the *possessory lien*. Under state law, a mechanic, FBO, repair station, or other business that has provided parts, labor, fuel, or storage for the aircraft is not required to release the aircraft to the owner without first being paid. Where such a business is holding the aircraft awaiting payment, it is said to have a possessory lien on the aircraft. Possessory liens are not required to be filed with the FAA Aircraft Registry, and under the law of most states there is no documentation of a possessory lien that one could file. Simply retaining possession of the aircraft pending payment perfects a possessory lien. Some states do allow persons and businesses that have performed such work without yet being paid to document the lien and the FAA Aircraft Registry will accept filing of such documents from those states. Other states do not, so these liens may or may not be revealed by the title search. Thus, before closing the deal to purchase an aircraft, the buyer should also inquire at the FBO or other facility where the aircraft is located whether there are any possessory liens against it for unpaid bills.

Aircraft Title Insurance

When purchasing an aircraft, it may be wise to purchase aircraft title insurance to protect against defects in the title, legal interests that were not revealed by a title search of the records of the FAA Aircraft Registry and the International Registry. Title insurance is most appropriate for corporate aircraft, as it is usually too expensive for transport category aircraft and the cost is difficult to justify for light single engine piston-powered general aviation aircraft.

Closing the Sale

If you decide to purchase the aircraft, it is a good practice to have a formal *closing* of the deal, much as you would when purchasing a home, with the buyer, seller, lending institution, and lienholders (or their representatives) present. Distant lienholders often arrange for the buyer's lending institution to serve as their *escrow agent*, sending lien releases to that institution to be recorded only after the funds to pay off the lien have been forwarded to the lienholder.

At the closing, the buyer should receive a signed *bill of sale* from the seller. This is an FAA form available free through most FAA offices and on the FAA website (*see* Fig. 11.5). If the seller is a corporation, check to be certain that the bill of sale has been signed properly. (Review the three mandatory elements of a proper corporate signature in Chapter 5.) If this signature is incomplete, the FAA Aircraft Registry will reject the document and refuse to re-register the aircraft to its new owner until a proper signature is obtained. 14 CFR §47.3(b) prohibits you from operating an aircraft that has not been registered to its owner. If the paperwork on the transaction is not perfect, this operates to ground your aircraft until the imperfection is corrected. At this point, Murphy's Law often kicks in and the seller drops dead or disappears before the documentation can be corrected. This results in your aircraft sitting on the ground while you spend thousands of dollars and months, if not years, getting a court order clearing the title so you can register and operate it without the missing signature.

The buyer should also receive *lien releases* signed by all lienholders who are executing these releases in exchange for that portion of the sale proceeds covering the balance of the debt still owed them.

If the contract of sale prepared by your lawyer or negotiated by lawyers for both parties (clearly expressing the warranties and exclusions

FORM APPROVED
OMB NO. 2120-0042
08/31/2008

UNITED STATES OF AMERICA
U.S. DEPARTMENT OF TRANSPORTATION FEDERAL AVIATION ADMINISTRATION

AIRCRAFT BILL OF SALE

FOR AND IN CONSIDERATION OF $ THE UNDERSIGNED OWNER(S) OF THE FULL LEGAL AND BENEFICIAL TITLE OF THE AIRCRAFT DESCRIBED AS FOLLOWS:

UNITED STATES REGISTRATION NUMBER **N**

AIRCRAFT MANUFACTURER & MODEL

AIRCRAFT SERIAL No.

DOES THIS DAY OF
HEREBY SELL, GRANT, TRANSFER AND DELIVER ALL RIGHTS, TITLE, AND INTERESTS IN AND TO SUCH AIRCRAFT UNTO:

Do Not Write In This Block
FOR FAA USE ONLY

PURCHASER

NAME AND ADDRESS
(IF INDIVIDUAL(S), GIVE LAST NAME, FIRST NAME, AND MIDDLE INITIAL.)

DEALER CERTIFICATE NUMBER

AND TO EXECUTORS, ADMINISTRATORS, AND ASSIGNS TO HAVE AND TO HOLD SINGULARLY THE SAID AIRCRAFT FOREVER AND WARRANTS THE TITLE THEREOF:

IN TESTIMONY WHEREOF HAVE SET HAND AND SEAL THIS DAY OF

SELLER

NAME(S) OF SELLER (TYPED OR PRINTED)	SIGNATURE(S) (IN INK) (IF EXECUTED FOR CO-OWNERSHIP, ALL MUST SIGN.)	TITLE (TYPED OR PRINTED)

ACKNOWLEDGMENT (NOT REQUIRED FOR PURPOSES OF FAA RECORDING: HOWEVER, MAY BE REQUIRED BY LOCAL LAW FOR VALIDITY OF THE INSTRUMENT.)

ORIGINAL: TO FAA:
AC Form 8050-2 (9/92) (NSN 0052-00-629-0003) Supersedes Previous Edition

Fig. 11.5. FAA aircraft bill of sale form.

of warranties agreed to) has not been signed, it must be signed by both the buyer and the seller at the closing. (The contract of sale is not the same thing as the bill of sale.)

If you're financing the purchase of the aircraft, the lender will require you to sign a *promissory note* and a *security agreement* (Fig. 11.2) giving the lender a security interest in the aircraft to secure payment of the loan.

Filings Required

The bill of sale, lien releases, and security agreement should then be filed with the FAA Aircraft Registry (usually by mail, although this is sometimes done in person on extremely expensive aircraft), along with an FAA form Aircraft Registration Application (*see* Fig. 11.6) signed by the new owner. None of these filings can be accomplished online. All must be submitted as hard copies with original signatures. In accordance with the Federal Aviation Drug Enforcement Assistance Act, the FAA will no longer accept aircraft registration applications that list a post office box or mail drop as the sole address. A street address or other physical location is required (although a P.O. Box may also be included). The pink copy of the Aircraft Registration Application ("pink slip") must be kept in the aircraft as the temporary registration certificate until the FAA Aircraft Registry issues a new Aircraft Registration Certificate in the new owner's name. It is prudent to assure that all of these documents have been mailed before operating the aircraft. (Also remember to ensure that liability and hull insurance on the aircraft has been bound and is in effect before starting the engine.) The pink slip is legally adequate as a temporary registration for flights within the United States, but international agreements require that you have the permanent registration on board before crossing international borders. If you anticipate an international flight shortly after closing the transaction and notify the FAA Aircraft Registry of this and the need for expedited handling, they are happy to provide you with a very quick turnaround on issuance and return of the new permanent registration.

An application for aircraft radio station license in the new owner's name must be filed with the Federal Communications Commission (FCC) in Harrisburg, Pennsylvania, if you intend to operate the aircraft across any international border, but not for operations wholly within the U.S. Most FAA field offices also stock free copies of this form.

If a 406 MHz emergency locator transmitter (ELT) is installed, that must be registered with the National Oceanic and Atmospheric Administration (NOAA), to facilitate search and rescue efforts in the event of activation. The registration form is available online at: *http://www.sarsat.noaa.gov/elt-form.pdf*

UNITED STATES OF AMERICA DEPARTMENT OF TRANSPORTATION
FEDERAL AVIATION ADMINISTRATION-MIKE MONRONEY AERONAUTICAL CENTER
AIRCRAFT REGISTRATION APPLICATION

CERT. ISSUE DATE

UNITED STATES
REGISTRATION NUMBER **N**

AIRCRAFT MANUFACTURER & MODEL

AIRCRAFT SERIAL No.

FOR FAA USE ONLY

TYPE OF REGISTRATION (Check one box)

☐ 1. Individual ☐ 2. Partnership ☐ 3. Corporation ☐ 4. Co-owner ☐ 5. Gov't. ☐ 8. Non-Citizen Corporation

NAME OF APPLICANT (Person(s) shown on evidence of ownership. If individual, give last name, first name, and middle initial.)

TELEPHONE NUMBER: (   )

ADDRESS (Permanent mailing address for first applicant listed.) (If P.O. BOX is used, physical address must also be shown.)

Number and street: _____

Rural Route: _____ P.O. Box: _____

CITY	STATE	ZIP CODE

☐ **CHECK HERE IF YOU ARE ONLY REPORTING A CHANGE OF ADDRESS**
ATTENTION! Read the following statement before signing this application.
This portion MUST be completed.

A false or dishonest answer to any question in this application may be grounds for punishment by fine and / or imprisonment (U.S. Code, Title 18, Sec. 1001).

CERTIFICATION

I/WE CERTIFY:

(1) That the above aircraft is owned by the undersigned applicant, who is a citizen (including corporations) of the United States.

(For voting trust, give name of trustee: _____), or:

CHECK ONE AS APPROPRIATE:

a. ☐ A resident alien, with alien registration (Form 1-151 or Form 1-551) No. _____

b. ☐ A non-citizen corporation organized and doing business under the laws of (state) _____ and said aircraft is based and primarily used in the United States. Records or flight hours are available for inspection at _____

(2) That the aircraft is not registered under the laws of any foreign country; and

(3) That legal evidence of ownership is attached or has been filed with the Federal Aviation Administration.

NOTE: If executed for co-ownership all applicants must sign. Use reverse side if necessary.

TYPE OR PRINT NAME BELOW SIGNATURE

EACH PART OF THIS APPLICATION MUST BE SIGNED IN INK.

SIGNATURE	TITLE	DATE
SIGNATURE	TITLE	DATE
SIGNATURE	TITLE	DATE

NOTE   Pending receipt of the Certificate of Aircraft Registration, the aircraft may be operated for a period not in excess of 90 days, during which time the PINK copy of this application must be carried in the aircraft.

AC Form 8050-1 (5/03) (0052-00-628-9007)

Fig. 11.6. FAA aircraft registration application form.

Tax and State Registration Requirements

The purchaser of the aircraft will have to pay either a *sales tax* or a *use tax* on the transaction in the purchaser's state of residence. If the sale took place in that state, then the sales tax that applies to other sales of goods in the state applies. However, if the aircraft was purchased out-of-state and then brought into the purchaser's home state, a use tax applies instead of a sales tax. (They're typically the same rate.) The law in most states provides that if the purchaser has paid a sales tax on the purchase in the state where the aircraft was purchased, that amount is credited against any use tax due in the purchaser's home state. If the amount of tax paid in the state of purchase is less than the amount due in the purchaser's home state, the purchaser must pay the home state the difference as a use tax. If a person paid a sales tax in the state of purchase equal to or greater than the use tax due in the purchaser's home state, the purchaser typically has no use tax liability in the aircraft's new home state, but receives no refund of any excess.

In most states, the aircraft will also be subject to some form of annual *personal property* tax. In many states, the procedure followed is similar to the annual registration of automobiles, with the aircraft owner paying both a *registration fee* (typically based upon the weight of the aircraft) and a *specific ownership tax* (a form of personal property tax having a prescribed rate for aircraft, often based upon the current blue-book value of the aircraft). In most states, at least a portion of these taxes is earmarked for airport development and provides a major source of funds that can be used to match federal funds to pay for airport improvements (discussed in greater detail in Chapter 13).

Under the law of most states, state revenue authorities automatically acquire a *tax lien* on aircraft for which these taxes have not been paid. Such a state law usually provides that upon request of state tax authorities, law enforcement officials (such as the county sheriff) may seize aircraft and sell them (usually at an auction called a *sheriff's sale*) to satisfy the owner's unpaid tax liability. As with the post-repossession sales previously discussed, if the sale brings more than the amount of the tax debt, the excess is paid to the aircraft owner.

In many states, failure to register and pay state taxes on aircraft is also a *misdemeanor* (a minor crime, as distinguished from a *felony*, a major crime). Punishments that can be meted out by the courts to recalcitrant tax evaders (in addition to the seizure and sale of the aircraft described above) typically include a fine or a jail sentence of up to one year.

When purchasing an aircraft, you should consult your accountant beforehand to determine which state taxes you will be liable for, as well as any federal taxes, tax credits, or accelerated depreciation benefits that may apply so that you can plan your budget accordingly.

If you are selling an aircraft on which you have taken depreciation for tax purposes, your accountant should be consulted to determine the potential tax consequences of the sale. If the aircraft's value has not actually depreciated at the rate used on your business's books of account (as is oftentimes the case), selling the aircraft at a price higher than its depreciated value may result in a *recapture of depreciation*. That will require an amendment of previous years' tax returns to reflect the actual depreciation experienced rather than the projection previously relied upon. This may mean that additional federal and state income taxes will have to be paid for previous years. In some instances, an aircraft may even fetch a higher price than you originally paid, in which case you might face additional income tax liability not only for such a recapture of depreciation but also for a *capital gain*.

But on the bright side, if you are able to satisfy the IRS that you have a valid business use for the aircraft, the IRS may allow at least some of the costs of ownership and operation as business expense deduction on your federal income taxes. The IRS very carefully scrutinizes such aircraft-related deductions to verify that they are *ordinary* (common in the business the taxpayer is engaged in, such as a traveling sales person), *necessary* (appropriate and helpful in the development of the taxpayer's business), and *reasonable* (the amount must bear a "reasonable and proximate relation to the production or collection of taxable income, or to the management, conservation, or maintenance of property held for the production of income"). Claiming aircraft-related deductions is virtually certain to prompt an IRS review of your return, at least the first time you do so, and well-documented proof that the aircraft use produced taxable income is essential to justify the deductions. Close coordination with your accountant is very important, here. Claiming aircraft-related entertainment expenses (such as taking clients on a fishing trip to foster goodwill) is viewed most skeptically by the IRS and frequently disallowed.

SUMMARY

Carefully following the procedures described in this chapter assures the buyer clear title to the aircraft and assures that both buyer and seller are quite clear on what legally enforceable promises have been made regarding the aircraft and its condition. Coupled with the technique of naming the lender as the *loss payee* on the aircraft's hull insurance coverage and obtaining a *lienholder's interest endorsement (breach of warranty endorsement)* on that policy as discussed in Chapter 6, these procedures assure the lender of payment of any balance on the loan, even if the aircraft is later destroyed in an accident along with its owner. The question of whether by virtue of being the holder of a recorded security interest in the aircraft the lender will have any exposure to liability if the aircraft is involved in an accident is directly and clearly answered in the negative by the Federal Aviation Act.

Having answered the questions of buyers, sellers, and lenders with which we began this chapter, we now turn to legal considerations in the leasing, time-sharing and management of aircraft.

12

Aircraft Leasing, Co-Ownership and Fractional Ownership

Leasing has become an increasingly popular method for corporate operators, flight schools, charter operators, the airlines, and even individuals to obtain the use of aircraft without making the substantial capital investment required to purchase them. Indeed, the U.S. airline fleet is now composed of far more aircraft leased than owned by the airlines operating them.

As in aircraft purchases, much of the litigation arising out of aircraft leases results from inadequate diligence in negotiating and documenting the details of the lease agreement. The "leaseback," a hybrid composite of sale and lease, has generated a volume of litigation entirely out of proportion to the popularity of its use.

Fractional Ownership has become a very popular and economical alternative to outright ownership, particularly for large and turbine-powered business aircraft. This alternative is not, however, without its limitations and pitfalls.

The purposes of this chapter are

1. to instill in you an appreciation of the differences between a lease and leaseback (and the special problems inherent in leasebacks),

2. to provide you with a methodical approach to negotiating an aircraft lease,

3. to equip you with a basic working knowledge of the legal aspects of fractional ownership, and

4. to build further upon your appreciation of the prudence of using the professional services of legal counsel in a preventive role in drafting the final version of agreements.

LEASING

Lease and Leaseback Distinguished

Some incorrect uses of lease terminology have permeated the aviation industry in recent years. It is important to use language precisely in aviation as well as in the law. A *lease* is an agreement, a contract that permits someone else to use an owner's aircraft. It is only where, as a part of the same "wrap-around" business deal, the buyer purchases the aircraft from the seller then turns around and leases it back to the seller for the seller's use, that the lease portion of this deal is correctly referred to as a *leaseback*. Not all leases are leasebacks; in fact, leasebacks represent the minority. It may help to think of a lease that is not tied to an aircraft purchase in this circular manner as a *lease forward* (*see* Fig. 12.1).

The drafting of a lease or leaseback agreement is another area in which it is prudent to have your attorney either draft the agreement or review the agreement offered to you by the other party and suggest changes that may be advisable to protect your interests. A little preventive lawyering at the drafting stage can avoid misunderstandings or disputes that might later necessitate expensive litigation having an uncertain outcome.

In any lease (forward or back), the aircraft owner is referred to in legal terms as the *lessor* and the user as the *lessee*. If you are the lessor, you should carefully check the credit rating of the prospective lessee before deciding to lease the aircraft to him. After all, you are entrusting him with an extremely valuable machine. If the lessee operates or has previously operated aircraft leased from others, inquire about their experiences with the lessee, especially timely payment and aircraft care and maintenance.

Another reason to check carefully the person or business you are considering leasing an aircraft to is the potential for seizure of the aircraft by law enforcement agencies if it is used for illegal purposes such as drug smuggling. The government expects aircraft owners not only to refrain from such activities themselves but also to exercise due diligence to ensure that others do not use their aircraft for such criminal activities. Even if the aircraft owner is not directly involved in the scheme, the aircraft may be seized and forfeited to the government if its owner

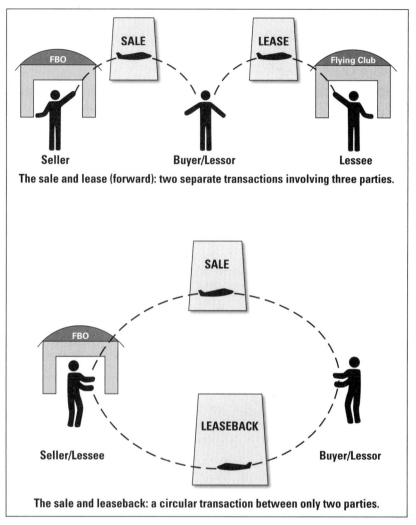

The sale and lease (forward): two separate transactions involving three parties.

The sale and leaseback: a circular transaction between only two parties.

Fig. 12.1. An aircraft lease ("lease forward") distinguished from a leaseback.

fails to take reasonable measures to ensure that the aircraft is not being used for such unlawful activities. It is not enough for the aircraft owner to have seen no evil.

Once the decision is made to enter into a lease, you may save on your attorney's fees by first agreeing with the other party to as many of the details of the lease as possible before going to your attorney to draft the lease. Your attorney will need the information contained in the following checklist to draft the lease agreement. If you bring all of this information with you to the first interview, it will save you considerable time and expense.

Aircraft Lease Checklist

1. *Description of the aircraft.* Manufacturer, model, manufacturer's serial number, and aircraft registration (N) number.

2. *Name and address of registered owner.* This must be exactly as it appears on the FAA aircraft registration certificate.

3. *Name and address of lessee.* If a corporation, be sure to provide the corporation's full legal name.

4. *Maximum certificated gross takeoff weight of the aircraft.* If more than 12,500 pounds, the lease must contain the truth-in-leasing clause required by 14 CFR §91.23.

5. *Who is the "operator" responsible for compliance with FARs governing aircraft operations?* Under the broad definition of *operate* contained in 14 CFR §1.1, the lessor could be held responsible for FAR violations committed by the lessee. A clear statement of responsibility for compliance with operational FARs in the lease may ameliorate that risk.

6. *Exclusive or nonexclusive use.* Does the lessee have the exclusive use of the aircraft during the term of the lease, or will the owner retain some right to use the aircraft from time to time? If the owner retains any right to use the aircraft during the term of the lease, how are scheduling conflicts that may arise between the owner and the lessee to be resolved?

7. *Inspections and maintenance.* Who is responsible for scheduling required inspections? Who is responsible to pay for those inspections, and how (directly or by deduction from lease payments)? Who has the authority to order maintenance? Are maintenance expenses estimated to exceed some set amount required to be approved by the owner before work begins? Are there any requirements as to who may perform the maintenance? Who will pay for the maintenance, and how (directly or by deduction from lease payments)?

8. *Other expenses.* Where is the aircraft to be based when it is not being flown or under inspection or maintenance? Will it be tied down outside or hangared at its base when not in use? Who pays for the hangar or tie-down expenses, and how? Who pays taxes and registration fees for the aircraft, and how? Who pays for fuel, additives, oil, and other lubricants consumed by the aircraft

and how? Who pays landing fees and other airport use fees, and how?

9. *Insurance.* Who provides aircraft insurance coverage for liability and hull and in what amounts? Will exclusions to that insurance be acceptable? What pilot qualifications will be required? Will a lienholder's interest endorsement (breach of warranty endorsement) be required to protect a lienholder having a security interest in the aircraft? Who will be named as insureds on the policy? To whom will the insurance company make payment (the loss payee) in the event of a loss covered by the hull insurance? What proof of insurance and notice of change or cancellation will be required to be provided, when, and to whom?

10. *Crew expenses.* Who will provide the flight crew and pay their salaries, expenses, workers compensation insurance, and unemployment compensation insurance?

11. *Lease payments.* What rent does the lessee agree to pay the lessor ($X per month, per Hobbs meter hour, etc.)? When, where, and how will this payment be made? Is some minimum monthly use or payment guaranteed by the lessee? Is there any provision to vary the amount of the lease payments to account for factors such as changes in fuel prices and/or inflation? Is either the lessor or lessee required to set aside reserve funds for engine overhaul and overhaul or replacement of other time/life limited components?

12. *Duration, renewal, and termination.* How long will the lease last? Who can terminate the lease sooner than that, and how? Can the lease be terminated only for specific reasons (such as nonpayment of rent or destruction of the aircraft)? Does the lessee have the option to renew the lease on the same terms for an additional term? If so, how must that be done, and when?

Special Considerations in Leasebacks

In my experience, leasebacks more frequently lead to disputes and litigation than other leases. In the ordinary aircraft lease (a lease forward), the lessor's primary motive is to earn income from the aircraft and the lessee's primary motive is to obtain the use of an aircraft without having to make the capital investment required to purchase one. Once the parties' motivations have been harmonized in a lease agreement, neither the lessor nor the lessee usually has any incentive to turn around and undermine that happy working of the lease.

That is not the case with a leaseback. Aircraft leasebacks developed primarily as an aircraft sales tool, the leaseback being offered as an incentive to encourage a person to purchase an aircraft she might not feel she could otherwise afford. Although in a leaseback, the seller/lessee may also have the same motivation as a lessee in a lease forward (to obtain the use of an aircraft without having to make the capital investment to purchase one), that is generally the lessee's secondary motive. The primary motive of the lessee in a sale and leaseback is to sell the aircraft. As we will see, the introduction of this motive may give the lessee an incentive to act later in ways that may undermine the happy working of the transaction. Additionally, the buyer/lessor may pay a substantially higher price for the aircraft when a leaseback is included in the deal than if it were not. Let's explore this in greater detail.

The Sales Pitch

The leaseback is typically offered by an FBO to a prospective aircraft purchaser who is vacillating over whether he can afford the aircraft as a final "carrot" to close a sale. Under the leaseback, the prospective buyer is told that he will receive income from the FBO's use of the aircraft in charter, flight training, and rental to other pilots to help cover the monthly payments for the aircraft's financing, inspections, and maintenance. He is told that the arrangement will also allow the new owner to deduct as business expenses depreciation, insurance, inspection, maintenance, and storage expenses associated with ownership of the aircraft.

Aircraft are typically sold on commission, and the dealer may receive as much as 25 percent of the purchase price for selling a new aircraft. If you were purchasing an aircraft without a leaseback, you would probably find some negotiability in the price. The dealer is usually willing to reduce the price by at least a portion of her commission on the theory that a percentage of something is better than all of nothing. Some dealers are required by their dealership agreement to purchase a certain number of aircraft from a manufacturer each year (customers or no). A dealer may have to finance the purchase of those aircraft through what is referred to as *floor plan financing* of her inventory. Dealers faced with aircraft in inventory have even been known to sell aircraft below cost in order to relieve the burden of the monthly payments of principle and interest on the floor plan financing. But where the purchaser wants to lease the aircraft back to the seller, the sale price usually becomes nonnegotiable, locked in at the dealer's list price for a new aircraft or "asking price" for a used aircraft. Thus, interjecting the leaseback into the transaction may deprive the buyer of the opportunity to negotiate purchase of the aircraft at a more favorable price.

The seller will usually include in the sales pitch calculations showing the prospective buyer the income-generating potential of the aircraft based upon some hypothetical monthly use figure and inspection and maintenance costs. When the seller actually presents the proposed leaseback agreement, however, it usually states that the seller/lessee does not guarantee any minimum monthly use or payment. The form lease offered by the seller/ lessee to the prospective buyer is usually either for only one year or without a fixed duration. It usually provides that either party may terminate the lease on relatively short notice (typically from ten to thirty days) without having to show good cause for cancellation. The form leaseback agreement offered by the seller/lessee also usually provides that all maintenance will be done by the seller/lessee's maintenance shop and at the seller/lessee's discretion, but at the owner's cost. It may provide that maintenance costs can be deducted from rental payments due, and if inspection and maintenance costs exceed the amount of rental payments due to the owner in a given month, the owner has to pay the seller/lessee the difference.

Typical Sad Experiences

The seller/lessee is likely to have competitors in the area who are also in the business of aircraft charter, rental, and flight training. In that competition, the FBO that has the newest aircraft available on its flight line enjoys a competitive advantage. Thus, the seller/lessee is continually faced with the competitive incentive to keep the newest and shiniest aircraft on its flight line. This puts an incentive on the seller/lessee to not keep the aircraft under leaseback for longer than two years, since an aircraft that has been in service for two years (and particularly one that has regularly been used by people who have no pride of ownership in that aircraft) is no longer a new aircraft either in actuality or appearance.

Further, and usually of greater importance, the incentive of commissions on sales (one of the rare opportunities for an FBO to earn a large chunk of quick cash) remains to motivate the seller/lessee to sell similar aircraft to other prospective buyers. If by negotiating a similar leaseback (and thus adding a newer aircraft to its flight line) the dealer can close another sale and make another sizable commission, the dealer is likely to seize that advantage. That may, of course, be to the detriment of the owner of a similar aircraft already leased back, since the newer aircraft may draw customers away from the older one, which will then see less use and generate less income for its owner.

There is also an incentive for the less than perfectly scrupulous seller/lessee to defer needed maintenance when the leased aircraft is in high demand for flight operations (particularly while the warranty is still good), then to attempt to catch up on deferred maintenance to provide an income to the seller/lessee's repair facility during periods when demand for the use of the aircraft is slow (such as seasons of inclement weather). Some FBOs have even been known to perform unnecessary maintenance or falsely bill aircraft owners for maintenance not performed. This can be very difficult for the aircraft owner to prove.

Judicious use of leasebacks can assure an FBO a steady supply of new aircraft on its flight line, producing income (without requiring capital investment) and producing handsome commissions on sales. On the other hand, the purchasers of these aircraft may find that their aircraft are being abused by the nonowners who are allowed to fly them, and that inspection and maintenance costs are considerably higher than forecast while income is less. They may find that as the aircraft's condition and appearance deteriorate (more rapidly than an aircraft used only by its proud owners), the FBO becomes less and less interested in having the bird on its flight line.

At this point, a disillusioned owner may turn to the FBO lessee and say, "This isn't working out as I expected, and I can't handle this financial burden any more. Will you please see if you can find someone to buy the airplane?" The dealer expresses regret at the owner's disappointment and the unforeseen series of events that led to this point, but finds a buyer and takes another commission on the resale. Then, adding insult to injury, the disillusioned owner may find that due to economic factors previously discussed, the aircraft has appreciated, or at least depreciated at a lesser rate than that scheduled by the owner's accountant, so that the owner has recaptured depreciation in the sale and now must file amended income tax returns and pay additional income taxes for the years the aircraft was owned.

Careful economic analysis may reveal that the prospective aircraft purchaser would be better off not to rely on a leaseback arrangement but to buy an aircraft only if able to meet the aircraft payments and expenses independently of any income that may be generated by the aircraft. This is particularly so if the purchaser is able to justify use of the aircraft in her own business or profession. The purchaser will then be in a position to bargain down the purchase price of the aircraft considerably. Such a purchaser will also be impervious to any reversals in the anticipated tax consequences of the purchase and use of the aircraft that could otherwise be unexpectedly precipitated by unilateral action of the lessee in prematurely terminating or declining to renew the lease. If the purchaser can then find another responsible party to share the use of the aircraft and its costs of ownership through a more traditional lease (lease forward) arrangement, that might make better economic sense. Even if that opportunity did not materialize, the purchase should have no catastrophic financial consequences for the new owner.

When is a Lease a Charter?

Some operators attempt to use leases to avoid the requirements of 14 CFR Parts 135 and 121. The FAA very closely scrutinizes *wet leases* whereby the aircraft owner leases the aircraft *with flight crew* to another user. The basic presumption applied by the FAA is that if the aircraft and crew are both provided by the same source, the transaction is not a lease, but a charter, so that the operation could not legally be conducted under the General Operating and Flight Rules of 14 CFR Part 91, but would be subject to the more stringent requirements of 14 CFR Part 135 or 121, depending on the size of the aircraft.

CO-OWNERSHIP

Because aircraft ownership is so costly, individuals often chip in together to buy an aircraft to share. This is not a partnership (in legal terms, a partnership is a form of business, only); it is *co-ownership*. Such owners are not partners (although this is a common misuse of the phrase, often heard around general aviation airports); they are *co-owners*. Because of the risk of vicarious liability associated with partnership (*see* Chapter 5), such owners would be well advised to clean up their language, introducing each other to the world as "co-owner of my aircraft," not "my aircraft partner." In order to avoid later disputes, the co-ownership agreement should also be encapsulated in a legal document (the final version written by your lawyer), signed by all of the co-owners clearly setting out responsibilities for costs, a means for resolving scheduling conflicts, and addressing the myriad other complications that can make for trouble later.

Fractional Ownership

Fractional ownership, a form that began in 1986 and continues to enjoy increasing popularity across a wide range of aircraft users, is a special kind of co-ownership. It began in the business aircraft world, as corporate operators moved into turboprops, jets and other large aircraft, but it's now becoming popular in the light piston-powered aircraft market as well.

For large and turbine-powered multiengine airplanes, 14 CFR §91.501(c)(1) and (3) provide a very narrowly drawn exception permitting operation under Part 91 under a *joint ownership* or a *time sharing agreement*. This avoids the considerable expenses and significant operating limitations associated with operating under Part 135 or 121, but with the limitation that only certain itemized expenses of the flight may be charged. Meticulous documentation of these charges must be maintained to show compliance with the rule. No similar exception is available to operators of small aircraft, single engine turbine-powered aircraft or piston-powered multiengine aircraft.

The economic and operational advantages offered by this exception to the FARs have spawned several aggressively marketed major fractional ownership programs. Some of these are offered by aircraft manufacturers such as Bombardier's FlexJet program and Sikorsky Helicopters' Sikorsky Shares to boost aircraft sales (over 1,200 aircraft sales valued at over $22 billion were attributed to these programs by 2007). Others are offered by charter operators such as Berkshire Hathaway's NetJets subsidiary (formerly Executive Jet Aviation) and aircraft fleet management services such as Flight Options (now merged with former airframe manufacturer Raytheon's Travel Air program) to promote their services. Fractional ownership is presently growing at a rate of 40 to 50% annually, with both corporate and wealthy individual buyers participating approximately equally. A true fractional ownership program includes four interlocking primary agreements:

1. The *aircraft purchase agreement* (between the seller and buyers),
2. A *joint ownership agreement* (among the buyers/owners),
3. An *aircraft management agreement* (between the buyers/owners and an aircraft management company), and

4. A *master interchange agreement* (between the buyers/owners of all aircraft owned by participants in the management company's fractional ownership program).

What each owner gets is access to an appropriate aircraft (not necessarily their own), without the associated management responsibilities for scheduling, crew (not included in the light piston fractional ownership programs), hangar, insurance, inspection and maintenance, at a cost that may be more favorable than either charter rates or full ownership.

Typically, the user buys that percentage of the aircraft that is expected to equal its annual use, with 50 flight hours equaling a 1/16th share. This is the smallest share offered in large and turbine-powered fixed-wing aircraft fractional ownership programs, though helicopter programs offer shares as small as 1/32nd. These are the smallest fractional shares permitted by 14 CFR §91.1001 (b)(10). Companies such as Air Shares Elite and Let's Fly now offer fractional or managed co-ownership programs for light general aviation aircraft in the U.S. In the light piston aircraft market, expect no more than four owners per fractionally-owned aircraft (Fig. 12.2).

Fig. 12.2. Fractional ownership and managed co-ownership are also now gaining popularity in the market for light general aviation aircraft.

Experience has shown that for fixed-wing aircraft, fractional owner-ship is economical for users who will need the aircraft at least 50 hours, but less than 200 hours annually. Users requiring less than 50 flight hours per year will typically find charter services (or, for light piston personal flying, aircraft rental) more economical, while those flying more than 200 hours annually will usually find outright sole ownership less costly than either charter or fractional ownership.

The four interlocking agreements establishing a fractional ownership can be quite complex (20–25 pages each is not unusual), and should be carefully reviewed by legal counsel before signing.

Analysis of FAA and NTSB accident data for U.S. registered turbine-powered aircraft during the eleven-year period from 1987 to 1998 shows that fractional ownership aircraft operations have been among the safest in aviation. However, safety concerns prompted the FAA to create the Fractional Ownership Aviation Rulemaking Com-mittee (FOARC). The committee included representatives of at least nine Part 135 operators, seven fractional ownership program managers, four aircraft manufacturers, three traditional Part 91 corporate flight departments, nine traditional aircraft management companies, and five industry trade associations along with the FAA, DOT and aircraft financing and insurance companies. The Civil Aviation Authority of the U.K and Transport Canada also participated in the committee's discussions, but recused themselves from the decision-making process.

In February of 2000, the committee presented its recommendations to the FAA. FOARC reached consensus that fractional ownership program operations should continue to be regulated under 14 CFR Part 91. However, the committee unanimously recommended FAA adoption of a new Subpart K to Part 91 to ensure adequate FAA oversight and surveillance of fractional ownership program managers equal to that experienced by Part 121 or 135 operators. Key features include:

1. clarification of responsibility for operational control,
2. crew flight and duty time limitations,
3. crew training comparable to Part 135 requirements,
4. requirement for a drug and alcohol abuse recognition program for all personnel performing safety-related functions,
5. aircraft equipment requirements by size, type and class of aircraft (cockpit voice recorder, flight data recorder, ground proximity

warning system, thunderstorm detection equipment or airborne weather radar, TCAS),

6. establishment of minimum runway length requirements,
7. weather reporting requirements for instrument approaches, and
8. requirement for an FAA approved maintenance and inspection program.

These FOARC recommendations were ultimately incorporated into the FAR governing fractional ownership and operation of large and turbine-powered aircraft (Subpart K of Part 91). Because most of these recommendations merely reflect best practices that were already being followed by the leading existing fractional ownership program managers, only the most marginal programs were adversely affected to any significant degree by this rulemaking.

PART IV

AIRPORTS, AIRSPACE, AND AVIATION SECURITY

13

Airports and Terminal Airspace

Following deregulation, airline operations multiplied radically at airports serving major metropolitan areas, especially those selected by airlines to serve as regional hubs for hub-and-spoke route systems. This strained airport capacity, resulting in incentives to build new airline airports and general aviation reliever airports and to expand existing airports in both categories.

The purpose of this chapter is to familiarize you with sources of power available to federal, state, and local governments to deal with the problems created by airport development and operation, particularly noise and safety issues; to review specific techniques and examples of applications of these powers that have succeeded and others that have failed; and to show the interplay of legal principles that determine the outcome when the rights of citizens come into conflict with the rights of their government.

Although safety is also a major concern of those living near an airport (a preponderance of aircraft accidents occur within a mile of the airport), most aviation litigation in the area of airports and airspace has focused on two problem areas: (1) aircraft noise and (2) keeping the airport's approaches clear of obstacles. Of these two, noise-related issues have accounted for the greater part of the litigation. In these cases, the courts struggle to weigh the rights of property owners against the public interest in safe and convenient air transportation.

SOURCES OF POWER

In the United States, all public airports that receive scheduled airline passenger service are owned and operated by state or local (city or county) governments or regional airport authorities having governmental powers.

Constitutional Powers

In their efforts to keep the approaches to these public airports clear of obstructions and to minimize costly aircraft noise-related lawsuits from airport neighbors, these governments have relied upon sources of power derived from both the Constitution of the United States and their inherent powers as proprietors of these airports (which are considered public utilities).

Eminent Domain

Under the power of *eminent domain*, governments have the right to take private land within their jurisdiction for public use (whether the landowner wishes to sell the land or not). The 5th Amendment to the U.S. Constitution requires, however, that when the government takes private property for public use, it must pay the landowner *just compensation*. If the landowner is unwilling to sell the property to the government or if the landowner and the government cannot agree on a fair price (just compensation), ordinarily the government files a *condemnation* lawsuit. A condemnation suit seeks a court order establishing the price to be paid and ordering transfer of title to the government upon payment of that price.

The Police Power

The *police power* is the government's right to adopt and enforce laws to protect the *public health*, *safety and welfare*. In the regulation of airports and airspace, this is the power that has been relied upon by state, regional and local governments as authority for adoption of *land use zoning* and *height zoning* ordinances in the vicinity of airports, as well as *noise ordinances*.

The Commerce Clause

The *commerce clause* of the Constitution, which gives the federal government the exclusive right to regulate interstate and foreign commerce, is the source of authority for all federal regulation of aviation. Judicial interpretations of the extent of this power have uniformly held that because even aircraft involved in purely local flying (such as aircraft observing and reporting on highway traffic for local news media, crop sprayers and sport flyers) operate in the same navigable airspace that may be used by aircraft traveling in interstate commerce (and could at least theoretically come into conflict with them), the FAA has the power to regulate those activities.

The Supremacy Clause

The *supremacy clause* to the Constitution has also sometimes come into play in these cases. The supremacy clause provides that where the federal government has adopted statutes or regulations governing some activity that it is authorized to regulate (such as aviation, under the commerce clause), then state, regional or local governments may not enact or enforce laws *conflicting* with federal law.

Proprietary Powers

In addition to these constitutional sources of power, the governmental entity that owns and operates the airport has a measure of authority as *proprietor* to regulate the use of that airport, much as the owner of a private airport would.

The Power to Tax

All governments have the inherent power to impose taxes on persons, property, and transactions within their jurisdiction. Taxes are a major burden on every person and business, and are often a key consideration in the location or relocation of business enterprises. Increasing property taxes, in particular, are often responsible for a private airport owner's decision to sell or develop the property for some other use.

The Power of the Purse

Proceeds of federal taxes on airline passenger tickets and aviation fuels have built up a multi-billion dollar *Aviation Trust Fund*. Congress, with the FAA's advice, budgets expenditure of this money for airport planning, development and improvement through a program of grants called the *Airport Improvement Program* (AIP). This may include providing funds to acquire land and aviation easements for noise abatement purposes and to soundproof existing buildings near the airport. Under that program, federal funds may be allocated to cover up to 95% of a project's costs. In this time of increased public focus on efficiency in government, grants under this program are becoming more difficult for non-hub airports to obtain. As we will see, these grants also come with some strings attached.

Many states have similar programs, typically funded by state aircraft fuel taxes, registration fees and specific ownership taxes, which may provide funds to cover that portion of a project not covered by federal funds. Many state grant programs also provide funding for airport projects that would not qualify for federal funding or for which it is not economical to go through the federal grant application process.

Additional federal funds are available under the Military Airport Program (MAP) for costs of converting closed military airfields to civilian airport use. MAP funds can be used for some projects not covered by the AIP.

CASES INVOLVING APPLICATION OF THESE POWERS

Through a narrative examination of the landmark cases, we will now examine how the law governing airports and airspace has evolved to its present state, observing the interplay of the powers described above with the legal rights of property owners in the vicinity of airports.

The Power of Eminent Domain

The very first aviation case decided by the Supreme Court of the United States, *United States v. Causby*, focused on airport and airspace issues. The Causbys were farmers whose principle source of income was raising chickens. Their home and chicken coops were located adjacent to a rural airport in North Carolina. That airport was not very busy, having some general aviation activity and a couple of airline DC-3 flights daily. Then World War II began. The federal government took over the airport and turned it into a heavy bomber-training base, operating around the clock with a high level of activity. A continuous stream of four-engine bombers spaced a minute or two apart roared over the Causbys' property day and night, with the landing approach bringing them as low as thirty feet over the Causbys' rooftop. The roar of the planes was deafening, and at night the landing lights illuminated the Causbys' bedroom brighter than day.

The brain of a chicken is apparently programmed to react to anything flying overhead as if it were a chicken hawk. Such a perceived threat drives chickens into a frenzy of activity. In this fashion, some 150 of the

Causbys' chickens had destroyed themselves in the process of crashing around their coops in a state of panic caused by the low-flying bombers (the Causbys were probably not bearing up much better themselves). Eventually, they (the Causbys, not the chickens) could take no more and hired a lawyer to sue the federal government. From this humble context would come the foundation of the law of airports and airspace in the U.S.

Courts are most comfortable deciding cases where a large body of legal precedent is available in the form of published decisions of other judges and appellate courts dealing with similar situations. Here, there were no such cases; this was a *case of first impression*, and the Supreme Court, having granted certiorari and recognizing the potentially far-reaching and long-lasting effect its decision would have upon the developing law of airports and airspace in this country, proceeded with great caution and deliberation.

In the quest for common law precedent, diligent judges and lawyers would sometimes even search back to times before it became fashionable to publish judicial decisions. A primary valid source of reference to the common law as it existed in those earlier times was the writings of the Roman Glossators who, around the time of Christ, had written rather extensive treatises on the common law. Reference back to these writings in *Causby* revealed a centuries-old facet of the common law known as the *ad coelum* doctrine, which, when translated from the original Latin (*Cujus est solum, ejus est usque ad coelum*) states that a person who owns a parcel of land owns not only the surface of that land but also the airspace above it, literally "to the sky" (*ad coelum*). This ancient legal doctrine had been relied upon from time to time to resolve the kinds of airspace disputes that arose prior to the advent of flying machines—for example, to determine the ownership of apples growing on branches of a land-owner's tree overhanging another's property or whether the landowner seeking maximum utilization of space might construct a building that although its foundation occupied only its owner's land, might legally have balconies or roof eaves extending over a neighbor's property.

The Supreme Court recognized, however, that application of this legal principle to the aviation situation would make flight virtually impossible; each property owner could demand that aircraft keep out of that landowner's airspace or pay a toll for transiting that "property." Relying upon the commerce clause and Congress's pronouncements in the Civil Aeronautics Act of 1938 (precursor to the Federal Aviation

Act of 1958), the Court held that navigable airspace is a public highway within the public domain, and that at least as it would affect the passage of aircraft, the *ad coelum* doctrine has no place in the modern world.

However, the Court went on to analogize from the constitutional law of eminent domain and terrestrial precedent, applying that law to afford the Causbys some relief for the damages they had suffered. By holding that in this situation the flights by aircraft owned and operated by the federal government were "so low and so frequent as to be a direct and immediate interference with the enjoyment and use of land," and because the value of the land was diminished as a result, these air operations constituted a *taking* of private property (in the nature of an *aviation easement*) for a public use, so that the Constitution required the federal government to pay the landowner just compensation for that taking. The Court held that the dollar amount of the just compensation would be the difference between the appraised value of the property before and after commencement of the oppressive overflights.

As previously noted, in an ordinary condemnation action, the government would have initiated the suit to take the property and determine the price. Since in this case it was the landowner who filed the suit seeking a judicial declaration that the government had *already* taken a property right and just compensation for that taking (a role reversal from the usual condemnation case), the Court characterized this lawsuit as an *inverse condemnation* case.

The next landmark case in the area, *Griggs v. Allegheny County*, would address the question of whether state, regional, and local governments would face similar liability for the impact of aircraft noise on landowners surrounding public civil airports. The Griggs's home was near the Greater Pittsburgh Airport, a county owned and operated airport served by several airlines. The county extended one of the runways almost to the Griggs's property line, so that airliners on approach to landing passed as low as eleven feet over the Griggs's chimney. The noise and vibration caused the plaster walls and ceilings to crack and toppled the Griggs's precious belongings from shelves and china cabinets. The Griggses hired an attorney, who filed an inverse condemnation suit against the county.

The Court held that facts were sufficiently similar to those in *Causby* that the county, as operator of this public airport, had taken an aviation easement over the Griggs's property through inverse condemnation, requiring the county to pay just compensation for the taking, to be measured by the appraised fair market value of the property before and after the runway extension that led to the radical increase in noise. The court also held that the airlines that were actually generating the noise had no liability to the landowners.

This decision alarmed many public airport operators, who feared that their budgets would be depleted by similar litigation. Thus, many attorneys for state, regional, and local governments were tasked with finding a way around the *Causby* and *Griggs* decisions.

The Police Power

In the Pacific Northwest, a new regional airline airport ("Sea-Tac") was about to be built in the Seattle-Tacoma area. In an apparent effort to circumvent potential liability for suits for inverse condemnation, the legislature drafting the statute authorizing the airport included an elaborate recital to the effect that the airport was created under the police power in the interest of the public welfare. When an adjacent landowner later filed an inverse condemnation suit, however, the court held that although building a public use airport is certainly a proper exercise of the police power, if the *effect* is to take private property rights for a public use, that exercise of the police power is also an exercise of the power of eminent domain, so that the governmental entity that owns and operates the airport must pay just compensation to property owners affected by the airport project.

This could be considered a corollary of the *duck rule*: Calling your duck an eagle doesn't make it one. The court will look not only at what a government claims it has done, but will also examine the actual effect of the government action, to decide whether there has been a taking of a private property right for a public use.

Shortly thereafter, in Riverside, California, the county was building a new general aviation airport (Ryan Field) and was concerned that the safety and utility of this public airport could be jeopardized if nearby property owners were allowed to erect structures that might block approach paths to the runway. Therefore, in the exercise of its police power, the county adopted *height zoning* restrictions that applied to property near each end of the runway to prevent landowners from building obstructions into the landing glide path. The maximum heights permitted proceeded outward and upward in a stair step fashion, only very low structures being permitted close to the runway and progressively higher structures permitted farther away. Sneed owned a parcel of some 234 acres immediately adjacent to the runway threshold. Under the new height zoning ordinance, the tallest structure that could be built on that portion of Sneed's property farthest from the end of the runway was twenty-four feet, and at the end closest to the runway a mere three inches!

Sneed's attorney filed suit (*Sneed v. County of Riverside*), and following the rationale of the cases we have already discussed, the court found that while building and operating the airport and keeping its approaches clear was certainly a valid exercise of the county's police power, this height zoning regulation was plainly intended to keep open a public right-of-way (aviation easement) for the passage of aircraft using this public airport. Therefore, although the zoning was a valid and permissible exercise of the police power, at least in Sneed's case (when the reasonable use of the airspace above his property was so drastically restricted), the height zoning ordinance *also* constituted a taking of his private property for a public use through the power of eminent domain, requiring the county to pay him just compensation.

Meanwhile, up the coast in Santa Barbara, California, Smith owned a large parcel of land that had been zoned, platted, and approved for development as a residential subdivision, although ground had not yet been broken for the development. The county decided to build an airline airport nearby and was appropriately concerned that if development of the residential subdivision were allowed to go forward, its residents would be annoyed by noise from the aircraft coming and going from the new airport, sue the county in inverse condemnation, and win. Therefore, the county government used its police power to enact a new *land use zoning* ordinance governing the uses to which property in the vicinity of the new airport could be put, the intent being to allow only land uses that were not as sensitive to noise as homes. Under this ordinance, Smith's property was rezoned from residential to industrial use.

Smith sued the county (*Smith v. Santa Barbara County*), claiming that this rezoning constituted a taking of his property for a public use, requiring the payment of just compensation. The court found that the ordinance was a valid exercise of the county's police power, adopted for the purpose of protecting the public health and welfare by preventing residential exposure to the adverse effects of aircraft noise. The court went on to note that unlike the height zoning ordinance in *Sneed*, the

Santa Barbara County land use zoning regulations did not impose height limits or evidence any intent to keep open a public right-of-way through the airspace (aviation easement). Thus, the court found that this land use zoning ordinance did not also involve any exercise of the power of eminent domain to take private property rights for a public use, so the county was not liable to pay the landowner compensation. That was probably just as well, since it turned out that industrial land in Santa Barbara County in such proximity to the city and transportation facilities was scarce and the value of the property actually increased as a result of the rezoning, so that even if an entitlement to just compensation had been found, the amount of that compensation would have been zero because the fair market value of the property had not been diminished. As a result of this decision, land use zoning is now a very popular tool used nationwide in new airport planning.

In the planning process, airport planners predict the airport's "noise footprint" as it will fall on surrounding land (Fig. 13.1). The sound level measurement method most commonly used today is "DNL," the average day-night sound level measure developed by the U.S. Environmental Protection Agency to permit comparison of noise levels from all types of urban sources. It measures ambient noise including aircraft noise and

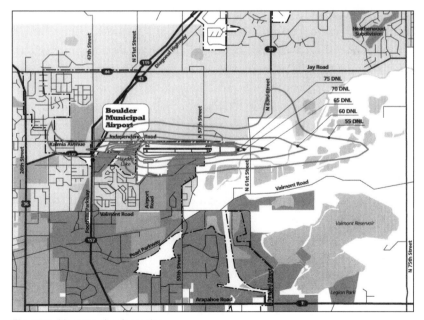

Fig. 13.1. Airport noise footprint.

other noises within the same community setting and imposes a penalty for nighttime (10:00 p.m.–7:00 a.m.) operations, the duration of noise events, and aircraft noise that is above the ambient background level. It is generally accepted that a DNL of 65 or higher is incompatible with noise-sensitive land uses such as homes, schools, churches, and hospitals. Thus, industrial, commercial, and some agricultural land uses are to be preferred within the 65 DNL noise contour. Airport industrial parks have been a particularly successful land use in these noisier areas, since a worker operating a turret lathe or other noisy machinery may be totally oblivious to the passage of a jetliner overhead and the proximity of the airport as a transportation hub may enhance the value of the property in an industrial application. For example, at Atlanta's busy Hartsfield International Airport, aircraft on short final for landing on runway 26R pass extremely low over a major Ford Motor Company automobile assembly plant without annoying the workers inside.

An increase of 10 decibels is perceived by humans as a doubling of the noise level. Therefore, airport planners now generally agree that where aircraft noise will be 75 DNL or greater, that land should be purchased outright and included within the airport's boundaries.

Use zoning, however, is a two-edged sword that may be used not only to protect airports from the encroachment of noise sensitive residential communities but also to protect residential communities from the encroachment of noisy airports. In New Jersey, Garden State Farms, Inc., was one of the early "agribusiness" corporate farming enterprises. The corporation sought a variance to the land use zoning ordinance of the county where the corporation's headquarters was located to permit construction of a heliport outside the headquarters building so that the corporation's executives might be more efficiently transported between the corporate offices and various operating locations around the state. However, the corporate headquarters was located adjacent to a residential area, and the residents objected to the heliport. The county authorities sided with the residents and refused to permit a deviation from the zoning law to allow construction of the heliport. The corporation sued (*Garden State Farms, Inc. v. Bay*), and the court held that state and local governments may also exercise their police power to protect the public health, safety, and welfare by land use zoning to exclude aircraft landing areas.

Injunctions for Nuisance

Sometimes residents who are annoyed by the proximity of an airport seek to obtain an *injunction* from a court to declare the operation of the airport a *nuisance* and order it to cease operation. Nuisance is another intentional tort, but generally a continuing one rather than an isolated incident. If a court finds a particular activity to constitute a nuisance, the court has the option either to award the plaintiff money damages or to issue an injunction prohibiting continuation of the activity that constitutes the nuisance.

Much of American law, as we have seen, derives from the law of England, and at the time of the Declaration of Independence, England had two separate sets of courts, each with its own separate body of law and powers: the *courts of law* and the *courts of chancery*. In the courts of law, judges trained in the common law applied the law. In the courts of chancery, however, judges selected for Solomonic wisdom (but usually untrained in the common law) "did equity"; that is, they issued orders that simply seemed fair. In this system, while the courts of law could enter judgments for money damages, orders for people to do or refrain from doing something were considered *equitable remedies* available only in the courts of chancery.

In the United States, the federal system and most state court systems now consolidate the two, with law courts having the authority to award either legal or equitable remedies. As a general rule, courts consider equitable remedies (which include injunctions) to be extraordinary remedies that should be awarded only if there is no adequate remedy at law—that is, if mere money will not suffice to compensate the plaintiff. Since injunctive relief is an equitable remedy, the court is primarily concerned with answering the question: "What is a fair result in this situation?" This may include a balancing of the interests of the public and of the parties to the lawsuit on imaginary scales of justice.

For example: The approach from either east or west to San Diego International Airport (Lindberg Field) brings aircraft over residential areas (*see* Fig. 13.2). When the airport opened and residents were appalled to find airliners roaring past their windows, they filed suit, seeking a judicial declaration that the operation of this municipal airport constituted a nuisance and asking for an injunction prohibiting operation of the airport (*Loma Portal Civic Club v. American Airlines*).

Fig. 13.2. Photo montage of airliners on final approach to San Diego's Lindbergh Field.

The court refused to hold that operation of the airport constituted a nuisance or to issue an injunction prohibiting its continued operation, finding that under *Causby* and *Griggs*, the landowners had an adequate remedy at law through suits in inverse condemnation to obtain payment of just compensation. The court held that such a suit was the only proper recourse of the landowners because the court found an "overriding public interest" in the operation of this public airport. No court has ever enjoined the operation of a publicly owned airport in the United States.

Privately owned airports, however, have not fared so well (Fig. 13.3). Some private airports have been found to constitute nuisances and have been enjoined against continuing operations. Considerations of fairness in these cases may take into account such factors as who came first, the airport or the complaining residents? If it appears that the airport was there first and the complaining residents "came to the nuisance," a judge might consider it unfair to order the airport to cease operation. In balancing the interests involved, the court may consider not only the rights and interests of the airport operator and complaining residents but also any public benefits from keeping the airport operational. If the airport is open to the public and the airport's attorneys can demonstrate

Fig. 13.3. Private airports do not enjoy the legal protection from noise-sensitive residential encroachment available to governments that own and operate airports. So as the area around a private airport is developed, resident complaints and rising property taxes may render continued operation of the airport uneconomical. Under those pressures, this one recently sold to a developer, who closed it as an airport and is developing it for a mixed-use commercial, retail and residential development.

that if this airport is closed, the city or county will need to build a public airport to replace it, the judge may see a public interest in allowing private enterprise to continue to fill that need. Some private airports have successfully fought off lawsuits seeking to enjoin their continued operation, while others have failed, and some have ceased operations rather than pay unaffordable damages to the surrounding residents following an adverse judgment finding the airport to constitute a nuisance.

The Power to Tax

Local governments have also effectively used their power to impose taxes on real property to force out private airports. In the typical scenario, a private property owner establishes an airport in a rural area well beyond the existing boundaries of a growing city. Property taxes in such an area (usually zoned for agricultural use, with airports being permitted) are usually quite low. But as the metropolitan area grows, residential subdivisions, businesses, and industrial developments creep ever closer to the airport. Eventually, typically as part of a city or countywide master land use plan, the area will be rezoned to accommodate residential or business development. While the airport will still have *grandfather rights* to continue operation as a *nonconforming use* despite the rezoning, property taxes will rise dramatically. Many such airports were financially marginal operations before the tax increase, and this sudden major increase in the cost of doing business often makes it uneconomical to continue at that location. In that circumstance, the airport owner will typically either sell out to a developer or decide to become one.

Noise Ordinances

The onset of a nationwide epidemic of aircraft noise related litigation was triggered by the introduction into airline service of the first generation of jets (Boeing 707, Douglas DC-8, and Convair 880). These aircraft were far noisier (and smokier) than the propeller-driven aircraft that preceded them (or later generations of jet airliners). This new noise burden spurred many communities that had long been neighbors of airports to defensive action.

The village of Cedarhurst, New York, was one such community. The village is located on Long Island, about a mile southeast of John F. Kennedy International Airport (JFK, formerly Idlewild). Several of JFK's runways point toward Cedarhurst. In response to citizen rage over the new noise level, the village government adopted a municipal ordinance that prohibited aircraft from flying over the village at less than one thousand feet above ground level (AGL).

A suit was filed challenging the validity of the ordinance (*Allegheny Airlines v. Village of Cedarhurst*). At trial, it was demonstrated through the use of FAA-approved instrument approach plates that many federally mandated instrument approach procedures leading to JFK required that aircraft overfly Cedarhurst at altitudes below one thousand feet AGL. The court found a pervasive federal regulatory scheme in the FAA's establishment of JFK arrival and departure routes as part of a nationwide system plan regulating interstate and foreign air commerce. Since the village ordinance prohibited aircraft from flying over the village below one thousand feet AGL, while the federal regulatory scheme mandated that aircraft fly over the village below one thousand feet AGL, the village ordinance was in direct conflict with federal regulations. Therefore, the court held that the supremacy clause of the Constitution rendered the municipal ordinance unenforceable.

Nearby, citizens of the town of Hempstead were also irate over this new burden of noise from JFK. When the *Cedarhurst* decision was announced, the town council appears to have instructed the town's attorney to find a way around that decision. Soon the town adopted a municipal noise ordinance setting decibel limits on the maximum noise anyone or anything (not only aircraft) could make in the town of Hempstead. The town promptly attempted to enforce the ordinance against aircraft flying overhead, inbound to JFK.

The validity of this ordinance too was soon tested in court (*American Airlines v. Town of Hempstead*). Expert testimony revealed that in order for a Boeing 707 overflying the town to avoid violating the town's noise limit, it would have to fly at an altitude of at least (surprise, surprise) one thousand feet AGL. Again, numerous FAA-approved instrument approach procedures leading to the airport required the aircraft to fly over the town at altitudes below one thousand feet AGL. Looking at this practical effect, the court found that the ordinance, *as applied against aircraft*, was in direct conflict with the federal regulatory scheme. The supremacy clause would prohibit the town from enforcing a noise ordinance against aircraft (although the town remained free to enforce the ordinance against terrestrial noise sources such as motorcycles, lawn mowers, leaf blowers, chain saws and the like).

Not far south, in the pine barrens of New Jersey, the government of the rural township of Lakewood adopted a noise ordinance virtually identical to Hempstead's. At the time, Parachutes, Inc. was operating a commercial skydiving school at the Lakewood Municipal Airport utilizing several World War II vintage Canadian-built Noorduyn Norseman jump planes, which in the author's personal observation are surely among the noisiest single-piston engine-powered aircraft ever conceived. These aircraft would take off from the Lakewood Municipal Airport, climb overhead in the immediate vicinity, drop their parachutists, and spiral back down to land, never straying more than a few miles from the airport.

When the township sought to enforce its noise ordinance against Parachutes, Inc., the corporation challenged the validity of the ordinance (*Parachutes, Inc. v. Township of Lakewood*). At trial, it was shown that the federal government exercised little control over the flight patterns of these aircraft. There was no control tower at the airport, and the only contact the jump planes were required to have with ATC was to report to New York Center one minute before each jump, advising them of the altitude from which the jump would be made, then later to advise when the last jumper had landed. The aircraft were free to climb and descend in the area at the pilot's discretion and were in no way constrained by federally mandated routings. Under these facts, the court found that the enforcement of the township's ordinance against the aircraft did not conflict with any regulatory scheme, so the supremacy clause did not come into play. Therefore, the court found enforcement of this noise ordinance against these aircraft legally valid. The corporation then replaced its Lakewood fleet with a quieter fleet of Cessnas and a DC-3, which enabled them to continue operations at that airport without violating the town's noise ordinance.

Proprietary Powers: Curfews and Restrictions on Airport Use

Meanwhile, back on the West Coast, the City of Santa Monica, California, owns and operates the Santa Monica Municipal Airport (SMO). Originally called Clover Field, this was one of the Los Angeles basin's earliest airports, developed long before the wisdom of noise compatible land use planning in the vicinity of airports became recognized, so the airport now appears as an aircraft carrier afloat in a sea of homes. Acting in its capacity as the *proprietor* of the airport, the city imposed a *curfew* on jet aircraft operations at the airport between the hours of 11:00 p.m. and 7:00 a.m. The validity of the curfew was challenged in court (*Stagg v. Santa Monica*, also known as *Santa Monica I* since this was only the beginning of a continuing series of legal battles at this airport). No airlines served Santa Monica, and this case appears to have caught general aviation interests napping. The court found that the jet curfew did not conflict with any federal regulatory scheme, so that the supremacy clause was no barrier, and that it was a valid exercise of the police power since it was intended to protect the public health and welfare by affording citizens a better night's sleep.

About this time, the U.S. Supreme Court decided that the time had come for it to render another decision updating the Court's thinking in the area of airport noise law. It decided to grant certiorari to hear the case of *Lockheed Air Terminal, Inc. v. City of Burbank*, arising out of attempts by the cities of Burbank and Glendale to regulate the noise of aircraft coming and going from an airport privately owned and operated by Lockheed Aircraft Corp. Unfortunately, the case was poorly chosen; it involved the only privately owned and operated airport in the country having interstate airline service, so the Court's laborious and intricate analysis had little general relevance to other airports. (In fact, shortly after the Court's decision was issued, Lockheed sold the airport to a regional airport authority—formed by the cities of Burbank, Glendale and Pasadena—which now operates it, so that the Court's decision no longer addresses even the facts of that previously unique airport.) As it would turn out, the most enduring contribution of *Lockheed v. Burbank* came in footnote 14 to the decision, which suggested that a governmental entity that owns and operates an airport may be legally able, *acting as proprietor*, to deny use of the airport to aircraft on the basis of noise considerations, as long as the exclusion does not discriminate against aircraft traveling in interstate or foreign commerce.

The City of Santa Monica (whose airport lay only about 15 air miles from Lockheed's) viewed that footnote as a green light from the Supreme Court, and in its capacity as proprietor of its municipal airport adopted five more restrictions in form of airport use regulations:

1. *Curfew.* Engine starts and takeoffs by *any* aircraft were prohibited between 11:00 p.m. and 6:00 a.m.
2. *Fixed wing flight training.* Touch-and-go landings, stop-and-go landings and low approaches were prohibited on weekends and holidays.
3. *Helicopter flight training.* Helicopter flight training was prohibited at all times.
4. *Noise limit.* Aircraft operations exceeding a 100-decibel single-event noise level (SENEL) were prohibited (and noise meters were installed off both runway ends).

5. *Jet prohibition*. All jets were prohibited from using the airport at all times. (The city even erected huge "NO JETS" signs off the approach ends of the runway.)

The validity of these new regulations was soon challenged in court (*Santa Monica Airport Association v. Santa Monica*, also known as *Santa Monica II*). Drawing on the preceding line of cases, the court held that the constitutional validity of regulations limiting the use of a public airport adopted by a governmental entity in its capacity as proprietor of that airport depends upon a three-step test:

1. Does the regulation affect interstate commerce? If not, then the regulation is constitutionally valid. If so, the court must then consider the next question.
2. Has the governmental entity acted within its jurisdiction, and is the regulation reasonable? If not, the regulation is unenforceable. If so, the court must proceed to question 3.
3. Local interests supporting the regulation must be balanced against the burden the regulation imposes on interstate or foreign air commerce. If the regulation does not discriminate between interstate (and/or foreign) and intrastate commerce and it has only slight adverse effect on interstate (and/or foreign), it will be valid. But if the regulation discriminates against interstate (and/or foreign) commerce or if the burden on interstate (and/or foreign) commerce is clearly excessive in relation to the local benefits, the regulation is void.

Applying this line of reasoning to each of Santa Monica's five new regulations, the court found that the first four imposed an "insubstantial burden, if any, on interstate commerce" and did not discriminate against interstate commerce, that the city was acting within its jurisdiction, and the regulations were reasonable to minimize the impact of noise from aircraft using the city's airport on the surrounding residential community during those times of night, weekends, and holidays when the need for leisure and rest in the community was the highest. Thus, the court found those first four regulations (curfew, limitations on fixed-wing flight training, ban on helicopter flight training, and noise limits) legally valid and enforceable. As to the fifth, the jet ban, however, it was proved that some jets (such as the Cessna Citation) were actually quieter than some piston-engine aircraft allowed to continue using the airport. The court thus found the jet ban to be void because it imposed an impermissible burden on interstate commerce and was unreasonable, banning some jet aircraft that were quieter than some piston aircraft that would have been allowed to continue to use the airport.

Buoyed by this decision, the City of Santa Monica almost immediately modified the single-event noise limit contained in the fourth of these regulations, reducing it from 100 decibels to 85 decibels, which virtually no powered aircraft could meet. The new regulation was also soon challenged in court (*Santa Monica III*).

Many national aviation organizations filed *amicus curiae* ("friend of the court") briefs siding with the airport users. The FAA also finally became concerned over the potential loss of a valuable general aviation reliever airport in the Los Angeles basin. The city had received federal airport improvement funds to aid in the airport's development over the years. To obtain federal funds, the city was required to sign a contract with the federal government, known as a *grant agreement*, in which the city agreed (among other things) to keep the airport open to the general public as an airport without discriminating against any aeronautical user or class of aeronautical user. At this point, the FAA notified the city that unless it backed off to a more reasonable single-event noise limit on aircraft, the FAA would consider the city to be in breach of its grant agreements and would take legal action to compel the city to repay all federal funds it had obtained.

Motivated by that specter, the city reached a settlement agreement with the federal government and aviation interests whereby the single-event noise limit was increased to 95 decibels, and it was further agreed that the airport would remain open without any further restrictions until the year 2015. One would think that would have been the end of it, at least until 2015, but in 2003 the city imposed a new landing fee schedule at the airport as part of the funding stream for its maintenance program for runways, taxiways and ramps. The fees, imposed on a per-landing basis, were on a sliding scale based on aircraft weight, ranging from 29 cents per 1,000 pounds for light aircraft up to $5.81 per pound for aircraft weighing 60,000 pounds or more. This could amount to about $325 per landing for a Gulfstream IV business jet as compared to less than $3 for a Citation 500/525. The FAA investigated and in a 2005 opinion sided with the aircraft operators, finding the fee schedule to be unreasonable and to result in unjust discrimination against one group of aviation users, in violation of the grant agreement. (By this point, general aviation interests appear to have stopped counting the number of Santa Monica disputes.) Santa Monica has since also tried to evict or keep out larger jets (such as actor John Travolta's Boeing 707), first by banning category C and D aircraft (having approach speeds greater than 121 knots and up to 166 knots at maximum certificated landing weight) from landing (subject to a $1,000 fine or up to 6 months in jail for each violation). When the FAA found that a violation of the grant agreement, the city next tried to accomplish the same thing by proposing to replace 300 feet of useable pavement on each end of the airport's single 4,973-foot long runway with a runway safety areas (RSA) composed of engineered material arresting system beds to prevent overruns, effectively shortening the useable runway to such an extent that category C and D aircraft could not use it. In 2008, the FAA found this proposed alteration would also violate the grant agreement.

The current state of the law in this area was most succinctly summarized in litigation arising out of the introduction of the now defunct Concorde supersonic transport (SST) into transatlantic service (*British Airways v. Port of New York Authority*). In deciding that case, the court held that regulation of commercial aviation in the United States is a two-tiered system:

1. Exclusive control of airspace allocation and use is concentrated at the national level, and state, regional, and local governmental entities are preempted from trying to regulate planes in flight.

2. The task of protecting the local population from airport noise, however, falls on the government operating the airport, and it may achieve this goal through acquisition of property and aviation easements, zoning for compatible land uses, and the issuance of reasonable, non-arbitrary, and nondiscriminatory rules governing use of the airport that do not impermissibly burden interstate commerce.

This two-tiered system has been uniformly followed by the courts in the latest litigation challenging the principle of federal preemption of the use of the navigable airspace and the regulation of airplanes in flight. In *Country Aviation, Inc. v. Tinicum Township*, the court struck down a local government's attempt to use its police power to enforce an aviation noise control ordinance against glider-towing aircraft operating at the privately owned Van Zant Airport, home to a glider club in Upper Bucks County, Pennsylvania. In *Banner Advertising, Inc. v. City of Boulder*, the Colorado Supreme Court struck down the City of Boulder's attempt to purge the city's skies of aircraft towing commercial advertising messages (usually over University of Colorado home football games) by a provision in the city's sign code. Huntington Beach, California, adopted a similar ordinance, but rescinded it following clarification from the FAA that it was in conflict with the FAA's exclusive control of the airspace. In *Gustafson v. City of Lake Angelus*, the court struck down a southeast Michigan city ordinance prohibiting operation by any aircraft below 500 feet over a lake owned by the city in a suit filed by a waterfront homeowner and seaplane pilot. In each of these cases, the court found the law to be long settled that except for reasonable noise control regulations adopted by airport proprietors, all state and local regulation of the noise of aircraft in flight is preempted by pervasive federal regulations governing airspace management and aviation noise control.

The Power of the Purse, Strings Attached: Grant Agreement Constraints

Where, however, the airport proprietor has accepted federal AIP airport planning and improvement grants, the assurances in the grant agreement further limit the proprietor's latitude to regulate and restrict the use of the airport. Most significantly, the airport proprietor must agree to keep the airport open for the use and benefit of the public and *"all types, kinds, and classes of aeronautical use on fair and reasonable terms without discrimination between such types, kinds, and classes unless prohibition or limitation of any given type, kind, or class of aeronautical use of the airport is necessary for the safe operation of the airport or necessary to serve the civil aviation needs of the public."*

These obligations typically continue for at least twenty years from the date of the last acceptance of federal aid. Thus, by accepting federal airport planning and improvement funds, the airport proprietor forfeits the right it would otherwise have to close the airport before the expiration of that twenty-year term and to exclude any particular type of aviation operation so long as it remains compatible with the safe and efficient operation of the airport.

The courts have uniformly held that only the FAA can sue to enforce these grant agreement assurances; that persons denied access to the airport do not have legal *standing to sue* as third-party beneficiaries of this contract to enforce its provisions. Thus, if an operator is denied access to a federally funded airport, the only available recourse is to file a written complaint of discrimination with the local FAA Airports

District Office (ADO). The ADO is required to investigate all complaints and determine whether the airport proprietor is in compliance with the grant agreement assurances. During the investigation, the FAA usually withholds any additional grant funds that may be forthcoming. If the FAA finds that the airport proprietor is in breach of the grant agreement assurances, future aid will be denied, and the United States may initiate litigation for *specific performance* (a court order that the proprietor comply with the grant agreement) or to recover federal funds previously furnished.

It is entirely within the FAA's discretion to decide how to resolve each complaint of discrimination on a case-by-case basis, and the FAA has demonstrated a high degree of practicality in analyzing these complaints. For example, if you were denied access to a small low-activity rural general aviation airport which had received federal funds where you proposed to operate an ultralight flight school, the FAA would likely side with you and prevail upon the airport authority to permit your proposed operation or face the consequences. On the other hand, if you complained that you were denied permission to conduct that same operation at Chicago's O'Hare International Airport, you would probably be laughed right out of the FAA office.

In recent years, the FAA has demonstrated both the will to aggressively enforce grant agreements as needed to protect recipient airports and admirable flexibility and creativity in working with airport authorities to amend the requirements of grant agreements where needed to foster and promote airport development. Denver's experience provides an excellent example. Like many airports, Denver's Stapleton International Airport had been built early in the last century, out in a country cow pasture, miles from downtown. So far out, in fact, that the airport (named for then-mayor Ben Stapleton) was derisively called "Stapleton's folly." Land use planning had not yet come into vogue, and within a few decades residential subdivisions crept up to the airport fence, an experience shared by virtually all airports built during that same era. Surrounding developments limited airport expansion, limiting the airport's capacity. The runways were too close together to permit simultaneous parallel ILS approaches in instrument meteorological conditions (IMC), so that bad weather at Denver (a major hub) caused delays to ripple throughout the country. This was stifling the growth potential of the region, and hostility between the airport and its noise-sensitive neighbors was escalating.

Denver got serious about following Dallas and Fort Worth's lead to leapfrog far beyond the built-up metropolitan area to buy a vast tract of grazing land and build a new airline airport with suitable easements and land use protection. But federal grants had steadily flowed into improvements at Stapleton, presenting two obstacles to the project. The city faced a real stretch to finance the new airport, even without having to repay the federal grants expended on Stapleton over the previous 20 years. If the FAA held the city to the grant agreement, there was no way the city could afford to build the airport needed for its future. Denver also saw that by keeping Love Field open to airlines, Dallas had stunted the initial growth of DFW. Denver wanted to completely close Stapleton as an airport the day the new airport opened, forcing all airline traffic to move to the new facility, but that would also run afoul of the grant agreement.

The FAA and its parent, the DOT, wanted the new airport to happen and to succeed. They agreed with the practical need to close Stapleton contemporaneously with the opening of the new airport. To facilitate the project, the FAA agreed to waive the Stapleton grant provisions.

At 34,000 acres, the Denver International Airport (DIA) (Fig. 13.4) has more land area than JFK, O'Hare and DFW combined. It opened during a snowstorm, and immediately accepted triple simultaneous ILS

Fig. 13.4. Mirroring the snowcapped Rockies, the distinctive white tent-roofed Jeppesen Terminal Building provides a stunning backdrop for this Southwest Airlines 737 taking off from Denver International Airport (DIA). (Photo provided courtesy of Denver International Airport)

approaches ("trips" in ATC lingo) to IFR minimums. (That practice, the first in the U.S., had originally been planned to phase in over a period of weeks, but on opening night, during a snowstorm, the "trips" started immediately.) The airport's layout allows aircraft to taxi between any runway and the terminal without crossing any other runway (by comparison, DFW averages 147 runway crossings per hour). Stapleton closed an hour or two after DIA opened, and its land is being redeveloped for non-aviation urban uses. DIA has since added a 16,000-foot runway (the longest public use runway in the U.S.) to accommodate takeoffs of the heaviest fully loaded jets under the highest density altitudes that occur on the hottest summer days (and permitting quadruple simultaneous ILS approaches to minimums). There's still room left over to add six more runways to the airport, if needed.

Chicago's recent abrupt closure of downtown lakefront general aviation reliever Meigs Field (accomplished by bulldozers destroying the runway in the middle of the night, without any prior notice to either the FAA or owners of aircraft then left stranded on the field) was hotly but unsuccessfully contested by general aviation interests, and succeeded only because of a set of provisions unique to that agreement. Those provisions were included in the agreement only because the city did not own the airport property, but operated it under a long-term lease from the landowner. It was these unique contract provisions, and not any lack of will on the part of the FAA, that stymied any effort to enforce the grant agreement and compel the city to keep the airport open when the lease expired. The closure of Meigs Field, though a serious and wasteful loss, should be seen as an aberration, not a portent of things to come, since aggressive FAA enforcement of grant agreements continues at other airports.

For example, the FAA demanded that Ocean City, Maryland, repay $13.3 million for 267 acres of land adjacent to the airport, originally purchased with federal aid money for the purpose of providing a noise buffer and expansion room for the airport but developed by the city instead as a golf course. The golf course (Eagle's Landing, rated one of the top 75 public courses in the U.S. by Golf Digest) had proved so profitable that the city decided not to go forward with two planned safety-related runway extensions that would extend into the land. The FAA also threatened to cut off existing grants of up to a half million dollars a year for maintenance of the airport.

The Complication of Political Boundaries

A government may exercise its power of eminent domain and police power only within its geopolitical boundaries. Airport noise and required clear zones, however, frequently cross those political boundaries. For example, in the Denver metropolitan area Denver International Airport is almost completely surrounded by another county and three of the area's four general aviation reliever airports abut a county line, so that in all cases a substantial portion of the noise generated by aircraft using these airports falls on cities and counties other than the airport proprietor and clear zones must be maintained outside the territorial jurisdiction of the airport's proprietor.

In such a case (or when the airport is operated by a regional airport authority not possessing the police power to zone), the cooperation of surrounding county or municipal governments must be obtained and nurtured. Through an *intergovernmental agreement* (IGA), the airport proprietor may obtain the commitment of surrounding governments to use their police powers to assure noise-compatible land uses in the area impacted by the airport, to add soundproofing requirements to applicable building codes, to deny building permits to incompatible uses, to height zone as appropriate to protect the required clear zones for air traffic, and to use their powers of eminent domain to acquire necessary land and aviation easements (typically at the airport proprietor's expense, which may include federal matching funds). In exchange for this commitment, the surrounding governments may exact a price, such as seats on the airport's governing board, a say in the airport's operations, layout and preferential runway use, and even a guarantee of public sector jobs at the airport for their residents.

ENVIRONMENTAL IMPACT

Airport development and its funding is considered a *major federal action that may affect the quality of the environment*, bringing into play the National Environmental Policy Act of 1969 (NEPA). NEPA requires preparation of an *environmental impact statement* (EIS) for projects that could affect the environment. Some states have adopted similar requirements for state and local projects that could affect the environment. These requirements may apply to improvements to existing airports as well as the development of new airports. Opponents of airport development have achieved some success in the courts in enjoining federal funding of airport projects where the EIS did not meet NEPA requirements. Further, if the study is viewed by those who stand to be adversely affected by the project as a "railroad job" working toward a foregone conclusion with little real consideration being given to citizen concerns, the intergovernmental cooperation necessary to success of the project becomes much more difficult to achieve. It is crucial that the study leading to the EIS be thorough, objective and legitimate and that it be completed as early as possible in the planning phase to avoid the risk of an injunction interrupting construction or financing of the project once ground has been broken.

Airports also require storage capacity for aviation fuels. Therefore, airport planners must take into account federal underground storage tank (UST) regulations promulgated under the federal Resource Conservation and Recovery Act (RCRA, pronounced "rickra"). Bringing aging fuel storage facilities into compliance has proved a major expense for many airports and has even caused some small fields to discontinue fuel service.

Concern over potential impacts of the global warming trend so clearly depicted in former vice president Al Gore's movie *An Inconvenient Truth* have focused worldwide attention on the need to drastically reduce the emission of the so-called *greenhouse gases* attributable to human activities that are deemed largely responsible for the trend. At this writing, proposed legislation is pending in Congress that would impose European Union-style cap-and-trade limits on carbon emissions. Although the airline industry is estimated to contribute only 2% of the total of these emissions, much of that is emitted in the upper atmosphere where it may have a disproportionately adverse effect. U.S. airlines' compliance costs are estimated at over $20 billion per year, a very significant negative impact on a struggling industry. At least one version of the proposed legislation exempts the airlines from coverage for this reason.

Regardless of what may be the outcome of that legislative process, airframe and engine manufacturers, airlines, energy companies, and government agencies are already making remarkable progress to reduce these emissions. Among the advances are procedural improvements in operations (such as continuous descent approaches that reduce fuel burn) and maintenance (such as frequently washing turbine engines), air traffic control (such as gate holds, direct routings and continuous descent approaches), aerodynamics and structures (such as weight saving through increased use of composites, as on the Boeing 787), engine efficiencies (with improvements to turbine engine design promising up to 20% fuel savings), and alternative fuels (some of which are showing increased power with decreased carbon emissions).

SOME OTHER SOLUTIONS THAT HAVE WORKED

Not all solutions to the twin problems of aircraft noise and keeping approaches to airports clear of obstacles have been found in the courts. The FAA has been very actively involved in the noise problem through regulation, funding, and procedures. Congress' enactment of the Airport Noise and Capacity Act of 1990 (ANCA), the first comprehensive federal statute addressing airport noise, required new air transport aircraft designs to be quieter and the phasing out of older, noisier jet transports or their silencing through engine replacement or "hush kits." ANCA prohibited airports from establishing new noise or access restrictions unless approved by the FAA or agreed to by the airport operator and all aircraft operators, but "grandfathered in" pre-existing restrictions. The FAA has worked with local airport operators to develop noise abatement procedures appropriate to specific locations, including runway use preferences that (winds permitting) route departures over the least noise-sensitive neighboring areas and establish climb and descent profiles to reduce aircraft noise (hopefully without compromising flight safety). Federal airport development funds have also been made available for the acquisition of land and aviation easements for noise abatement and clear zone purposes and for the soundproofing of buildings affected by airport noise.

Once upon a time, a residential area of palatial homes lay between the Los Angeles International Airport (LAX) and the Pacific Ocean. With the introduction of jets into airline service, residents of that area began to file and win inverse condemnation suits against the city of Los Angeles (proprietor of LAX). The jet noise and smoke (early airline jets trailed quite a plume of black smoke and this was before mechanical clothes dryers became popular, when most people still dried their laundry outside on a clothesline) destroyed the quality of life in the area. When Congress amended the legislation governing federal funding of airport improvements to permit these federal funds (which may cover up to 95% of a project's costs) to be used to purchase land and aviation easements for noise-abatement purposes, the city of Los Angeles went on the offensive. The city targeted this noise-impacted community for maximum federal funding (then 90%, which was approved), then condemned and purchased the entire residential area and removed all of the homes. The area is now a popular state beach.

In Dallas, Texas, the Love Field airport is quite convenient to downtown. At one time, Dallas banks became engaged in a competition to build higher and higher office towers. 14 CFR Part 77 requires that before constructing anything that could be an obstacle to aircraft, the sponsor must notify the FAA. Upon receipt of such a notice, the FAA performs an *obstruction analysis* to determine the effects of the project on flight operations at the airport. The FAA then issues one of three determinations: (1) that it has no objection to the proposal, (2) that it has no objection to the proposal *if* certain conditions are met (such as the realignment of a traffic pattern), or (3) that the proposal is objectionable because it would adversely affect air navigation. The FAA, however, neither permits nor prohibits the proposed construction, leaving that decision to the local government having jurisdiction over zoning and the issuance of building permits in the area.

In the case of one of Dallas's proposed skyscraper banks, the FAA found that the structure would constitute an obstruction to air navigation, requiring decommissioning of instrument approaches to Love Field from the southeast. The FAA did not prohibit the construction but merely announced its finding and plans, which were well publicized in the local media. This would have greatly reduced the utility of this popular airport, and the bank apparently soon felt the brunt of considerable resentment from the local business community over the prospect of the bank's depriving them of the convenient use of this airport. The bank quickly yielded to public opinion, announcing that why, shoot, everybody knew that they were the biggest and best bank in Dallas, and they didn't have to build some silly skyscraper to prove it. The airport's approaches remained unobstructed.

Washington, D.C.'s Reagan National Airport (Fig. 1.3) has long been considered a noisy annoyance by its Virginia neighbors. In an effort to improve the situation without resorting to regulation, the airport's owner/operator (then the FAA) announced a *"voluntary jet curfew,"* requesting that corporate jets voluntarily refrain from using the airport between 11:00 p.m. and 7:00 a.m. When the voluntary program took effect, not all corporate jet users "volunteered." But then the local newspaper published the names of the major corporations whose jets, by choosing not to participate in the voluntary curfew, had awakened the airport's neighbors. The airport's neighbors wrote letters to those corporations, expressing their displeasure, often vowing not to do business with those corporations again, and sometimes highlighting the strength of their convictions by enclosing the severed remains of credit cards the corporation had issued to the writers. The corporations swiftly responded to this public reaction, and it was not long before "voluntary" participation in the curfew reached the 100 percent level.

Noise complaints are often triggered by pilots executing a lower than normal approach to an airport, "dragging it in under power." 14 CFR §91.129(e)(3) requires that when operating in Class D airspace, an airplane approaching to land on a runway served by a visual approach slope indicator or precision approach path indicator (VASI or PAPI) shall maintain an altitude at or above the glide slope until a lower altitude is necessary for a safe landing. The city of Santa Monica has installed a "PAPI-cam" at SMO, where the precision approach path indicator is set to project a 4-degree glide slope. It incorporates a video camera and theodolite that record and measure the descent profile of every VFR approach to runway 21. If a neighbor calls the airport to complain about a low approach and review of the video tape shows the aircraft to have been more than 1.5 degrees below the glide slope when within two miles of the airport, the pilot receives a warning letter from the airport manager. A second violation by the same pilot is referred to the FAA for counseling or enforcement action. A special benefit of the system is that it is a truly unbiased observer that can also disprove neighbors' complaints by confirming that the aircraft was not below the glide slope.

The Teterboro, New Jersey, airport (TEB) is a designated general aviation reliever airport serving the New York/New Jersey area. Beginning flight operations in 1919, TEB is the oldest operating airport in the area and since the early 1960s has been one of the busiest business jet bases on the East Coast. The airport, which is operated by the Port Authority of New York and New Jersey, has long experienced a love/hate relationship with the surrounding community. The community loves the reported 1,137 jobs at the airport, the 15,554 other jobs it creates, and the $1.8 billion it generates in annual economic activity in the region, but hates the noise it generates in the process (especially at night, when most people are trying to sleep). This tends to be a typical relationship between airports and their neighbors. As proprietor of TEB, the port authority imposed some noise-level restrictions on departures from the airport that vary according to the time of day and continue in effect because they predate ANCA. The restrictions are enforced by a "three strikes and you're out" compliance program. If an aircraft departing the airport exceeds the applicable noise level, the airport manager sends the operator a violation letter. If the operator receives three violations in a two-year period, that aircraft is banned from the airport forever. Although ostensibly barred by ANCA from adopting tougher restrictions, TEB also recently succeeded (at least for now and with the help of congressional legislation) in banning aircraft having a maximum takeoff weight (MTOW) of more than 100,000 lbs. Ostensibly adopted to protect runway, taxiway, and ramp pavement life, local officials and their congressional representative openly stated that the real purpose of the ban was to protect the community from the noise of the increasingly popular Boeing Business Jet derivative of the 737 (MTOW 171,000 lbs). Also, in an effort to reduce the increasing local antagonism toward the airport, the Teterboro Airport Working Group—composed of representatives of the aviation industry, the airport's governing agency (the Port Authority of New York and New Jersey), and state and local politicians—agreed to a voluntary 11 p.m.–6 a.m. curfew. Such voluntary agreements are not affected by ANCA. In the first 2 years of the program, the number of night operations decreased by 16% and the airport publicly handed out "Good Neighbor Awards" to those TEB-based operators that had never violated the voluntary curfew.

Continuous descent approaches (CDA) are now being widely used for fuel saving and airport area noise reduction. On a CDA, aircraft meeting Required Navigation Performance standards are able to begin a smooth and stable descent at reduced power from cruise altitude up to 120 miles from the airport and all the way to landing, eliminating the throttle jockeying necessitated by step down approach procedures previously in common use, and resulting in fuel savings and noise reduction.

SUMMARY

Publicly Owned Airports

The *governmental entity that owns the airport* can:

1. As proprietor, impose curfews and other reasonable limitations on the use of the airport as long as these limitations are not

discriminatory against or unduly burdensome on interstate or foreign commerce and are reasonable.

2. Condemn and purchase land and aviation easements within their jurisdiction in the vicinity of the airport, through the power of eminent domain (and seek federal airport improvement funds to aid in financing those purchases).

3. Impose land use zoning and height zoning on land within their jurisdiction in the vicinity of the airport under the police power (but may have to pay just compensation to some landowners if height zoning diminishes their property values).

4. Add soundproofing requirements to building codes applicable to construction in areas impacted by airport noise and pay to soundproof existing structures in that area (and impose passenger facility charges and seek federal airport improvement funds to aid in financing that soundproofing).

5. Enter into Intergovernmental Agreements with other local governments to accomplish items 2 through 4, above, beyond the jurisdiction of the airport-owning government.

6. Close the airport, unless federal airport aid funds have been received, in which case they may have to be repaid, unless a Denver-style deal can be struck with the FAA, or the FAA may seek court-ordered specific performance to require the owner to keep the airport open to the public.

Even the airport proprietor has no control of overflights by aircraft not using the airport.

Citizens can file *Causby* suits in inverse condemnation for taking of an aviation easement over their property or suits for damages in tort (nuisance) and can recover money damages (in the amount by which the value of the property was reduced by virtue of airport operations) but cannot obtain an injunction to close or restrict the airport.

Governments can also use-zone airports out of their jurisdiction.

Adjacent governments that do not own the airport can do nothing.

Privately Owned Airports

The private *airport owner* can:

1. Purchase adjacent lands or aviation easements over them, but only if the owners are willing to sell. (Private landowners do not have the power of eminent domain and therefore cannot condemn and take the property of other private landowners.)

2. Impose limitations on use of the airport without limit unless federal airport development funds have been accepted (which is now possible for private airports open to the public where the FAA has designated the airport as a general aviation reliever airport needed to draw general aviation traffic away from a busy airline hub airport in the area).

Citizens can bring suit against the airport owner for nuisance and obtain a judgment for money damages or an injunction compelling the airport to cease operations.

The *local government having jurisdiction over the property* can preclude construction of an airport by land use zoning or render the continued operation of an established private airport uneconomical by raising property taxes.

Adjacent governments not having jurisdiction over the property can do nothing.

14

FAA Regulation of Airspace

Through the Federal Aviation Act of 1958, Congress empowered the FAA Administrator to regulate the use of the navigable airspace as he in the exercise of his discretion deems necessary in order to assure the safety of aircraft and the efficient utilization of such airspace.

The FAA accomplishes this primarily through rulemaking published in 14 CFR Part 71, which establishes:

Class A Airspace. Positively controlled airspace above Flight Level (FL) 180, where the turbines cruise under IFR.

Class B Airspace. "Upside-down wedding cake" configurations of positively-controlled airspace to protect aircraft arriving and departing from airports serving a high volume of airline traffic.

Class C Airspace. Protecting aircraft using medium-sized commercial airline airports.

Class D Airspace. Protecting traffic at smaller airports having air traffic control towers.

Class E Airspace. For en route air navigation below FL 180 and for instrument operations at airports not having an air traffic control tower.

Special Use Airspace. Airspace which FAA has ceded control over to another agency. Examples include:

- *Restricted Areas* where activities incompatible with the safe flight of civil aircraft (such as artillery or missile firing, aerial gunnery and bombardment) are conducted (R-2601 at Ft. Carson, Colorado, is an example).

- **Prohibited Areas** established for national security reasons (P-56, encompassing the White House and Capitol buildings in Washington, D.C., for example).

- **Warning Areas** to alert pilots to hazardous activities in international airspace (the FAA term "warning area" is synonymous with the ICAO term "danger area"). W-72, located 3–12 miles off the Virginia coast, is an example.

- **Military Operations Areas (MOA)** to notify pilots of areas where the armed forces regularly conduct such operations as air combat maneuvering ("dogfighting"), intercepts, aerobatics and low-level tactics. Civilian pilots operating under VFR may choose as a matter of prudence to avoid flight through MOAs during military operations, since the military pilots may not be able to devote much of their attention to scanning for nonparticipating traffic during this type of flying. LaVeta MOA in Southern Colorado, where jet fighters engage in simulated air combat, is an example.

- **Alert Areas** to inform pilots of areas where a high volume of pilot training or an unusual type of aeronautical activity is regularly conducted. A-260 at the U.S. Air Force Academy in Colorado, which has an extraordinarily high level of flight training in powered airplanes and gliders as well as parachuting packed into a small area, is an example.

- **Controlled Firing Areas** are established instead of restricted areas where the gunnery or rocketry activities are of short duration and can be immediately suspended on notice of an intruding aircraft.

- **Military Training Routes (MTR)** alert pilots of civil aircraft to routes along which the FAA allows high-speed flight below 10,000 feet MSL by military aircraft.

- **Air Defense Identification Zones (ADIZ)** established around U.S. borders and, since the terrorist attacks of 9/11, Washington, D.C., and **National Security Airspace** over such potential terrorist targets as nuclear plants (Fig. 14.1) and chemical facilities impose special requirements for penetration by civil aircraft and subject aircraft to interception by military aircraft for visual identification (Fig. 14.2).

The FAA may also impose *temporary flight restrictions* (TFRs) by Notice to Airmen (NOTAM). These typically cover areas to be visited by the president, vice president and other security-sensitive public figures as well as space flight operational areas (such as Cape Canaveral,

Fig. 14.1. As a result of post 9/11 terrorism concerns, the airspace above and surrounding this nuclear powerplant is now likely national security airspace.

Fig. 14.2. Attention no civilian pilot wants: an unauthorized airspace intrusion may get you a fighter escort to a welcoming committee of law enforcement or Secret Service officers and FAA inspectors who will have lots of questions for you. (U.S. Air Force photo)

Vandenberg, and Edwards Air Force Bases). Temporary flight restrictions are also designated in areas where nonparticipating aircraft might interfere with disaster relief, law enforcement, or fire fighting aircraft operations. They are also imposed where an unsafe congestion of sightseeing and other aircraft might otherwise occur above an event (such as the Super Bowl).

Temporary flight restrictions are also sometimes announced by NOTAM pending establishment and charting of restricted airspace. An example occurred in August of 1993, when the U.S. Customs Service installed an aerostat (balloon) bearing a radar system, tethered near Glencoe, California, by a 15,000-foot unlighted and difficult-to-see cable to detect low-flying drug smugglers.

Since 9/11/01, implementation of TFRs has been a major tool used by the FAA in coordination with the DHS, TSA and Secret Service to help address domestic security concerns. TFRs have been established to help protect events gathering large open-air assemblies of people (including, for example, major sporting events such as NASCAR races, college football bowl games and a variety of professional games).

The FAA may also establish *Special Flight Rules Areas (SFRA)* where restrictions to flight apply. Examples include the Washington, D.C., area (which, immediately following 9/11, was established via the temporary flight restriction process as an Air Defense Identification Zone—the only one within U.S. borders—and after a 7-year rulemaking process converted to a permanent SFRA) and Grand Canyon National Park, discussed later in this chapter.

What remains is *Class G Airspace* (formerly known as *uncontrolled airspace*), an endangered species.

SECURITY CONTROL OF AIR TRAFFIC AND AIR NAVIGATION AIDS (SCATANA)

On September 9, 1950, Congress directed the FAA's forerunner, the CAA, to develop and implement plans for security control of air traffic whenever U.S. security is endangered. At that time, Cold War tensions between the U.S. and the communist bloc were escalating, and the Russians were building a potentially formidable long-range bomber force. The concern was that enemy bombers might penetrate U.S. air defenses by hiding in the radar shadow of civilian airliners and home in on their targets navigating by reference to U.S. radio aids to navigation, such as VORTACs, and that the presence of civilian aircraft in the battle space could confuse or interfere with air defense efforts.

The plan, called *SCATANA*, short for *Security Control of Air Traffic and Air Navigation Aids*, was developed in cooperation with the Department of Defense (DOD), and updated over the years. It was never actually implemented, however, until the surprise terrorist air attacks on the U.S. on Tuesday, September 11, 2001, presented a national security scenario no one had foreseen or planned for.

Immediately following those attacks, the President and Congress in essence declared the entire U.S. national airspace system National Security Airspace and the FAA implemented SCATANA. All civilian air traffic in contact with ATC was diverted to the nearest suitable airport, usually an airport some distance outside any major metropolitan area or likely target complex. Then all civilian aircraft were grounded. Some who didn't get the word were met and escorted to a nearby airfield by interceptors. The Civil Air Patrol, operating as the official civilian auxiliary of the U.S. Air Force, was allowed back into the air almost immediately, transporting relief supplies and equipment for the search, rescue, and recovery efforts and taking digital aerial photos to aid in that effort. CAP aircrews reported the eerie sensation of landing at JFK International Airport in a Cessna 182 laden with special equipment requested by the searchers and having the gigantic airport all to themselves. It would be days before airline and other civilian IFR operations were permitted to resume, and civilian VFR operations were gradually phased back in over a period of weeks, by which time many new TFRs and a new ADIZ around Washington, D.C., were in place. Since then new TFRs have been appearing and disappearing like bubbles in boiling water, often faster than notice of their existence or demise can be communicated to pilots. The problem has been exacerbated by the practice of establishing a TFR having a radius of 3 to 30 miles at each location to be visited by the president, vice president, and opposition candidate during the presidential election campaign and that can be an enormous number of locations. At this writing, the FAA has gotten better at providing timely notice, but errant pilots have illegally intruded into special-use airspace thousands of times since the attacks. Some have been intercepted by fighters (Fig. 14.2) and escorted to a ground reception by FAA, law enforcement and/or Secret Service agents, and some have faced criminal charges (*see* Chapter 15) or FAA certificate action. It is a tribute to the professionalism and good judgment of those responsible for enforcement of national security airspace that no pilot making such an error has yet been mistaken for a terrorist and shot down, as I write this sentence.

Considering the scope of the attack, while pilots and passengers were inconvenienced and aviation businesses lost a great deal of money, the adverse effect on civil aviation could have been much worse.

Implemented in response to a national security emergency other than the one for which it was designed, SCATANA worked remarkably well.

COMPETITION FOR AIRSPACE

FAA airspace allocation regulations, like all other FARs and other federal regulations, are subject to requirements of the federal *Administrative Procedure Act* (APA). The APA requires (except in an emergency) that the agency first publish a proposed regulatory change as a *Notice of Proposed Rulemaking* (NPRM) in the *Federal Register*, and provide a reasonable opportunity for public comment before adoption. Where the FAA considers a potential rule likely to be particularly controversial or expects that its development might benefit more than usual from outside input, it may first issue an *Advance Notice of Proposed Rulemaking* (ANPRM) to help focus the issues.

The APA also allows citizens to petition the FAA (and other federal agencies) to change existing regulations.

Like real estate, airspace is a finite resource. Many different interest groups within the aviation community assert demands for use of a share of this resource for their activities. Earthbound interests—such as the broadcasting industry, which has a need to erect tall signal transmission towers rising into the navigable airspace—also compete for the right or privilege to use a share of this resource.

Tall structures and activities on the surface such as gunnery and spacecraft launches may conflict with aviation activities. Various aviation activities may be incompatible in the same airspace: military high-altitude dogfight training, unless carefully coordinated and controlled, may conflict with airliners cruising en route, while low-level high-speed military flying may pose a hazard to general aviation fliers.

Low-flying aircraft may interfere with the solitude sought by back country hikers and campers, spiritualists and residents of rural areas and may disturb wildlife, hunters and domestic animals.

The APA rulemaking procedures make it possible for all views to be voiced and considered in each instance.

AOPA (the Aircraft Owners and Pilots Association) frequently weighs in to object to proposals to erect tall transmission towers into the navigable airspace, especially near major metropolitan areas, and to proposals to set aside for military use airspace needed for general aviation's peregrinations. The FAA often provides for public hearings in addition to the required opportunity for written comment where proposals are particularly controversial.

Wilderness Airspace

All aircraft are *requested* to maintain an altitude no lower than 2,000 feet above the surface of National Parks, National Monuments, National Seashores, National Recreation Areas, and Scenic Rivers administered by the National Park Service. National Wildlife Refuges, Big Game Refuges, Game Ranges, and Wildlife Ranges administered by the U.S. Fish and Wildlife Service benefit from identical requests. So do Wilderness and Primitive Areas administered by the U.S. Forest Service. Boundaries of these areas are depicted on VFR aeronautical charts, and the vast majority of general aviation pilots honor the request.

However, many visitors on the ground in Grand Canyon National Park complained that aircraft noise was diminishing the quality of the national park experience and traumatizing wildlife. These complaints prompted Congress in 1987 to mandate an FAA and Department of the Interior study of the problem and led to *Special Federal Aviation Regulations* (SFAR) in the vicinity, imposing *"flight free zones"* (not to be confused with the diametrically opposite concept of free flight) over large areas of the park, prohibiting overflight below 10,500 feet MSL except in emergencies. Park overflights were confined to narrow corridors within which minimum flight altitudes ranging from 5,000 feet MSL to as high as 14,500 feet were mandated. Since implementation of this SFAR, visitor complaints about aircraft noise in the Grand Canyon dropped by 80% (Fig. 14.3). Some complaints continue to be received, however, and the FAA and Department of Interior continue to adjust airspace use requirements over the park.

Fig. 14.3. View of Grand Canyon National Park from the air.

Over 40 aviation businesses from Arizona, California, Nevada, Utah and New Mexico provide aerial tours of Grand Canyon National Park to almost a million tourists annually, about a fifth of the park's visitors. During peak summer vacation months, air tours exceed 10,000 flights a month over the park. The industry accounts for approximately 300 pilot jobs and generates over $250 million in economic impact. Air tour operators, who in response to increasing restrictions organized into an association, note that experience under the SFAR eliminated the impact of aircraft noise on more than 99% of the park's ground visitors. They also point out that air tours relieve congestion at the canyon's rim, contribute nothing to the erosion of trails, and provide equal access to visitors with disabilities. They note further that some 60% of the aerial tourists are foreigners on vacation and that commercial air tours provide an opportunity for visitors to enjoy park vistas when time or physical constraints might otherwise preclude them. Others have expressed concern that high-density altitude conditions typical of the area's hot summers, resulting in reduced performance, make it impossible for some aircraft (particularly helicopters) to climb to required or proposed minimum overflight altitudes, necessitating lengthy circumnavigation of the park's meandering boundaries.

Since then, visitors to other National Parks, such as Rocky Mountain National Park in northern Colorado (Fig. 14.4) as well as the entire multi-island state of Hawaii, successfully brought pressure to bear on the FAA and Department of Interior to restrict overflights (particularly commercial air tours).

The FAA and National Park Service (NPS) are now developing Grand Canyon-style regulations to restrict at least commercial air tour operations over thousands of square miles of as many as 345 National Parks.

Only successful aviation lobbying efforts in Congress recently stopped agency plans to close and abandon the entire network of wilderness airstrips on federal lands in Idaho and Utah, cherished by many for emergency and recreational use.

Fig. 14.4. Westbound across Corona pass, Colorado's Rocky Mountain National Park with the over 14,000-foot-tall Long's Peak appear beyond the author's wingtip.

NASA's focus on technological solutions to aircraft noise reduction (*see* Chapter 1) are important and timely not only to airports but in the wild as well, for unless great strides are made in quiet aircraft propulsion, increasing restrictions to overflight of these areas of protected wilderness must be expected. Environmental interests can be expected to continue to mount an organized, methodical and aggressive campaign to pursue expansion of such restrictions. Aviation interests must be prepared to take full advantage of the opportunities offered by the APA rulemaking and legislative processes to respond in kind.

Dispute Resolution

Resort to the courts is rarely useful in these controversies. If the FAA and other agencies involved fail to follow procedures required by the APA, a court may set aside the agency's decision and remand the matter to the agency for reconsideration in accordance with proper procedure. This is typically an empty ritual. Having once made up its mind on a subject, an agency is likely to reach the same decision after complying with a judicial mandate to start over at square one and jump through the correct sequence of procedural hoops.

Once the agency has reached its decision through the prescribed process, the courts are unlikely to reverse the decision. In such a case, the court cannot substitute its judgment for that of the agency, but must defer to agency judgment and expertise. The court can review the agency's decision only to determine whether it is an arbitrary and capricious abuse of the agency's discretion. So long as the record shows some rational basis for the agency's decision, the court must affirm it, even if it disagrees.

Thus, presenting the most logical and persuasive argument to the agency at every opportunity is crucial. Once the agency announces its final decision, the courts are unlikely to overturn it. Petitioning Congress to change the law may then be the only potential recourse.

Effectiveness in the administrative and legislative arenas frequently depends heavily upon not only advocacy (legal and otherwise), but also diplomacy and consensus building skills. Reason may still prevail in either forum where claim of legal rights fails. A couple of successful examples from my personal experience may be illustrative.

When the FAA published (as an advance notice of proposed rulemaking under the APA) its "*straw man*" initial proposal for the configuration of the Terminal Control Area (TCA, now Class B airspace) for the new Denver International Airport (DIA) then under construction, an extremely diverse group of representatives of users of the area's airspace came together to form an ad hoc user group. The FAA cooperated by providing ATC and airspace specialists on request, to help the group understand the regulatory and procedural constraints and considerations that were required to be respected in the airspace design, but otherwise kept hands off and did not attempt to influence the group's deliberations. As could be expected, there was initially considerable distrust and disrespect between representatives of aviation interests as diverse as the airlines, military, area airport operators, general aviation pilots and a variety of air sports, all jockeying to protect "their" airspace needs. But as they worked together over a period of months, listening to each other's concerns and capabilities, mutual respect developed and consensus was reached on an optimal airspace configuration. The group presented its written (and diagrammed) recommended configuration (far different from the initial FAA "straw man" proposal) to the FAA, with detailed explanations and justifications for each recommended change. The FAA then scheduled several public hearings, where the initial FAA proposal and the group's counterproposal were briefed, questions taken and answered and comments received. In the end, the airspace design implemented by the FAA was almost identical to that developed by the user group.

When the Colorado Air National Guard transitioned to F-16s at the same time many U.S. military bases were being phased out while the armed forces' operations tempo was increasing, the need was recognized to reconfigure the entire web of military special use airspace in the state to accommodate the expanding and changing demand for realistic air combat and surface attack training. The National Guard Bureau's design effort came to be known as the Colorado Airspace Initiative. A coalition of interested parties formed an ad hoc working group including a variety of interested parties who might be affected by the air operations, including general aviation (represented by the Colorado Pilots Association), farmers and ranchers, back-country hikers and environmentalists, real estate developers, rural residents, and even monks from a monastery located along a proposed low-level route (Fig. 14.5). This group, too, met weekly for several months, with technical support as requested from the National Guard Bureau and FAA, came to understand each other's

Fig. 14.5. A serene scene: This family ranch in Colorado's San Luis Valley abuts the soaring Sangre de Cristo range of the Rocky Mountains. Now imagine the serenity disrupted by the sudden intrusion of a formation of F-16s flying near the speed of sound at 300 feet or less over the ranch house and you can well imagine how the family might feel about that airspace use.

concerns, and reached consensus on a recommended tailoring of the initial design of the complex airspace to minimize the adverse effects of the operations on the people and creatures living below. While this group's recommendations were not all adopted into the final airspace design, enough were that all participants agreed that their time was well spent in the effort.

15

Crimes and Aviation Security

While terrorism (particularly since the attacks within the United States on September 11, 2001) has brought greater public attention to the subject, civil aviation has been the target or arena for a variety of criminal activity almost since its inception. As mentioned in Chapter 1, the first reported crime against aviation occurred in France in 1784, when an early gas balloonist was accosted by a sword-wielding young man who forced his way into the basket of the balloon and demanded the aeronaut take him aloft.

In the U.S. today, a variety of federal criminal laws are specifically directed at protecting aircrews, passengers, aircraft, ATC and air navigation facilities, airports, and the general public against terrorism and other criminal behavior. The federalization of air carrier airport security and new focus on general aviation security have given rise to rapid growth in jobs in aviation security, in both the public and private sectors. New laws that restrict civil liberties in the interest of national security are being challenged in the courts, though at this writing, no such case has yet climbed far enough up the judicial ladder to establish published precedent.

The purpose of this chapter is to introduce you to those federal laws specifically directed toward civil aviation and some constitutional considerations in criminal law enforcement in aviation. Some states have also adopted criminal laws specific to aviation. Under the principle of federal preemption discussed in Chapter 13, where these do not conflict with federal law, they are generally also enforceable. General criminal laws, both federal and state, sometimes also apply in an aviation scenario. For example, the federal law that makes it a crime to make a false statement applies not only to FAA applications for pilot and medical certificates, pilot logbook entries that could show currency or qualification, and inspection and maintenance entries in aircraft logbooks (discussed in Chapters 2 and 3) but to a host of documents and records required by or submitted to any of the myriad federal agencies. As another example, a state law making reckless endangerment of others a crime can be enforced against aviators operating aircraft so as to create a hazard to persons on the ground, and state charges of manslaughter or criminally negligent homicide may result if a fatal accident results. In order to convict a person of a crime, the government must prove its case *beyond a reasonable doubt*, a tougher standard than the preponderance of evidence standard that applies in civil litigation, but not one that requires prosecutors to overcome any alternative theories no matter how far-fetched that defense lawyers may advance.

JURISDICTION

Jurisdictional issues can be especially complex in the case of crimes committed aboard aircraft in flight. Because aircraft can quickly cross state and national borders and because it may be difficult to determine exactly where the aircraft was positioned at the moment a crime was committed aboard (indeed, the offense itself could span several states or nations and cross the high seas) it could be difficult to establish that a particular state or nation actually had jurisdiction to prosecute the offense.

Citations below are to the U.S. Code (USC), the compilation of all laws enacted by Congress that are currently in effect. For example, Title 18 of the U.S. Code, section 37 is cited as 18 USC 37. The code can be accessed on line through the Government Printing Office website at *http://www.gpoaccess.gov/uscode/* or several other sources easily located with any of the internet search engines in common use. The two titles of the code most relevant to this chapter are Title 18, Crimes and Criminal Procedure, and Title 49, Transportation.

Special Aircraft Jurisdiction of the United States (49 U.S.C. 46501)

To simplify jurisdictional issues, Congress enacted legislation providing for the *special aircraft jurisdiction* of the United States. This special aircraft jurisdiction extends to crimes committed aboard (1) any civil aircraft of

U.S. registry (that is, having an N-number), (2) U.S. military aircraft, (3) any other aircraft *within* the U.S., and any aircraft outside the U.S. that has either its next scheduled destination or last point of departure in the U.S. Where the crime is committed while the aircraft is on the ground, state government may have concurrent jurisdiction over the offense under state law. In such a situation, state and federal prosecutors will typically confer to agree which will prosecute. The prosecution of in-flight crimes, however, falls exclusively within federal jurisdiction.

Violence at International Airports

Congress has also provided, at 18 USC 37, for jurisdiction enabling the United States to prosecute individuals for certain crimes of violence occurring at international airports, even under some circumstances where the international airport is on foreign soil (Fig. 15.1). Here is the actual text:

(a) Offense.—A person who unlawfully and intentionally, using any device, substance, or weapon

(1) performs an act of violence against a person at an airport serving international civil aviation that causes or is likely

Fig. 15.1. U.S. courts have jurisdiction over crimes committed at international airports even, under certain circumstances, where the crime was committed in another nation.

to cause serious bodily injury (as defined in section 1365 of this title) or death; or

(2) destroys or seriously damages the facilities of an airport serving international civil aviation or a civil aircraft not in service located thereon or disrupts the services of the airport, if such an act endangers or is likely to endanger safety at that airport, or attempts or conspires to do such an act, shall be fined under this title, imprisoned not more than 20 years, or both; and if the death of any person results from conduct prohibited by this subsection, shall be punished by death or imprisoned for any term of years or for life.

(b) Jurisdiction.—There is jurisdiction over the prohibited activity in subsection (a) if—

(1) the prohibited activity takes place in the United States; or

(2) the prohibited activity takes place outside the United States and

(A) the offender is later found in the United States; or

(B) an offender or a victim is a national of the United States (as defined in section 101(a)(22) of the Immigration and Nationality Act (8 U.S.C. 1101 (a)(22)).

(c) Bar to Prosecution.—It is a bar to Federal prosecution under subsection (a) for conduct that occurred within the United States that the conduct involved was during or in relation to a labor dispute, and such conduct is prohibited as a felony under the law of the State in which it was committed. For purposes of this section, the term "labor dispute" has the meaning set forth in section 2(c) of the Norris-LaGuardia Act, as amended (29 U.S.C. 113 (c)), and the term "State" means a State of the United States, the District of Columbia, and any commonwealth, territory, or possession of the United States.

The bar that appears in subparagraph (c), above is important, for as we shall see in Chapters 16 and 17, emotions frequently run high in labor disputes and can provoke ordinarily calm and thoughtful people (including aviation and aerospace professionals) to intemperate acts. While these acts may violate state criminal statutes, they are not subject to federal prosecution under this provision.

Some of the laws discussed below proscribing specific aviation-related crimes also address special jurisdictional issues that may arise in their enforcement.

AVIATION-SPECIFIC FEDERAL CRIMES

Crimes relating to aviation fall into two general categories: those relating to aviation security and those more focused on safety, though the concepts of safety and security often overlap.

Security-Related Crimes

We'll begin with the security-related crimes, since these appear to be drawing the greatest focus of law enforcement and the heaviest penalties these days.

Violation of national defense airspace (49 U.S.C. 46307)

It is not only an FAR violation, but also a federal crime to knowingly or willfully violate national defense airspace. This could include not only an ADIZ or National Security Area, but also certain Prohibited Areas and TFR airspace established for national security reasons. (*See* Chapter 14.) Violators are subject to fines, imprisonment of up to one year, or both. (Unless otherwise indicated, the potential maximum fine for crimes discussed in the chapter is $10,000 per violation.)

Destruction of aircraft or aircraft facilities (18 U.S.C. 32)

This law makes criminal a broad range of deliberate acts against aircraft (Fig. 15.2), air navigation facilities, airport facilities, and people. These may include not only acts of terrorism and sabotage, but also violence sometimes committed by drunken and/or angry passengers or damage done by vandals. Because the law is so pervasive as to preclude thorough and accurate summarization or paraphrasing, here is the complete text:

(a) Whoever willfully—
   (1) sets fire to, damages, destroys, disables, or wrecks any aircraft in the special aircraft jurisdiction of the United States or any civil aircraft used, operated, or employed in interstate, overseas, or foreign air commerce;
   (2) places or causes to be placed a destructive device or substance in, upon, or in proximity to, or otherwise makes or causes to be made unworkable or unusable or hazardous to work or use, any such aircraft, or any part or other materials used or intended to be used in connection with the operation of such aircraft, if such placing or causing to be placed or such making or causing to be made is likely to endanger the safety of any such aircraft;

Fig. 15.2. Warning posted on airport fence about federal felony of disabling aircraft.

(3) sets fire to, damages, destroys, or disables any air navigation facility, or interferes by force or violence with the operation of such facility, if such fire, damaging, destroying, disabling, or interfering is likely to endanger the safety of any such aircraft in flight;

(4) with the intent to damage, destroy, or disable any such aircraft, sets fire to, damages, destroys, or disables or places a destructive device or substance in, upon, or in proximity to, any appliance or structure, ramp, landing area, property, machine, or apparatus, or any facility or other material used, or intended to be used, in connection with the operation, maintenance, loading, unloading or storage of any such aircraft or any cargo carried or intended to be carried on any such aircraft;

(5) performs an act of violence against or incapacitates any individual on any such aircraft, if such act of violence or incapacitation is likely to endanger the safety of such aircraft;

(6) communicates information, knowing the information to be false and under circumstances in which such information

may reasonably be believed, thereby endangering the safety of any such aircraft in flight; or

(7) attempts or conspires to do anything prohibited under paragraphs (1) through (6) of this subsection; shall be fined under this title or imprisoned not more than twenty years or both.

(b) Whoever willfully—

(1) performs an act of violence against any individual on board any civil aircraft registered in a country other than the United States while such aircraft is in flight, if such act is likely to endanger the safety of that aircraft;

(2) destroys a civil aircraft registered in a country other than the United States while such aircraft is in service or causes damage to such an aircraft which renders that aircraft incapable of flight or which is likely to endanger that aircraft's safety in flight;

(3) places or causes to be placed on a civil aircraft registered in a country other than the United States while such aircraft is in service, a device or substance which is likely to destroy that aircraft, or to cause damage to that aircraft which renders that aircraft incapable of flight or which is likely to endanger that aircraft's safety in flight; or

(4) attempts or conspires to commit an offense described in paragraphs (1) through (3) of this subsection; shall be fined under this title or imprisoned not more than twenty years, or both. There is jurisdiction over an offense under this subsection if a national of the United States was on board, or would have been on board, the aircraft; an offender is a national of the United States; or an offender is afterwards found in the United States. For purposes of this subsection, the term "national of the United States" has the meaning prescribed in section 101(a) (22) of the Immigration and Nationality Act.

(c) Whoever willfully imparts or conveys any threat to do an act which would violate any of paragraphs (1) through (5) of subsection (a) or any of paragraphs (1) through (3) of subsection (b) of this section, with an apparent determination and will to carry the threat into execution shall be fined under this title or imprisoned not more than five years, or both.

Aircraft Piracy (49 U.S.C. 46502)

Congress enacted this law to criminalize what is commonly called *hijacking* but is formally referred to in both U.S. and international law as *aircraft piracy*. In this statute, Congress defines the offense as follows:

> *"aircraft piracy"* means seizing or exercising control of an aircraft in the special aircraft jurisdiction of the United States by force, violence, threat of force or violence, or any form of intimidation, and with wrongful intent.

The statute goes on to make a failed *attempt* at aircraft piracy also a crime, even if the attempt was made when the aircraft was not in flight. The punishment for either committing or attempting aircraft piracy is *at least* 20 years imprisonment or, if the death of someone other than the hijacker results, death or life imprisonment. The statute extends the special aircraft jurisdiction of the U.S. to any hijacking in which either: (1) a national of the United States was aboard the aircraft, (2) an offender is a U.S. national, or (3) an offender is afterwards found in the U.S.

Interference with cabin or flight crew (49 U.S.C. 46504)

Flight attendants and flight deck crewmembers are increasingly called upon to deal with unruly passengers, so much so that a new phrase has been coined to describe the phenomenon: *"air rage."* Such abusive passenger behavior can be a federal felony under this law:

> An individual on an aircraft in the special aircraft jurisdiction of the United States who, by assaulting or intimidating a flight crew member or flight attendant of the aircraft, interferes with the performance of the duties of the member or attendant or lessens the ability of the member or attendant to perform those duties, or attempts or conspires to do such an act, shall be fined under title 18, imprisoned for not more than 20 years, or both. However, if a dangerous weapon is used in assaulting or intimidating the member or attendant, the individual shall be imprisoned for any term of years or for life.

Carrying a weapon or explosive on an aircraft (49 U.S.C. 46505)

This statute makes it a federal felony for a person to either: (1) board or attempt to board an airliner with a dangerous weapon concealed on their person or in a carry-on item, or (2) place, attempt to place, or attempt to have someone else place a loaded firearm, explosive or incendiary device aboard an airliner. Starter pistols, used in sporting events to fire a blank cartridge to signal the start of a foot race, are specifically included in the category of dangerous weapons, so traveling sports officials sometimes run afoul of this law. In this era of heightened and well-publicized airport security, it is truly amazing how many seemingly ordinary airline passengers continue to enter airport security screening with a prohibited weapon (usually a handgun—I'm not talking about nail clippers) on their person or in carry-on luggage. Often, the lame excuse is that the passenger usually travels by ground and simply forgot he had a gun in his bag. Unbelievable! Where the violation was deliberate, the offender can be fined or imprisoned for not more than 15 years. Most non-deliberate (read: stupid) violations are compromised to a civil fine of $10,000 or less, so long as authorities believe the passenger's story and are satisfied that he has learned his lesson. The TSA collects over $1 million in fines each year for violations of this statute, but if a passenger cops an attitude and chooses instead to try to defend the charge by asserting his (and virtually all of these offenders are male) Second Amendment constitutional right to keep and bear arms, both prosecution and conviction are inevitable. The statute makes exceptions for law enforcement officers and others authorized to carry arms in an official capacity as well as others authorized by FAR. The law does not apply to *unloaded* firearms in hold (checked) baggage inaccessible to passengers, so long as the passenger first notified the airline of the presence of the weapon.

False information (49 U.S.C. 46302)

Making a false report of an impending attempt to commit aircraft piracy (hijacking), interfere with flight crew or attendants, or carry weapons or explosives aboard an aircraft is also punishable under federal law by a civil penalty (fine) of up to $10,000.

This statute applies not only to deliberate hoaxes, but also to ill-considered attempts at dark humor by passengers. Law enforcement and the judiciary have zero tolerance for such humor, and the courts have uniformly held that the First Amendment guarantee of freedom of speech does not apply to this situation, analogizing it to shouting a false warning of fire in a crowded theater. Joke, wisecrack, or otherwise smart off to security personnel or others at the airport about hijacking, weapons or explosives, and you are guaranteed prosecution under this section.

Entering aircraft or airport area in violation of security requirements (49 U.S.C. 46314)

This statute makes it a federal crime for a person to deliberately enter an aircraft or air carrier airport area in violation of security requirements (including, but not limited to passenger and baggage screening requirements). Punishment includes a fine or imprisonment up to one year, or both, except that if it is proved that the violator also intended to commit a felony under federal or state law while within the secured area, imprisonment can be for as long as ten years.

Safety and Drug-Related Crimes

Pilots operating in air transportation without an airman's certificate (49 U.S.C. 46317)

Formerly, the only punishment the federal government could impose upon an unlicensed person piloting an aircraft was a civil penalty (fine). When this proved insufficient to deter some persons (particularly pilots whose certificates had been revoked for smuggling drugs by air) from flying, Congress enacted this law:

(a) General Criminal Penalty.—An individual shall be fined under title 18 or imprisoned for not more than 3 years, or both, if that individual—

   (1) knowingly and willfully serves or attempts to serve in any capacity as an airman operating an aircraft in air transportation without an airman's certificate authorizing the individual to serve in that capacity; or

   (2) knowingly and willfully employs for service or uses in any capacity as an airman to operate an aircraft in air transportation an individual who does not have an airman's certificate authorizing the individual to serve in that capacity.

(b) Controlled Substance Criminal Penalty.—

   (1) Controlled substances defined.—In this subsection, the term "controlled substance" has the meaning given that term in section 102 of the Comprehensive Drug Abuse Prevention and Control Act of 1970 (21 U.S.C. 802).

   (2) Criminal penalty.—An individual violating subsection (a) shall be fined under title 18 or imprisoned for not more than 5 years, or both, if the violation is related to transporting a controlled substance by aircraft or aiding or facilitating

a controlled substance violation and that transporting, aiding, or facilitating—

(A) is punishable by death or imprisonment of more than 1 year under a Federal or State law; or

(B) is related to an act punishable by death or imprisonment for more than 1 year under a Federal or State law related to a controlled substance (except a law related to simple possession (as that term is used in section 46306(c)) of a controlled substance).

(3) Terms of imprisonment.—A term of imprisonment imposed under paragraph (2) shall be served in addition to, and not concurrently with, any other term of imprisonment imposed on the individual subject to the imprisonment.

Lighting violations involving transporting controlled substances by aircraft not providing air transportation (49 U.S.C. 46315)

When drug runners began to endanger other aircraft by turning off their running lights (in violation of the FARs) in an attempt to avoid detection when flying at night, Congress made that action also a serious crime:

(a) Application.—This section applies only to aircraft not used to provide air transportation.

(b) Criminal Penalty.—A person shall be fined under title 18, imprisoned for not more than 5 years, or both, if—

(1) the person knowingly and willfully operates an aircraft in violation of a regulation or requirement of the Administrator of the Federal Aviation Administration related to the display of navigation or anticollision lights;

(2) the person is knowingly transporting a controlled substance by aircraft or aiding or facilitating a controlled substance offense; and

(3) the transporting, aiding, or facilitating—

(A) is punishable by death or imprisonment for more than one year under a law of the United States or a State; or

(B) is provided in connection with an act punishable by death or imprisonment for more than one year under a law of the United States or a State related to a controlled substance (except a law related to simple possession of a controlled substance).

Interference with air navigation (49 U.S.C. 46308)

Speaking of lighting, Congress also made it a federal felony for a person to attempt to mislead aircraft by displaying a false air navigation facility light or signal or interfering with the operations of a true air navigation facility light or signal (that could include radio aids to navigation and ATC voice commands). Persons who shined laser pointers at aircraft, presenting a danger of flight crew distraction and even eye injury, have also been arrested and charged under this statute. Violators are subject to fine or imprisonment for up to five years, or both.

Aircraft registration violations (49 U.S.C. 46306)

Smugglers have been known to also violate FARs regulating registration of aircraft, trying to conceal their activities by changing registration numbers and supporting aircraft documents and enabling nonstop long-range flights by installing illegal fuel tanks (water bed mattresses in the cabin are one popular field expedient). When the FARs alone proved insufficient to deter these practices, Congress made them federal felonies, as well, providing not only for imprisonment of offenders but also for seizure and forfeiture of the aircraft. Because this is another particularly extensive and intricate law not amenable to accurate summarization, its full text is reproduced here:

(a) Application.—This section applies only to aircraft not used to provide air transportation.

(b) General Criminal Penalty.—Except as provided by subsection (c) of this section, a person shall be fined under title 18, imprisoned for not more than 3 years, or both, if the person—

(1) knowingly and willfully forges or alters a certificate authorized to be issued under this part;

(2) knowingly sells, uses, attempts to use, or possesses with the intent to use, such a certificate;

(3) knowingly and willfully displays or causes to be displayed on an aircraft a mark that is false or misleading about the nationality or registration of the aircraft;

(4) obtains a certificate authorized to be issued under this part by knowingly and willfully falsifying or concealing a material fact, making a false, fictitious, or fraudulent statement, or making or using a false document knowing it contains a false, fictitious, or fraudulent statement or entry;

(5) owns an aircraft eligible for registration under section 44102 of this title and knowingly and willfully operates, attempts to operate, or allows another person to operate the aircraft when—

    (A) the aircraft is not registered under section 44103 of this title or the certificate of registration is suspended or revoked; or

    (B) the owner knows or has reason to know that the other person does not have proper authorization to operate or navigate the aircraft without registration for a period of time after transfer of ownership;

(6) knowingly and willfully operates or attempts to operate an aircraft eligible for registration under section 44102 of this title knowing that—

    (A) the aircraft is not registered under section 44103 of this title;

    (B) the certificate of registration is suspended or revoked; or

    (C) the person does not have proper authorization to operate or navigate the aircraft without registration for a period of time after transfer of ownership;

(7) knowingly and willfully serves or attempts to serve in any capacity as an airman without an airman's certificate authorizing the individual to serve in that capacity;

(8) knowingly and willfully employs for service or uses in any capacity as an airman an individual who does not have an airman's certificate authorizing the individual to serve in that capacity; or

(9) operates an aircraft with a fuel tank or fuel system that has been installed or modified knowing that the tank, system, installation, or modification does not comply with regulations and requirements of the Administrator of the Federal Aviation Administration.

(c) Controlled Substance Criminal Penalty.—

    (1) In this subsection, "controlled substance" has the same meaning given that term in section 102 of the Comprehensive Drug Abuse Prevention and Control Act of 1970 (21 U.S.C. 802).

    (2) A person violating subsection (b) of this section shall be fined under title 18, imprisoned for not more than 5 years, or both, if the violation is related to transporting a

controlled substance by aircraft or aiding or facilitating a controlled substance violation and the transporting, aiding, or facilitating—

(A) is punishable by death or imprisonment of more than one year under a law of the United States or a State; or

(B) that is provided is related to an act punishable by death or imprisonment for more than one year under a law of the United States or a State related to a controlled substance (except a law related to simple possession of a controlled substance).

(3) A term of imprisonment imposed under paragraph (2) of this subsection shall be served in addition to, and not concurrently with, any other term of imprisonment imposed on the individual.

(d) Seizure and Forfeiture.—

(1) The Administrator of Drug Enforcement or the Commissioner of Customs may seize and forfeit under the customs laws an aircraft whose use is related to a violation of subsection (b) of this section, or to aid or facilitate a violation, regardless of whether a person is charged with the violation.

(2) An aircraft's use is presumed to have been related to a violation of, or to aid or facilitate a violation of—

(A) subsection (b)(1) of this section if the aircraft certificate of registration has been forged or altered;

(B) subsection (b)(3) of this section if there is an external display of false or misleading registration numbers or country of registration;

(C) subsection (b)(4) of this section if—

(i) the aircraft is registered to a false or fictitious person; or

(ii) the application form used to obtain the aircraft certificate of registration contains a material false statement;

(D) subsection (b)(5) of this section if the aircraft was operated when it was not registered under section 44103 of this title; or

(E) subsection (b)(9) of this section if the aircraft has a fuel tank or fuel system that was installed or altered—

> (i) in violation of a regulation or requirement of the Administrator of the Federal Aviation Administration; or
>
> (ii) if a certificate required to be issued for the installation or alteration is not carried on the aircraft.

(3) The Administrator of the Federal Aviation Administration, the Administrator of Drug Enforcement, and the Commissioner shall agree to a memorandum of understanding to establish procedures to carry out this subsection.

(e) Relationship to State Laws.—This part does not prevent a State from establishing a criminal penalty, including providing for forfeiture and seizure of aircraft, for a person that—

(1) knowingly and willfully forges or alters an aircraft certificate of registration;

(2) knowingly sells, uses, attempts to use, or possesses with the intent to use, a fraudulent aircraft certificate of registration;

(3) knowingly and willfully displays or causes to be displayed on an aircraft a mark that is false or misleading about the nationality or registration of the aircraft; or

(4) obtains an aircraft certificate of registration from the Administrator of the Federal Aviation Administration by—

> (A) knowingly and willfully falsifying or concealing a material fact;
>
> (B) making a false, fictitious, or fraudulent statement; or
>
> (C) making or using a false document knowing it contains a false, fictitious, or fraudulent statement or entry.

Transporting hazardous material (49 U.S.C. 46312)

Intended to prevent accidents such as the ValuJet accident discussed in Chapter 4, this criminal statute puts real teeth into enforcement of the regulations governing transportation of hazardous materials ("hazmat") by air. It is curious that although it is a fundamental principle of law enforcement that every person is presumed to know the law, Congress specifically provided in this provision that ignorance of this law is no excuse for violating it (although it may be considered by the court in mitigation of sanction):

(a) In General.—A person shall be fined under title 18, imprisoned for not more than 5 years, or both, if the person, in violation of a regulation or requirement related to the transportation of hazardous material prescribed by the Secretary of Transportation under this part—

(1) willfully delivers, or causes to be delivered, property containing hazardous material to an air carrier or to an operator of a civil aircraft for transportation in air commerce; or

(2) recklessly causes the transportation in air commerce of the property.

(b) Knowledge of Regulations.—For purposes of subsection (a), knowledge by the person of the existence of a regulation or requirement related to the transportation of hazardous material prescribed by the Secretary under this part is not an element of an offense under this section but shall be considered in mitigation of the penalty.

Fraud involving aircraft or space vehicle parts in interstate or foreign commerce (18 U.S.C. 38)

This law was enacted by Congress at the urging of then DOT Inspector General Mary Schiavo to deal with a growing problem of so-called "bogus parts" finding their way into certified aircraft and presenting a serious safety problem. Some of these parts were manufactured to look like actual certified aircraft parts, although they did not meet certification standards, while others were actually certified parts that had been removed from service because they had reached time/life cycle limits. In either case, the part was passed off as a useable (yellow tagged) part, when in fact it was not. In use, however, these parts failed and accidents resulted. Here is the actual language of this rather complicated law:

(a) Offenses.—Whoever, in or affecting interstate or foreign commerce, knowingly and with the intent to defraud—

(1)

(A) falsifies or conceals a material fact concerning any aircraft or space vehicle part;

(B) makes any materially fraudulent representation concerning any aircraft or space vehicle part; or

(C) makes or uses any materially false writing, entry, certification, document, record, data plate, label, or electronic communication concerning any aircraft or space vehicle part;

(2) exports from or imports or introduces into the United States, sells, trades, installs on or in any aircraft or space vehicle any aircraft or space vehicle part using or by means

of a fraudulent representation, document, record, certification, depiction, data plate, label, or electronic communication; or

(3) attempts or conspires to commit an offense described in paragraph (1) or (2), shall be punished as provided in subsection (b).

(b) Penalties.—The punishment for an offense under subsection (a) is as follows:

(1) Aviation quality.—If the offense relates to the aviation quality of a part and the part is installed in an aircraft or space vehicle, a fine of not more than $500,000, imprisonment for not more than 15 years, or both.

(2) Failure to operate as represented.—If, by reason of the failure of the part to operate as represented, the part to which the offense is related is the proximate cause of a malfunction or failure that results in serious bodily injury (as defined in section 1365), a fine of not more than $1,000,000, imprisonment for not more than 20 years, or both.

(3) Failure resulting in death.—If, by reason of the failure of the part to operate as represented, the part to which the offense is related is the proximate cause of a malfunction or failure that results in the death of any person, a fine of not more than $1,000,000, imprisonment for any term of years or life, or both.

(4) Other circumstances.—In the case of an offense under subsection (a) not described in paragraph (1), (2), or (3) of this subsection, a fine under this title, imprisonment for not more than 10 years, or both.

(5) Organizations.—If the offense is committed by an organization, a fine of not more than—

(A) $10,000,000 in the case of an offense described in paragraph (1) or (4); and

(B) $20,000,000 in the case of an offense described in paragraph (2) or (3).

(c) Civil Remedies.—

(1) In general.—The district courts of the United States shall have jurisdiction to prevent and restrain violations of this section by issuing appropriate orders, including—

(A) ordering a person (convicted of an offense under this section) to divest any interest, direct or indirect, in any enterprise used to commit or facilitate the commission of the offense, or to destroy, or to mutilate and sell as scrap, aircraft material or part inventories or stocks;

(B) imposing reasonable restrictions on the future activities or investments of any such person, including prohibiting engagement in the same type of endeavor as used to commit the offense; and

(C) ordering the dissolution or reorganization of any enterprise knowingly used to commit or facilitate the commission of an offense under this section making due provisions for the rights and interests of innocent persons.

(2) Restraining orders and prohibition.—Pending final determination of a proceeding brought under this section, the court may enter such restraining orders or prohibitions, or take such other actions (including the acceptance of satisfactory performance bonds) as the court deems proper.

(3) Estoppel.—A final judgment rendered in favor of the United States in any criminal proceeding brought under this section shall stop the defendant from denying the essential allegations of the criminal offense in any subsequent civil proceeding brought by the United States.

(d) Criminal Forfeiture.—

(1) In general.—The court, in imposing sentence on any person convicted of an offense under this section, shall order, in addition to any other sentence and irrespective of any provision of State law, that the person forfeit to the United States—

(A) any property constituting, or derived from, any proceeds that the person obtained, directly or indirectly, as a result of the offense; and

(B) any property used, or intended to be used in any manner, to commit or facilitate the commission of the offense, if the court in its discretion so determines, taking into consideration the nature, scope, and proportionality of the use of the property on the offense.

(2) Application of other law.—The forfeiture of property under this section, including any seizure and disposition of the property, and any proceedings relating to the property, shall be governed by section 413 of the Comprehensive Drug Abuse and Prevention Act of 1970 (21 U.S.C. 853) (not including subsection (d) of that section).

(e) Construction With Other Law.—This section does not pre-empt or displace any other remedy, civil or criminal, provided by Federal or State law for the fraudulent importation, sale, trade, installation, or introduction into commerce of an aircraft or space vehicle part.

(f) Territorial Scope.—This section also applies to conduct occur-ring outside the United States if—

(1) the offender is a natural person who is a citizen or perma-nent resident alien of the United States, or an organization organized under the laws of the United States or political subdivision thereof;

(2) the aircraft or spacecraft part as to which the violation relates was installed in an aircraft or space vehicle owned or operated at the time of the offense by a citizen or permanent resident alien of the United States, or by an organization thereof; or

(3) an act in furtherance of the offense was committed in the United States.

Obstruction of Justice (18 U.S.C. 1519)

As we have often seen in high-profile criminal cases, people who suspect that the government is investigating them for some misdeed tend to quickly shift into cover-up mode, destroying or falsifying documents that prosecutors might be able to use to prove their crimes. This infuriates investigators, prosecutors, judges and juries. It inevitably adds a charge of obstruction of justice to the criminal charges brought against them and often carries a more severe sentence than the underlying crime. The federal crime that falls under this name is actually a variety of crimes, depending on different facts, but the one that applies to these facts says:

> Whoever knowingly alters, destroys, mutilates, conceals, covers up, falsifies, or makes a false entry in any record, document, or tangible object with the intent to impede, obstruct, or influence the investiga-tion or proper administration of any matter within the jurisdiction of any department or agency of the United States or any case filed under title 11, or in relation to or contemplation of any such matter or case, shall be fined under this title, imprisoned not more than 20 years, or both.

SEARCH OF AIRLINE PASSENGERS

The law of search and seizure as applied to the screening of airline passengers continues to evolve as terrorists and other criminals continue their efforts to find ways to penetrate security defenses and smuggle weapons, explosives, and components aboard airliners and security agencies continue to strive to defeat such efforts.

Pre-Boarding Screening

In the U.S., airline passenger screening was first mandated by federal law in 1973 in response to a rash of hijackings to Cuba. Most published cases to date dealing with application of the criminal law in the aviation context arose out of encounters between passengers and security personnel in the vicinity of the passenger screening magnetometer at airline airports. These cases have typically involved the discovery of either a prohibited weapon or contraband during the screening process.

The courts have consistently held that the screening of airline passengers and their baggage by magnetometers and other devices constitutes a "search" within the meaning of the 4th Amendment to the Constitution of the United States. That amendment provides:

> The right of the people to be secure in their persons, houses, papers, and effects, against *unreasonable* searches and seizures, shall not be violated, and no Warrants shall issue, but upon probable cause, supported by Oath or affirmation, and particularly describing the place to be searched, and the persons or things to be seized. (*Emphasis supplied.*)

The U.S. Supreme Court has read this amendment broadly, inferring from it a general (if limited) *right to privacy*. These protections are not limited to our homes, but travel with us wherever we go (including the airport). So how can TSA personnel legally search us without a warrant every time we go to board an airliner? Because the courts have recognized certain classes of warrantless searches as reasonable, including but not limited to: (1) searches carried out with the *consent* of the person being searched and (2) *emergency administrative searches*. The courts have held these two exceptions applicable to the pre-boarding airline passenger-screening program. In this era of international terrorism, when terrorists so frequently choose civil airliners as targets for destruction or to seize for the taking of hostages or use as weapons, the passenger pre-boarding screening program is considered an emergency administrative search, and passengers who present themselves at the airport's security checkpoint for pre-boarding screening are deemed to consent to that search. The case law previously held that a passenger who does not consent to the search must be free to turn around and depart the area without adverse consequences. Post 9/11 judicial decisions in this area are narrowing, if not entirely eliminating that option, recognizing that it would allow terrorists or others planning an attack to freely probe airline security for weaknesses they could exploit, without fear of consequences.

Thus, where such a lawful search of a passenger or baggage detects a prohibited weapon or explosive, the search will pass subsequent judicial scrutiny, the weapon or explosive will be deemed legally seized, and the passenger can be convicted of the crime of carrying or attempting to carry a weapon or explosive aboard an aircraft.

Sometimes, though, the pre-boarding screening search will turn up not a prohibited weapon, but contraband such as illegal drugs. In these cases, the courts must consider the specific facts of the situation to determine whether the scope of the search was reasonable. The purpose of the passenger-screening program is to prevent passengers from carrying weapons or explosives aboard airliners. If the item of contraband found was of sufficient size and texture that it might have been or contained a weapon or explosive device, the courts have generally refused to suppress that evidence in a subsequent criminal trial. For example, where a small amount of marijuana was found inside a sealed letter-size envelope in a passenger's carry-on bag, the court found that the action of security personnel in opening the envelope constituted an unreasonable search, since it was too small to contain a weapon or explosive device. Where, however, a metal foil wrapped "brick" of hashish was found, the court found it reasonable for security personnel to unwrap the hard package to assure that it did not contain, for example, plastic explosive. In the latter case, the evidence was found admissible to prosecute the passenger for felony possession of narcotics or a controlled substance.

Likewise if the passenger sets off the magnetometer alarm, submits to further search by hand-held (wand) magnetometer, pat down or other physical search that reveals contraband other than a weapon or explosive device, the search will be deemed valid and the evidence seized admissible at trial.

However, given the increasing miniaturization of weapons (the 9/11 terrorists succeeded in gaining control of the aircraft using simple box cutters), explosive devices (less than a pound of Czech-manufactured Semtex plastic explosive, a favorite of terrorists, concealed in a portable "boom box" tape deck inside a checked bag is believed to have destroyed Pan Am flight 103 in flight over Lockerbie, Scotland, in 1985), chemical or biological agents (such as the envelopes of anthrax powder sent through the mail to members of Congress shortly after the 9/11 attacks), I fully expect this distinction to wane. As weapons and explosive devices are becoming miniaturized and terrorists are known to be exploring the alternative of carrying small components of weapons and explosive devices aboard aircraft to assemble in flight, courts can be reasonably expected to find searches of ever-smaller areas reasonable, at least at the airport passenger screening area.

Meanwhile, a variety of promising (if expensive) new technologies are being introduced to more rapidly, efficiently and thoroughly identify, scan and track airline passengers, bags and cargo. It is reasonably to be expected that the courts will also consider use of these devices to constitute a search, but will find the search reasonable unless it goes too far. Examples of arguable unreasonableness might be the millimeter wave and backscatter X-ray imaging devices now in use by the TSA. Designed to detect even non-metallic items concealed under passengers' clothing, the original version demonstrated by the manufacturer was so sensitive that the passenger's body image displayed to the operator was as clear and anatomically-detailed as a full strip search. This clearly went too far and raised what should have been an entirely predictable and understandable public uproar over passengers' constitutional right to privacy. The manufacturer has since modified the equipment by digitally placing an electronic "fig leaf" of pixels on key areas of the image in hope of gaining passenger acceptance without compromising detection capabilities. In current use, passengers are afforded the option of being screened by this device or the more conventional magnetometer. Meanwhile, use of baggage "sniffers" such as thermal neutron analysis (TNA) devices that detect chemical traces of explosives and lower-tech search dogs with similar capabilities to screen bags (both checked and carry on) appear reasonable.

Before Reaching the Secured Area

Law enforcement efforts view pre-boarding screening as the last chance to deter attacks, and are increasingly focusing on earlier deterrence opportunities, especially on the unsecured areas of airport premises, where persons would not under current court decisions be deemed to have consented to search or subject to emergency administrative searches.

At airports (as elsewhere in modern society), arrays of video cameras monitored by security personnel are commonplace (Fig. 15.3). Such observation is not considered by the courts to be a search, but could raise right-to-privacy issues if used in areas where people of normal sensibility would reasonably expect privacy, such as restrooms.

Searches on Reasonable Suspicion

Outside secured areas, the general law allows a law enforcement officer to stop, question and frisk an individual whose behavior or appearance

Fig. 15.3. Video surveillance is becoming increasingly pervasive worldwide and is an integral part of airport security. In the eyes of the law, it does not constitute a search, and used discretely it does not violate reasonable expectations of privacy.

gives rise to *reasonable suspicion*. This is known as a *"Terry stop*," after *Terry v. Ohio*, the U.S. Supreme Court case that first articulated the standard. The facts, as later articulated by the officer, must be such that they would lead a reasonable person to suspect that the individual may have committed or may be about to commit a crime. Examples of bases for reasonable suspicion approved by the courts have included wearing a bulky coat on a warm day, looking about furtively, appearing nervous, and attempting to evade or avoid contact with the officer.

A risk inherent in such searches is that the officer's prejudices may lead to suspicion the officer deems reasonable, but that are based on such factors as race, color, religion, national origin, or sex (*profiling*). Although unlawful, such searches are far from unheard of. Americans of African descent have received the brunt of such abuse of the *Terry* doctrine, so much so that many if not most (especially young males) have experienced being pulled over by a police officer without any visible reason other than DWB (driving while black). Such experiences do not endear our justice system to the recipients.

Today, it is certainly a tempting knee-jerk reaction to recent terrorist activity to single out persons of Middle Eastern origin and Muslims for special suspicion and scrutiny in the airline screening process. After all, every recent hijacker of a U.S. aircraft was of Middle Eastern origin and a follower of a version (some would say perversion) of Islam. But in fact the overwhelming majority of Middle Easterners, Muslims included, are peaceful and law-abiding citizens fully worthy of the protections against racial and religious stereotyping and discrimination that are so central to our most basic American concepts of fairness and justice. The American Civil Liberties Union (ACLU) and others have shown profiling to be ineffective and counterproductive, typically failing to catch the guilty while antagonizing the innocent. In 1996, President Clinton signed into law an act mandating creation of the Computer Assisted Passenger Screening System (CAPS), since widely used by the airlines. Although the factors the system considers to flag certain passengers for heightened scrutiny are classified, the Department of Justice has given public assurances that CAPS does not record or consider a passenger's race, color, national origin, religion or gender. Assuming that to be true (and I have no reason to suspect that it is not), there do not appear to be any constitutional or other legal impediments to use of this system. Likely CAPS indicators are behavior-focused, and may include such things as a pattern of frequent travel to destinations known to harbor or train terrorists or buying a one-way ticket with cash. The federal government has also given the airlines secure access to its list of individuals suspected of having terrorist connections (*"terrorist watch list"*), to aid in airline efforts to identify passengers who may merit increased scrutiny. This, too, is likely constitutionally sound.

Airport law enforcement officers are also being trained in observational techniques that could allow a proper *Terry stop* of persons based on their behavior before they reach the passenger screening station. Here, too, the criteria are a closely held secret but we are assured that they are based on observable behaviors, not racial or religious profiling.

Airlines have implemented *baggage resolution* programs to assure that no checked bag is carried aboard an airliner unless the passenger who checked it has also boarded (although many of the current generation of terrorists have shown no reluctance to die in the commission of a terrorist act, and some appear to welcome such an opportunity for instant martyrdom, in the past explosive-laden bags have been checked by passengers who then failed to board the flight or disembarked short of their ticketed destination). These programs, which match every bag to a passenger, without regard to any characteristic of the passenger, also appear legally sound.

Airport Entry Security Checkpoints

At certain alert levels, airport authorities implement checkpoints to control vehicular access to the terminal's parking structures and curbside passenger pickup and drop-off areas. Although no case arising out of such a security stop and vehicle check has yet reached publication, one would expect the same principles governing passenger pre-boarding screening discussed above to apply, that is to say that the stop and security check would likely be deemed an emergency administrative search, and that so long as adequate advance signage alerted the driver of the necessity to consent to search in order to enter the airport it would be deemed a search pursuant to consent, and the search was also conducted in a reasonable manner, the search would be found lawful and any contraband seized would be admissible in evidence.

General Aviation Security and Passenger Screening

At the request of the TSA, general aviation associations including Aircraft Owners and Pilots Association (AOPA), the Airport Consultants Council (ACC), American Association of Airport Executives (AAAE), Experimental Aircraft Association (EAA), General Aviation Manufacturers Association (GAMA), Helicopter Association International (HAI), National Air Transport Association (NATA), National Association of State Aviation Officials (NASAO), National Business Aviation Association (NBAA) and U.S. Parachute Association (USPA) banded together as the General Aviation Airport Security Working Group to provide industry input to the TSA's Aviation Security Advisory Committee (ASAC).

This diverse group, broadly representing a wide variety of general aviation interests, reached consensus on a thorough and extensive set of recommended guidelines or best practices for security enhancements at the nation's privately and publicly owned and operated general aviation landing facilities. They include recommended security procedures for charter operations, flight schools, airports and airspace. These recommendations were delivered in October of 2003, and were largely adopted by the TSA as non-regulatory Security Guidelines for General Aviation Airports, available free on the TSA web page. The TSA had previously implemented a national toll-free hotline that the general aviation community can use to report any "out-of-the-ordinary" event or activity at general aviation airports. The hotline, reached by dialing (866) GA SECURE, is operated by the National Response Center. The center serves as a centralized reporting point and relays reports to the appropriate local, state, and federal agencies. The TSA has also adopted a rule imposing enhanced security measures on the half-dozen air-taxi operators providing private charters using aircraft weighing 95,000 pounds or more.

Meanwhile, in the absence of any federal mandate, general aviation industry, aircraft and airport operators took a proactive, cooperative approach to the problem, proceeding with development, dissemination, and voluntary implementation of security recommendations, programs and practices, many of which are now incorporated into the new TSA guidelines as "best practices." The AOPA developed a nationwide Airport Watch system that includes airport warning signs (Fig 15.4) and feeds reports to the National Response Center, as well

Fig. 15.4. Airport watch programs, such as this AOPA-sponsored example based on successful neighborhood watch programs, do not raise legal issues so long as suspicious activities are reported to law enforcement for investigation, rather than being dealt with vigilante style by watchful participants.

as educational literature and a training videotape to educate pilots and airport employees on improving aircraft and airport security. Knowing that money laundering enables terrorist operations, GAMA, in conjunction with the Treasury Department and in consultation with manufacturers, aircraft finance companies, used-aircraft brokers and fractional-ownership companies, developed and published Guidelines for Establishing Anti-Money Laundering Procedures and Practices Related to the Purchase of General Aviation Aircraft. The National Agricultural Aviation Association (NAAA) produced an educational program called the Professional Aerial Applicators Support System (PASS) specifically addressing security of aerial application operations. (In addition, NAAA members have undergone several industry-wide FBI background investigations since 9/11/01.) The National Association of Flight Instructors (NAFI) developed a series of security recommendations and best practices for flight schools and flight instructors. USPA disseminated detailed security recommendations to its 219 skydiving clubs and centers across the U.S., most of them based on general aviation airports, aimed at enhancing the airport watch program and ensuring the security of jump aircraft. At least to the extent that these measures are voluntarily implemented and any observed security concerns are referred to sworn law enforcement officers (LEOs) for investigation rather than triggering any vigilante-style response, they do not appear to raise significant legal issues.

Large Aircraft Security Program

The TSA's proposed Large Aircraft Security Program (LASP), announced in late 2008 by a notice of proposed rulemaking without any apparent prior input from persons or organizations knowledgeable about general aviation, would impose a whole range of expensive and burdensome requirements on Part 91 operators of aircraft weighing more than 12,500 lbs. Those requirements include criminal history record checks for crew members, matching passengers to TSA watch and no-fly lists, checking passengers and baggage for dangerous weapons or prohibited items, and paying for biennial third-party security audits. That last item amounts to outsourcing security oversight, an inherently governmental function. These proposed requirements provoked an adverse response from the general aviation alphabet groups, who considered them unrealistic, unwarranted, and oppressive. At this writing, TSA is belatedly consulting the general aviation organizations and promises to issue a new NPRM before issuing a final rule.

Compliance with TSA Security Directives (SD) is mandatory but such directives are exempt from the advance and final publication and public comment requirements of the Administrative Procedure Act (APA). In December 2008, without having consulted general aviation organizations, the TSA issued Security Directive 1542-04-08F, requiring airports served by commercial air carriers to perform background checks and issue badges to all persons having unescorted access to secure areas, such as ramps, including the passengers and crews of general aviation aircraft. The badging programs were to be airport-specific, so that general aviation pilots and passengers would have to obtain a separate badge from every airport they might wish to use, a mind-boggling prospect. In the spring of 2009, implementation began at 13 Colorado airports having some commercial air carrier service. Arriving general aviation passengers and crews not badged at the airport were required to remain within the "footprint" of the aircraft unless escorted through the operations areas. The Directive stirred an immediate hornets' nest of adverse reaction from the general aviation community and its representative organizations, which petitioned DHS Secretary Janet Napolitano to withdraw the directive. Neither the DHS nor TSA has acted on this request, and implementation of the directive continues at this writing.

In June 2009, this episode, combined with the TSA's near-simultaneous rough handling of the LASP program, gave rise to proposed legislation in the U.S. House of Representatives called the General Aviation Security Enhancement Act of 2009 (H.R. 3093), sponsored by Representative Charlie Dent, that would require the TSA to create a rulemaking committee with general aviation stakeholders and engage in a negotiated rulemaking process prior to implementing security measures for the industry (specifically including the LASP and other aircraft and airport operator security programs), absent a credible and urgent threat.

At this writing, the bill has been referred to the House Homeland Security Committee's Subcommittee on Transportation Security and Infrastructure Protection.

PART V

LABOR AND EMPLOYMENT LAW

16

Labor and Employment Law, Generally

Employment law is the fastest-growing area of litigation in America, today. A web search on the subject yields almost 69 million hits, up from 3.5 million only five years ago, when I wrote, "That figure could well have doubled by the time you read these words." Even I am astonished. Every business of significant size has its own personnel department, staffed with human resources professionals versed in the complexities and pitfalls of this body of law. Among aviation businesses, managers are now facing employment-law problems as frequently as FAR compliance issues, if not more often.

Unionized work forces are characteristic of the giant companies in the aerospace industry today, such as major airframe and engine manufacturers, and on the increase in major general aviation companies such as FBO chains, fractional, and charter operators. As the global economy recovers and competition for skilled employees resumes, employees of significant aviation enterprises are seeking union representation to gain the advantages offered by collective bargaining to improve their pay and working conditions.

The purpose of this chapter is to provide you a working knowledge of fundamental principles of labor and employment law, to prepare you to avoid common but costly mistakes made by employers uneducated on the subject.

Employment law principles discussed in this chapter apply to all American businesses, not only aviation enterprises. Labor law principles under the National Labor Relations Act (NLRA) discussed here apply to all American businesses, including aviation and aerospace businesses,

Fig. 16.1. Preparing this airliner for departure, contract catering and fuel service employees are working under the NLRA, while airline employee baggage handlers, passenger service agents, dispatchers, and flight deck and cabin crews are working under the RLA. Each employee specialty group is likely represented by a different labor union.

except for the railroads and air carriers (including charter and emergency medical air service operators), which are governed by the Railway Labor Act of 1926 (RLA), discussed in Chapter 17. Where the RLA is silent on a subject, judges often turn to the NLRA and cases decided under it even in air carrier cases. (Fig. 16.1.)

EMPLOYMENT LAW

As used in this text, the term *employment law* refers to law applicable to all employment situations, regardless of whether the employees are represented by a union, while *labor law* refers to the organization, election, representation, and collective bargaining of labor unions.

Employment at Will

As a general rule, unless a collective bargaining agreement (contract) between the employer and employees' union is in force, employers have the right to terminate (fire) employees for any reason (or for no apparent reason). Collaterally, employees have the right to quit their jobs for any reason (or for no apparent reason). This is referred to as *employment at will.*

The job insecurity inherent in the doctrine of employment at will is a major incentive for employees to unionize.

Legislatures and courts have, however, made some exceptions to this general rule. Employers have been found liable in civil suits for *wrongful discharge* where:

1. the action is in violation of a law prohibiting discrimination, or
2. the action is contrary to public policy, such as when the employee has been discharged for:
   a. missing work because summoned to serve on a jury, or
   b. in *retaliation* for refusing to give false testimony to a court or administrative agency, or
   c. in retaliation for reporting illegal conduct of an employer to law enforcement or administrative agencies ("*whistleblower protection*"), or
   d. in retaliation for engaging in union activity protected by law, or
3. the employment is deemed not really at will, because the company's personnel policy or oral or written statements promising job tenure, relied upon by the employee in good faith, are found by the court to have created an *implied contract* of long-term employment.

Prudent employers having non-unionized employees require new hires to sign agreements that their employment is at will, and exercise great care in choice of words in employee handbooks, position announcements and discussions to avoid statements that might later be construed as creating an implied contract for long-term employment.

Plaintiffs who have won wrongful discharge suits against former employers have been awarded: (1) reinstatement of their job, (2) back pay, (3) money for damage to their professional reputation, and even (4) money damages for mental anguish suffered as a result of the termination.

Hiring

The hiring process is fraught with peril for the employer, who must take great care to comply with the intricacies of myriad federal anti-discrimination laws, which are discussed here. Some state laws provide employees even greater protection than these federal laws.

The *Civil Rights Act of 1964*, as amended by the *Equal Employment Opportunities Act of 1972*, prohibits employers from discriminating in employment and compensation against any individual because of the person's *race, color, religion, sex or national origin* (these are referred to as *protected classes*). *Title VII* of the act requires both the company and the union to assure that any collective bargaining agreement provides for fair representation and equal opportunity for employees regardless of race, color, religion, sex or national origin. The Equal Employment Opportunity Commission (EEOC) is the federal administrative agency primarily responsible for enforcing compliance with these laws. Some states have enacted laws that add sexual orientation to the list of protected classes. In 1991, Congress amended the Civil Rights Act to allow victims of unlawful discrimination to recover compensatory and punitive damages up to $300,000 each, in addition to job reinstatement and back pay. Congress specified that in these cases, compensatory damages include money damages for the pain and suffering of discrimination and that where the employer's discrimination was intentional, punitive damages are appropriate if the discrimination was with "malice or with reckless or callous indifference to the federally protected rights of others."

The *Equal Pay Act*, also administered by the EEOC, prohibits employers from paying different rates of pay for the same job, based on gender or race.

The *Age Discrimination in Employment Act (ADEA)* prohibits employment discrimination against individuals over age 40 and also prohibits employers from imposing a mandatory retirement age. The act provides exceptions for certain specified occupations. These exceptions include airline pilots, whose retirement remains mandatory at age 65.

The *Americans with Disabilities Act (ADA)* applies to public and private employers having more than 15 employees. The act prohibits employment discrimination against qualified individuals with disabilities. A person is considered disabled under the ADA only if he or she has a physical or mental impairment that substantially limits one or more *major life activities*. Major life activities include such functions as caring for one's self, performing manual tasks, walking, seeing, hearing, speaking, breathing, learning or working. Some of the impairments the courts have found covered by the ADA include vision, hearing, and speech impairments; orthopedic impairments; cerebral palsy; epilepsy; muscular dystrophy; multiple sclerosis; cancer; heart disease; diabetes; mental retardation; emotional illness; specific learning disabilities; tuberculosis; AIDS and HIV infection; *past* drug addiction; and alcoholism.

A disabled person is protected by the ADA only if otherwise qualified for the job. A "*qualified individual*" is one who can accomplish the *essential functions* of the job, with or without *reasonable accommodation.* Essential functions of the job are generally those included in a written job description. If an individual can perform those essential functions without needing any change in the work process or work environment (accommodation), the ADA prohibits the employer from discriminating against the person because of the disability. If some accommodation is needed, the ADA requires the employer to provide it, within reason. This requires at least a good faith best effort. It does not require the employer to do the impossible or suffer an undue hardship. Factors to determine whether a proposed accommodation would impose an undue hardship on the employer include:

1. Nature and cost of accommodation,
2. Size and resources of the facility affected,
3. Size and financial resources of employer overall,
4. Type of operation, composition, and structure of work force (non-financial), and
5. Impact of accommodation on operation.

Changes to the workplace that could be readily accomplished with little difficulty or expense, such as a simple wheelchair ramp or a magnifying lens for a computer screen, would be considered reasonable and thus required by the ADA. If the employee's disability is obvious, the employer has an affirmative duty to provide reasonable accommodation even if the employee has not requested it.

If an employer believes (and can clearly and convincingly articulate a reasonable basis for the belief) that an individual with a disability cannot perform the job without creating a *direct threat* to his own safety or the safety of others, the employer is not required to hire the person.

The *Immigration Reform and Control Act (IRCA)* shifts much of the burden of immigration law enforcement from the federal government to employers by making it illegal for an employer to hire, recruit, refer for a fee, or continue to employ an alien who the employer knows is not eligible to work in the U.S. IRCA requires employers to verify and maintain records of each new employee's identity and work eligibility. These records must be kept for three years after employment or one year after termination, whichever is longer. Thousands of U.S. companies have been fined millions of dollars for violations of this act.

Additional statutory requirements apply to employers having government contracts. Executive Order 11246 requires contractors to develop *affirmative action programs* including specific goals and timetables for recruiting, selecting, training, and promoting minorities and women, although this was recently narrowed to apply only to employers having 250 or more employees and federal contracts totaling $1 million or more. This executive order is administered by the Department of Labor's *Office of Federal Contract Compliance Programs (OFCCP)*, whose powers include termination of federal contracts and barring violators from future federal contracts. The OFCCP can also award back pay to individuals who show an actual loss due to the violation. The *Vocational Rehabilitation Act of 1973* and the *Disabilities Act of 1991* require holders of federal government contracts in excess of $2,500 to develop *affirmative action programs* to employ and advance individuals with disabilities. The *Vietnam Era Veteran Readjustment Assistance Act* requires employers with government contracts of $10,000 or more to take affirmative action to employ and promote qualified and disabled veterans who served during that era. The *Military Selection Act* mandates that employers reemploy veterans to the position they held before entering the armed forces, at the same seniority, status and pay.

Wages, Hours, Benefits, and Working Conditions

The *Occupational Safety and Health Act (OSHA)* requires all employers to provide a safe and healthy workplace. The act created the Occupational Safety and Health Administration (OSHA) under the Department of Labor. OSHA has adopted and vigorously enforces an extensive body of regulations to this end. OSHA regulations impose stiff fines on employers for violations, and permit an employee to refuse to work "if a reasonable person would conclude he faced an immediate risk of death or serious injury."

The *Fair Labor Standards Act (FLSA)* outlaws employment of children under age 16, provides a federal minimum wage (which Congress periodically increases, $7.25 per hour at this writing) and stipulates that certain employees (*"non-exempt employees"*) must receive overtime pay of one-and-one-half times the normal pay rate when they work over 40 hours per week. Time off (*compensatory or "comp" time*) cannot be used as a substitute for overtime pay. Other (*"exempt"*) employees do not qualify for the act's overtime pay benefit. All employees are considered non-exempt (that is, they are entitled to overtime pay) unless the employer proves the employee to be exempt.

Five basic categories of employees are recognized as exempt under certain circumstances: (1) executive, (2) administrative, (3) professional, (4) computer, and (5) outside salespeople. Within these categories, to qualify as exempt, an employee must receive at least a minimum salary specified by regulation ($455 per week, at this writing) and have certain primary duties.

To qualify for the executive employee exemption, the employee's primary duties must include managing the enterprise or a department or subdivision of the enterprise; regularly directing the work of at least two other full-time employees; and having the authority to hire and fire other employees, or the employee's recommendations as to the hiring, firing, advancement, promotion or other change of status of other employees must carry weight. To qualify for the administrative employee exemption, the employee's primary duties must include performance of office or non-manual work directly related to the management of general business operations of the employer or the employer's customers; and must include the exercise of discretion and independent judgment with respect to matters of significance. There are two recognized categories of professionals who may be exempt: *learned professionals* and *creative professionals*. To qualify for the learned professional employee exemption, the employee's primary duty must be the performance of work requiring advanced knowledge (defined as work which is primarily intellectual in character and which includes work requiring the consistent exercise of discretion and judgment); the advanced knowledge must be in a field of science or learning; and the advanced knowledge must be customarily acquired by a prolonged course of specialized intellectual instruction. To qualify for the creative professional employee exemption, the employee's primary duty must be the performance of work requiring invention, imagination, originality or talent in a recognized field of artistic or creative endeavor.

To qualify for the computer employee exemption, an hourly fee (currently not less than $27.63 per hour) may be substituted for the minimum weekly wage. The employee must be employed as a computer systems analyst, computer programmer, software engineer or other similarly skilled worker in the computer field and the employee's primary duty must consist of: the application of systems analysis techniques and procedures, including consulting with users, to determine hardware, software or system functional specifications; the design, development, documentation, analysis, creation, testing or modification of computer systems or programs, including prototypes, based on and related to user or system design specifications; the design, documentation, testing, creation or modification of computer programs related to machine operating systems; or a combination of the aforementioned duties, the performance of which requires the same level of skills.

For overtime entitlement calculations, a workweek is defined as 168 consecutive hours or seven consecutive days, not necessarily a calendar week. It does not matter whether the employer asked the employee to work overtime or a supervisor merely voiced no objection when noticing a non-exempt employee putting in extra hours. If the employer knows or has reason to believe that employee was continuing to work, overtime is earned.

This is a well-camouflaged potential pitfall for employers. Without any claim for overtime being mentioned, well-meaning, loyal, non-exempt employees may come to work early, work through lunch, or work late to complete a task or project. In the culture of the company, such demonstrations of dedication may routinely draw expressions of appreciation from supervisors and even help such employees advance ahead of clock-watching peers. But the company's statutory liability for overtime pay nonetheless accrues, a financial bomb waiting to explode. If the employee later becomes disgruntled and seeks legal advice, becomes concerned about the adequacy of provisions for retirement income and seeks ways to supplement that income, or complains to labor regulators, the company may be hit with a substantial judgment for back pay, with interest, plus penalties. Multiply that by the number of non-exempt employees who worked for the company during years of inattention to FLSA overtime requirements and it should be readily apparent that the liability could be catastrophic in magnitude. A clearly written policy should be adopted and enforced by the company, specifying who has authority to approve how much overtime and under what circumstances. Supervisors must be trained and motivated to be especially watchful to observe and prevent employees from accruing unauthorized overtime, no matter how well intentioned or voluntary the act (Fig. 16.2).

For calculation of the overtime rate, all compensation must be included in the regular rate of pay (not merely the employee's regular hourly pay rate). This may include pay incentives such as attendance and productivity bonuses and commissions.

Compliance with FLSA overtime requirements is a complex but important task for corporate personnel departments. Employers are moti-

Fig. 16.2. Is this aircraft mechanic smiling because he knows that the FLSA entitles him to collect a nice nest egg of back overtime pay that his employer does not yet realize it owes?

vated by overtime costs to classify the maximum number of employees as exempt, but excessive zeal in this area has resulted in millions of dollars in back pay judgments against employers. Tight control of overtime worked and compensation paid is crucial to avoid such unwanted results.

Employers in the restaurant, agricultural, tourist and medical industries are exempt from FLSA overtime provisions.

As we settle into this information age, many workers have the ability to accomplish much of their work anywhere there is a source of electricity and internet connectivity: office, home, hotel, vehicle, cafe or internet coffee shop, and to do that work at any time of day. A great many employees yearn for the personal freedom such working arrangements offer. Employers can benefit from such working arrangements, too, as they may enable the employer to get the work done with less overhead cost for providing office or other working space. The difficulty, if not impossibility, of assuring compliance with the overtime provisions of the FLSA (along with OSHA's position that in such cases, OSHA safety requirements extend to the home or wherever else the work is done) have thus far put such working arrangements beyond the reach of non-exempt employees. A good source for current FLSA law and implementing regulations is the Department of Labor website: *www.dol.gov.*

Additional compensation legislation applies to employers having federal contracts. The *Walsh-Healey Act* requires employers with federal contracts over $10,000 to pay overtime anytime an employer works more than 8 hours in a day. The *Davis-Bacon Act* requires employers holding federal construction project contracts of $2,000 or more to pay the prevailing wage rate for that particular geographic area. (In most urban areas, this will be the union wage.)

Sexual Harassment

The EEOC has declared *sexual harassment* a form of *sex discrimination* prohibited by the Civil Rights Act. The EEOC recognizes two categories of workplace behavior as prohibited sexual harassment: *quid pro quo* and *hostile work environment. Quid pro quo* (Latin meaning "this for that") harassment involves demands or suggestions of sexual favors in exchange for such benefits as a job or promotion, or to avoid adverse actions such as being fired or laid off. A hostile work environment may be created by verbal abuse, sexist remarks, touching, leering or ogling. Both categories of sexual harassment are prohibited so long as the conduct (whether physical or verbal) is both *unwelcome* and *of a sexual nature*. The courts now regularly hold businesses liable for sexual harassment of their employees. This includes sexual harassment not only by co-workers in the company, but also by customers, vendors and others having work-related contact with the employee. Employer liability may accrue even if the employer was unaware of the harassment, so employers must take the initiative, encourage everyone in the company to be on the lookout for and report incidents of sexual harassment and other prohibited discrimination, thoroughly investigate each such report, and act on it in a timely and proper manner upon conclusion of the investigation.

In aviation, flight attendants are probably the employees most continuously exposed to risk of unwelcome sexual comments and advances from passengers and coworkers. If the airline fails to take reasonable steps to protect them, this may create a hostile work environment, a form of sex discrimination recognized by the EEOC as prohibited by the Civil Rights Act, and the airline employer can be held legally liable to the employee.

Discipline, Suspension and Termination

Although the doctrine of employment at will discussed earlier affords employers the general right to suspend or fire non-unionized employees for any reason or for no reason at all, there are important limits. Even employees at will cannot be subjected to adverse job actions for discriminatory reasons (within the protected classes), or in retaliation for activities protected by law. Even in employment at will states, employers should document every disciplinary action (including counseling) taken against an employee, including the reason for the discipline, in the worker's personnel file. Employment lawyers representing employers call this "building a *paper fortress*," while those representing employees use the more derisive term "*papering the file*." In my experience, jurors tend to disbelieve an employer's testimony about an employee's work record and the reason an employee was fired, unless it's clearly documented in the personnel file. Employers (and there are still many in the small business community) who try to handle all employee problems by an off-the-record chewing out leave their companies wide open to judgments for wrongful discharge.

Insuring Against Wrongful Discharge Claims

Because employment litigation has become so frequent, and because most general liability policies exclude coverage for these claims, employers are well advised to purchase *employment practices liability insurance*.

Layoffs and Reductions in Force

Under the *Worker Adjustment and Retraining Notification Act* (*WARN*, also known as the *Plant Closing Act*), enacted in 1989, most private sector employers that employ 100 or more full-time employees are required to give employees at least 60 days advance notice of impending closing of a facility or layoff of 50 or more employees in one location.

NON AIR CARRIER LABOR LAW

The *National Labor Relations Act* (*NLRA*, also known as the *Wagner Act*) applies to most private-sector employers *except the railroads and air carriers* (these will be discussed in the next chapter). The NLRA gave employees the right to organize without interference by the employer and to bargain collectively (through a union of their choice) with the employer. Congress' intent in enacting the NLRA was to equalize bargaining power between employers and employees and thereby minimize the disruption to interstate commerce caused by labor disputes. The NLRA created the *National Labor Relations Board (NLRB)* to adopt and enforce regulations implementing the act. Major provisions of the NLRA include the following:

1. Guarantees *employee rights* to:
   a. *organize* into unions of their own choosing,
   b. *assist* such labor unions,
   c. *bargain collectively* with their employer through a union of their own choosing (which, upon election, becomes the *exclusive bargaining representative* of that group of employees, called a "*bargaining unit*"), and
   d. *strike* or take other concerted action.
2. Prohibits *employers* from engaging in *unfair labor practices* made illegal by the act, including:
   a. *interfering* with employee rights guaranteed by the act,
   b. *discriminating* against union members or employees pursuing their rights under the act,
   c. attempting *to dominate or interfere* with employee unions, and
   d. *refusing to bargain in good faith* with employee representatives.
3. Provides for NLRB to:
   a. determine the *appropriate bargaining unit* (*craft or class of employees*) (i.e.: aircraft sheet metal workers, aircraft fuelers)
   b. oversee union organizing efforts to prevent unfair labor practices, and
   c. when at least 30% of employees in an appropriate bargaining unit authorize a union to represent them, determine who is entitled to vote (non-supervisory employees) and conduct elections by secret ballot to select a union to represent those employees.

The *Taft-Hartley Amendments* to the NLRA, enacted to correct an imbalance in labor's favor, added the following provisions:

1. Prohibits *secondary strikes or boycotts* (aimed to force one employer to cease doing business with another employer),
2. Establishes employee *right to refrain* from any and all union activities except union shop provisions in any valid collective bargaining agreement,
3. Prohibits *union unfair labor practices*, including:
   a. restraint or coercion of employees in exercise of their rights,
   b. discrimination against an employee for not engaging in union activities, and

c. refusal to bargain in good faith with the employer.

4. Empowers states to enact *right to work laws* outlawing union shop requirements in collective bargaining agreements, to allow employees to refrain from joining the union.

Examples of private-sector employee unionization under the NLRA in the aerospace industry include virtually all non-management employees of the major aircraft and component manufacturers and, most recently, flight instructors employed by Embry-Riddle Aeronautical University's Daytona Beach campus and Flight Safety International and employees of several major FBO chains. Flight instructors surely rank among the most underpaid highly skilled workers, so it will be interesting to see whether the ERAU and Flight Safety examples will be followed elsewhere in the industry.

The NLRA, as amended, narrowly circumscribes a company's options to resist employee efforts to unionize. Frequently, efforts to unionize result from long-standing employee dissatisfaction with the company's treatment of and apparent attitude toward its employees. Once union organizing efforts begin, there is little the company can legally do to resist because of the unfair labor practice prohibitions of the NLRA. Those companies that have been most successful in avoiding unionization of their workforces have been proactive in management–employee relations over the long term. Issues that, if allowed to fester, make employees receptive to union organizing efforts include not only substandard wages and benefits, but also more subjective feelings of unfairness and lack of interest in worker well-being on the part of management.

Such issues lend themselves to preventive management by the company, to prevent development of worker dissatisfaction that may lead to employee efforts to unionize. Fundamental is the necessity to pay wages and provide benefits that are competitive with other employers of such employees. An FBO that wishes to keep its aircraft mechanics, and keep them unrepresented by a union, must compete in wages and benefits not only against other FBOs in the area, but also with the airlines, corporate flight departments, fractional operators and even automobile dealerships and shops.

Feelings of unfairness arise where employees perceive that management is inconsistent, arbitrary or unresponsive or shows favoritism in handling disciplinary cases. Adoption and even-handed implementation of a formal, published grievance procedure with provision for progressive discipline in most cases can go a long way toward preventing or healing employee feelings of management unfairness.

Failure to keep open effective lines of communication between management and employees can also lead to dissatisfaction. A perception (accurate or not) that management does not care about the rank-and-file employees and is disinterested in hearing their views, suggestions and concerns leaves the workforce ripe for union organizing efforts. There is no substitute for listening to the workers. Suggestion boxes, company newsletters, hot lines, and opportunities for face-to-face dialogue between workers and management can be very effective in keeping workers content and also yield benefits in productivity. Formal and honest performance evaluations also provide an important opportunity for truthful and meaningful communication.

Training supervisors in company policies and procedures and in interpersonal skills can pay off in the company's effort to avoid feelings of unfairness and keep the lines of constructive communication open. Skilled and trusted supervisors can also keep management informed of the extent of union sentiment among workers and convey messages from management to the workers, within the extremely narrow bounds of content permitted by the NLRA and NLRB.

Companies may also legally adopt and enforce a *no solicitation/no distribution rule* placing certain restrictions on union organizing activities in the workplace. For example, such activities may be limited to non-working time (such as breaks and mealtimes) and non-working areas (break rooms, cafeterias, locker rooms, parking lots). Reasonable limits can be placed on where literature can be posted. Care must be taken to enforce the rule uniformly against all forms of solicitation and distribution; not merely those associated with union activities. The same rules must apply and be enforced against, for example, posting or distributing in the workplace literature promoting sales of cosmetics, homes, vehicles, and event tickets as against literature promoting union activities.

Federal Government Employees

Executive Orders signed by Presidents Kennedy and Nixon extended collective bargaining rights to most federal government employees. These were replaced by the *Civil Service Reform Act* enacted by Congress in 1978, which affords federal government employees rights virtually identical to private sector employees covered by the NLRA, with two important exceptions: (1) federal government employees do not have the right to strike, and (2) all collective bargaining agreements with federal employees must contain a grievance procedure providing for final resolution by binding arbitration.

The *Office of Personnel Management (OPM) (www.opm.gov)* establishes the rules regulating federal civilian employment procedures and practices, the *Federal Labor Relations Authority (FLRA) (www.flra.gov)* oversees the unionization and collective bargaining of federal employees, and the *Merit System Protection Board (MSPB) (www.mspb.gov)* hears appeals of federal employee grievances, such as those filed by terminated air traffic controllers.

Following close on the heels of enactment of the Civil Service Reform Act, the Professional Air Traffic Controllers' (PATCO) strike of 1981 was the first declared strike against the federal government. President Reagan stood fast against the unlawful strike, resulting in the FAA firing about 12,000 strikers and the courts imposing crippling fines against union leaders and the union and jailing some union leaders. The union was decertified and dissolved and no organization of federal employees has dared to defy this law since. FAA air traffic controllers have reorganized under a new union, the National Air Traffic Controllers Association (NATCA), an affiliate of the powerful AFL-CIO.

State and Local Government Employees

Most public airports are owned and operated by local and regional governmental entities and are managed, operated and maintained by public employees. State laws governing the union representation and bargaining rights of public employees vary widely. Most states allow public employees the right to union representation and some degree of collective bargaining (though the permissible scope of bargaining is typically limited and varies among the states). Most, if not all, states deny the right to strike to at least those public employees who are deemed essential to the public safety and welfare (such as police, firefighters, medical personnel and, in some states, teachers). Some aviation jobs may fit into this category, as well.

17

Air Carrier Labor Law

In the wake of economic deregulation of the airlines, numerous new air carriers—commuter, regional, and trunk—started business using nonunion labor and paying wages substantially below scales then paid by existing ("legacy") airlines (which were bound by contracts previously negotiated with elected union representatives). Competitive pressures led to "hardball" renegotiation of virtually all unionized airlines' pay and benefit scales. In nonunion airlines, discontent over persistent low pay and difficult working conditions has led to increasing interest of employees in unionizing to gain the strength of collective bargaining with management. As the industry consolidates, airline mergers and acquisitions are complicated by the necessity to merge workforces operating under different union contracts. Airline pilot unions are also now in a consolidation phase, with the Air Line Pilots Association (ALPA) aggressively courting pilots presently represented by a company union.

Meanwhile, in the general aviation industry, some activities have also seen growth and consolidation that has attracted union organizing efforts. Examples include charter and fractional operators, emergency medical aviation operators, FBO chains, and pilot training companies. The diverse nature of services offered by some of these companies frequently raises the question of whether the company and its employees are subject to the regulatory jurisdiction of the NLRB under the NLRA or the NMB under the RLA.

The purpose of this chapter is to equip you with a practical working knowledge of procedures in the air carrier industry for jurisdictional determinations, unionizing employees, contract negotiations, disciplinary actions against employees, changing unions, and dealing with employee issues in mergers and acquisitions.

THE RAILWAY LABOR ACT

Labor relations in the air carrier industry are governed by (of all things) the Railway Labor Act of 1926 (RLA), which Congress made applicable to air carriers in 1936. The purpose of this statute is to minimize interference in interstate commerce caused by labor disputes in the mass transportation industries while insuring transportation employees' right to engage in collective bargaining and collective action.

Jurisdiction

Under the statutory language of the 1936 amendment to the RLA, the Act applies to:

> …every *common carrier by air engaged in interstate or foreign commerce*, and every carrier by air transporting mail for or under contract with the United States Government, and every air pilot or other person who performs any work as an employee or subordinate official of such carrier or carriers, subject to its continuing authority to supervise and direct the manner of rendition of his service. (*Italics supplied*.)

Faced with the question of whether a particular enterprise and its employees fall under the RLA or the NLRA, the NLRB defers to the NMB to investigate and determine whether the business fits within the definition of a *common carrier by air engaged in interstate or foreign commerce*. If the NMB determines that the company fits that definition, it takes jurisdiction under the RLA; if not, the NLRB takes jurisdiction under the NLRA.

To make that determination, the NMB applies a two-pronged test: (1) the *function test* asks whether the work is of a nature traditionally performed by employees of air carriers, and (2) the *control test* asks whether a common carrier exercises direct or indirect control over the work.

Applying the two-pronged test, the NMB has asserted jurisdiction over, as examples:

- Companies providing scheduled air service,
- Air charter companies,
- Air ambulance services,
- A fractional aircraft operator also holding a 14 CFR Part 135 operating certificate, and
- FBOs providing air taxi, charter, and on-demand air transport along with aircraft rental, refueling, and aircraft maintenance.

But the NMB has determined that it does not have jurisdiction over, as examples:

- An air tour operator operating entirely within a single state,
- A scheduled air carrier operating entirely within a single state,
- A company that trains pilots and flight engineers,
- A company providing ground services to airlines, including reservations, cleaning, fuel and maintenance, and
- A company providing airport and airline food catering.

In a curious historical artifact, UPS (which began as a trucking company) is under NLRB jurisdiction and the NLRA, while FedEx (which began as an air carrier) is under NMB jurisdiction and the RLA. At this writing, there is hotly-contested legislation pending in Congress to remove FedEx's freight and ground units from RLA coverage and move them under the NLRA.

Distinguishing RLA Features

General characteristics of the RLA include:

1. ***Union or agency shops.*** If a majority of the workers in a particular craft or class (such as pilots, aircraft mechanics, flight attendants, customer service representatives, ramp workers or aircraft dispatchers) vote to be represented by a union, union dues (or an equivalent service fee for those who prefer not to be listed on the union's membership roll) will be automatically withheld (by a *dues check off*) from the paychecks of all workers in that craft or class, and the union will become the exclusive bargaining agent of all of them. The RLA prohibits "*yellow dog*" contracts whereby employees agree not to join a union.

2. ***Compulsory mediation and opportunity for binding arbitration.*** Procedures for the resolution of major disputes between airlines and their employees' union focus on mandatory mediation and the opportunity for a resolution by binding arbitration if mediation fails.

3. ***Postponement of right to strike.*** The parties are prohibited from resorting to self-help (the employees or union from striking or engaging in non-strike work actions such as sickouts, the air carrier from unilaterally changing pay scales or other terms and conditions of employment, locking out union employees and hiring permanent replacement workers) until the major dispute resolution process spelled out in the act has been completed.

These are mandatory and exclusive remedies, administered by the National Mediation Board (NMB). The National Labor Relations Board (NLRB) has no jurisdiction over air carrier labor controversies.

There are two basic types of air carrier labor law cases: *representation cases* and *disputes*.

Representation Cases

In order to raise and test employee interest in unionizing, the union usually mounts an organizing campaign that may include the distribution of leaflets, informational picketing, mass meetings and speeches, even radio and television advertising. The union will then circulate authorization cards to prospective members. It is unlawful for the air carrier to interfere in any way with the union's efforts to organize the employees. Air carrier management is also prohibited from informing the workers that management prefers one union over another. If 35% of the employees who are found eligible to vote sign authorization cards, an election is justified.

Once a union believes it has sufficient support among the workers to win, it petitions the NMB to hold an election. The NMB investigates the responsibilities and authority of various workers in the particular craft or class to determine which of them are "labor" (allowed to vote in the election) and which are "management" (prohibited from voting in the election). For example, an air carrier's pilots might include not only the line pilots (labor) and a chief pilot (management) but also flight instructors and company check airmen (whose authority in one company may look more like management but more like labor in another). Once the NMB has decided who can vote, an election is held under NMB supervision, and those who are qualified to vote cast ballots for or against representation by the union. If a simple majority of qualified voters cast ballots and a simple majority of those who voted cast their ballots in favor of the union, the NMB certifies that union as the official bargaining representative for that craft or class of workers.

Once a union has been certified, it has the exclusive authority to represent all of the air carrier's employees in that craft or class (including those who would rather not be so represented and who voted against unionization). But correlative to that right, the union also has the *duty of fair representation* of all of the air carrier's employees in that craft or class (including those who voted against unionization) in bargaining with the employer.

Upon certification, the union will enter into negotiations with company management for an employment contract covering that craft or class of employees. At this stage, both sides have a legal *duty to bargain in good faith*. Many (but not all) unions' bylaws require that once union representatives and management have negotiated a new contract, the union must present the contract to the affected members for their vote to ratify or reject the agreement. In that case, if a simple majority of the affected members vote to ratify the contract, all are bound by it (Fig. 17.1). If a simple majority votes to reject the contract, the union's representatives must return to the bargaining table and resume contract negotiations with the airline.

Fig. 17.1. As a result of successful collective bargaining by their chosen union, ALPA, United Airlines pilots, such as the one seen here performing a preflight inspection, enjoy the best pay and benefits in the industry. An AFL-CIO affiliate, ALPA represents about 60,000 pilots at 50 U.S. and Canadian airlines.

The RLA does not establish a procedure for decertifying a union in the event that the employees become disaffected with their union. Absent a statutory procedure, it has become customary in the industry in such a case to hold a new election in which an individual (rather than a union) is voted in to represent the employees instead of their previous union. The newly elected person then resigns and the goal of returning to unrepresented status is accomplished.

Disputes

After an employment contract has been agreed to, disputes may arise. Disputes between the union and the airline are divided into two categories: *minor disputes* and *major disputes*.

Minor Disputes

Minor disputes (also referred to as *grievances*) involve disputes over the interpretation or application of the employment contract. Most minor disputes involve company discipline of employees. For example, the pilots' contract requires pilots to report for duty one hour prior to the scheduled departure time for their flight to obtain a briefing and trip documentation from the dispatcher and perform the pre-flight inspection of the aircraft. A pilot arrives late, so that the air carrier has to call in a reserve pilot and the flight is delayed. The company suspends the rule breaker for thirty days without pay as punishment.

The RLA requires that the employment contract provide for the creation of a *System Board of Adjustment* to resolve minor disputes that arise under the contract, such as the foregoing example. A typical System Board in the airline industry includes two members selected by the airline and two members selected by the union. The board's procedures should also be set out in the contract. Where an employee has a legitimate claim that the company has breached the employment agreement, the union must represent the employee in the grievance hearing of the System Board. This representative may be a union representative, rarely a lawyer. If in the tardy pilot example the employment contract specifically provided for some lesser penalty for a first offense of tardiness or (if the contract is silent regarding penalties) other employees have done the same thing but received lesser penalties from the airline, the pilot would have a valid claim.

As you might suspect, the equal balance between union and management representation on the System Board often leads to deadlock, with management representatives voting to uphold the company's action and union representatives voting to soften or reverse it. The contract should provide a way to break such deadlocks; most provide for the selection of a neutral arbitrator to decide the case. The RLA provides that if a System Board is unable to resolve a minor dispute, something called the National Air Transportation Board can be convened. This has never been necessary, although there have been many thousands of minor disputes resolved by System Boards (or tie-breaking arbitrators) in the well over seventy years the RLA has applied to the airline industry.

Under the RLA, minor disputes cannot be brought before the courts except in the rare instance where delays or procedural irregularities in the handling of an employee's case by the System Board amount to a deprivation of the employee's right to *due process of law*. Due process of law has generally been held to include these rights: (1) to have a hearing before a fair and impartial decision maker, (2) to have adequate notice of the nature of the charges and of the time and place of the hearing to allow one to prepare, (3) to be represented by legal counsel if one chooses, (4) to testify and present witnesses and evidence on your behalf, and (5) to cross-examine witnesses for the opposition.

Both management and coworkers may dislike a particularly obnoxious employee. In such a case, System Board members on both sides may be tempted to "railroad" the obnoxious employee by having a hearing at a time or place the employee cannot attend or by giving the employee little or no notice of the hearing. In such an extreme case, a court would hold that the employee had been denied due process of law and would send the case back to the board to afford the employee a proper hearing with reasonable notice.

Major Disputes

Major disputes involve the negotiation of either a new employment contract or a change to the existing contract. The RLA's mandatory procedure for resolving major disputes is often referred to by attorneys and labor negotiators as the "*Kabuki Theater*," after the ancient Japanese style of drama that consists of ritual in the extreme, exalting form over substance.

Until this entire procedure has been completed, the RLA requires that the status quo be maintained. (Collective bargaining agreements under the RLA do not expire, having only an *amendable date*, after which either party can propose amendments, triggering the major dispute resolution process (Kabuki Theater). Both the air carrier and the union must continue to work together under the existing contract (or, if the employees are newly unionized and this is the first contract to be negotiated, under the company's preexisting terms and conditions of employment) as the major dispute resolution process proceeds.

Consider this example of a major dispute: Faced with price competition from nonunionized air carriers, management of a unionized air carrier seeks the pilots union's agreement to wage reduction concessions which would reduce the company's operating costs and allow the company to compete by reducing its prices. Since this would involve a change in the existing contract, it is a major dispute. The RLA requires the air carrier and the union to follow this procedure (the "Kabuki Theater") to resolve any major dispute:

1. The party desiring the change (in this example, the air carrier) must notify the other side (in this example, the union) of the proposed change, in writing. This is often referred to as a *Section 6 notice*, after the RLA section that imposes this requirement.

2. Both sides must then confer within 30 days and bargain in good faith in a genuine effort to negotiate their differences. Trade-offs and counter proposals are often brought up at this stage, which continues until at least one of the parties believes that negotiations have reached an impasse.

3. If the parties are unable to resolve the controversy by negotiation, either side can request mediation by the NMB. In mediation, as distinguished from arbitration, the federal mediator has no authority to enter an order deciding the case but can only serve as an intermediary between the company and the union to help them reach an agreement. The NMB can hold the parties in mediation until the mediator declares an impasse. Mediators are reluctant to declare an impasse, as it is an admission that the mediator has failed to accomplish his mission. Being held in mediation by a stubborn mediator far beyond the time all meaningful progress toward an agreement has ceased can be enormously frustrating to the parties. Nowhere is this frustration more vividly described than in Aaron Bernstein's book, *Grounded: Frank Lorenzo and the Destruction of Eastern Airlines*, listed in the bibliography.

4. If the mediator is unable to bring the parties to an agreement and declares an impasse, the NMB will offer the opportunity

for binding arbitration. If both parties agree, a panel of three arbitrators will be selected to hear the views of both sides and decide the result, and the parties will be bound by the decision, whether they like the result or not. If they have agreed to submit the dispute to binding arbitration, the arbitrators' decision is final and cannot be appealed. In air carrier labor disputes, it is extremely rare for the parties to agree to binding arbitration.

5. However, if either party rejects binding arbitration as a method of resolving the dispute, there is a mandatory 30-day "cooling off" period during which the parties must continue to maintain the status quo. Although not a part of the RLA's mandatory procedure, it has become an NMB practice at this stage to offer the parties an opportunity for *supermediation*. Supermediation is a meeting with one of the three presidential appointees to the NMB, designed to bring visibility and political pressure to bear on the parties to reevaluate their positions one last time. An opportunity for supermediation is rarely turned down by the parties.

6. Once the cooling off period is up, if the parties have still not reached an agreement, they are free to resort to self-help. (In this example, that would mean that the company could unilaterally reduce the employees' pay scales, the employees could strike and picket the company, and/or the company could lock the strikers out and hire permanent replacements).

The only event that could further delay those rights would be if the president of the United States decided to convene a *Presidential Emergency Board (PEB)* as a last effort to aid the parties in reaching an agreement without the transportation disruptions inherent in a strike. The president has the authority to convene a PEB only if the NMB advises him that an emergency exists because a threatened work stoppage involves the transportation service of an entire region of the country (for example, if an airline was the sole regional carrier) and may cause substantial interruption of interstate commerce. It is entirely in the president's discretion to decide whether to convene an Emergency Board. If the president does convene the Emergency Board, the parties must continue to work under the previous contract or terms of employment until the board completes its investigation and hearing and reports its finding (which must be issued within sixty days). The board's findings are not binding on the parties but may be persuasive. At this stage, each side is trying to assess how a strike will turn out. Will passengers and members of other unions honor or cross the picket lines? Will other unions join in sympathy strikes? How much will it cost the company to train and rely upon newly hired replacement pilots and any union members who may choose to not go on strike (collectively, *strikebreakers* or *scabs*)? In the past, the airlines had a Mutual Assistance Plan (MAP) of strike insurance under which a struck carrier would receive funds from the other participating carriers not shut down by the work stoppage. These plans were outlawed by the Airline Deregulation Act of 1978. Once the PEB issues its findings another 30-day *cooling off period* begins, during which the parties are still required to continue to work under the status quo.

The Emergency Board's findings will have been widely reported in the news media, and pollsters for both sides will sample public opinion. Discussions will be had with other unions so that each side may gain a more accurate approximation of what is likely to happen in the event of a strike. It is hoped that this new dose of reality may enable the parties to reach an agreement. If, however, at the end of this last 30-day "cooling off" period they have still not reached agreement, they are free to resort to self-help without further interruption or delay.

Injunctions. If the air carrier, the union, or employees acting independently of the union (*wildcat strikers*) refuse to follow these RLA procedures and act to change the status quo prior to exhaustion of this complete ritual sequence, the other side may file suit in court to obtain an injunction. An injunction would compel persons who made the change to return to the status quo ante until this Kabuki Theater process has been completed. In the case of a premature strike, the injunction compelling employees to return to work is usually reported in the news media as a *back-to-work order*. If the injunction is issued but not obeyed, violators (the union, union leadership, and striking members) are exposed to fines and/or imprisonment for *contempt of court*. The same would apply to the company and its managers if it were to prematurely lock out strikers and begin hiring permanent replacements.

Strikes and Their Lasting Consequences. Few things provoke us humans to a more emotional response than a threat to our job. The animosity generated in a major dispute between an air carrier and a union must be experienced to be believed. Seemingly unflappable silver-haired professional pilots may be provoked to fits of rage. Unions may orchestrate "safety campaigns" designed to raise consumer fears that the air carrier, operated largely by new hires, is unsafe. Crimes, sabotage of aircraft and threats, intimidation, and even physical violence against strikebreakers

Fig. 17.2. It takes tightly orchestrated teamwork to keep an airline moving safely and efficiently. Bitter labor disputes can jeopardize that teamwork, and disruptions may continue even after the dispute is officially resolved, as festering resentments linger.

are not unheard of. The FAA puts a much closer watch on air carriers involved in labor disputes to try to assure that public safety is not compromised. Even if the dispute is ultimately settled, its adverse effects may be long lasting, especially where the air carrier has hired permanent replacement workers who remain with the company after strikers return to work (Fig. 17.2). The industry abounds with stories of pilots who refuse to acknowledge or speak to such former "scabs," even when a member of the same flight crew where open cockpit communication is essential to flight safety. There are even stories of other crewmembers playing dirty tricks on former strikebreakers, such as by deliberately entering an incorrect altitude into the altitude alerter to mislead the other pilot into an altitude deviation and FAA enforcement action. This may be understandable, given that in our society what we do for a living is not only our means of survival but also our identity. (Ask anyone to "tell me about yourself," and the first thing they are likely to say is what they do for a living: "I'm an airline pilot.") While such extreme vehement behavior may be understandable, it is unwise and unprofessional.

If your means of survival and your identity are threatened, you may find yourself in the emotional grip of primitive base instincts that provoke such ugly and dangerous behavior. Finding yourself in such a situation, I hope you will argue in the appropriate time and venue for your principles but draw the line at any behavior that could jeopardize flight safety and never cross that line.

Mergers and Acquisitions

Frequently, one of the most difficult challenges facing a merger between air carriers (or acquisition of one carrier by another) is that of merging the two workforces into one. Differences in employee compensation, benefits, seniority, qualifications and training must be reconciled. This task is made doubly complex where different unions represent similar employees in the two companies. Major dispute resolution procedures continue to govern the process and employees' rights while labor and management work toward agreement over these thorny issues. Modern air carrier merger and acquisition agreements typically provide for a phasing-in period. Employees coming from the carrier that provided lesser pay and benefits enter the new carrier's workforce on a separate scale that is programmed to catch up and merge with that of the acquiring carrier's previous employees over a period of years.

Where a craft of employees (such as aircraft mechanics) of one of the merged carriers are unionized but their counterparts at the other carrier are not, the NMB long followed carte blanche the practice of ruling that whichever group was largest at the time of the merger determined whether the merged airline's employees in that craft would be deemed represented by the union and covered by the existing collective bargaining agreement or not. Likewise where a craft of employees of the merging carriers were represented by different unions and working under existing collective bargaining agreements, the bigger group would absorb the smaller. In the recent merger of Northwest Airlines into Delta, the NMB abandoned that practice in favor of what can only be described as an unpredictable ad hoc case-by-case decision process, rendering the impact of the merger on union representation of the employees unpredictable.

Bankruptcies

Although as a general rule collective bargaining agreements under the RLA do not expire, being perpetual subject to amendment by the parties, there is one exception often resorted to by management in desperate circumstances: in proceedings for reorganization of companies under Chapter 11 of the Bankruptcy Code, bankruptcy judges are empowered to order modification or termination of collective bargaining agreements and often wield that power in their efforts to restructure the company to improve its chances of survival in today's hypercompetitive marketplace. Of all major U.S. airlines that were in existence before deregulation, only American Airlines has not resorted to bankruptcy since then and some have done so more than once. Typical court-imposed cutbacks in labor costs for airlines reorganizing in bankruptcy include deep pay cuts, reduced health care benefits, and modification or termination of pension plans.

KEY AVIATION ORGANIZATIONS

AERONAUTICAL REPAIR STATION ASSOCIATION, 121 N. Henry Street, Arlington, VA 22314-2903. (*www.arsa.org*) The voice of aviation maintenance and modification facilities before the FAA, NTSB and other federal agencies.

AEROSPACE MEDICAL ASSOCIATION, 320 South Henry Street, Alexandria, VA 22314-3524. (*www.asma.org*) A scientific association promoting knowledge of aviation, space, and environmental medicine. Publication: *Aviation, Space and Environmental Medicine* (monthly).

AEROSPACE INDUSTRIES ASSOCIATION, 1000 Wilson Blvd., Suite 1700, Arlington, VA 22209-3928. (*www.aia-aerospace.org*) The trade association for aircraft, spacecraft and component manufacturing.

AIRCRAFT OWNERS & PILOTS ASSOCIATION, 421 Aviation Way, Frederick, MD 21701. (*www.aopa.org*) Promotes the interests of general aviation, particularly in regulatory, airspace, and airport access matters. Publication: *AOPA Pilot* (monthly).

AIR LINE PILOTS ASSOCIATION, 1625 Massachusetts Avenue N.W., Washington, DC 20036. (*www.alpa.org*) The largest union of airline pilots. Publication: *Air Line Pilot* (monthly).

AIRPORTS COUNCIL INTERNATIONAL, P.O. Box 16, 1215 Geneva 15—Airport, Switzerland. (*www.airports.org*) An association of the world's airports founded to promote cooperation.

AIR TRANSPORT ASSOCIATION, 1301 Pennsylvania Avenue, Washington, DC 20006-5206. (*www.airlines.org*) Represents the interests of major airlines. Publication: *Air Transport* (annual).

AMERICAN ASSOCIATION OF AIRPORT EXECUTIVES, 601 Madison St., Alexandria, VA 22314. (*www.aaae.org*) Promotes professionalism in civil aviation airport management. Publications: *Airport Magazine* (bimonthly), *Airport Report* (bimonthly).

AMERICAN BAR ASSOCIATION FORUM COMMITTEE ON AIR & SPACE LAW, 750 North Lake Shore Drive, Chicago, IL 60611. (*www.abanet.org/forums/airspace*) Members of the ABA having a special interest in air and space law. Publication: *Air & Space Lawyer* (quarterly).

AMERICAN INSTITUTE OF AERONAUTICS & ASTRONAUTICS, Suite 500, 1801 Alexander Bell Dr., Reston, VA 20191-4344. (*www.aiaa.org*) Promotes the advancement of the scientific, technical, and engineering aspects of aeronautics and astronautics. Publication: *Aerospace America*.

AVIATION INSURANCE ASSOCIATION, 400 Admiral Blvd., Kansas City, MO 64106. (*www.aiaweb.org*) An association of aviation insurance professionals. Publication: *The Binder* (quarterly).

CIVIL AVIATION MEDICAL ASSOCIATION, P.O. Box 2382, Peachtree City, GA, 30269-2382. (*www.civilavmed.com*) A professional association composed primarily of FAA-designated Aviation Medical Examiners. Publication: *CAMA Bulletin* (quarterly).

EXPERIMENTAL AIRCRAFT ASSOCIATION, EAA Aviation Center, 3000 Poberezny Rd., Oshkosh, WI 54902. (*www.eaa.org*) Represents the interests of sport aviation particularly. Publication: *Sport Aviation* (monthly).

GENERAL AVIATION MANUFACTURERS ASSOCIATION, 1400 K Street N.W., Suite 801, Washington, DC 20005-2485. (*www.gama. aero*) Trade association representing the interests of manufacturers of general aviation fixed wing aircraft and components and promotes public appreciation of general aviation's contribution to the economy. Publications: *General Aviation Statistical Data Book* (annual), *Shipment Reports* (quarterly).

INTERNATIONAL AIR TRANSPORT ASSOCIATION, 800 Place Victoria, P.O. Box 113, Montreal, Quebec H4Z 1M1, Canada. (*www.iata.org*) The organization of international airlines. Numerous publications.

INTERNATIONAL CIVIL AVIATION ORGANIZATION, 999 University St., Montreal, Quebec H3C 5H7, Canada. (*www.icao.int*) An agency of the United Nations standardizing aviation technical standards and procedures and promoting safety, uniformity, and efficiency in air navigation worldwide. Numerous publications.

INTERNATIONAL COUNCIL OF AIR SHOWS, 751 Miller Dr., Suite F-3, Leesburg, VA 20175. (*www.airshows.aero*) The organization of airshow producers, promoters, and performers. Publication: *ICAS News* (monthly).

INTERNATIONAL SOCIETY OF AIR SAFETY INVESTIGATORS, 107 E. Holly Ave., Suite 11, Sterling, VA 20164. (*www.isasi.org*) Promotes professionalism in the investigation of aircraft accidents. Publication: *Forum* (quarterly).

LAWYER-PILOTS BAR ASSOCIATION, P.O. Box 1510, Edgewater, MD 21037. (*www.lpba.org*) An organization of lawyers who are also pilots, many of whom practice aviation law. Publication: *LPBA Journal* (quarterly).

NATIONAL AIR TRANSPORTATION ASSOCIATION, INC., 4226 King Street, Alexandria, VA 22302. (*www.nata.aero*) Trade association of FBOs, Part 135 operators, and related suppliers and manufacturers. Numerous publications.

NATIONAL ASSOCIATION OF FLIGHT INSTRUCTORS, EAA Aviation Center, P.O. Box 3086, Oshkosh, WI 54903-3086. (*www.nafi@eaa.org*) Represents the interests of certified flight instructors and promotes professionalism in flight instruction. Publication: *NAFI Foundation Newsletter* (bimonthly).

NATIONAL ASSOCIATION OF STATE AVIATION OFFICIALS, Washington National Airport, Hangar 7, Suite 218, Washington, DC 20001. (*www.nasao.org*) Encourages cooperation and mutual aid among local, state, and federal governments to improve air transportation. Publication: *NASAO State Aviation Newsletter* (monthly).

NATIONAL AGRICULTURAL AIRCRAFT ASSOCIATION, 1005 E Street, S.E., Washington, DC 20003-2847. (*www.agaviation.org*) The trade association for agricultural aviation operators.

NATIONAL BUSINESS AIRCRAFT ASSOCIATION, INC., 1200 18th Street N.W., Suite 400, Washington, DC 20036. (*www.nbaa.org*) Represents the interests of corporate and other business users of aircraft. Numerous publications.

NATIONAL EMS PILOTS ASSOCIATION, P.O. Box 2128, Layton, UT 84041-2128. (*www.nemspa.org*) Represents the interests of pilots employed in emergency medical service aviation, promotes safety in those operations. Publication: *Air Net* (monthly).

NATIONAL TRANSPORTATION SAFETY BOARD BAR ASSOCIATION, P.O. Box 957, Edgewater, MD 21037. (*www.ntsbbar.org*) An organization of attorneys, in private practice and in government service, practicing before the NTSB.

THE NINETY-NINES, INC., 4300 Amelia Earhart Rd., Oklahoma City, OK 73159. (*www.ninety-nines.org*) The international organization of women pilots. Publication: *Ninety-nine News* (monthly).

ORGANIZATION OF BLACK AIRLINE PILOTS, 8630 Fenton St., Suite 126, Silver Spring, MD 20910. (*www.obap.org*) A non-profit organization to enhance, advance, and promote educational opportunities in aviation.

PROFESSIONAL AVIATION MAINTENANCE ASSOCIATION, 400 North Washington St., Suite 300, Alexandria, VA 22314. (*www.pama.org*) A professional association of aviation maintenance personnel. Publication: *PAMA News*.

SOCIETY OF AUTOMOTIVE ENGINEERS, 400 Commonwealth Drive, Warrendale, PA 15096-0001. (*www.sae.org*) A professional engineering society establishing aerospace technical standards. Numerous publications.

UNIVERSITY AVIATION ASSOCIATION, 3410 Skyway Drive, Auburn, AL 36830-6444. (*www.uaa.auburn.edu*) A professional organization representing collegiate aviation education. Publication: *UAA Newsletter* (bimonthly).

WOMEN IN AVIATION, INTERNATIONAL, Morningstar Airport, 3647 State Rt. 503 South, West Alexandria, OH 45381-9354. (*www.wai.org*) A non-profit organization dedicated to encouragement and advancement of women in all aviation fields and interests. Publication: *Aviation for Women* (monthly).

BIBLIOGRAPHY

Adamski, A. & T. Doyle. *Introduction to the Aviation Regulatory Process* (5th ed). Plymouth: Hayden-McNeil, 2005. A thorough overview of U.S. legislation relating to civil aviation, the aviation regulatory process and Federal Aviation Regulations.

Bernstein, A. *Grounded: Frank Lorenzo and the Destruction of Eastern Airlines.* New York: Simon & Schuster, 1990. An inside view of the most bitter airline labor dispute in U.S. history, showing workings of the "Kabuki Theater" major dispute resolution process in context. Available in reprint in paperback.

Bor, R. & T. Hubbard. *Aviation Mental Health.* UK: Ashgate, 2006. An authoritative and practical guide to the assessment, treatment, care and management of the mental health of pilots and other professional groups within aviation, written for health and human resources practitioners working in the airline industry.

Cathcart, D. *Aircrash Litigation Techniques.* Charlottesville: Michie, 1985. Although written for trial lawyers, this treatise contains many interesting insights into the workings of the law in finding fault and apportioning liability in aviation accident cases.

Congress of the United States, Office of Technology Assessment. *Safe Skies for Tomorrow: Aviation Safety in a Competitive Environment.* July 1988. A thought provoking examination of the roles of government and private industry in improving aviation safety in the wake of deregulation of airline economics.

DeHaan, W. *The Optometrist's & Ophthalmologist's Guide to Pilots' Vision.* Boulder: American Trend, 1982. Has an especially good section on obtaining FAA certification even if your uncorrected vision falls below FAA standards.

Dempsey, P. & L. Gesell. *Air Commerce and the Law.* Chandler: Coast Aire Publications, 2004. A *tour de force* written by two of aviation's foremost scholars. Particularly strong in air carrier economics and related regulatory theory and practice.

Dempsey, P., A. Goetz & J. Szyliowicz. *Denver International Airport: Lessons Learned.* New York: McGraw-Hill, 1997. A detailed and thoroughly-researched narrative of the development of the new Denver International Airport (DIA) by three brilliant University of Denver professors who watched it all happen.

Dempsey, P., R. Hardaway & W. Thoms. *Aviation Law and Regulation.* Austin: Butterworth Legal Publishing, 1992. A two-volume loose-leaf comprehensive overview of virtually all aspects of U.S. aviation law, written by three distinguished law professors for use as a law school text and reference for practicing attorneys. Also available as an abridged single-volume bound paperback text for student use.

Eichenberger, J. *General Aviation Law* (2d ed). New York: McGraw-Hill, 1997. A very readable inexpensive paperback book of advice written by an experienced aviation lawyer, pilot, and adjunct professor at Ohio State University.

Ellis, James E. *Buying and Owning Your Own Airplane* (2d ed). New-castle: Aviation Supplies & Academics, 2004. A good review of the many practical considerations involved in purchasing and insuring a personal airplane.

Ericsson, L. *Aviation Insurance.* Portland: Oregon State Bar, 1983. Written primarily for lawyers, this work includes extensive citations to legal precedents interpreting many features of aviation insurance policies. The author, now deceased, was a renowned aviation lawyer and one of the underwriters at Lloyds.

Gesell, L. & P. Dempsey. *Aviation and the Law* (4th ed). Chandler: Coast Aire, 2005. A basic textbook relying heavily on oversimplified and sometimes inaccurate briefs of historic aviation cases.

Hardaway, R. *Airport Regulation, Law & Public Policy.* Westport: Greenwood, 1991. The most complete work on airport law to date.

Hopkins, G. *The Airline Pilots: A Study in Elite Unionization.* Cambridge: Harvard Univ. Press, 1971 & 1998. A fascinating and insightful historical study of the founding and development of the Air Line Pilots Association of the AFL-CIO.

The Journal of Air Law and Commerce. Dallas: Southern Methodist University. A wide-ranging scholarly law journal on domestic and international developments in aviation law.

The Journal of Aviation/Aerospace Education & Research. Daytona Beach: Embry-Riddle Aeronautical University. A scholarly publication for educators and researchers as well as for professionals in the aviation and aerospace industry, particularly oriented toward non-engineering elements.

The Journal of Air Transportation Worldwide. Omaha: University of Nebraska at Omaha. A scholarly journal for the airline industry, featuring a good variety of domestic and international issues. Available in print and online. (email: *journal@unomaha.edu*)

Kaps, R. *Air Transport Labor Relations*. Carbondale: Southern Illinois University Press, 1997. The seminal college text on airline labor relations under the RLA.

Kaps, R., J. Hamilton & T. Bliss. *Labor Relations in Aviation & Aerospace*. Carbondale: Southern Illinois University Press, 2011. The aviation and aerospace industries and their related government agencies encompass the full range of the three federal statutes and several government agencies regulating labor relations. This book focuses on the aviation/aerospace industry and related government agencies, exploring in detail the unique laws and practices applicable to each segment of that set of interlocked industries highly dependent on technologically skilled labor. An accompanying study guide with supplemental readings and instructors manual make the set suitable for use in undergraduate and graduate courses.

Komons, N. *Bonfires to Beacons: Federal Civil Aviation Policy under the Air Commerce Act 1926–1938*. Washington: U.S. Government Printing Office, 1978. The definitive work on this seminal era of federal regulation and support of civil aviation.

Kreindler, L. *Aviation Accident Law*. New York: Matthew Bender, 1990. Written for practicing attorneys, this three-volume set is one of two tours de force minutely detailing the law governing liability for aviation accidents, especially airline accidents. Written by one of the legends of aviation accident litigation.

Lawrence, H. *Aviation and the Role of Government* (2d ed). Dubuque: Kendall/Hunt, 2008. A very complete and readable presentation of the involvement of the federal government in regulating aviation and fostering its development, interwoven with historical developments in the field.

Margo, R. *Aviation Insurance: The Law and Practice of Aviation Insurance* (3d ed). London: Butterworths, 2000. Although written primarily for lawyers, this extraordinarily well-annotated treatise, international in scope, contains an especially insightful chapter on the aviation insurance market.

Pollard, D. *Handbook of Aeronautical Inspection and Pre-Purchase*. Victoria: Trafford, 2005. A short and concise review of the elements of a thorough pre-purchase aircraft inspection and the elements of airworthiness.

Rayman, R. *Clinical Aviation Medicine* (4th ed). New York: Professional Publishing, 2006. Written for the aviation medical examiner, a thoroughgoing overview of the relationships between various health problems and flying. Incorporates USAF standards.

Schiavo, M. *Flying Blind, Flying Safe*. Avon Books, 1997. A scathing indictment of FAA airline safety regulatory and enforcement efforts written by an outspoken and controversial former Inspector General for the U.S. Department of Transportation.

Speciale, R., *Fundamentals of Aviation Law*. New York: McGraw-Hill, 2006. Written by a highly experienced aviation lawyer and pilot, this college text makes extensive use of well-edited court decisions to demonstrate application of the principles of aviation law by the courts.

Speiser, S. & C. Krause. *Aviation Tort Law*. Rochester: Lawyers Cooperative, 1978. Written for the practicing attorney, this is the other of the two three-volume tours de force on liability for aircraft accidents written by legendary aviation accident litigators.

Thoms, W. & F. Dooley. *Airline Labor Law: The Railway Labor Act and Aviation After Deregulation*. New York: Quorum Books, 1990. A good overview of the subject, well illustrated with cases.

The Transportation Law Journal. Denver: University of Denver. A scholarly law journal touching on the full spectrum of transportation law: air, surface and marine.

Weber, L. *International Civil Aviation Organization: An Introduction*. Netherlands, Kluwer Law International, 2007. A thorough overview of ICAO, its mission, organization, and functioning.

Wells, A. & B. Chadbourne. *Introduction to Aviation Insurance and Risk Management* (3d ed). Malabar: Krieger Publishing, 2007. Intended as an undergraduate text in aviation insurance, about half the work consists of an appendix that reproduces sample aircraft insurance policies.

Wright, R. *The Law of Airspace*. Indianapolis: Bobbs-Merrill, 1968. Although dated, this treatise written primarily for lawyers is the foundation for any exploration of this area of the law.

INDEX

General Aviation Airport Security
  Working Group   326
General Aviation Revitalization Act
  (GARA)   108, 152
general aviation security   301
general partnership   115–120
global positioning systems (GPS)   14
government contractors   107
government liability   191–201
grand cabotage   29
Grand Canyon National Park, and
  aircraft noise   295–297
grandfather rights   270
grant agreement   275
grant agreement constraints   277
grievances, in labor law   354
*Grounded: Frank Lorenzo and the
  Destruction of Eastern Airlines*   356
Guidelines for Establishing Anti-
  Money Laundering Procedures   327

Hail Endorsement   148
hangarkeeper's liability   135, 151
hazardous materials   26
hazardous waste   24
health changes   84
hearing   65
hearing standards   77–78
height zoning   258, 263
helicopters   136
hijackings   30, 184, 308, 320
hindsight review   126
hiring   335–337
Hoover Bill   68
Hoover, Bob   68
horror factor   37
hostile work environment   342
hot air balloons   95
Huntington Beach, California   277
hush kits   9, 283
hypersonic transport   18

Immigration Reform and Control Act
  (IRCA)   337
implied contract   335
implied warranties   227–228
incidents, reporting of   208
independent contractors   126
injunction   358

injunctions for nuisance   267
injury   97, 98
Inspection Authorization (IA)   230
instrument landing systems (ILS)   14
insurance
  See also aviation insurance
insurance adjuster   133, 155
insurance broker   131, 134, 147–149
insurance principles
  minimizing risk   133–134
  spreading the risk   133–134
intelligence, sharing of   5
intentional torts   92
  See also liability
interference with air navigation   312
intergovernmental agreement
  (IGA)   281
Internal Revenue Service (IRS)   126
international airports, violence at
  303–304
International Air Transport Association
  (IATA)   4, 31–32
  clearinghouse function of   32
international cargo
  liability for   177–179
International Civil Aviation
  Organization (ICAO)   4, 25–30
  Annexes   26
international passengers   167, 173–176,
  183
International Registry   224
interrogatories   112
intrastate operations of air carriers
  21–22
inverse condemnation case   262
investigation of violations   39–72
invitation to hang yourself   53

John F. Kennedy International Airport
  (JFK)   270
joint and several liability   100
Joint Family Support Operations Center
  (JFSOC)   214
joint ownership   250
joint ownership agreement   250
jury instructions   170
just compensation   258
Justice, Department of   22

possessory lien 232
power of the purse 259
power to tax 259–268
Practices Related to the Purchase of
  General Aviation Aircraft 327
pre-boarding screening 320–325
premises liability 151
prepurchase inspection 217, 230
Presidential Emergency Board
  (PEB) 357
priority search certificate 224
privacy, right to 320
privately owned airports 268
privatization of the ATC 13
Production Type Certificate 10, 199
product liability
  coverage 152
  lawsuits 109
Professional Air Traffic Controllers'
  (PATCO) strike 347
profiling, racial 324
prohibited weapon 320
promissory note 123, 234
proprietary powers 259, 272
prosecution and appeal
  and Federal Aviation Administration
    (FAA) policy 61
prospective interests 224
proximate cause 97, 98–100
punitive damages under the Warsaw
  Convention 183
punitive or exemplary damages 195

Quick-Cert 78
quid pro quo 342

radio aids to navigation 14
radio beacons 14
Railway Labor Act of 1926 (RLA)
  334, 350–358
ramp checks 41–43
recapture of depreciation 238
recertification 69
reexamination, of pilot 38
registration
  role of Federal Aviation
    Administration (FAA) in 10
registration fee 237

regulation
  international 25–32
  role of Federal Aviation
    Administration (FAA) in 3
reinsurance 133
remedial training 34
rescission 229
res ipsa loquitur 102
res judicata, doctrine of 101
Resource Conservation and Recovery
  Act (RCRA) 282
revocation 68
right to control and direct 126–128
right to privacy 320
right-to-work laws 345
risk, assumption of 104, 172
risk management 129
  See also aviation insurance
risk management plan 131
risk management tool 159
Riverside, California 263
Rocky Mountain National Park 297

sabotage 30
SabreTech, Inc. 92
Safer Skies initiative 16
safety and drug-related crimes
  310–318
sales pitch 246
sales tax 237
same-day medical certification 78
San Diego International Airport 267
Santa Barbara, California 264
Santa Monica Municipal Airport
  (SMO) 272
scabs 359
Seattle-Tacoma airport 263
Section 6 notice 356
security agreement 219, 234
security, airports 11
security checkpoints, airport 325
Security Control of Air Traffic and Air
  Navigation Aids (SCATANA)
  292–294
Security Guidelines for General
  Aviation Airports 326
security interests 219
  perfection and priority 220
security-related crimes 305–310
seizure and forfeiture 314

transport jets and noise levels   8–9
trespass   94, 95
TSA Security Directives (SD)   328
Type Certificate   10, 199

ultrahazardous activity   103
umbrella policy   154
underground storage tank (UST)
   regulations   282
Underwriters at Lloyds, The   132
underwriting   132–133
unemployment compensation
   insurance   125
Uniform Commercial Code (UCC)
   217–239
      on disclaimer of warranties   228
      on express and implied warranties
      225–227, 228
unionization   333
union or agency shops, under Railway
   Labor Act of 1926 (RLA)   351
U.S. Customs   23
use tax   237

very light jets (VLJs)   20
vicarious liability   110
Victims Compensation Fund   201
video surveillance   323
Vietnam Era Veteran Readjustment
   Assistance Act   338
vision standards   77–78
Vocational Rehabilitation Act of 1973
   338

wages, hours, benefits, and working
   conditions   338
Wagner Act   343
waiver of subrogation
   endorsement   145
Walsh-Healey Act   342
warbirds   160
warehousemen's liens   219
War, Hi-Jacking, and Other Perils
   Exclusion Clause   145
warranties   225–229
   breached   229
   disclaimer of   228
   express   225–228
   implied   227–228
warranty   218
warranty law   103
war risk exclusion clause   145
Warsaw Convention   167, 173–190
   damages under   183
Washington, D.C., Reagan National
   Airport   284
weather and accidents   198
wet leases   249
whistleblower protection   335
Whitcomb winglet   17
wide-area augmentation systems
   (WAAS)   14
wildcat strikers   358
wilderness airspace   295
willful misconduct   183
William J. Hughes Technical
   Center   16
winglets   18
Worker Adjustment and Retraining
   Notification Act (WARN)   343
workers compensation insurance   125
wrongful discharge   335

yellow dog contracts   351